INTRODUCTION
TO THE
MIDDLE WAY

Buddha Shakyamuni

༄༅། །དབུལ་ལ་འཇིགས་པའི་རྩ་བ་དང་འགྲེལ་པ།

སྐྲ་བའི་ཤལ་ལུང་རྡོ་རྗེ་མེད་ཤེལ་ཕྲེང་

བཞུགས།།

པདྨ་ཀུ་རའི་སྐྲ་བསྒྱུར་མ་ཐུན་ཚོགས་ནས་

སྐྲ་བསྒྱུར་ཞུས།།

The Padmakara Translation Group gratefully acknowledges

the generous support of the Tsadra Foundation in

sponsoring the translation and preparation

of this book

INTRODUCTION
to the
MIDDLE WAY

Chandrakirti's Madhyamakavatara

with commentary by
Jamgön Mipham

TRANSLATED BY THE
PADMAKARA TRANSLATION GROUP

SHAMBHALA
BOSTON & LONDON
2002

Shambhala Publications, Inc.
Horticultural Hall
300 Massachusetts Avenue
Boston, Massachusetts 02115
www.shambhala.com

9 8 7 6 5 4 3 2

Printed in the United States of America

∞ This edition is printed on acid-free paper that meets the
American National Standards Institute Z39.48 Standard.
Distributed in the United States by Random House, Inc.,
and in Canada by Random House of Canada Ltd

Library of Congress Cataloging-in-Publication Data
Candrakirti.
[Madhyamakavatara. English]
Introduction to the middle way: Candrakirti's Madhyamakavatara;
with commentary by Ju Mipham.—1st ed.
p.   cm.
Includes bibliographical references and index.
ISBN 1-57062-942-0
1. Mādhyamika (Buddhism)—Early works to 1800.
I. Mi-pham-rgya-mtsho, 'Jam-mgon 'Ju, 1846–1912.
Dbu ma la 'jug pa'i 'grel pa zla ba'i zhal lun dri med 'shel 'phren
English.   II. Title.
BQ2910.M3622 E6   2002
294.3'85—dc21
2002017668

Contents

SUPPLEMENTARY DISCUSSIONS APPEARING IN THE TEXT

Foreword

THIS COMMENTARY on Chandrakirti's *Madhyamakavatara* was compiled from the notes and oral teachings of Kunkhyen Lama Mipham by Kathok Situ Rinpoche and Khenpo Kunzang Pelden at the request of Shechen Gyaltsap Rinpoche. Mipham Rinpoche was Mañjushri in person, and his disciples, the scholars who compiled this text, were themselves learned and accomplished masters. We can therefore be confident that the teachings contained in this book are not merely of academic interest; they have been transmitted to us by masters who perfectly understood and actualized their meaning. They are the expression of an authentic tradition that goes back to Chandrakirti and Nagarjuna themselves. It is interesting to recall that Kathok Situ Rinpoche recognized and brought up Jamyang Khyentse Chokyi Lodro, the previous incarnation of Dzongsar Khyentse Rinpoche, while Shechen Gyaltsap Rinpoche was the root teacher of Kyabje Dilgo Khyentse Rinpoche. It is therefore with great pleasure that we in the Padmakara Translation Group are able to present in translation these instructions, which are so closely associated with the lineage of our own teachers.

The *Madhyamakavatara* itself is a wonderful text, a product of the golden age of Buddhism in India, when the writings of learned masters were composed and assessed according to strict rules. In order to be acknowledged and proclaimed, these writings had to pass the stringent test of other qualified masters, who were appointed by the king, so that when they were finally published, their authority and reliability were guaranteed. Their ensuing celebrity was therefore well founded and was not merely the outcome of publicity and popular opinion. Why is this so important? It is important because, once we are sure that a writer is trustworthy, we know that we are in touch with the authentic tradition. Through Mipham Rinpoche we have access to Chandrakirti and through him to Nagarjuna. Through Nagarjuna, we may enter the Prajñaparamita and thus the very essence of the Buddha's teaching.

Of course, Madhyamika is challenging. It is not something that we can hope to understand in a single reading. It requires discipline, concentration, and repeated effort. It is good to remember that Chandrakirti and Shantideva did not become great panditas overnight. They and all the great scholars of the lineage studied the teachings with courage and perseverance. And if at times the study of Madhyamika seems arduous and difficult, we should remind ourselves that the fruit that we may reap from our endeavor is extremely worthwhile and will serve us well—far better perhaps than the relaxed and casual daydreaming that is so often a feature of our meditation!

We in Padmakara have attempted to translate these texts in accordance with the wishes and instructions of Dzongsar Khyentse Rinpoche, who, with immense kindness and in order to continue the tradition of teaching established here by Kyabje Dilgo Khyentse Rinpoche, made visits to Dordogne over several years and gave a complete instruction on the *Madhyamakavatara*. In offering this translation to him, we would like to express our deep gratitude as well as our prayers for his long life and the continuous increase of his enlightened activities.

Jigme Khyentse
Dordogne, 2001

INTRODUCTION
TO THE
MIDDLE WAY

Translators' Introduction

THIS BOOK is the result of a translation project that grew out of a series of teachings on Chandrakirti's *Madhyamakavatara* given by Dzongsar Khyentse Rinpoche in Dordogne, France, in the course of four summer seminars in 1996 and from 1998 to 2000. Although the exposition was based on a commentary composed by the fifteenth-century Sakya master Gorampa Sonam Senge, when a translation of the root verses was called for, it was specified that it should be made according to the commentary of the nineteenth-century Nyingma master Jamgön Ju Mipham. Since the translation of Chandrakirti required constant reference to an authoritative source, we decided to make a complete translation of Mipham Rinpoche's commentary as well and to offer it here as a key to understanding the general meaning of the root text.

Madhyamika is challenging.[1] It is many-faceted and, at first, hard to understand. Throughout its long history, it has been variously interpreted, and dissension has given rise to systems and subsystems. In India and Tibet, it has been the object of intensive study within an elaborate and sophisticated educational system redolent of the scholasticism of medieval Europe. Despite its apparent difficulty, it is nevertheless considered, at least in Tibet, to be central to the correct understanding of Mahayana Buddhism, and this importance is perhaps reflected in the fact that, down the centuries, it has been the focus of fierce debate between scholars and schools. The discussion has often turned on difficult points of logic and epistemology; and it is unfortunate that, especially in more recent centuries, this has not infrequently degenerated into acrimony and the hardening of positions along sectarian lines.[2]

A first encounter with this material can prove disheartening, even worrying, given that Chandrakirti tells us that liberation from samsara is impossible without a correct understanding of Madhyamika. Its literary expression, whether in the translations of traditional texts or in the expositions of Western scholars, is dry and daunting and often presupposes a knowledge that the general reader and practitioner does not possess or have time to acquire. Perhaps one reason for the difficulties encountered is that, in the study of Madhyamika, the preliminary steps are often passed over too hastily, and one finds oneself provided with answers long before one has had time to get the questions clear. One may well turn for help to the latest doctoral thesis, for example, only to find oneself submerged in difficult and abstruse technicalities, the sense of which is not always evident. Philosophical reflection, on the other hand, is important and interesting only to the extent that its practical relevance is perceived. And in the case of Madhyamika, the essential points are easy to miss; one so often fails to see the wood for the trees.

The products of Western scholarship are, to be sure, impressive, and it is true that the academic establishment, especially in America, has seen an increase, over the last thirty years, in the numbers of students of Buddhist philosophy who are themselves committed and practicing Buddhists.[3] Nevertheless it is still possible to find scholars, oblivious or indifferent to the living tradition, who are happy to repeat the age-old misconception that Madhyamika is a species of nihilism, some even going so far as to say that it is incompatible with the pursuit of spiritual values. In any case, the learned disquisitions of academics do not as a rule provide the kind of help most needed by aspirants on the path. So it is worth remembering that with Madhyamika, as with all other aspects of the Buddhist teachings, the key to understanding is not normally to be found in an unaided reading of texts. Experience shows, at least in the case of the group of people attending the summer teachings in Dordogne, that the easiest and most effective kind of introduction is to be found in the oral exposition of a qualified master.

Fortunately for us, we had in Dzongsar Khyentse Rinpoche a scholar as well as a talented and entertaining teacher. Perfectly qualified in the subject, he had studied for years at the feet of some of the greatest living exponents of Tibetan Buddhism. He was able to take us by the hand and show us the essential meaning of Madhyamika, pointing out its vital relevance to our lives and to our spiritual aspirations. He succeeded in drawing a large crowd of curious listeners, presented them with a difficult subject for which they had no preparation whatever, and transformed them into a class of enthusiastic students.

Perhaps the secret of his success was that, in slowly introducing his audience to a difficult text and the unusual, sometimes complicated ideas that it contained, he constantly reminded his listeners of the essential import and relevance of the Madhyamika teaching. He made the point on several occasions that, now that the period of Buddhism's introduction to the West is almost over, it is of great importance to consolidate and deepen the correct study and practice of the Doctrine according to an authentic tradition. Of first importance in this procedure must be the establishment of the view, the correct understanding of the nature of phenomena: the objects and situations that surround us in our daily lives and the thoughts and emotions that occupy and agitate our minds. The view, as presented in the Madhyamika texts, is the indispensable foundation of a stable and fruitful spiritual development. From the outset, it gives a clear idea of where the practice should lead and is a powerful tool for dealing with doubts and difficulties. Considerable intellectual effort is certainly required, but it leads to solid, tangible results. A correct understanding of the view imparts confidence and independence; it is like creating a suit of armor for oneself. It helps in the development of a clear-sighted, enduring devotion toward the teacher and the teachings, immune to whatever vagaries and difficulties may occur.

Another reason for studying the classic philosophical texts, we were told, is that they provide a firm criterion of doctrinal authenticity. There is a story that once when Atisha was in Tibet, he received news of the death of the master Maitripa. He was deeply grieved, and on being questioned about the reasons for his sorrow, he replied that Buddhism was in decline in India and that everywhere there was syncretism and confusion. Until then, Atisha continued, there had been only two masters in the whole of India, Maitripa and himself, capable of discerning the correct teaching from the doctrines and practices of the reviving Hindu schools. The time is sure to come, Dzongsar Khyentse Rinpoche commented, and perhaps it is here already, when there will be an analogous situation in the West. Only the correct establishment of the view will enable one to find one's way through the religious confusion of the modern West and to distinguish authentic Buddhism from the New Age "self-help" versions that are already taking hold.

Furthermore, a correct understanding of Madhyamika provides an excellent foundation and brings into focus the entire range of Mahayana practice. The view is none other than the absolute aspect of bodhichitta, indissociable from compassion, its relative aspect. The one cannot be perfected without the other. Compassion can never be mastered without the view of emptiness; wisdom can never be brought to completion without the perfection of compassion. Dzongsar Khyentse Rinpoche remarked significantly that just as the practice of guru yoga is said to be the life of the Vajrayana, *lojong*, the mind training, is the heart of Madhyamika.

Given the presence of Mipham Rinpoche's commentary, there is no need here for a detailed introduction to the *Madhyamakavatara* itself. The reader may, however, be interested by the following reflections, the aim of which is to give a general summary of Madhyamika in terms of its essential meaning and its historical development in India and Tibet.

Chandrakirti and the Madhyamakavatara

Although Chandrakirti lived approximately five centuries after Nagarjuna, that is, roughly halfway through the period in which their tradition was extant in India,[4] the *Madhyamakavatara* is often used as a convenient text with which to embark on the study of Madhyamika. Of the two elements that make up the treatise's title, *Madhyamaka* means "middle" or "middle way" and is in fact a reference to the *Mulamadhyamaka-karikas*, or *The Root Stanzas on the Middle Way*, composed by Nagarjuna. *Avatara* means literally "to descend" or "to go down into." It is cognate with the Sanskrit word *avatar* and is to be found in such titles as the *Lankavatara-sutra* (*The Sutra of the Journey into Lanka*) and the *Bodhicharyavatara* (*The Entry into the Ways of Enlightenment*) by Shantideva. The title of Chandrakirti's text therefore means "an entrance or introduction to (Nagarjuna's stanzas on) the Middle Way." It is what Tibetan scholarship defines as a general meaning commentary and provides a conspectus or summary of the overall meaning of Nagarjuna's great masterpiece. The *Madhyamakavatara* may therefore be contrasted with Chandrakirti's later work, the *Prasannapada*, which also comments on Nagarjuna's text but in much greater detail. In fact, although the *Madhyamakavatara* is actually of greater length than the *karikas*, its presentation of emptiness is actually simpler and less extensive in terms of subject matter and demonstration. Chandrakirti discusses fewer arguments but at greater length, in a manner more adapted to the beginner.[5]

The *Madhyamakavatara* is, therefore, a good place to start. Moreover, in addition to providing an accessible introduction to the teaching of Nagarjuna, it also gives a wider overview of the Madhyamika teaching as this developed in the centuries that followed him. Chandrakirti takes into consideration, for example, the position of the Chittamatra school, the other great stream of the Mahayana tradition, which came into prominence after Nagarjuna's time. And following the later division between the Prasangika and Svatantrika approaches to the Madhyamika dialectic, it was the Prasangika teaching of Chandrakirti that came to be accepted by all four schools of Tibetan Buddhism as the summit of Buddhist tenet systems.

Although the main theme of the *Madhyamakavatara* is the presentation of wisdom according to the view of Nagarjuna, it is important to advert to other aspects of the text, which, though subsidiary, are also important. It should be noted, for instance, that the dialectic is presented as an integral part of the Mahayana, the Buddhism of the great vehicle. At the beginning of the text, Chandrakirti emphasizes that the seed and accompaniment of the realization of wisdom is compassion, the desire to release beings from suffering. The twin aspects of ultimate and relative bodhichitta are never separate. Moreover, the exposition of the view is set within the framework of the ten *paramita*s and these are correlated with the ten Bodhisattva grounds of realization or *bhumi*s. Finally, buddhahood itself is made the subject of a detailed presentation at the conclusion of the text.

The Origins of Madhyamika and the Buddha's Silence

When beginning the study of a complicated subject, it is often helpful to isolate a comparatively simple key idea that can provide a vantage point from which to view the whole terrain and that might serve later on as a landmark as one tries to thread one's way through the subsequent labyrinth. As suggested by the Indian scholar T. R. V. Murti and corroborated by Mipham Rinpoche in the introductory section of his commentary on the *Madhyamakalankara*, one such idea is to be found

in the characteristic attitude of the Buddha when confronted by a certain kind of question. He remained silent, refusing to answer or to express an opinion. These questions, usually fourteen in number, are
mentioned on several occasions in the Pali canon. They are of a specifically metaphysical character and deal with subjects that of their nature lie beyond the possibility of common experience and empirical
verification. On most occasions, they are posed by the wandering asce-
tic Vacchagotta and are as follows:

> *Whether the universe has a beginning, or not, or both, or neither.*
> *Whether the universe has an end, or not, or both, or neither.*[6]
> *Whether the Buddha exists after death, or not, or both, or neither.*
> *Whether the self is identical with the body or different from it.*

To each of his questions, Vacchagotta receives no answer or else,
more pointedly, a negative reply to all four alternatives. He is thus
faced with another, more fundamental question: Why is it that the
Buddha refuses to be drawn into a discussion about such apparently
fundamental topics, on which other thinkers had been more than
ready to express their views? The silence of the Buddha has traditionally been interpreted as profoundly significant. Correctly understood, it constitutes a seminal anticipation of the Madhyamika, in
both meaning and method. It was expressive of a profound insight of
the Buddha, and its subtle implications were to be fully elucidated in
the writings of Nagarjuna. Conversely, the Madhyamika is to be understood as the exploration and systematic expression of the Buddha's silence.

The fourteen unanswered questions are typical examples of the
fundamental attempt, present in most philosophies, to go beyond
the data of the phenomenal world in order to discover some kind of
transcendent ground or reality that will explain the nature of things
as they appear to us and the reason for their existence. Unlike commonsense reflection, which bases itself on concrete evidence and is
interested not so much in what things are but in how they work,
metaphysics tries to find out the reality behind appearances. And it is
evident that in an inquiry that extends beyond the field of phenomenal appearance, there can be no appeal to the objective data provided
by the senses. The only possible course is deduction, reasoning from

effect to cause. And since the conclusions arrived at cannot be verified empirically, their plausibility must rest exclusively on the quality of the arguments employed and on logical coherence alone. This kind of activity has occupied the minds of philosophers for thousands of years and represents a deeply rooted tendency of the human mind, which yearns for knowledge and the satisfaction and sense of security that this brings. Faced with the mystery of the cosmos, the spirit naturally tries to interpret what it encounters; and where knowledge is lacking, it will fill the void with speculation or myth. When one surveys even the little that is known of philosophical and religious history, and the successive attempts put forward to account for the world and our experience of it, one cannot but marvel at the sheer inventiveness of the human imagination.

Of course, in view of the fact that reason and logic seem to work well enough in the context of day-to-day existence, one is naturally inclined to think that, given a sound basis in experience and adopting a careful method of argument, it ought to be possible to reason one's way to conclusions that, even in the absence of material evidence, *must* be true. But here we encounter a paradox, which points to the precarious nature of such an assumption. At least on this point, the eighteenth-century European philosopher Immanuel Kant is in full agreement with Nagarjuna and the Buddha himself: the use of pure reason extended beyond the empirical sphere results not in knowledge but in antinomies, that is, contradiction. It is a fact that equally plausible and coherent arguments may be constructed upon the same premise only to arrive at diametrically opposite conclusions. One philosopher will propound an attractive thesis to show that the cosmos had a beginning in time; another, with equally persuasive reasons, will prove the contrary. No one has ever succeeded in inventing a rational philosophy that is wholly incontrovertible. A procedure that appears to give us truth in fact produces only theory and opinion. And since, where metaphysics is concerned, verification is ruled out, there being no objective evidence available to compel the assent of all parties, it is clear that, in such a procedure, conflict between contrasting opinions is not only inevitable but endless. The problem, it seems, lies not in the quality of this or that line of reasoning but in the very constitution of reason itself. We are thus led to the possibly unpalatable conclusion that any attempt to express the transcendent in the empirical terms of thought and word cannot but fail. It produces illusion and not knowledge. It is in the light of such reflections that the Buddha's silence is best interpreted.

In other passages in the sutras, where the Buddha refers to his meeting with Vacchagotta, he makes it clear that the problem lay not in the difficulty of the subject but in the very nature of the question and the expectation that it implied. Vacchagotta was looking for either an affirmative or a negative reply. But what if the truth lies in neither of these alternatives? To reply according to the terms laid down by the questioner cannot but falsify the issue and make matters worse. The question "Is the self identical with the body?" demands an answer of yes or no. Yet neither of these answers is true, for there is no such thing as a self. Reflecting on this, Vasubandhu observed, "Since such a self is totally nonexistent, how could the Buddha have declared whether it was the same or different from the body? It is as though Vacchagotta had asked: 'Are the hairs of the tortoise bristly or smooth?'"

It is clear that the encounter between the Buddha and Vacchagotta was dominated by the latter's incapacity. Vacchagotta had posed a question in terms such that no true answer could be returned. A question framed according to the categories of ordinary experience demands an answer similarly expressed. But when the inquiry itself concerns matters that transcend experience, it is clear that silence is the only possible response. If further communication is to take place, it is first necessary to bring the questioner to the understanding that the question itself is faulty and must not be pursued in its present form. This is the purpose of the Buddha's silence, and this, as we shall see, is precisely the function of the Madhyamika dialectic.

When at the end of their interview the disconsolate Vacchagotta asked whether the Buddha had, after all, any theory of his own, the latter replied: "The Tathagata, O Vaccha, is free of all theories. But this, Vaccha, does the Tathagata know: the nature of form, of how form arises and passes away, the nature of feeling (and so on through the five aggregates). Therefore the Tathagata has attained liberation and is free from attachment, inasmuch as all imaginings, or agitations, or false notions, concerning a self and anything pertaining to a self have gone, faded, ceased, have been given up and abandoned."[7] It would be easy to misread this passage as a simple rejection of metaphysics and a slightly condescending admonition to stick to the simple practice of self-scrutiny and attentive living. But the message is much more profound than this. It is precisely because the Buddha does not immerse himself in theories about phenomena that he is able to discern their true nature, and it is this very discernment that confers liberation. To know things as they truly are is to free oneself from their tyranny. On the other hand, to elaborate theories about phenomena is not only to become engrossed in endless cogitation and verbiage; it is to veil the nature of phenomena even more and to fall even further beneath their spell. One becomes ever more entangled in what can only be productive of further frustration and sorrow.

"To hold that the world is eternal," the Buddha declared, "or to hold that it is not, or to agree to any other of the propositions that you adduce, O Vaccha, is the jungle of theorizing, the wilderness of theorizing, the tangle of theorizing, the bondage and the shackles of theorizing, attended by ill, distress, perturbation, and fever. It does not lead to detachment, passionlessness, tranquillity, and peace, to knowledge, and to the wisdom of Nirvana. This is the danger I perceive in these views, which makes me discard them all."[8]

It is important to assimilate this passage in its entirety. For although it expresses an unambiguous rejection of futile theorizing, it nevertheless indicates a truth that lies beyond the ordinary mind and becomes accessible precisely when theories are laid aside. It points, in other words, to a reality that transcends ordinary thought processes but is nevertheless still knowable. To say that it is possible to know something that is beyond thought carries the important, indeed astonishing implication that there is in the mind a dimension that in the vast majority of living beings is wholly concealed, the existence of which is not even suspected. As the Buddha says, it is passionless, tranquil, peaceful; it is the knowledge and wisdom of nirvana. This, the teachings say, is the true nature of the mind, which is discovered and actualized in enlightenment. Nagarjuna suggests[9] that it is a state so subtle and so profound that in the first moments after his awakening, the Buddha remained silent and declined to teach, perceiving that there was little chance of ordinary beings' understanding him. Moved by the entreaty of Brahma Sahampatti, the Buddha, as we know, relented and began his compassionate mission for those who might be trained. And in words that resonate down the centuries, he declared: "Open to them are the doors to deathlessness, O Brahma. *Let those who have ears throw off their old beliefs.*"

These old beliefs undoubtedly refer not only to the belief in the self but to all theories and constructions of the ordinary mind, the inventions of philosophy and of religion, which operate according to the procedures of affirmation and negation and the two extreme viewpoints of existence and nonexistence. No one, so the Buddha and the Madhyamika affirm, can hold to either of these views and hope to be free. It is necessary to analyze such false trails and, having discovered their inner contradiction, to abandon them. Only then can one progress beyond samsara. When, in a meeting that Nagarjuna mentions explicitly in the *karikas*,[10] Katyayana asked the Buddha for a teaching about the correct view, the latter replied that ordinary beings are used to thinking dualistically, in terms of affirmation or negation. In dealing with themselves and the phenomena that surround them, they think and speak in terms of "it is" and "it is not." They take things and situations to be "really real" or "really not real." They cling to them, act accordingly, and wander through the transient joys and sorrows of samsara, high and low, in heaven, hell, or any of the other six realms. But for those who have wisdom and correctly perceive the truth of how phenomena arise, abide, and pass away, the Buddha said, there is no "is" and no "is not." "That things exist, O Katyayana, is one extreme. That they do not exist is another. But I, the Tathagata, accept neither 'is' nor 'is not,' and I declare the truth from the Middle Position."

This position, this "Madhyamika," is the Buddha's Middle Way. On earlier occasions, it had been formulated ethically, as the path of moderation between the extremes of indulgence and excessive asceticism. Here is it expressed "philosophically" as the middle position between eternalism and nihilism, affirmation and negation. Confronted by Vacchagotta, the Buddha remained silent, refusing to involve himself in the inept attempts of philosophy and religion to reach beyond the world. This is exactly the attitude of Madhyamika. On the issue of transcendent reality, it adopts the Buddha's reserve and does not formulate a position. Rather, by a systematic analysis, whereby every possible position is exposed as false, the busy, restless mind (which, in failing to recognize its own nature, fails also to recognize the true status of phenomena) is reduced to silence. Conceptual construction must be stilled if the perfection of wisdom is to manifest; the mind must be brought to the Buddha's silence for liberation to be possible.

The Development of the Madhyamika School

In the final stanza of the *karikas*, Nagarjuna wrote: "I bow to Gautama, who out of compassion set forth the sacred Dharma for the rejection of all theories." The self-confessed mission of Madhyamika is to undermine the misrepresentations of philosophy and religion, the fruit of the discursive mind's deep-rooted tendency to elaborate theories in an attempt to explain phenomena, both of the outer world of things and the inner world of thought and emotion. In the hands of Nagarjuna, it is primarily a critique of other Buddhist tenet systems and secondarily, by implication, of the Hindu schools of ancient India. In the centuries that followed the Buddha's passing away, perfectly valid attempts were made to synthesize his teachings and facilitate their practice. But all of them, from the Madhyamika point of view, fall short to a greater or lesser degree, on the one all-important issue: the ultimate status of phenomena. All of them, in one way or another, affirm something to which they attribute real and ultimate existence.

In itself, therefore, Madhyamika is not a philosophy so much as a critique of philosophy. Its task is to examine the attempts of reason to give an account, in terms of thought and word, of "the way things really are" and to demonstrate its failure, showing that it is not in words and concepts that the nature of reality can be expressed. In this respect (but in this respect only) Madhyamika has been accurately compared with the philosophy of Kant.

In being a system of pure criticism, Madhyamika has no positive content of its own. Its evolution therefore cannot be assessed in terms of doctrinal elaboration and change. The history of Madhyamika is consequently no more than the account of the system's relationship with other philosophies. This is why the presentations of Madhyamika found in texts like the Wisdom chapter of Shantideva's *Bodhicharyavatara* and in the *Madhyamakavatara* itself, instead of being formal philosophical expositions, consist of a list of arguments with which other systems have been refuted. As Murti has observed, a study of the Madhyamika "shows the stresses and strains to which philosophy was subject in India down the ages."[11]

The development of the Madhyamika system, from its appearance in the second century C.E. till the disappearance of Buddhism from India in the twelfth, falls into three or four periods. The first is that of systematic exposition, achieved by Nagarjuna and his immediate disciple Aryadeva. The second stage (in the course of the sixth century) is marked by the appearance of two subschools, or rather tendencies, the Prasangika and Svatantrika, occasioned by the divergence of the masters Buddhapalita and Bhavaviveka in their approach to debate procedure and other connected issues. This period was brought to an end, or rather another period was inaugurated, about a hundred years afterward by Chandrakirti, who, in defending Buddhapalita and refuting Bhavaviveka, endeavored to establish *prasanga*, or consequential arguments, as the normative procedure in Madhyamika debate when defining the view. As we shall see, this entailed a quite specific attitude both to the position and the role of logic in such procedures as well as to a presentation of the conventional truth. Finally, the last important development in the Madhyamika, and of Indian Buddhist philosophy generally, was brought about by the great abbot Shantarakshita and his disciple Kamalashila. This consisted of a synthesis of the two great tenet systems of the Mahayana, namely, the Madhyamika and Chittamatra (Yogachara), as ways of presenting the ultimate and relative truth respectively. It was Shantarakshita and Kamalashila who established the Buddhist sutra teachings in Tibet in the eighth century, and it was their brand of Madhyamika that was to prevail there until the translation of Chandrakirti's work by Patsap Nyima Drak and others at the beginning of the twelfth century. Long extinct in its country of origin, Madhyamika has remained a living tradition in Tibetan Buddhism until the present day.

Nagarjuna and Aryadeva

Nagarjuna, the founder of Madhyamika, "elucidated the sutras of ultimate meaning through the sheer strength of his own genius, without recourse to other commentaries."* His work marks a new departure in the history of Buddhism. His name is inseparably linked with the teachings of the Mahayana and especially with the Prajñaparamita sutras, which, according to tradition, he recovered from the land of the Nagas where they had been preserved from decline until a time more

---

* See Longchen Yeshe Dorje, *Treasury of Precious Qualities* (Boston: Shambhala Publications, 2001), pp. 257–58.

propitious for their effective propagation. The Prajñaparamita literature is enormous; Madhyamika may be regarded as its essential and
systematic expression.

Nagarjuna is said to have been a prolific writer, and his total output was no doubt far greater than the works that have survived and
can be attributed to him with certainty. Following the conventions of
Tibetan scholarship, his writings are collected into three main
groups: the texts on reasoning (*rigs tshogs*), the collection of hymns
(*bstod tshogs*), and the collection of discourses (*gtam tshogs*). Of these,
the most important in the present context are the six texts of reasoning. These are the *Mulamadhyamaka-karikas,* or *The Root Stanzas on the
Middle Way*; the *Yuktishastika*, sixty stanzas dealing with the principles
of logic; the *Shunyatasaptati*, seventy stanzas on the doctrine of emptiness; the *Vigrahavyavartani*, a defense in verse of the Madhyamika
method and a refutation of objections; the *Vaidalya-sutra*, a prose
work delimiting the use of logical categories; and the *Vyavaharasiddhi*,
which is a discussion of the conventional truth.

Nagarjuna's masterpiece, the work in which he laid the foundations
of his system, is of course the *Mulamadhyamaka-karikas*. Here, his principal task is to analyze and undermine the categories and assumptions
implicit in the earlier Buddhist tenet systems. By this is meant the
Vaibhashika and Sautrantika schools, which, although they differ in
certain important respects, display, from Nagarjuna's point of view,
the same kinds of faults and may in the present context be grouped together as the Abhidharmika system. In brief, Nagarjuna represents
these earlier schools as having misunderstood, or only partially understood, the meaning of the Buddha's teaching.

When, as we have seen, the Buddha heeded the entreaty of Brahma
and began to teach, he did not, of course, immediately set forth the
truth in all its purity according to the level of his own understanding.
He realized that this would have been far beyond the capacity of his
hearers. Out of compassion, he set forth a doctrine suited to their
powers, which was designed to draw them onto the path and foster
their spiritual growth. His first task was to wean them away from the
gross, naïve understanding of worldly beings: their unquestioning belief in the personal self and the reality of substances—physical objects
extended in space and psychic experiences extended in time. He therefore spoke about the five aggregates, the six senses, and their objects

and associated consciousnesses, showing, for example, how the human person can be analyzed without residue into form, feelings, perceptions, conditioning factors, and consciousness. Despite the ingrained tendency of all sentient beings to assume the existence of a self and to cling to it, analysis shows that, no matter how hard one searches, no self can ever be found. In the same way, by observing the impermanence of physical things and mental events, one can come to an understanding that phenomena, however solid and unchanging they may appear, are in a state of constant, momentary flux. On the basis of this insight, one can begin to dissolve the attachment one has to things and loosen the fetters that bind one in the round of suffering.

In creating the first synthesis of the Buddha's teaching, the Abhidharmika schools took his teaching about the aggregates and so on at its face value. Of course, they correctly grasped his primary message, namely, the denial of the personal self, but insofar as the Buddha had indeed spoken of the aggregates, *ayatana*s, and so forth, they understood him to imply that these were real. On this basis, incorporating the ideas of gross and subtle impermanence, but overlooking the Buddha's admittedly less frequent but nevertheless significant statements that the aggregates and so forth are themselves illusory, they elaborated a theory of really existing, partless particles of matter and instants of consciousness. And it was within this framework that they understood the doctrine of the two truths. Broadly speaking, the relative or conventional truth refers to the gross, physical objects, together with the thoughts and emotional states that we encounter in waking life, while the ultimate truth consists of the momentary but irreducible particles of matter and instants of consciousness. As a method for undermining naïve commonsense assumptions, the Abhidharmika embodies a profound and sophisticated tool.

Nevertheless, Nagarjuna's primary objective in the *karikas* is to show that the Abhidharmika synthesis is fatally flawed and in fact misrepresents the Buddha's meaning. Step by step, the various categories (production, movement, the sense powers, aggregates, elements, and so on), so crucial to the coherent structure of the Abhidharmika tenets, are relentlessly dismantled and shown to be empty of real existence, while the arguments adduced to support belief in them are refuted as untenable absurdities. Chandrakirti comments that the twenty-seven chapters of the *karikas* are in fact a continuous, ongoing debate. Each successive chapter embodies an answer to a possible objection that could be raised in defense of the position demolished in the preceding section.

It is obviously not possible to discuss the *karikas* in any great detail here, but it is of some interest to review, however cursorily, a few of the text's most salient features, since this throws light on the work of Chandrakirti and the later tradition generally. In what was to become the standard procedure in Madhyamika literature, the work begins with a discussion about causation. It is, however, important to bear in mind that, in this context, causes are understood exclusively in a substantial or material sense.[12] The discussion, in other words, is about how things come into being and evolve.

Nagarjuna begins by showing that, appearances to the contrary, the everyday notion that real effects are produced by real causes is mistaken; it cannot possibly be true. Causes and effects, so much a feature of existence, are, he says, essentially definable only in terms of mutual dependence; they are not real things in themselves. To say that something has real existence in itself is to say that it is an autonomous, circumscribed entity, separate in all respects from other things. This is, as a matter of fact, how we habitually view things in the ordinary transactions of everyday life. We feel that we are self-contained individuals and relate to other self-contained individuals. We encounter objects, some pleasant, some unpleasant, which we try to acquire or avoid accordingly. More or less complicated situations arise, which themselves seem individual and real. We are happy and we suffer. To the uncritical observer, life consists of blocks; it is a collection of individual, discrete realities. But this is an illusion. In its anxiety for reassurance and security, the mind reifies situations and things, which it clings to and manipulates in its hopeless quest for lasting satisfaction. In order to expose this procedure as the false trail that it is, Nagarjuna relentlessly demonstrates the inconsistencies inherent in what ordinarily passes for common sense; he shows that the normal "worldview" is in fact riddled with contradiction. It is important to understand, however, that he is not trying to deny our experience of production and change, or of anything else in the phenomenal world. That would be absurd; the world-process is all around us constantly, undeniably. The objects of his critique are not the empirical facts of existence that inescapably appear to us but the assumptions that we make about these facts. We think that real things give rise to real things; that real things come into being and pass away. But this notion of real, individual, self-contained entity is something that we impose on the raw material of experience. It is a figment of our imagination; in fact there are no real things in this sense. Self-contained entities can never change and can never enter into relation with other entities. The notions of coming into being or passing away cannot be meaningfully applied to them. Thus the first stanza announces: "No things are produced anywhere at any time, either from themselves, from something else, from both, or from neither." The mere fact of "coming into being" excludes real entity and vice versa. The true status of the phenomena that we experience is not, therefore, to be found in their supposed real entity, but in their relatedness, their interdependence with all other phenomena. This is Nagarjuna's interpretation of the doctrine of dependent arising, understood not in the sense of a temporal sequence (as in the Hinayana interpretation of the doctrine of the twelvefold chain of dependent production), but in the *essential dependence* of phenomena. This interdependence undermines the notion of individual, intrinsic reality in things; it is the very antithesis of "thingness." Phenomena, being the interplay of interdependent factors, are unreal. Their interdependence (*pratityasamutpada*) is their emptiness (*shunyata*) of inherent existence.

Production or change, in the sense of the inner transformation of things, gives way, in the second chapter, to a consideration of change in the sense of movement. Compared with the more or less subtle processes involved in physical change, one might have thought that so obvious a fact as physical movement would be easy enough to describe. And yet, by a process of ingenious arguments, Nagarjuna shows that this too is beyond rational explanation. By a minute examination of the categories of space traversed, space yet to be traversed, moving body, and so forth—understood as real according to the common view of things—he demonstrates that reason is powerless to account for even the simplest of events, the displacement of a thing from one location to another. The whole of the second chapter of the *karikas* is an astonishing and disconcerting performance, and the reader is forced to acknowledge that what had previously been taken as the straightforward certainties of existence is nothing but a tissue of naïve and ultimately untenable assumptions. The entire worldview of common sense is shown to be completely incoherent.

If we follow Nagarjuna's arguments carefully, we can see—we are unable to deny—that they make sense. Nagarjuna is saying that if we think that the things of the world (ourselves included) are as they appear, self-existent and solid, we are not in touch with reality; we are living in a world of mirages. Phenomena appear to be real, but they are insubstantial, dreamlike. Given, however, that our perceptions are commonly shared, we might be tempted to dismiss Nagarjuna's ideas as no more than a curious paradox with little relevance to the facts of experience. Life, after all, goes on regardless of the theories of philosophers. Nagarjuna could be right, we may say, but since we all concur in our dreamlike experiences, why question them? What, finally, is wrong with the way we perceive things?

The answer is that there is nothing "wrong" with it; the issue is not a moral one. We are not condemned for being in samsara. To believe that phenomena are solid, real entities is not a "sin"; it is only a mistake. But it is a mistake with unfortunate consequences. In his first teaching following his enlightenment, the Buddha did not speak, though he could have done so, about the dreamlike nature of samsaric existence. Instead, he referred to a more pressing, less deniable problem, namely, that existence—the samsaric dream—is, as a matter of fact, painful. Beings suffer; they are not satisfied. Whatever may be the true nature of phenomena, we cannot deny that our lives are plagued by the ills of birth, sickness, old age, and death, the inescapable accompaniments of existence. It is true that suffering may be suspended by moments of happiness. But these turn out to be fragile and are marked by a transience so intrinsic as to render them, in the larger view, meaningless. Caught in the dream, unaware that they are dreaming, ordinary worldly beings endlessly try to manipulate phenomena in the interests of security and fulfillment. They do this by trying to create the conditions of material and emotional satisfaction and, if they are religious, by striving to create the causes of happiness in the hereafter, whether in terms of "going to heaven" or of securing a favorable rebirth in their future existences. Undoubtedly, the happiness thus produced is both good and necessary, but it is still samsara. It is still part of the dream; it is not the final answer, not liberation. For samsara to disappear, its cause must be identified and arrested. The Buddha is saying that a lasting solution cannot possibly lie in the reorganization of the dream, in a mere rearrangement of the furniture. A better plan is to recognize our state of deception—the fact that we are dreaming—and to wake up. And to wake from the dream, it is necessary to understand the nature of phenomena.

Throughout the *karikas*, Nagarjuna's critique is directed at the categories adopted by the Abhidharmika schools: the sense powers, aggregates, ayatanas, and so on. These too are shown to be hollow and dreamlike. To the non-Madhyamika, this is highly disturbing, for Nagarjuna seems to be undermining the doctrine itself. Everything is denied. Nothing is real; nothing makes sense. It is not surprising that in both ancient and modern times, Madhyamika has been stigmatized as philosophical and moral nihilism. The twenty-fourth chapter (perhaps the most important of the *karikas*) therefore opens with an expression of these qualms. If everything is empty, there is neither arising nor destruction. It follows that there is no such thing as the Four Noble Truths. Without the Four Noble Truths, there can be no wisdom, and the qualities of elimination and realization are impossible. Therefore the spiritual path is fruitless and meaningless. Attainment is out of the question. There is no such thing as liberation and enlightenment. There are no enlightened beings. There is no Doctrine and no Spiritual Community. The teaching on emptiness is therefore a rejection of the Three Jewels. Emptiness is the destruction of the Dharma. Good and evil and all the conventions of ordinary life are utterly negated and without significance.

These are the objections that Nagarjuna has been expecting and wanting. The whole gist of the *karikas* in the previous chapters in fact leads to this and is the cue for Nagarjuna to turn the objection on its head and show not only that emptiness is compatible with the spiritual path, but that it is precisely the factor that makes spiritual growth possible. In order to do this, he must expound his own teaching on the two truths, the single most important element in the Madhyamika. It is impossible, he says, to grasp the teaching of the Buddha without a correct understanding of the way the two truths are differentiated. There is no liberation without the realization of emptiness, the ultimate truth; there is no approach to the ultimate without correctly relying on the conventional. The doctrine of emptiness, however, is a double-edged sword, and Nagarjuna is the first to speak of its dangers. Understood correctly, it leads to liberation; understood wrongly, it can be a source of spiritual and moral degeneration—as dangerous as a poisonous snake badly handled or a powerful spell ineptly applied. The teaching on the two truths is indeed profound and subtle, and it is important for the reader to reflect upon the explanations of an authoritative source.[13] For the purpose of this introduction, it will perhaps be helpful to advert to the following important point.

We have seen already how, in the Abhidharmika system, the awareness of the impermanence of extended phenomena and mental events had implied a theory of indivisible particles of matter and instants of consciousness. This involved a distinction between two levels of reality: the gross, extended objects that populate our perceptions and constitute the phenomenal world, and the "real" entities that underlie appearance but are not experienced. All philosophy of any degree of sophistication is obliged to make a distinction between fact and appearance; intelligent reflection necessarily leads to the awareness that phenomena cannot actually be the way they seem.[14] From the Madhyamika point of view, conventional truth comprises the things and transactions of everyday life—or, to use an expression more in line with Sanskrit and Tibetan usage, the things and events of the phenomenal world are themselves "conventional truths." When analyzed, these same phenomena are found to be empty of unitary, intrinsic being. This is their ultimate truth. We have seen that emptiness, the ultimate status of things, the middle position beyond the categories of "is" and "is not," is by definition inexpressible in thought and word. "The ultimate," as Shantideva said, "lies not within the reach of intellect, for intellect is grounded in the relative."[15] This does not mean, however, that the ultimate is somehow remote from phenomena, floating free, as it were, in an absolute dimension of its own. The ultimate is said to be beyond the world only because it is veiled by the appearances of the world—and for ordinary beings, appearances *are* the world. In fact, the ultimate is not separate from phenomena; it is the very nature of phenomena. The ultimate is what the conventional really is; the conventional is the way the ultimate appears. The two truths are never separate; they merge and coincide in phenomena. The difference is not ontological but epistemic. According to Madhyamika, the distinction is not in the object; it is a matter of recognition within the cognizing subject. The objective distinction of the two truths corresponds to the views of other systems, which by a process of reasoning, beyond the possibility of experience, arrive at some putative entity considered to be ultimately real (*prakriti*, for instance, or the indivisible particle, the *alaya*, *atman*, God, the first cause, and so on). For these systems, the two truths are two separate entities.

Thus far, we have been considering Nagarjuna. We have seen that the focus of his attention had been mainly the tenets of the Abhidharmika schools. It was left to his foremost disciple and successor, Aryadeva, to apply the same dialectic to the refutation of the Samkhya and Vaisheshika schools of Hinduism, which he does in his chief work *The Four Hundred Stanzas*.[16] Aryadeva was formidable in debate, and it was in large measure thanks to him that the position of the Madhyamika system was consolidated in the face of opposition both Buddhist and non-Buddhist. Chandrakirti remarks that in their view, Nagarjuna and Aryadeva agree in all respects. Tibetan scholarship refers to them as "Madhyamikas of the founding texts,"* for it is in relation to their writings that the later Madhyamika subschools defined themselves.

A Difference of Method: Buddhapalita, Bhavaviveka, and Chandrakirti

Around the turn of the sixth century, an important disagreement occurred about the method whereby the Madhyamika view was to be established in debate. This question had important ramifications concerning the manner in which the relative truth was to be explained and how, within that context, the ultimate truth was to be presented. One side of the debate was represented by Buddhapalita, who had confined himself to the exclusive use of consequential arguments (*prasanga*). He was opposed by Bhavaviveka, who maintained that, in debate with non-Madhyamikas about the ultimate nature of phenomena and in order to establish one's view beyond doubt, the adduction of mere consequences was insufficient. It was both possible and necessary to prove one's point positively by means of independent inferences (*svatantra-anumana*) adduced in syllogistic form. The fact that Buddhapalita returned no answer to this critique gave rise to the story that he had been intimidated by Bhavaviveka's princely rank. However,

* *gzhung phyi mo'i dbu ma pa.*

there are reasons for believing that he was already dead by the time the latter launched his attack.

Bhavaviveka was a famous scholar with an encyclopedic knowledge of the different philosophical and religious schools of his time, both Buddhist and non-Buddhist. It is evident, too, that he was deeply interested in questions of formal logic, the study of which had been developing in India from the third century onward. And it has been suggested that the movement Bhavaviveka inaugurated was an attempt to create a bridge between the Madhyamika and the philosophical movement that reached its climax in the logical reforms of Dignaga and Dharmakirti.[17]

The division between the Prasangikas and the Svatantrikas is a large question and in certain respects highly technical. Fortunately, there exist a number of learned studies in English on this subject, and the interested reader is invited to refer to them.[18] For the present purposes, we will attempt a summary of the main issues.

To begin with, it is useful to bear in mind that the final aim of Madhyamika, as of all other Buddhist teachings, is soteriological. Its sole purpose is to lead beings to ultimate freedom. As Nagarjuna said, it is only through the understanding and realization of the ultimate truth that freedom from suffering can be gained. Impelled by their vows of bodhichitta, Nagarjuna and the great Madhyamika masters who followed him were concerned, therefore, not only with the realization of the truth for themselves, but also with the communication of this truth to others. The disagreement between the Prasangikas and the Svatantrikas turns on precisely this question: how is the view to be established and what is the best and most effective way of indicating it to others?

The disagreement between Bhavaviveka and Buddhapalita arose out of the interpretation of the very first stanza of the *karikas*: "No things are produced anywhere at any time, either from themselves, from something else, from both, or from neither." Cast in a form that harks back, it will be remembered, to the fourteen unanswered questions, the primary dilemma between the first two alternatives (production from self and production from other) is expanded into a tetralemma (*catuskoti*) by the addition of two more alternatives intended to exhaust the entire range of possibilities. These four alternatives, which provide the framework for Chandrakirti's later discussion of phenomenal emptiness in the *Madhyamakavatara*, were usually associated, emblematically, with four schools of Indian philosophy: the Samkhya, the Buddhist Abhidharmika, the Jaina, and the Charvaka respectively. We are to imagine a discussion between a Madhyamika and the representatives of four types of philosophical realism, who believe that there is at least something, the intrinsic existence of which must be accepted. The purpose of the Madhyamika critique is to demonstrate their mistake and to produce in their minds an understanding of the emptiness of all phenomena. How is one to go about this? The Prasangikas and Svatantrikas disagree as to the best approach.

Buddhapalita refuted the Samkhya theory simply by pointing out that it entailed an absurd consequence. His argument, which is reiterated exactly in the *Madhyamakavatara*, runs roughly as follows. The Samkhyas believed that everything arises through modulations occurring in the primal substance, prakriti. All effects are therefore, in the most fundamental sense, identical with their causes. Buddhapalita argued that this assertion is untenable. To say that things arise "from themselves" is absurd, because if they already exist (being identical with their causes), no further coming into existence is needed. If, on the other hand, "coming into existence" is part and parcel of the supposedly produced thing, its production must be as unending as the produced thing itself. The Samkhya account is therefore incompatible with causality, either in theory or in fact. It is not necessary, at this stage, to enter into the details of Buddhapalita's argument. The point is that he disposes of the Samkhya claim simply by showing that it involves contradictions and is therefore unviable. In refuting the Samkhya view, he does not substitute a theory of his own.

Bhavaviveka objected that Buddhapalita's procedure was logically deficient. The latter, he said, should have supported his contention by supplying a reason and an example. He complained, moreover, that the Samkhyas were being dealt with too summarily. They had their own arguments against the Buddhist critique, which Buddhapalita was failing to address. Finally, the simple negation of the Samkhya view by showing its untenable consequences was too open-ended. It could be taken to imply that Buddhapalita entertained an alternative position, which, since he was a Madhyamika, was not the case. Simply to adduce a consequence, therefore, leaves room for doubt in the opponent's mind. In order to remedy these defects, Bhavaviveka argued that when refuting the Samkhya, it was both possible and necessary to prove Nagarjuna's proposition (as given in the first stanza of the *karikas*) in terms of a syllogism—an independent syllogism, indeed, that expressed the contention in a self-contained manner, without reference to the opinion of the interlocutor. Bhavaviveka evidently thought that this kind of approach would be more effective in convincing the opponent and helping him accept the Madhyamika view. The kind of formulation he proposed took the standard form of a syllogism as laid down in Indian logic: subject, predicate, reason, and so on.[19] When used in debate, the syllogism is, or should be, founded on commonly accepted elements established by valid cognition, thereby deriving its cogency from basic premises shared by both parties. Such an argument is intended to convey real knowledge and induce conviction. To this standard format, Bhavaviveka added a touch of his own, namely, the rider "on the ultimate level" or "ultimately."* The reasons for this addition will become clear in due course.

Buddhapalita no doubt represented a conservative element in the Madhyamika tradition.[20] In confining himself to consequences, and in being evidently reluctant to involve himself in the sophistications of logic and epistemology as these were developing at his time, he emulated Nagarjuna, who had employed consequential reasoning very often (though not exclusively) in the *karikas*, and who, in the *Vigrahavyavartani*, had been careful to confine the use of logic to the level of conventional truth, implying the illegitimacy of using it to establish anything transcending that sphere. Unlike Bhavaviveka, who was a popular and influential teacher, Buddhapalita appears to have had few disciples. It was left to Chandrakirti in the following century to defend him and to stem the Svatantrika tide.

As we have seen, the purpose of prasanga is to refute a position, not by stating a more plausible counterposition but by exposing a consequence unwanted by the proponents—on the basis of arguments that the proponents themselves accept. In adopting this strategy, the Prasangika debater is not committed either to the immediate conclusion of the argument or to the principles invoked in the course of the investigation. It is only necessary for the proponents to accept them, the only object being to enable them to see for themselves the falsity of

---

*Skt *paramarthatah*, Tib *don dam par* or *yang dag par*.

their position and to abandon it. The position of the adversary is not destroyed, as it were, from outside, by arguments adduced independently by the Madhyamika. It is shown instead to be intrinsically absurd, so that it collapses, so to speak, under its own weight. By using this technique in discussions concerning the ultimate status of phenomena, the Prasangikas are able to undermine the false notions of their opponents and to indicate the truth indirectly, without having to verbalize a position of their own.

Why is this last point so important? In order to answer this question, we must digress slightly. We have already seen that the Buddha himself had declared the ultimate truth to be beyond the scope of the ordinary mind. But though the ultimate is not to be expressed in thought and word, it can be indirectly indicated by demarcating the limits of conceptual construction and suggesting that there is, nevertheless, "something" beyond. In this procedure, logical arguments are used to demonstrate that when reason attempts to give an accurate account, in absolute terms, of "the way things are," it leads to antinomies and contradiction. This is the method of Nagarjuna and of Chandrakirti. Even if reason is unable to encompass reality, it can at least convince itself that it is unequal to the task and that the ultimate is to be approached and realized by means other than philosophical cogitation. Reason understands, inferentially, that the ultimate truth exceeds its powers of comprehension and expression. The Madhyamika approach is, in other words, a *via remotionis*, to borrow a term from Christian theology: the dialectic approaches its goal by showing all that the ultimate is not; its purpose is to demolish the theories produced by the ordinary mind and to reveal the hollowness of their pretensions. The use of reasoning to demonstrate its own inadequacy is not, to be sure, an attractive prospect for the rationalist. In one sense, it is a bewildering discovery, and it did indeed prove the sticking point for Kant. Having understood the limitations of pure reason, he found of course that this purely intellectual achievement was unable to remove what he called the transcendental illusion: the impression, and therefore the constant temptation to think, that thought is able to lay hold of perfectly perspectiveless objectivity. He doubted that it could ever be removed, that the mind could ever pass beyond it.[21] He could never countenance the possibility of *jñana*, the nondual wisdom in which the ultimate is known directly without the mediation of thought.[22] He failed, in other words, to appreciate the immense spiritual significance of his discovery and, as Murti aptly observes, ended by putting it to a trivial purpose.[23] This was a mistake that Nagarjuna and the Madhyamikas did not make. And they did not make it because they had at their disposal not just the intellectual tools of their own brilliant minds but also their spiritual training on the Buddhist path and the realization of the masters who had transmitted it to them.

A perception of the limitations of thought may seem, as we have said, a sorry conclusion to the philosophical enterprise—until one notices that the implications for the mind that reaches this conclusion are immense. The very fact that the discovery is possible points to something beyond the ordinary intellect. To realize, by thought, that there is an ultimate truth that is not the object of thought is no ordinary finding. It is not just the negative conclusion of dialectical analysis, but also the discovery of a wholly new dimension in the mind itself. When the mind realizes emptiness, it overcomes the subject-object dichotomy. It does not just break through the appearances that conceal the ultimate status of phenomena; it also penetrates the veils of mental construction that had concealed its own true nature and had made the misperception of phenomena possible. When the true nature of phenomena is discovered, the mind's nature also stands revealed, for the realization of emptiness is the experience of nondual wisdom. Looked at from this point of view, the final outcome of Madhyamika analysis is not a negative but a profoundly positive experience.

Chandrakirti's defense of Buddhapalita and his refutation of Bhavaviveka are to be found in his detailed commentary on the *karikas* entitled the *Prasannapada*.[24] Here he considers each of the objections brought against Buddhapalita by Bhavaviveka and refutes them all on technical grounds.[25] To begin with, he rejects as unfounded the charge that Buddhapalita's use of consequences is inadequate because it fails to supply a reason and example. In fact a consequential argument can be restated in the form of what is technically known as an inference accepted by the opponent,* whereby the import of the consequence can be expressed in a syllogism in which both reason and example are present by implication. In being an extension of the consequence, the inference accepted by the opponent is based on elements that need only

---

* *gzhan la grags pa'i rjes dpag.*

be agreeable to the opponent, not to the proponent, in the debate. It is
thus not to be confused with an independent inference in the terms of
which the acceptance of the proponent is implied. Like the consequence, the inference accepted by the opponent does not compromise
the proponent in the way that an independent inference does.

This fact, Chandrakirti argues, also acquits Buddhapalita of the second charge brought by Bhavaviveka, namely, that he fails to address
the objections advanced by the Samkhyas. In fact, these objections are
of necessity only advanced against a position positively expressed, that
is, in an independent argument. This does not occur in the case of the
inference accepted by the opponent.[26]

Finally, that Buddhapalita's consequential argument implies a contrary position that inadvertently undermines his Madhyamika stance
is categorically denied. The meaning and purpose of the consequence
are clear from the context, and Buddhapalita's words are to be understood according to his evident intention.[27] A consequential argument,
Chandrakirti insists, is perfectly adequate to the task of refuting the
false position. If the adversary refuses to accept defeat even after it has
been shown, on principles already acceptable to him, that his view is
untenable, it is clear that the further adduction of an independent argument would serve no purpose. If the opponent still maintains his
position even after its incoherence is laid bare, it is clear that he does so
for motives that cannot be rational. Either he is too dull to understand
the refutation or he clings to his position out of prejudice. This being
so, it is futile to discuss further.

These are undoubtedly complex questions. The point to retain, however, is that Chandrakirti's objective is to defend a method of communication whereby proponents of Madhyamika can debate on matters
concerning the ultimate truth without having to verbalize positions of
their own, thereby betraying the Madhyamika's most important principle, namely, that the ultimate status of things is ineffable.

Having vindicated Buddhapalita, Chandrakirti turns to his as-
sailant. "Bhavaviveka wishes only to parade his knowledge of the logical treatises. He adduces independent syllogisms, despite the fact that
he claims to hold the Madhyamika view. The Madhyamika system, to
be sure, creates lots of difficulties for such a would-be logician. He
makes one mistake after another."[28] According to the rules of logic,
when an independent syllogism is framed, its validity depends on the

fact that its terms denote exactly the same thing for both parties in the debate. This, Chandrakirti argued, is impossible in any discussion between a Madhyamika and a realist philosopher (such as the Samkhya) when the subject of discussion is the ultimate status of phenomena. A viable independent syllogism presupposes the existence of objects that both sides accept. But the whole purpose of the Madhyamika is to show that no such objects exist. In situations of this kind, therefore, the Madhyamika debater cannot use independent syllogisms without being fatally compromised. The Madhyamika teaching on the two truths, which is not accepted by the opponent, necessarily excludes any community of understanding with the realist concerning the existential status of phenomena. This being so, the Madhyamika is unable to advance an independent syllogism, without the syllogism itself, according to the rules of logic, being defective. If the two parties use the same terms but in effect mean different things by them, it is obvious that they are talking at cross-purposes; common understanding is ruled out. In brief, therefore, Chandrakirti castigates Bhavaviveka not only for compromising his Madhyamika principles but also for being an incompetent logician.

In defense of Bhavaviveka, it may be said that he was not unaware of the difficulties involved in his position, and it seems clear that the characteristic orientation of the Svatantrikas with regard to logic and the conventional truth is adopted with a view to consistency. The fundamental teaching of Madhyamika is the rejection of the ultimate existence of all entities. Like the Prasangikas, the Svatantrikas are concerned to communicate this view to non-Madhyamikas. Unlike the Prasangikas, they seek to do this not by consequences alone but by the use of logic and the making of positive statements—adducing, as we have seen, independent syllogisms that are based on elements commonly acceptable, on the conventional level, to both parties. In so doing, the Svatantrikas take a conciliatory step toward the opponent. In other words, they introduce the Madhyamika view in terms easier for ordinary people to understand. The motivation, as we have seen, is a good one, but the step cannot be made without compromise, and this consists in the creation of a provisional separation of the two truths.

Bhavaviveka and those who followed him say that whereas, on the ultimate level, phenomena have no reality whatever, on the conventional level, they do possess a certain existence (though not a true existence), and this is proved by the operation of conventional reasoning. Common sense can, for instance, distinguish a "real" object from an optical illusion. It does so on the basis of functionality (real water is drinkable, mirage water is not, and so on). Therefore, when phenomena are said to be without inherent existence, the Svatantrikas add the proviso "on the ultimate level." Conventionally, for the Svatantrikas (at least those who follow Bhavaviveka), phenomena do have a kind of "natural existence according to their characteristics."* When investigated by conventional reasoning, they are "found"; one can discuss them and entertain theories about them. For Bhavaviveka, therefore, meaningful discourse is still possible on the level of the conventional truth. Although ultimately empty, conventional phenomena can nevertheless be talked about without absurdity. It is still possible to philosophize, and this can be utilized to good purpose, in giving disciples a correct orientation and leading them gradually on the path. Thus the theory of partless particles, as presented in the Abhidharmika schools, is provisionally accepted. What the Abhidharmikas had taken to be ultimate truth remains valid, but only conventionally valid, for the Svatantrikas.

Chandrakirti and the Prasangikas will have none of this. For them no compromise is possible. The ultimate, being ineffable, is falsified by any attempt to express it. To separate the two truths is to deviate from Nagarjuna's meaning. Therefore, *when establishing the view and in debate,* the Prasangikas express no position, no thesis. In debate, they confine themselves to consequential arguments, the reduction to absurdity of the opponent's position; the ultimate truth is indicated only indirectly by the demolition of theories. For the Prasangikas, therefore, it is neither desirable nor possible to elaborate a theory of the conventional truth. Unlike Bhavaviveka, who discusses along Sautrantika lines, and unlike Shantarakshita, who presents the conventional truth in terms of the Yogachara view, Chandrakirti refers to the conventional as being simply the unexamined phenomena of ordinary experience, accepted as true by the common consensus. The Prasangikas do not care to theorize about the conventional. They do not philosophize. This does not, of course, mean that they acquiesce in the ignorant opinions of worldly people, who believe firmly in the reality of the phenomenal

---

*rang mtshan nyid kyis sgrub pa.

and personal selves. It does mean, however, that, as a method of approach to the ultimate truth and as a medium with which to communicate with worldly people, the Prasangikas simply accept, without analysis, the things and events occurring in everyday experience.

As forms of philosophy, the four theories of production given in the tetralemma all claim to give an accurate account of conventional experience. All can be shown to be logically incoherent and are, the Prasangikas say, a source of confusion. Far from giving a sensible explanation of the world, their solutions are obscure and far-fetched. In Chandrakirti's opinion, they are quite irrelevant (as philosophy often is) to the perceptions and concerns of ordinary folk. No ordinary person consciously advocates either the theory of the Samkhyas or that of the Buddhist Abhidharmika—production explained in terms either of identity or difference of material causes and effects. A man who deposits a drop of semen in the womb of his wife will point to the baby nine months later and say, "I produced this child." The difference between baby and semen is routinely overlooked. In the same way a gardener points to the flowers that "he planted," whereas in actual fact he planted only seeds. In practice, therefore, people do not acknowledge a separation between material cause and material effect. On the other hand, if you ask someone whether the food they eat and the feces they excrete are the same, they will certainly say that there is a difference. They are very far from accepting the Samkhya theory. On the level of *what actually happens*, it is impossible to say that cause and effect are either the same or different. The only thing one can and must allow is that, in experience, production does occur. Everyone is agreed about this and, as an account of the conventional, this is, for the Prasangikas, quite sufficient.

Indeed, in situations where one is trying to penetrate to the ultimate status of phenomena, the introduction of theories as a means of explaining the working of the phenomenal world fogs the issue and actually undermines the correct approach to the conventional truth. Far from elucidating the conventional, Chandrakirti says, theories actually undermine it. It is the conventional itself—what actually happens—that is the means of entering the ultimate. To create a theory as a way of explaining the mechanics of the conventional does not help to introduce the ultimate; it merely complicates the matter. Therefore theories are dangerous, for they obscure the conventional; they hinder the

procedure whereby one can "see through" the conventional appearance of phenomena and perceive their lack of intrinsic "thingness."
Chandrakirti says that to create a theory about the conventional is in a
sense to "destroy" the conventional; it produces an account that, however coherent it may be, is always at variance with what we actually experience. As such, it is at best irrelevant to the task in hand, namely, to
perceive the true nature of phenomenal appearance. At worst it is a
hindrance and a trap. The image often evoked is that of a man climbing a tree. Before he has caught hold of the branch above, it is inadvis-
able for him to move off the one below. In weaving their theories, this
is precisely what philosophers do. To create a theory about the conventional is in a sense to move away from the conventional as experienced
(which alone is the gateway to the ultimate). The progression from the
conventional to the ultimate is rendered more difficult by the invention of ill-conceived hypotheses.

The following parable, borrowed from Bertrand Russell, may further illustrate this important point.[29] If I go up to a nuclear physicist
and ask him to describe for me the physical constitution of a table, I
will receive a long and learned answer, all about magnetic fields and
atomic and subatomic particles moving around at great speed. These,
he assures me, are the real constituents of the table; the object in the
corner is little more than an optical illusion. On the other hand, if I approach the same scientist unannounced and simply ask whether there
is a table in the room, he will, without a moment's hesitation, point
and say: "It's over there, can't you see it?" However accurate the scientist's earlier description may be, it has clearly not interfered with his
perceptions. But now let us extend the parable further and imagine the
same physicist trying to use his bank card to get money from a cash
machine outside a bank, and let us suppose that there is something
wrong with the card, with the result that the machine swallows it and
produces no money. Before long he will become annoyed and start
beating on the machine with the same degree of frustration as any ordinary nonscientist. And I would be ill advised, at this point, to try to
comfort him by reminding him that, after all, the bank card he has lost
and the bank notes he has failed to receive are no more than a mass of
subatomic particles. Sophisticated as the physicist's theory may be, it
has done nothing to free him from the suffering and perturbation always liable to manifest in the course of conventional transactions. In

the same way, the propounding of theories about the conventional does nothing to remove the tyranny of phenomenal appearance. And the use of independent syllogisms, and the acceptance of conventionally existent entities, which this entails, necessarily implies a theoretical explanation of the conventional—of the kind that, in the above example, seemed only to intensify (when mentioned inappropriately) the impotent fury of the frustrated scientist.

Therefore, in discussions about the reality or otherwise of phenomena, the Prasangikas restrict the terms of discussion to the position propounded by the non-Madhyamika opponent. They do not allow themselves, by the use of logical arguments, to become involved in an exchange that might give the impression that they believe in the real existence of the topic under discussion. It must be stressed that in the debates between the Madhyamika and other philosophies, the only point of issue is real existence. The opponents, Samkhya, Buddhist, and so on, all contend in one way or other that something exists. The Madhyamikas deny this. Therefore, for Madhyamikas to discourse about phenomena as if they believed in their real existence would, the Prasangikas say, necessarily weaken the force of their argument.

It is important to be aware that a discussion about a thing's existence is radically different from a discussion about a thing's attributes. The standard example used to illustrate this point is the debate about the nature of sound. Buddhists find themselves in disagreement with certain Hindus who believe that sound is permanent, part of the primordial structure of the universe, and so on. The two positions are in total opposition. But in the discussion, both parties are agreed on one thing, namely, sound itself. Sound as a phenomenon can be observed by Buddhist and Hindu alike, irrespective of the ideas they have about it. However complicated the discussion may become, the situation is clear: both parties are referring to *sound*; they are disagreeing about its properties.

Discussions about existence, by contrast, are much less straightforward. And it may be observed in passing that the problem at hand evidently concerns the question of whether existence is a predicate. This topic has had a long and interesting career in the history of Western philosophy, and the matter is still not settled. But since Western Buddhist scholars never seem to advert to it, and since the traditional texts formulate the matter differently, it would perhaps be hazardous to insist upon it too much in the present context. Briefly, the point is that when two people are debating the qualities of sound, for instance, they can both accept sound as the basis of the discussion without preempting the issue and committing themselves to conclusions that are yet to be established. Whatever the facts of the case, no illogicality is involved in saying, "Sound is either permanent or impermanent." It must be one or the other, of course, but this remains to be demonstrated. There is nothing, however, in the notion of sound itself that logically excludes either permanence or impermanence; and in an inquiry of this kind, one may analytically separate a subject from its properties, even though they are not separable in experience. One might suppose that the situation is exactly parallel in the statement "Sound is either existent or nonexistent." But this is an illusion created by the verbal structure of the sentence. Whereas sound, as a fact of experience, can be considered separately from its permanence or impermanence, it cannot be considered, with the same propriety and in the same way, in isolation from its existence. We may conceivably have a permanent sound, or an impermanent sound. But we cannot conceivably have a nonexistent sound—that is, a sound that has no existence—since a nonexistent sound is not a sound; it is just nothing. On the other hand, as soon as an object is consciously indicated, existence, or belief in existence, is logically implied.

Consequently, the Prasangikas conclude, in a debate about the existence of phenomena, if instead of confining oneself to an examination of the validity of the opponent's view, one makes an assertion about the phenomenon in question, this very fact is liable to imply that one acquiesces in the thing's existence. In such debates, therefore, the Prasangikas say that one must abstain from expressing an independent position of one's own on pain of already falsifying one's own position and misrepresenting the case.

Madhyamika in Tibet

However effective Chandrakirti may have been in vindicating the method of Buddhapalita and refuting Bhavaviveka, it is clear that he did not succeed in convincing all his contemporaries. There is no doubt that the Svatantrika method remained popular. Shantarakshita himself, who in his synthesis of the Madhyamika and Yogachara schools represents the last great stage in the development of Buddhist philosophy in India, made use of independent syllogisms as Bhavaviveka had done several centuries before. He is therefore classified as a Svatantrika, although, as we shall see, this question is more complex than it appears. It was, in any case, Shantarakshita and his disciple Kamalashila who, at the invitation of King Trisong Detsen, carried the Buddhist sutra teachings to Tibet, with the result that the Madhyamika doctrine first established there was Yogachara-Svatantrika, in which form it was to flourish for approximately four hundred years. Only in the twelfth century, when Patsap Nyima Drak translated the works of Chandrakirti, did the Prasangika really take hold in Tibet.

According to *The Blue Annals*, Patsap was born in Penyul but left Tibet while still a child. He grew up in Kashmir and India, where he studied at the feet of numerous famous and important scholars. He returned to Tibet around 1160 and embarked on a career of translation and teaching. He expounded in particular the six logical treatises (*rigs tshogs*) of Nagarjuna and, in collaboration with the Indian pandita Kanakavarman, translated Chandrakirti's *Prasannapada* and the *Madhyamakavatara*, together with its autocommentary, as well as the commentary on the *Yuktishastika* by the same author. From slender beginnings he became an influential teacher, and his return home marked a turning point in the study of Madhyamika in Tibet.

The introduction of Prasangika ideas was the focus of intense interest. Convinced that they were in possession of a more accurate and profound understanding of Nagarjuna's doctrine, the early Tibetan Prasangikas attacked the Svatantrika establishment with the enthusiasm of missionaries. They encountered a sturdy resistance. The period of persecution inflicted by King Langdarma (836–841) had been followed by an intense religious and scholastic renewal. And in the intervening period, before the return of Patsap, the Madhyamika had been closely studied, mainly according to the tradition laid down by Shantarakshita and Kamalashila, but also following the works of Bhavaviveka, which had also been translated in the early period. A number of great scholars had been involved in this enterprise, and by the twelfth century the Svatantrika view was well able to resist, at least for the time being, the wave of novelty. The master Chapa Chökyi Senge, for example, whose interpretation of Dignaga and Dharmakirti was to form the basis of the logic tradition still upheld by the Gelugpa school, was a formidable debater and defended with brilliance the Svatantrika view against Prasangika innovation. He composed several expositions of the Madhyamika system and numerous refutations of Chandrakirti. It is recorded that, on one occasion, he encountered in debate, and defeated, the celebrated Indian Prasangika master Jayananda.[30]

Be that as it may, the Prasangika view gained ground in Tibet and eventually triumphed. Even before the translation of Chandrakirti by Patsap, the Prasangika view was advocated by Atisha, whose role in the development of Tibetan Buddhism can scarcely be exaggerated; and it became intimately associated with the mind-training teaching of the Kadampas, which exerted a pervasive influence throughout the tradition. In their different ways, all four schools of Tibetan Buddhism have adopted the Prasangika approach—the teaching of Nagarjuna, as interpreted by Chandrakirti—as the highest view on the sutra level. Svatantrika was driven into the shade, and nowadays, especially in the New Translation schools, it is relegated to the doxographical literature, in the context of which it is studied largely as a lower view to be examined and surmounted by students on their way to mastery of the Prasangika system. It is comparatively rare for the original writings of Svatantrika authors—even of Shantarakshita—to be studied at first hand.

Mipham Rinpoche and the Prasangika-Svatantrika Distinction

It is therefore of some interest, before finishing with this topic, to advert to the attitude of Mipham Rinpoche toward the Svatantrika teaching, specifically in the form advocated by Shantarakshita. Naturally, this finds its full expression in the great commentary on the *Madhyamakalankara*, which is one of Mipham's great masterpieces, but it is appropriate to mention it briefly here, since not only does the view of Shantarakshita represent the final development of Madhyamika in India, but it also profoundly qualifies the Nyingma understanding of the relationship between Prasangika and Svatantrika, and of Madhyamika in general.

In the context of modern Madhyamika scholarship, dominated as it is by the Gelugpa and Sakyapa schools, the position of Mipham Rinpoche is liable to appear unusual, certainly unfamiliar. It is not, however, a personal eccentricity. One of the main reasons for

Mipham's scholarly work was to revive and reexpress the teachings characteristic of the Nyingma school; his understanding of Madhyamika is rooted in the tradition of the Old Translations. Without going into excessive detail, it is possible to summarize the Nyingma attitude (as expressed by Mipham Rinpoche) toward Madhyamika by saying that it accommodates the Prasangika approach current in Tibet after the translation of Chandrakirti's works, without betraying its original allegiance to the teaching of Shantarakshita. And in this connection, one may advert to the paradox, with regard to the works of these two masters, occasioned by the fact that chronologically the order of translation in Tibet was the reverse of the order of composition in India. After Patsap, Chandrakirti seemed "new" in Tibet and Shantarakshita seemed "old," whereas it was the teaching of the latter that represented the final development of Madhyamika in India at a time when Buddhism was still at its zenith.

So far in this introduction, in distinguishing the teachings of Buddhapalita, Bhavaviveka, and Chandrakirti and their followers, we have followed the common convention of speaking about Svatantrikas and Prasangikas. These terms are the Sanskrit renditions, contrived by Western scholars, of two Tibetan terms (*rang rgyud pa* and *thal 'gyur pa* respectively). It is important to realize that the Svatantrika-Prasangika distinction, as such, is the invention of Tibetan scholarship, created as a convenient method for cataloging the different viewpoints evident in Madhyamika authors subsequent to Chandrakirti's critique of Bhavaviveka. There is no evidence that these two terms were ever used by the ancient Indian Madhyamikas to refer either to themselves or to their opponents. Moreover, although the Svatantrika and Prasangika viewpoints differ on a number of interconnected issues, the actual terminology refers, as we have seen, to the characteristic method of debate adopted when the question of the ultimate status of phenomena is at issue. This divergence was emphasized by Chandrakirti in the first chapter of the *Prasannapada*, from which it follows that the terminological distinction "Svatantrika-Prasangika" became current in Tibet only from the twelfth century onward. Convenient as it may be, it is not without its difficulties.

If the Madhyamikas are differentiated solely according to whether they use independent syllogisms or confine themselves to consequences, a twofold division results, with Buddhapalita and

Chandrakirti on one side and Bhavaviveka and Shantarakshita on the other. The identification of the view of Chandrakirti and Bud-dhapalita is natural, but the placing of Bhavaviveka and Shantara-kshita in one undifferentiated category is problematic. Historically, Bhavaviveka and Shantarakshita are separated by a period of about two hundred years, while Chandrakirti appeared approximately midway between them. Given that these three masters were scholars of the first magnitude, and given Shantarakshita's knowledge of the entire philosophical and religious field, as evidenced in the *Tattvasam-graha*, it is difficult to explain how, if Shantarakshita is merely con-tinuing the Svatantrika stance of Bhavaviveka, he should have been so oblivious of Chandrakirti's critique—a development in the history of Madhyamika of which he could not conceivably have been igno-rant. However convenient, the Svatantrika-Prasangika distinction, made exclusively in terms of debate procedure, is not wholly ade-quate as an account of the evolution of Madhyamika or as a general description.

There is, however, another set of criteria for distinguishing between the approaches of these three Madhyamika masters, namely, their way of speaking about the conventional truth. We have seen that one of the reasons Chandrakirti objected to Bhavaviveka's innovation was that, according to the rules of logic, independent syllogisms commit their user to an implicit and compromising acquiescence in the existence of the elements referred to. Bhavaviveka was apparently aware of this, and we have seen that, in the interests of consistency, his use of the inde-pendent syllogism went hand in hand with a view that, on the conven-tional level, phenomena do indeed enjoy a certain existence "according to their characteristics." By contrast, Chandrakirti's quite different at-titude toward the role of *pramana* in establishing emptiness reflects his rejection of any kind of existence at any level. In the doxologies written in Tibet during the earlier period—that is, before the discovery of the teaching of Chandrakirti—the two kinds of Madhyamika known to Tibetans at that time were defined not according to debate proce-dure but on the basis of the attitude evinced toward the conventional truth, namely, the Sautrantika-Madhyamika and the Yogachara-Madhyamika.[31] This method of classification could theoretically be en-larged to accommodate the position of Chandrakirti, namely, that of the Madhyamika that accepts the common consensus as the conventional truth.*

The conventional truth corresponds to the world of everyday experience. It is the dimension, the field of perception, so to speak, in which ordinary beings live and interact. Viewed in the light of their soteriological aims, the attitude of Madhyamikas toward the conventional is largely a matter of communication. In trying to introduce beings to the Middle Way (the wisdom of the Buddha as expressed by Nagarjuna, by which alone samsara is destroyed and liberation gained), different approaches are both possible and necessary. This is what we would expect of any Buddhist system. Beings differ in their capacities and requirements; the form in which the teachings are expressed varies accordingly.

The characteristic approach of Chandrakirti and Buddhapalita is clear. When debating the final status of phenomena, they are content merely to deconstruct the false opinion; they refrain from verbalizing a position of their own. In the same way, they abstain from elaborating a theory of the conventional. Ultimately, phenomena are empty by their nature; conventionally, they appear by the force of dependent arising. The appearances of the common consensus are accepted, without analysis, as the conventional truth. No theory is advocated as to the nature of phenomena, and no sort of existence is attributed to them on a provisional basis. This approach seems simple and straightforward. In practice, it is less so.

A realist may hold to the view, let us say, that phenomena truly exist in the way that they appear. But in undermining this notion, the Prasangika does not intend to show that phenomena do not exist. On the contrary, the true status of phenomena lies wholly beyond both existence and nonexistence. It is subtle, inexpressible in thought and word. The Prasangika method, whereby the consequence is adduced without further comment, offers few concessions to the slow-witted and is obviously not without an element of risk. Admittedly, the destruction of one position, by reduction to absurdity, is not taken in isolation; it is accompanied by the negation of the other alternatives of

* Respectively *mdo sde spyod pa'i dbu ma pa, rnal 'byor spyod pa'i dbu ma pa,* and *'jig rten grags pa'i dbu ma pa.*

the tetralemma. Nevertheless, the Prasangika does no more than expose the inadequacy of the opponent's position. The effectiveness of the consequential method depends as much on the acuity and honesty of the opponent as it does on the accuracy and cogency of the argument. Whether or not the opponent "gets it" and realizes the point that the Madhyamika is making, and whether or not he or she is then able to apply it to good purpose, depends not only on intelligence but also on merit, the positive orientation and receptiveness of the mind, which is the result of training in virtue on the path. It is merit that empowers the mind and renders it apt not only to understand in an intellectual sense, but also to progress into the direct experience of wisdom itself. It is therefore said that the Prasangika approach, which, by a process of austere annulment of all intellectual positions, constitutes a direct introduction to the ultimate truth in itself, is appropriate for persons of the highest spiritual faculties, a qualification, incidentally, that is not to be confused with mere intellectual acumen.

By contrast, the Svatantrikas make use of independent syllogisms and thus adopt a "position" with which to interpret conventional experience (Sautrantika in the case of Bhavaviveka, Yogachara in the case of Shantarakshita). Their approach is gradual; it makes allowances for the needs of beings who must be led along the path. In such a context, the two truths must be distinguished, unpacked, and presented in terms of words and concepts. In the nature of things, this distinction, whereby the conventional is contrasted with the ultimate is—can only be—confined to the level of conventional truth. From the ultimate point of view, no distinctions of any kind can be made; it is only on the conventional level that the analytical investigation of phenomena takes place. Furthermore, two kinds of analysis are differentiated, depending on their object. On the one hand, there is ultimate or absolutist reasoning, which investigates and establishes the ultimate status or emptiness of phenomena. On the other hand, there is conventional reasoning, which determines whether a given object is "real" or "illusory" according to the general scheme of things accepted in the common consensus.

It is on the conventional level also that a further important distinction is made, this time with regard to the ultimate truth. In itself, the ultimate is utterly ineffable. It is beyond the ordinary mind and cannot

become the object of a cognition in which there is a separation between subject and object. This is the "ultimate in itself."* It is experienced by nondual wisdom and can never be expressed in thought and
word, themselves the preserve of the conventional. The ordinary mind
can, however, point to the ultimate indirectly, describing it, for example, as the counterpart of the conventional. This is the approximate ultimate.† It is the concordant image of, or gateway to, the ultimate
truth in itself.

As methods of introduction to emptiness, the ultimate condition of
phenomena and of the mind, the Prasangika and Svatantrika approaches are adapted to two kinds of beings: those who are able to enter into the ultimate truth in itself directly, without the intermediary
step of the approximate ultimate truth (*cig char pa*), and those who
must progress toward it gradually (*rim bskyed pa*). It may be thought
that Prasangika is superior to Svatantrika, but if there is a hierarchy of
levels, this refers only to the respective capacities of the disciples concerned, where the difference is one of merit. It is not a reflection on the
quality of the approaches themselves, which, Mipham Rinpoche argues, are both indispensable and equally valuable. Neither are they in-
terchangeable. The direct approach is useless for someone who must
progress gradually; the gradualist approach is unnecessary for one who
is able to perceive directly.

Furthermore, the adoption of these different methods reflects the
compassionate activity of the masters concerned, not their own personal realization. With regard to the ultimate truth, all Madhyamikas,
of whatever complexion, are in full agreement. Mipham Rinpoche observes that the ultimate in itself, beyond the domain of words or concepts, is what the Aryas see by stainless wisdom in their meditative
equipoise; on this level, neither Prasangikas nor Svatantrikas make assertions of any kind, and there is no differentiating them. The distinction comes only with regard to the conventional, for it is here alone that
the Svatantrikas make their statements about the ultimate (the approximate ultimate). "A person who, by dint of practice, thus attains the experience of the ultimate truth in itself may be called either Prasangika

---

* *rnam grangs ma yin pa'i don dam.*
† *rnam grangs pa'i don dam.*

or Svatantrika depending on the way he or she makes assertions with regard to the postmeditation period. But one should know that in the ultimate realization there is no difference between them. They both enjoy the wisdom of the Aryas."[32] It is thus meaningless to place the Madhyamika masters themselves in a hierarchy according to the manner in which they instruct beings. In their own right, Buddhapalita, Bhavaviveka, Chandrakirti, Shantarakshita and so on are all equal—they are all, we might say, Prasangikas, possessed of the highest view.

For Mipham, therefore, Prasangika and Svatantrika are two approaches to be understood in harmony; they are not diverging views. This point is brought out very clearly in the introduction to his commentary on the *Madhyamakalankara*, which has been described as one of the most profound texts on Madhyamika ever written. Having referred to the eighty-ninth stanza in the sixth chapter of the *Madhyamakavatara*, where Chandrakirti says that the source of phenomenal experience is the mind itself, Mipham Rinpoche comments:

To say [on the contrary] that the phenomenal world does not arise from one's mind necessarily implies the belief that it is caused by something else. And since this involves the assertion that beings are bound in samsara or delivered from it through causes other than their own minds, it will doubtless cause one to fall into non-Buddhist tenet systems. It is therefore established step by step that if there is no external creator and no external world, extramental objects are but the mind's projection. This assertion that conventionalities are "only the mind" exists in all the Mahayana schools.

Why is it then that glorious Chandrakirti and others do not posit the conventional level in this way? As was explained above, when he establishes the ultimate in itself, which accords with the field of wisdom of Aryas while they are in meditative equipoise, it is sufficient for him to have, as the object of assessment, the phenomena of samsara and nirvana as they appear and are referred to on the empirical level, without examining them. Since, from the very beginning, these phenomena are beyond the four conceptual extremes, it is not necessary for him to enter into a close philosophical investigation of the way phenomena appear on the conventional level. When one assesses appearances with words and concepts, one may, for instance, say that phenomena exist or do not exist, that phenomena are or are not the mind. But however one may assert them, they do not exist in that way on the ultimate level.

Therefore, with the consequences of the Prasanga reasoning, which investigates the ultimate, Chandrakirti is merely refuting the incorrect ideas of the opponents. And given that his own stance is free from every conceptual reference, how could he assert a theory? He does not. In this way, he can refute, without needing to separate the two truths, whatever assertions are made as to existence and nonexistence. In the present Svatantrika context, since assessments are made with the reasoning specific to each of the two truths, one cannot refute or establish anything *without* separating these same two truths. But in Chandrakirti's tradition, assessment is made using the valid reasoning, which investigates the ultimate nature of the two truths—the ultimate in itself. As Chandrakirti quotes from a scripture in his autocommentary to the *Madhyamakavatara*: "On the ultimate level, O monks, there are no two truths. This ultimate truth is one."

Therefore from the beginning, the honorable Chandrakirti emphasizes and establishes the ultimate in itself. He does not do away with mere appearances, for these are the ground for his absolutist type of investigation, the means or gateway to the ultimate. He therefore takes them as a basis of debate and establishes them as being beyond all conceptual extremes. Then, in the postmeditation period, he establishes or refutes all the propositions concerning the path and result in accordance with the way they are assessed by the two kinds of reasoning. And thus even the Prasangikas do not invalidate the conventional level. They assert conventional phenomena as mere appearances (*rkyen nyid 'di pa*) or simply as dependent arisings. If, with regard to these mere appearances, an investigation is made using conventional reasoning, the Prasangikas do not deny the manner in which samsara and nirvana are produced through the forward and backward progression of the twelve interdependent links of existence. They show that phenomena arise dependently through the power of the pure or impure mind. And in this way they clearly express the tenet of mind-only.

In the present text (*Madhyamakalankara*) by the great abbot Shantarakshita, emphasis is placed on the approximate ultimate. The two truths are, to begin with, distinguished; each of them is assessed with the appropriate kind of valid cognition and each is established as having assertions proper to it. Finally, the ultimate truth in itself, which is completely free from all assertion, is reached. These two approaches (Svatantrika and Prasangika) belong respectively to those who follow the gradual path and those whose realization is not gradual but immediate. And since the essence of Shantarakshita's approach is the ultimate-in-itself, he does indeed possess the ultimate and essential view of the Prasangikas. And what he says in the text itself is in perfect agreement with the view of the glorious Chandrakirti.[33]

Mipham Rinpoche and The Word of Chandra

Mipham Rinpoche was born in 1846 into an aristocratic family in the east of Tibet. His father belonged to the Ju clan, and the ancestors of both his parents had been ministers to the kings of Derge.[34] The circumstances of his birth entailed the advantage of material independence. And although Mipham Rinpoche was eventually to be acknowledged as an undeniable, indeed spectacular embodiment of Manjushri himself, he was never recognized as a *tulku*. He was therefore unhampered by the responsibilities and ties, both political and economic, that are often associated with that prestigious rank. He was able to devote himself exclusively to the pursuit of the Dharma in both study and practice.

He took his first monastic vows at the age of twelve at Jumo Horsang Ngakchö Ling, which was a dependency of the great monastery of Shechen Tennyi Dargye Ling in Kham. Conspicuous intelligence and aptitude for study soon distinguished him. An eighteen-month retreat on Manjushri, begun at the age of fifteen, marked a turning point in his intellectual and spiritual development. His practice was attended by signs of unusual accomplishment, and it is said that from that moment he was able to assimilate easily and without labor the entire range of Buddhist learning. The troubles provoked by the war in Nyarong obliged him to leave home. He traveled first to Golok in eastern Tibet and thence, on pilgrimage, to Lhasa, during which he spent a month at the great monastic university of Ganden. There, he was able to observe at first hand the scholastic methods of the Gelugpas, for which he acquired a lasting admiration. This was the first of many travels in the course of which he received instructions from many great masters. Mipham's most important teachers were Patrul Rinpoche, Jamyang Khyentse Wangpo, and Jamgön Kongtrul Lodrö Thayé, the founding fathers and principal exponents of a new and vigorous movement that was to revitalize the Dharma in the east of Tibet and beyond. This was the so-called Rimé (*ris med*) movement, the essence of which was an endeavor to collect and preserve, in a spirit of nonsectarian impartiality, all the spiritual lineages of Tibetan Buddhism, especially those that at that time were threatened with extinction. Mipham Rinpoche was to become one of the most talented and learned exponents of this tradition. By no means confined to philosophy and religion, the scope of his interests was universal, ranging from the *Kalachakra-tantra*, on which he composed an immense commentary, to the intricacies of traditional divination, ranging en route through such subjects as poetry, music, medicine, political theory, and even the arts of love (although, as Gendun Chöpel was to observe, as a chaste upholder of the monastic vows, his contribution to this last subject was essentially speculative).

In accordance with the free spirit of the Rimé movement, Mipham frequented masters of every lineage. He studied logic with Loter Wangpo, one of the greatest Sakya masters of the nineteenth century, and received from him the transmission of the *tshad ma rig gter*, the important work of Sakya Pandita that marks the beginning of the "new logic school." Similarly, he received teachings on the *Madhyamakavatara* from the celebrated Gelugpa master Bumsar Geshe Ngawang Jungne. He was invariably praised by his teachers for his incomparable intelligence. After examining Mipham on his understanding of Chandrakirti, Ngawang Jungne exclaimed to the monastic entourage that though he was the one with the title of *geshe*, he had not even a trace of Mipham's brilliance. In short, Mipham studied and mastered the entire spectrum of Tibetan Buddhism according to the traditions of both the Old and New Translations. As his biographer observed, he "moved like a fearless lion in the company of the greatest scholars, effortlessly explaining, debating, and composing commentaries."[35]

Nonetheless, he had a special love for the Nyingma tradition, which he treasured above all else. He is reported to have said that his youth had been marked by meetings with great and wonderful teachers of both the old and new traditions and that, thanks to the blessing of his yidam deity rather than his own studies, he had been able to comprehend whatever text he came upon.[36] He observed that at the beginning, he found the texts of the New Translation traditions easier to assimilate. But though he found the Nyingma texts more difficult, he never doubted that they were of great significance. "And for that reason," he remarked, "my wisdom ripened fully." Later on he was to discover, to his satisfaction, that the profoundest points of doctrine were "all to be found in the teachings deriving from the lineages of the Old Translations."

Jamyang Khyentse Wangpo requested Mipham to compose text-books for the benefit of the Nyingma tradition. He was to create, in other words, a series of commentaries covering the whole range of the sutra teachings. This included not only the Madhyamika, with important commentaries, for example, on the Wisdom chapter of the *Bodhicharyavatara* and the *Madhyamakalankara*, but also commentaries on the five texts of Maitreya and Asanga, logic, and so on. This invitation to compose is interesting in itself not only because it shows there was a need for such texts but also because, as Mipham himself remarked, it attests to the fact that there does indeed exist a specifically Nyingma approach to these sutra topics. Overshadowed perhaps by the enormous output of the later schools, the sutra tradition of the Old Translations harks back to the first dissemination of the Dharma in Tibet, set in motion by Shantarakshita. A characteristic feature of the Nyingma teaching is an insistence that a balance is to be struck between the traditions of the profound view (Nagarjuna) and of vast activities (Asanga), as illustrative of the experience of the Aryas in meditative equipoise and in postmeditation respectively. This in turn implies that the teachings of the second and third turnings of the Dharma wheel are to be regarded as complementary; not only the scriptures of the second turning but also those of the third are to be classified as definitive in meaning.[37]

The re-presentation of a specifically Nyingma position on philosophical and logical questions did not fail to provoke a reaction from the other schools. It could scarcely be otherwise. It is well known that debate plays an important role in the Buddhist scholastic tradition, and down the centuries the Tibetans have shown themselves to be the worthy inheritors of the Indian tradition of disputation. The Sakyapas and Gelugpas, in particular, are famous for excelling in this art. Its aim is to sharpen the mind's discriminative powers with a view to a deeper grasp of difficult and subtle doctrines, and, taken within the framework of spiritual training, it has been productive of spectacular results, on both the intellectual and religious levels. Nevertheless, it is obvious that a practice in which emphasis is placed primarily on intellectual acumen is not without its dangers. In the heat of controversy, pure motivations may be forgotten; and in situations where traditions and reputations are to be defended and where sponsorship and perhaps careers are in question, it is not always possible to avoid sophistry, arrogance, and vindictiveness. These are the occupational hazards of academic life the world over. Traditional and institutional allegiances may well breed prejudice and narrowness. Destructive sectarian intolerance of the kind that the Rimé movement was in part designed to combat was one of the least attractive features of Tibetan society during the nineteenth and early twentieth centuries, and it materially contributed, as the present Dalai Lama has observed, to the eventual catastrophe.

It is clear that Mipham Rinpoche had no interest in disputation as such. Neither could a polymath of such wide-ranging interests and capacity be expected to involve himself in narrow, factional attitudes. He is recorded as saying that he composed his commentaries for two reasons only: in obedience to the command of his teacher and because the sutra traditions of the Nyingmapas were in a pitiful state of decline and in danger of extinction. No longer a source of light, he said, they had become little more than "the painting of a lamp," to the point where many Nyingmapas were themselves unaware even of their existence. It had become common practice, in philosophical subjects, to adopt the methods of other schools, so that few even wondered what the specifically Nyingma teachings might be.

One has only to read Mipham Rinpoche's writings to see that the spirit of faction is completely foreign to him. He is wholly free from a desire to vilify the positions of other schools, still less to criticize their spiritual endeavors. His remarks are never personal and his tone, though firm and occasionally ironic, is never vituperative. This impartial search for the truth did not fail to elicit a warm response in sincere and sensitive minds, as is well illustrated by the famous debate between Mipham and the Gelugpa scholar Lozang Rabsel, following the composition of the *Norbu Ketaka*, Mipham's commentary on the ninth chapter of the *Bodhicharyavatara*. The exchange was marked by mutual respect and good humor.[38] Kunzang Pelden records that by the end of the exchange, the minds of the two scholars had mingled perfectly and they complimented each other with expressions of mutual admiration.[39] It is not surprising that Mipham came to be universally respected in all the great monasteries of Eastern Tibet and attracted disciples from all four schools.

Jamyang Khyentse Wangpo once exclaimed, "At the present time, there is no one in the whole world more learned than Lama

Mipham!" Although he appeared at the very end of the period of Dharma in Tibet, it seems beyond question that Mipham is to be placed among the very greatest luminaries of the entire Tibetan tradition—in the same category, some would say, as Sakya Pandita and Tsongkhapa themselves.[40] Whereas throughout its history, the Nyingma tradition has produced teachers and scholars of the first rank, its importance in the development of Tibetan learning has frequently been overshadowed by the activities of other schools. The reason for this appears to be mainly cultural and circumstantial,[41] and it is no doubt the origin of the vulgar error that all Nyingmapas are tantric practitioners who know nothing of scholarship—which is as much a caricature as to say that all Gelugpas are logicians who never meditate. In this connection, there is no doubt that, in addition to his immense labors on the tantra side, Mipham Rinpoche attempted and succeeded in preserving and refocusing the Nyingma approach with regard to the sutra teachings. His importance for the Nyingmapas can scarcely be exaggerated, and, grounded in the wider perspective of the Rimé movement, his influence on subsequent generations of scholars has been decisive.

Nevertheless, a remark recorded in *The Essential Hagiography*[42] suggests that toward the end of his life Mipham was occasionally overtaken by a sense of disillusionment—a sadness that in the event he had been unable to achieve all that he had hoped. Perhaps he was wearied by the defense and counterattack entailed in the controversies aroused by his writings—time-consuming and largely futile at a moment when the teachings themselves were under threat. For Tibet indeed, time was running out. The generation following Mipham Rinpoche was to be the last in Tibet that would have the freedom to pursue the goal of spiritual perfection unhindered.[43] No doubt, like other great lamas of his time, Mipham noticed the lengthening shadows and sensed the uncertainties of the approaching end. Not long before his death, in a rare moment of self-disclosure, he acknowledged his own dignity as a great Bodhisattva who had appeared intentionally in the world for the sake of others. His incarnation, he said, had been meant for the benefit of Buddhism in general and for the Nyingma tradition in particular. But the Nyingmapas, owing to their lack of merit, were troubled by obstacles, not excluding his own ill health, which had been protracted and serious. Although a number of his intended writings had been completed, he said, other important projects remained unrealized (including a general study on Madhyamika).

Although in an introduction of this kind, one is naturally primarily concerned with Mipham Rinpoche's scholarly achievements, failure to mention his spiritual accomplishments would be a serious omission. As with other great masters of the Rimé tradition, it is said of him that if one looks at his scholarly writings one would think that he spent all his time in study; if one looked at his spiritual works, one would think they were written by one who spent his entire life in meditation. It is certainly true that, in addition to writing and teaching, Mipham Rinpoche spent many years in strict meditative retreat. His innumerable pith instructions bear witness to his absolute mastery of the view of the Great Perfection. The circumstances of his death attested to his supreme accomplishment.[44]

The Word of Chandra

It was no doubt in order to fulfill Mipham Rinpoche's wishes, whether stated or implied, that some of his closest disciples endeavored, after his death, to supplement his work as much as possible by assembling unfinished writings and lecture notes and casting them in a completed form. The collected works therefore contain a number of posthumous items. These include a commentary on the *Mulamadhyamaka-karikas*,* and also the commentary on the *Madhyamakavatara* included in this volume.

The redaction of *The Word of Chandra* was made by Kathok Situ Chökyi Gyamtso assisted by Khenpo Kunzang Pelden. Their editorial strategy, however, has not merely been to assemble from the author's notes and unfinished fragments a complete commentary of Chandrakirti's text. Fortunately, they have also included a number of lengthy passages, connected only indirectly with the root verses, in which Mipham expatiates more generally on Madhyamika and related issues. It is obvious that, as good disciples, the editors were unwilling to omit anything that the master had uttered, and they have done their utmost to include every recorded comment that Mipham made on the different occasions that he taught on the *Madhyamakavatara*.

*dbu ma rtsa ba'i mchan 'grel gnas lugs rab gsal klu dbang dgongs rgyan.

It is understandable in such circumstances that the purely formal considerations of elegant arrangement are subservient to the preservation of content. No claim is made that the commentary represents the form that the book might have taken if Mipham Rinpoche had been able to write it out for himself; and it must be admitted that the passages added by the editors to the actual commentary on the root verses have made for a repetitiousness that the author himself would have undoubtedly abbreviated and streamlined. On the other hand, in view of the importance and difficulty of the material in question, especially for the unfamiliar reader, the frequent reiteration of certain themes is no bad thing. Nevertheless, it seems fair to say that the added passages are liable to create a distorted impression and that certain topics probably did not occupy Mipham's attention to the obsessive degree that the repetitions might suggest. Because the passages are of intrinsic interest and because the reason for their inclusion at a given point in the commentary is not always obvious, we have marked them by subtitles and indentation. They can thus be easily identified or passed over as the reader wishes. These passages are listed at the end of the table of contents.

The tenor of these passages is polemical, and the object of attack is a series of ideas mainly characteristic of the Gelugpa school. These include questions about the nature of the realization of the Shravakas, the valid establishment of phenomena,* and the concept of disintegration as a positive entity.† The most important issue, however, to which Mipham Rinpoche returns again and again, is the Gelugpa presentation of the notion of "true existence."‡ Although it is impossible for us to give an adequate assessment of this controversy, we will attempt to outline the positions of Mipham Rinpoche and his opponents as follows.[45]

One of the most well known features of Je Tsongkhapa's presentation of Madhyamika is its special emphasis on the conventional truth and an insistence that, while the purpose of Madhyamika is to reveal the emptiness of all phenomena, its correct understanding is nevertheless grounded in the commonsense perceptions of the world. This

---

*tshad grub.
†zhig pa dngos po.
‡bden grub.

goes hand in hand with a particular understanding, along realist lines, of logic and epistemology rooted in the interpretation by Chapa Chöseng of the teaching of Dignaga and Dharmakirti.[46] The commonsense experience of the external world provides the starting point on the basis of which the mind progresses from the conventional to the ultimate truth. Tsongkhapa seems to have been particularly averse to any approach favoring an idealist or "mind only" explanation of experience. Essential to his presentation of Prasangika is the clear identification of the object of negation (*dgag bya*), which must be distinguished from the basis of negation (*dgag gzhi*). The basis of negation is the conventional phenomenon as it is commonly perceived; the object of negation is the true existence of that phenomenon. Therefore, according to Tsongkhapa, "conventional existence" and "true existence" are to be clearly differentiated. Only the latter is negated by absolutist reasoning, the kind of analysis aiming to establish the ultimate status of phenomena.

In distinguishing true existence from conventional existence, Tsongkhapa's intention was to guard against an exaggeration, a tendency toward a nihilistic interpretation of emptiness. To assert the emptiness of phenomena is not to deny phenomena completely. Though empty of intrinsic nature, things are not nothing. To acknowledge conventional existence while denying true existence is presumably a way of preserving this important truth, and in the Gelugpa system, it is a crucial point to distinguish—first intellectually, and eventually by direct experience—the difference in phenomena between the basis of imputation (the conventional phenomenon) and that which is imputed (the truly existent phenomenon).[47] On the other hand, Tsongkhapa himself acknowledges that this distinction is so subtle as to be beyond the detection of beginners in the practice. Only on the path of seeing does it become possible for the mind to differentiate clearly the basis of imputation from that which is imputed.

Whatever the merits of this distinction, therefore, it is clear that it is not without its dangers. This is openly acknowledged by many Gelugpas themselves. For as a basis of the path, a distinction is propounded that is perceptible only to those who are far advanced upon that same path. The majority of people are very far from being able to tell the difference between the mere existence of phenomena and their true existence. It stands to reason, therefore, that to distinguish them and then to insist that only the latter is the object of negation may easily be misconstrued as meaning that only the "true existence" of phenomena is refuted and not phenomena themselves. The object of Madhyamika investigation thus becomes a sort of hornlike excrescence superimposed on phenomena, to be refuted by a process of intellectual acrobatics, while phenomena themselves (and with them all the attachments that bind us in samsara) are left unscathed and active. As the great Gelugpa master Jangya Rolpa'i Dorje said:[48]

> Our great intellects these days,
> Leave things appearing clearly on one side
> And look for hares with horns as something to refute.
> Old grandmother[49] will run away from them!

This and other admonitions by representatives of the Gelugpa tradition suggest that the misinterpretation alluded to was not uncommon. As the reader is about to discover, Mipham Rinpoche attacked it tirelessly as a pernicious distortion that actively hinders the experience of the absence of conceptual construction,* which alone is the hallmark of the true realization of emptiness. It is clear, however, that Mipham's attack was not directed at Tsongkhapa personally, about whom he invariably speaks in respectful terms. His critique, like that of Gendun Chöpel in his *Ornament of Nagarjuna's Meaning*, is directed at a possible misrepresentation of Tsongkhapa's meaning, resulting in what Jeffrey Hopkins refers to as a pedagogical fault.[50] The assertion that "the pot is not empty of pot but of true existence"—by someone for whom the distinction between the object of negation and the basis of negation means nothing on the experiential or even intellectual level—far from calling into question the apparent reality of phenomena, tends instead to confirm the deep-rooted habitual belief in substantial reality. In the last analysis, it is a species of realism. It involves a separation of the two truths and is *in practice* indistinguishable from Bhavaviveka's Svatantrika assertion that phenomena, though empty ultimately, exist according to their characteristics on the conventional level.

*spros bral.

Given Mipham's generally positive assessment of Svatantrika, one might have expected him to show a certain leniency in this matter. But he is uncompromising and has no time for what he considers to be a complete aberration. It should be remembered that his remarks are made in the context of the *Madhyamakavatara*. And, as tradition dictates, he advocates the view of the author on whose work he is commenting. That is, he takes a strictly Prasangika stance and censures what is, from a Prasangika point of view, an illegitimate procedure. It is a mistake, Mipham says, to claim to be a Prasangika when one separates the two truths, analyzes the conventional, and so forth. This is, to be sure, the way of the Svatantrikas—and, from Mipham's point of view (as expressed in his commentary on the *Madhyamakalankara*), they are not at fault, for they distinguish and employ the two kinds of reasoning in relation to their proper objects. To do otherwise—to use, for example, absolutist reasoning to disprove only what does not exist even conventionally—results in a muddle that obscures the crucial point, namely, the demonstration that phenomena are indeed empty by their nature. As we have seen, that this may have dangerous consequences was acknowledged not only by Gendun Chöpel, admittedly a controversial figure, but also by Jangya and Tendar Lharampa. It has received attention too from Western Gelugpa scholars, some of whom even go so far as to suggest a political dimension to a realistic distortion of the doctrine of emptiness.[51] Summing up the issue in the introductory section to his commentary on the *Madhyamakalankara*, Mipham suggests (possibly not without a smile) that the tendency of Prasangikas in Tibet to lapse inadvertently into the view of the Svatantrikas perhaps reflects a karmic pattern (*tendrel*) set in motion by the fact that Madhyamika first appeared in Tibet in its Svatantrika form.

The Textual Outline

In conclusion to these somewhat diffuse reflections, it is necessary to draw the reader's attention to the textual outline (*sabche*)* of Mipham's commentary, which, as the author himself declares in the concluding verses, is of particular importance. The creation of a

*sa bcas.

sabche is an essential feature of Tibetan commentarial technique. In its traditional form, it is almost invisibly embedded in the body of a text, but is in fact a sort of tree structure—sometimes of astonishing complexity—according to which the subject matter and the various levels of argument are arranged. It can be regarded as a sort of interpretative grid that can be placed across the root text, thus giving a complete overview of its contents. Sometimes, as Mipham Rinpoche remarks, the sabche is no more than a table of contents, but at its best it constitutes a sophisticated tool of textual analysis and expresses the entire attitude and orientation of the commentator toward his subject. It is the skeleton upon which the body of the commentary is built and is in fact the commentary itself in its most essential form. "When in doubt," Khenpo Pema Sherab often advised us, "always go to the sabche." It is common practice for Tibetan scholars, when studying a text, to commit the sabche to memory (possibly as a preliminary to the memorization of the entire commentary!). This done, the entire subject matter is mastered. Moreover, in the course of textual exposition, each new teaching session normally begins with the recitation of the sabche covering the part of the text already commented upon in order to refresh the memory and to place the following sections in their proper context. The sabche is thus an invaluable study tool, for which reason we have reproduced it, albeit in a slightly simplified form, not only in the text itself but also as a separate document preceding the text. Whereas the commentary on the *Madhyamakavatara* presented in this volume consists of Mipham Rinpoche's lecture notes as compiled by his disciples after his death, the sabche, as the concluding verse makes clear, is the work of his own hand and encapsulates the essence of his teaching on Chandrakirti's text.

Acknowledgments

The translation of these two texts, of Chandrakirti on the one hand and of Mipham Rinpoche on the other, has been a considerable challenge. It would have been wholly impossible without the support of our teachers and friends. Speaking for ourselves, we can make no claims to scholarship. Nevertheless, in the attempt to produce an accurate translation, we have been fortunate in being able to consult numerous eminent authorities, both lamas and khenpos.

First and foremost, we would like to thank Dzongsar Khyentse Rinpoche himself, whose precious, deeply enjoyable instructions allowed us, the students of the Dordogne summer school, a taste of the Madhyamika teachings—leading us, in his inimitable way, to Chandrakirti himself and his radiant introduction to the "great and teeming waters of the mind of Nagarjuna."

In addition, and once again, we are very deeply indebted to the kindness of Jigme Khyentse Rinpoche and Alak Zenkar Rinpoche for their help with difficult points. Most particularly, we would like to thank Khenchen Pema Sherab of Peyul monastery in India, who with great erudition and patience gave us indispensable help with many complex and profound passages in Mipham Rinpoche's commentary. Finally, we are grateful to Khenpo Jamyang Ösel of Dzongsar Institute, who attended the seminar in 1999 when he gave explanations and answered questions. Of course, all inaccuracies, misunderstandings, and ineptitudes of expression are our responsibility alone.

The translators, Helena Blankleder and Wulstan Fletcher of the Padmakara Translation Group, would like to thank Jenny Kane, Burkhard Quessel, and Dominique Side for their generous help in providing reference material.

PART ONE

Madhyamakavatara

Chandrakirti

Outline of the Madhyamakavatara

One

PERFECT JOY

Homage to Mañjushri Kumara—tender, glorious, ever-youthful!

1   The Shravakas and those halfway to buddhahood are born from
       the Mighty Sage,
    And Buddhas take their birth from Bodhisattva heroes.
    Compassion, nonduality, the wish for buddhahood for others' sake
    Are causes of the children of the Conqueror.

2   Of buddhahood's abundant crop, compassion is the seed.
    It is like moisture bringing increase and is said
    To ripen in the state of lasting happiness.
    Therefore to begin, I celebrate compassion!

3   Beings think "I" at first, and cling to self;
    They think of "mine" and are attached to things.
    They thus turn helplessly as buckets on a waterwheel,
    And to compassion for such beings I bow down!

4   Beings are like the moon in rippling water,
    Fitful, fleeting, empty in their nature.
    Bodhisattvas see them thus and yearn to set them free.
    Their wisdom is beneath compassion's power.

5   Through dedication with Samantabhadra's prayer,
    They rest in *Perfect Joy,* the first of all the grounds.
    And, henceforth, gaining this, they take
    The name of Bodhisattva and are thus renowned.

6   For they are born the offspring of the Tathagatas.
    Three fetters they have utterly forsworn.
    Fulfilled in supreme joy, these Bodhisattvas have
    The power to shake a hundred worlds.

7   From ground to ground they stride; their steps lead ever higher.
    All paths to lower realms have now been closed.
    The states of common beings are no longer theirs,
    Their level likened to the eighth stage of the Aryas.

8   With perfect bodhichitta as their aim, though dwelling on the First,
    Those born from Buddha's speech they now surpass,
        Pratyekabuddhas too;
    They soar above them by their merit's growing strength
    And by their wisdom also when on *Far Progressed.*

9   The initial cause of perfect buddhahood
    Is generosity, which here is now preeminent.
    With joy the Bodhisattvas give their very flesh—
    A sign whereby the unseen is inferred.

10 All living beings yearn for only happiness,
    And yet there is no human joy without enjoyment of possessions.
    The latter in their turn arise from generosity.
    This Buddha knew and so spoke first of giving.

11 Meager in compassion and with harsh and ruthless minds,
    Beings seek their self-regarding gain;
    And yet the riches they pursue, the healing of their ills,
    Are fruits of generosity alone.

12 Indeed it is through acts of generosity
    That they are swift to meet with noble beings.

They cleanly cut the stream of birth and death,
And journey into peace, possessed of such a cause.

13 To those who keep in mind their pledge for beings' good,
A joy from giving comes without delay.
For those who have, and those who lack, compassion,
All talk of generosity is thus of highest moment.

14 The merest thought or sound of someone crying "Give!"
Will bring to children of the Conqueror a joy
Unknown to Arhats even when they enter into peace—
How shall we speak of when they give up everything?

15 Because they suffered when they cut and gave away their flesh,
They see within their minds the pains endured
By others caught in hell and other states;
They therefore swiftly strive to cut away all pain.

16 Giving, void of giver, gift, receiver,
Is called a paramita that transcends the world.
But when attachment to these three occurs,
The teachings have defined it as the perfect act of worldly ones.

17 Abiding firmly in the minds of Bodhisattvas—
Holy beings endowed with lovely light—
This Joyful ground is like the Water-Crystal Gem*
That scatters the obscuring dark and reigns supreme.

Here ends the first ground or stage in the cultivation of absolute bodhichitta.

---

* The moon.

Two

IMMACULATE

1   The qualities of perfect discipline are theirs, and thus
    They spurn disordered conduct even in their dreams.
    The actions of their body, speech, and mind are pure;
    They practice tenfold virtue on the sacred path.

2   Indeed, their path of virtue in its tenfold aspect,
    Now perfected, is extremely pure.
    And ever-radiant like the autumn moon,
    Their discipline is lovely in its soothing light.

3   If discipline is looked upon as truly and by nature pure,
    This very thing deprives it of its purity.
    The Bodhisattvas thus are always and completely free
    From dualistic thoughts and hence the three concerns.

4   The fruits of generosity enjoyed in lower realms
    Occur through fracturing the limbs of discipline.
    When capital and interest are both wholly spent,
    There is no further prospect of a future yield.

5   If, when free and dwelling in a wholesome state,
    We make no effort to remain therein,
    We'll fall into the depths and then, deprived of freedom,
    How shall we escape and rise again?

6   Thus, having set forth generosity,
    The Conqueror went on to speak of discipline.
    For qualities that spring up in the fields of discipline
    Will yield unending fruits of happiness.

7   Common folk and speech-born Shravakas,
    And those established on the path of self-enlightenment,
    The children of the Conqueror also—their final excellence
    And high rebirth derive from discipline alone.

8   The ocean and a corpse do not remain together;
    Good fortune and calamity do not keep company.
    Likewise the great ones, who have perfect discipline,
    Decline the company of dissolute behavior.

9   Restraint, the agent, and the object of the same—
    All discipline observed with these three thoughts
    Is said to be a perfect worldly deed;
    But when these three are absent, it transcends the world.

10 Deriving from the radiant moon of discipline—the glory of the
        world,
    While yet transcending it—the Bodhisattvas, free from stains, are
        now immaculate.
    And like the moonlight in the autumn sky,
    They soothe away the sorrows from the minds of wanderers.

Here ends the second ground or stage in the cultivation of absolute bodhichitta.

Three

LUMINOUS

1 Because the fire that burns the wood of all phenomena produces
  light,
  The third ground has been called the *Luminous.*
  Here, the offspring of the Conqueror behold
  A copper-colored glow as of the rising sun.

2 Their foes may torture them, though they be innocent,
  Dismembering their bodies piece by piece,
  And cut their flesh and bones in lingering pain—
  But this serves only to confirm their patience for their butchers.

3 For Bodhisattvas, those who see the absence of the self,
  Agent, object, time, and manner of the wounds—
  All things are like the image in a glass.
  By understanding thus, all torments are endured.

4 If you respond in anger when another harms you,
  Does your wrath remove the harm inflicted?
  Resentment surely serves no purpose in this life
  And brings adversity in lives to come.

5 For it is taught that harms endured
  Exhaust the fruits of wrongs committed in the past.
  But damage done to others is itself a source of pain,
  For thus you plant the seeds of future woe.

6 Indeed all anger felt toward a Bodhisattva
  Destroys within an instant merits that arise

Through discipline and giving of a hundred kalpas.
No other evil is there similar to wrath.

7   For wrath disfigures face and form and leads to evil states;
It robs the mind of judgment to distinguish good from ill.
Intolerance is swift to drive you to the lower realms.
But patience, anger's foil, is source of every good.

8   Patience makes you beautiful and dear to holy beings.
Through patience you are skilled in knowing right from wrong.
In afterlives you will be born as human or divine,
And negativity will have no hold on you.

9   Common folk and Bodhisattvas both,
Who understand the good of patience and the ill of wrath,
Abandon anger swiftly and forever,
Adopting patience praised by noble ones.

10   But patience, even pledged to perfect buddhahood,
If practiced with the three concerns, is bound within the world.
Yet practiced without reference, this the Buddha said,
It leads beyond the world, transcendent, perfect.

11   The Bodhisattvas on this ground enjoy clairvoyance and samadhi.
Desire and anger here are wholly rooted out.
They are at all times able to subdue
The cravings of this kingdom of desire.

12   These first three virtues, giving and the rest,
The Buddha praised, in general, for the householders.
Through these is gathered what is known as merit,
The source of the enlightened rupakaya.

13   Luminous and shining like the sun,
Such Bodhisattvas utterly remove all darkness from themselves.
Their wish is then to scatter others' gloom.
Upon this ground, they know no anger, though their minds are
    keenly sharp.

Here ends the third ground or stage in the cultivation of absolute bodhichitta.

Four

RADIANT

1   Virtues, all without exception, follow in the train of diligence,
The source of wisdom and of merit, both accumulations.
Since it blazes with the light of diligence,
This ground, the fourth, is known as *Radiant*.

2   For here the offspring of the Tathagatas have a radiance born
From thorough meditation turned toward enlightenment.
Their shining light is brighter than the morning's copper glow;
The views of self are utterly removed.

Here ends the fourth ground or stage in the cultivation of absolute bodhichitta.

Five

HARD TO KEEP

1 The Great Ones on the ground called *Hard to Keep*
   Cannot be overcome by all the hosts of demons.
   Strong in concentration, excellent in mind,
   In subtle grasp of truth they have great skill.

   Here ends the fifth ground or stage in the cultivation of absolute bodhichitta.

Six

CLEARLY MANIFEST

1   On *Irreversibly Advancing*,[52] the mind abides in evenness—
    Proceeding irreversibly toward the qualities of perfect buddhahood.
    Dependent coarising, in its truth, lies open, manifest;
    The Bodhisattva dwells in wisdom and achieves cessation.

2   A single man endowed with eyes
    Can lead unseeing multitudes with ease to where they wish to go.
    And so it is with wisdom, here;
    It takes the sightless virtues, guiding them to Victory.

3   One who grasped profound and ultimate reality,
    Through force of reasoning and by the light of scripture,
    Was the Noble Nagarjuna; and following his tradition,
    As this still exists, I will proceed to speak.

4   Certain simple, ordinary people,
    When they hear of emptiness, will feel
    A joy that leaps and surges in their hearts.
    Their eyes will fill with tears, the hairs upon their skin stand up.

5   Such people are the vessels for the teaching;
    They have the seed of wisdom, perfect buddhahood.
    The final truth should be revealed to them,
    In whom ensuing qualities will come to birth.

6   Embracing perfect ethics, they will constantly abide therein,
       And give with generosity, compassion nurturing,
       Will steep themselves in patience, with their merits wholly pledged
          to buddhahood,
       That they might bring all wanderers to freedom.

7   They will venerate the perfect Bodhisattvas
       And have mastery of ways profound and vast,
       Attaining, step by step, the ground of Perfect Joy.
       All those who thus aspire should hearken to this path!

8   Not from self, and how from something else?
       Not from both, and how without a cause, can things arise?
       If from themselves phenomena emerge, there's nothing gained.
       And furthermore, a thing once born cannot repeat its birth.

9   For if you think existent entities can once again arise,
       The growth of plants and other things could never happen in this
          world.
       And seeds would reproduce *themselves* until the end of time,
       For how could shoots arise to do away with them?

10 A shoot that's different from the seed that causes it—
       In shape and color, virtue, taste, and ripening—could not exist, if
          what you say is true.
       And if the former entity gives place to something else,
       Indeed, what comes of their identity?

11 If your seed's not different from the shoot we see before us,
       The shoot, not different from the seed, should likewise be
          invisible.
       Or if the two are really one, then like the shoot, the seed should be
          perceived.
       And thus your theory we cannot countenance.

12 It's only when the cause is gone that products of this cause are seen.
       And thus no normal person thinks that cause and fruit are one.

The view that things are self-produced, when well examined, fails—
Both in itself and in the light of everyday experience.

13   If things are self-produced, begetter and begotten—both are one;
     Identical also the maker and his work.
     But they are not the same, so self-production we reject.
     For the unwanted consequences we have lengthily explained.

14   If something can arise from something other than itself,
     Well then, deep darkness can arise from tongues of flame,
     And anything could issue forth from anything.
     For "nonproducer," like "producer," is an "other."

15   What can be produced, you say, is, for that reason, called "effect."
     And what has power to generate, though other, is accounted cause.
     Things are continuities, you say, born from what gives rise to them;
     And rice plants cannot come from something alien, like barley seeds.

16   Barley, lotus, blossoms of the *kimshuka*—you do not think of them
     As source of rice plants, and indeed they have no power to be.
     They share no likeness, are not members of the same continuum.
     Now rice seeds, being other, differ also from their shoots.

17   Seed and shoot are not coincident, occurring at a single time.
     So how can seed be "other," in the absence of a correlate?
     And so it is not proved that shoots derive from seeds.
     The view that things derive from other than themselves should
         thus be spurned.

18   You say that, like the crossbar of a weighing scales,
     The ends of which go up and down and cannot but be seen as
         moving all at once,
     A thing that is produced arises as its cause subsides.
     Now, this is true if seed and shoot are synchronous, but they are not.

19   For if a thing is being born, it tends to birth; it is not yet.
     And what is ceasing still exists, for it is tending to destruction.

Now how can such a case be likened to a weighing scales?
To speak about production, when there's nothing that produces,
    has no sense.

20   If consciousness of sight arises at the same time as its stimuli
     (The eye, the object, and the simultaneous perception),
     It's other and already present. Why should it arise again?
     Because it does not yet exist, you say. The faults of such a theory
         we've already shown.

21   And if producers are the cause of products other than themselves,
     Is what they generate *existent, nonexistent, both,* or *neither*?
     If existent, why is a producer needed, and if nonexistent, what does
         the producer do?
     If both, again, what use is it? If neither, yet again, what purpose
         does it serve?

22   Ordinary humanity, you say, takes common sense as truth.
     To what avail, therefore, is this philosophy?
     That things arise from other than themselves is evident to all.
     And therefore it is true. What need have we of reasonings?

23   All objects may be seen in truth or in delusion;
     They thus possess a twin identity.
     The Buddha said the ultimate is what is seen correctly;
     The wrongly seen is all-concealing truth.

24   Deluded vision has, it's said, a double face,
     According to the organ's good or impaired functioning.
     Perceptions that derive from faulty faculties,
     Compared with what the healthy senses know, are held to be
         mistaken.

25   And everything the six undamaged senses grasp
     Within the ordinary experience of the world
     Is held as true, according to the world.
     The rest, according to the world, is false.

26   The "Self" as it's imagined by the Tirthikas,
      Enveloped as they are in ignorance's sleep,
      And mirages and tricks of sight—are all construed as real,
      Though they have no reality in ordinary experience.

27   Whatever is perceived with dimmed, defective sight
      Has no validity compared with what is seen by healthy eyes.
      Just so, a mind deprived of spotless wisdom
      Has no power to contradict a pure, untainted mind.

28   The nature of phenomena, enshrouded by our ignorance, is
          "all-concealed."
      But what this ignorance contrives appears as true.
      And so the Buddha spoke of "all-concealing truth,"
      And thus contrived, phenomena are "all-concealing."

29   Those who suffer from an eye disease
      Will falsely think they see black lines and other things,
      But healthy eyes will see "what is the case."
      Suchness, we should understand, is similar to this.

30   If ordinary perception yielded true and valid knowledge,
      Suchness would be seen by common folk.
      What need for Aryas then? What need for noble paths?
      It's wrong to take the foolish mind as validly cognizing.

31   In every aspect, ordinary experience has no validity;
      The ultimate, therefore, is not thereby refuted.
      Empirical phenomena consensus will approve,
      And all denial of them consensus will negate.

32   And so a man who merely left his seed
      Will say: "This is the child I fathered!"
      Likewise people think: "This tree is what I planted."
      Thus common practice too denies "extraneous production."

33   Because the shoot's not other than the seed,
      When shoots arise the seeds are not destroyed.

Because the shoot and seed are not identical
One cannot say that when the shoot is there, the seed exists as well.

34   If things depended truly on specific attributes,
      Denial of these same attributes would mean things are discounted.
      Emptiness would cause phenomena to disappear.
      But this does not make sense—which shows that things lack real
          existence.

35   Thus, if such phenomena are analyzed,
      Apart from suchness as their nature, nothing else is found.
      And so the truth of everyday convention
      Should not be subjected to analysis.

36   In absolute analysis, no reasoning admits
      Production from another or from self.
      And reasoning cannot uphold it even as conventional.
      What comes, then, of your theory of production?

37   Empty things, reflections and the like,
      Dependent on conditions, are not imperceptible.
      And just as empty forms reflected in a glass
      Create a consciousness in aspect similar,

38   So too all things, though empty,
      Strongly manifest within their very emptiness.
      And since inherent nature is in neither truth,
      Phenomena are neither nothing nor unchanging entities.

39   Since actions are without inherent, true cessation,
      Even though there is no *universal ground*, they can produce effects.
      Indeed, some acts may be completed long ago,
      But you should know that they will bear their fruit.

40   A fool when waking from his dream
      Remains attached to things he dreamed about.
      In such a way, from finished acts that are without reality
      Resultant fruits will also manifest.

41 While nonexistent objects are all equal in their unreality,
    Black lines are only seen by those who suffer from an eye disease,
    While other (nonexistent) things will not appear to such an invalid.
    It's thus that we should understand that ripened acts do not again
        bear fruit.

42 While evil acts are seen to be the source of baneful fruits
    And good results are seen to come from virtuous deeds,
    The wise, for whom there is no good or ill, are free;
    And we are warned against investigation of the karmic process.

43 That the universal ground, that persons do exist,
    That skandhas only are existent things—
    All these are teachings given for those
    Who cannot understand the deepest meaning.

44 The Buddha, free of thinking that the aggregates composed a self,
    Did yet say "I" and spoke of "these my teachings."
    In such a way, though *things* are certainly without inherent being,
    He taught expediently and said that they exist.

45 Finding no perceiving subject and no thing perceived,
    And understanding that the triple world is merely consciousness,
    The Bodhisattvas, you affirm, abide in wisdom,
    Knowing that the mind alone is ultimate reality.

46 Just as from the mighty sea, you say,
    The waves appear, called forth by blowing winds,
    Likewise from the seed of all, the universal ground,
    Mere consciousness arises through its own potential.

47 And thus dependent nature, "other-powered,"
    Is cause of things that are but imputations.
    This nature is what manifests—there are no things outside the mind.
    This does indeed exist, but lies beyond the sphere of intellect.

48 But what example can you give of mind without an outer world?
    It's like a dream, you say, but this we must examine.

I hold that, even when I dream, my mind does not exist.
The example that you give has therefore no validity.

49   But when we wake, you say, we can recall our dreams. This shows
          the mind exists.
      But then it follows that the objects of our dreams exist likewise.
      For just as you remember that you dreamed,
      You also can remember what you dreamed about.

50   In sleep, you say, there is no visual consciousness and thus no
          object seen;
      The mental consciousness alone is operative.
      Its aspects are assumed to be existing outwardly—
      And as with dreams, so too with waking life.

51   But just as "outer objects," in your dream,
      Are unproduced, the consciousness beholding them is likewise
          unproduced.
      The faculty, the object seen, the consciousness that they create—
      These three indeed are all deceptive fancies.

52   For hearing and the rest, these three are likewise unproduced.
      And as in dreams, so also in the waking state,
      Phenomena are false illusions—indeed, there is no mind,
      There are no objects, and there are no senses.

53   Both when we are awake and when we are not roused
      From sleep, these three appear to be.
      These same three melt away when from our dreams we stir,
      And so it is when waking from the sleep of nescience.

54   The minds of those who suffer from defective sight
      Behold black lines, the symptom of their malady.
      For them this consciousness and object are both true;
      For those with healthy sight, both terms are false.

55   If mind exists without an object of cognition,
      Then even those without the malady,

When looking at the place where lines are seen, should see them too.
They do not. Therefore no such mind exists!

56   For those with healthy sight, you say, the mind's potential
     Is not ripe, and this is why they do not see;
     It's not because there is no object that the mind does not perceive.
     But this potential has no being, thus this mind is not established.

57   Potential cannot be in what is actual;
     With what is not yet born it cannot be aligned.
     No owner can there be of what does not exist,
     Or such could be ascribed to childless women's sons!

58   You say that consciousness will manifest and thus it has potential.
     We say that since there is now no potential, there will be no
        consciousness.
     Phenomena arising in a mutual dependence
     Do not have true existence, so the Holy Ones have said.

59   If consciousness emerges from a ripened potency already passed,
     It will have come from a potential that's extraneous to itself.
     And since the instants of this continuity are alien to each other,
     Anything and everything can come from anything.

60   You may reply that while the sequence does consist of different
        things,
     The sequence in itself is one and integral.
     But if you think your argument is firm, it's now your task to
        prove it,
     For extraneous items do not make a continuity.

61   Qualities ascribed to Upagupta and Maitreya
     Are distinct and cannot be assigned to one continuum.
     Phenomena that differ by their varying particulars
     Do not compose a single continuity.

62   You say that from the potency for visual consciousness
     This consciousness arises wholly and at once.

This potency, on which this consciousness is founded,
Is what is thought of as the eye: the material visual power.

63 People think, you say, that it is from the senses that perceptions
    come,
Not knowing that when colors are beheld,
It's due to mental seeds, not outer stimuli, that things are seen.
The outer world they apprehend, you say, is but their mind.

64 In dreams, the objects seen are not outside the mind;
The mind assumes their aspects through its ripened potency.
And as with dreaming, so with waking life, you say,
The mind exists without external objects.

65 But just as in a dream, when eyes are closed,
The mental consciousness of color does occur;
Why is it that a blind man does not see without his eyes,
Through ripening likewise of his mental seeds?

66 The potential of the mental consciousness, you say, matures in
    dreams;
It does not ripen in the blind man's waking state.
But why should we not say that just as the potential of the mental
    consciousness
Does not mature in waking life, it does not do so either in a dream?

67 For just as eyelessness does not cause such a ripening
When we are dreaming, neither should our sleep.
And so you must concede that even in a dream, both sense and object
Are the causes of mistaken mental consciousness.

68 However you may answer and whatever you may say,
It all appears to us as mere hypothesis,
Which brings the disputation to a close.
The Buddha never taught that things existed truly.

69 Instructed by their master, yogis meditate
And see the ground as strewn with skeletons. But even then

The object, sense, and consciousness are all perceived as
    unoriginate;
The teachings thus describe it as a mental construct without true
    existence.

70   If such unpleasant mental objects are
    As any other object that you say is mind,
    When others look on them, they should perceive accordingly.
    And yet such objects are not false.

71   Like one who suffers from an eye disease,
    A *preta* will perceive a river as a stream of pus.
    Briefly, just as knowledge objects, so the mind—
    It should be understood that both are nonexistent.

72   Now if there is dependent nature, empty of duality,
    Without an object, and devoid of subject,
    Who or what could know of its existence?
    It will not do to say "It is, but is not known!"

73   Now, that this nature "self-experiences" is quite unproved.
    And if you say it's proved by later memory,
    The evidence you give to prove what is unproved
    Itself remains unproved and thus supplies no proof!

74   Reflexive self-awareness is, of course, a fact,
    But there can be no memory remembering—the moments are
        extraneous.
    For it would be as though the unknown were remembered.
    This reasoning disproves all other claims.

75   For us, the thing that now recalls its object
    Is not, in fact, distinct from that which, in the past, experienced.
    For our part, we agree with ordinary convention—
    Memory is the thought that "I have seen."

76   If thus reflexive self-awareness has no true existence,
    What cognizes your dependent nature?

Indeed, the agent, object, act are not a single thing;
Thus talk of "self-experience" is not acceptable.

77 If, unknowable and unoriginate,
Dependent nature has a true existence,
Why don't you accept the childless woman's son?
Wherein has he offended you?

78 Since dependent nature has not even slight existence,
What then is the cause of relative phenomena?
Because you are besotted with substantiality,
You gainsay all the facts of ordinary life.

79 Except the path expounded by the honored master Nagarjuna,
There is no means to reach transcendent peace.
All others fail to grasp the truths of suchness and
    conventionality,
And therefore liberation lies beyond their reach.

80 Conventional reality therefore becomes the means;
And by this means, the ultimate is reached.
Those who do not know how these two differ
Err in thought and take mistaken paths.

81 Unlike you, who think dependent nature is a true existent,
Even for the all-concealing relative we make no claims.
And yet, to gain the fruit, we speak in harmony with worldly folk
And grant that things exist, though they do not.

82 If, as for the Arhats—those who dwell
In peace, abandoning the aggregates—
There were no objects in the sphere of everyday experience,
We in turn would never say that things exist within the world.

83 If you think the world does not refute you,
Try now to deny the worldly view:
Argue and debate with ordinary people—
The strongest is the one that we will follow!

84   Advancing irreversibly upon the *Clearly Manifest*,
      Such Bodhisattvas understand the triple world as merely
         consciousness.
      Because they know there is no self or permanent creator,
      They understand that the creator is the "mind alone."

85   In order to increase the wisdom of the wise
      And clarify his thought, the Buddha, knowing all, expounded
      In the sutra of the Journey into Lanka diamond words
      That crush the heathen teachings, lofty like the mountains.

86   For in their books and treatises,
      The heathen teachers postulate creators, personal or otherwise.
      But since he found no evidence for them,
      The Buddha said that mind alone is maker of the world.

87   For just as "One who blossoms into Suchness"
      Refers to one who "blossoms and is purified,"
      The sutra speaks of "mind alone" because the mind is chief within
         the world.
      That form does not exist is not the scripture's sense.

88   You say that, knowing that phenomena are mind alone,
      The Buddha has refuted all external forms aside from this.
      But why then, in that very sutra, did the Mighty One proclaim
      That mind was born from karma and from ignorance?

89   The vast array of sentient life,
      The varied universe containing it, is formed by mind.
      The Buddha said that wandering beings are from karma born.
      Dispense with mind and karma is no more.

90   Though form exists indeed,
      It does not, like the mind, create.
      A creator other than the mind is thus denied,
      But form itself is not refuted.

91   While dwelling in the realm of ordinary experience,
      Five aggregates exist, on this we're all agreed.

But these do not occur for yogis
Who have gained the primal wisdom they desired.

92   If form does not exist, do not affirm the mind;
If mind exists, then form should not now be denied.
When teaching Prajñaparamita, Buddha taught that neither has
    existence,
But in the Abhidharma he declared that both exist.

93   Although you disregard our system of two truths,
Your "real phenomenon" is now disproved; it cannot be established.
And you should know that, in our view and from the very first,
Phenomena are ultimately unborn, and yet relatively they are born
    indeed.

94   The sutra* says that outer things have no reality—
It is the mind that manifests in various ways.
This teaching that dismisses outer forms was only a device
To counteract the strong attachment that we have to things.

95   The Buddha gave such teachings as expedients;
Their nature is provisional, as reason shows.
This sutra makes it clear that scriptures of like kind
Belong among the texts to be interpreted.

96   For once the outer objects of cognition are disproved,
The Buddhas have declared, the knowing mind is easily refuted.
Perceiver is discounted with the percept;
The outer world was thus negated first.

97   The way in which the teachings were bestowed should be discerned.
The sutras that explain things other than the ultimate
Were taught contingently, to lead upon the path;
While those that speak of voidness should be understood as
    ultimate.

---

* The *Lankavatara-sutra.*

98   Production from both self and other we cannot accept,
      For it displays the defects of the theses just explained.
      Empirically it is not found, nor yet in terms of suchness.
      Neither kind of origin is separately sustained.

99   If things arise in total absence of a cause,
      It follows that at all times, everything can come from anything.
      If that were so, then worldly people would not gather seeds,
      In all their myriad ways, to cultivate their crops.

100   If wanderers were not themselves the cause, then like the scent
          and color
      Of the lotus in the sky, there would be no perception of the universe.
      And yet this world appears in all its brilliance.
      Conclude therefore that, like the mind, the world derives from
          causes.

101   How can you say the elements, which are the object of your mind,
      Compose the latter's nature? This surely cannot be!
      And how can you with minds so thickly clouded
      Ever comprehend aright what lies beyond this world?

102   For when you say there's nothing after death,
      The nature of phenomena you understand amiss.
      Your view is based upon, coordinated with, the body you possess;
      It's just as when you say the elements are all that is.

103   The elements do not exist, as we have generally shown,
      When proving, as we have above, that not from self, nor other,
      Nor from both, nor yet without a cause does birth occur.
      Refuted thus, the elements are lacking all existence.

104   Since not from self, from other, nor from both at once,
      Nor yet without reliance on a cause do things emerge, they are
          deprived of entity.
      Dense ignorance enshrouds the world as though by massing clouds;
      Because of this, phenomena are misperceived.

105   Those who have defective eyes perceive black lines, a double moon,
      The colors of the peacock's tail, a swarm of bees—illusions all!
      It's thus the unwise are enslaved by faults of ignorance,
      Perceiving with their minds the multitude of composite
          phenomena.

106   "Karma comes about through ignorance; when ignorance is
          banished karma also"—
      To think like this betrays most certainly the uninformed.
      The sunlight of right understanding clears the darkness of
          confusion.
      The wise have realized emptiness, and thus they are set free.

107   If things, you say, did not exist in ultimate reality,
      Conventionally, too, they would be like a childless woman's son.
      But this is not the case, you say,
      And claim phenomena by nature do exist.

108   To those who suffer from an eye disease
      Black lines appear, though they have no arising.
      So now you should debate and prove them false
      And then refute the ones who suffer from the ills of ignorance.

109   As when you dream or see a city in the clouds,
      A mirage of a pool, an optical illusion, or an image in a glass,
      The things you see are unproduced, are all without existence.
      But how do you perceive them? It should not be possible!

110   Though ultimately things are unproduced,
      This does not mean that, like a barren woman's child,
      They are not seen or found within this world.
      Your argument is therefore inconclusive.

111   In itself, a barren woman's child is never born,
      And this is true both ultimately and according to the world.
      And likewise, by their nature, all phenomena
      In common truth and ultimately are indeed unborn.

112 Our Teacher, for this reason, has proclaimed
       That from the outset, all phenomena are peace—
       Are unproduced, transcending, by their nature, every pain.
       And so we say that true production there has never been.

113 Though pots and suchlike have no ultimate existence,
       They certainly exist according to the general consensus.
       And likewise the conclusion does not follow
       That phenomena are like a barren woman's son.

114 And therefore since phenomena are not produced
       Uncaused, nor are the handiwork of God,
       Do not arise from self, from other, nor from both these things,
       They do indeed emerge dependently.

115 And so things are produced dependently;
       The theories just mentioned cannot be believed.
       The argument that all "arises in dependence"
       Cuts in pieces all mistaken views.

116 Such notions come when true existence is ascribed to things—
       Which we have just disproved by our analysis.
       These theories therefore cannot now occur,
       As fire cannot arise when there's no fuel.

117 Common folk are fettered by their thoughts;
       Without such concepts, yogis are set free.
       The very halting of discursiveness is fruit
       Of true analysis, the wise have said.

118 The arguments contained within our treatises were not contrived
           through love of disputation.
       They set forth suchness only for the sake of freedom.
       They are not to be blamed if, while expounding emptiness,
       They show the falseness of discordant doctrines.

119 Attachment to one's own belief,
       Aversion for another's view: all this is thought.

Once clinging and aversion are dispelled
Through reason and analysis, we will be swiftly freed.

120   Perceiving that all faults and all afflictions
      Flow from the idea of the transitory composite,
      And knowing that its focus is the very self,
      This self is what the yogi will disprove.

121   Non-Buddhists hold the self is what experiences.
      It's permanent, does not create, it is devoid of *gunas* and of all
          activity.
      With minor variations on this single theme,
      The heathens separate themselves in different schools.

122   But since it is unborn, just like the barren woman's child,
      This self is utterly unreal.
      It cannot be regarded as the base for ego-clinging,
      For even in the relative it cannot claim existence.

123   Indeed the various aspects of this self,
      As heathen masters teach in all their treatises,
      Are countered by their common maxim that the self is unoriginate.
      Therefore these aspects also are revealed as nonexistent.

124   And thus there is no self existing separate from the aggregates;
      Divided from the aggregates there is no self to grasp.
      The common man does not ascribe his sense of "I" to such a source.
      He does not know of such a self, and yet he thinks: "I am."

125   And we may see that beings born as beasts for many ages
      Never apprehend a self unborn and permanent.
      And yet they clearly have a sense of "I."
      Thus, separate from the aggregates, there is no self.

126   A self that's different from the aggregates does not exist;
      The referent for the notion "I" is thus the aggregates alone.
      Now some believe the five together are the basis for the view of "I,"
      While others hold this basis is the mind alone.

127   But if the self were equal to the aggregates,
       It must, since these are many, be a multiplicity.
       And it would be substantial, visible like every other thing,
       And not at all a simple misconception.

128   Nirvana once attained, the self would be extinguished,
       And prior to this, a self would rise and vanish every instant.
       Without an agent, there would be no karmic fruit,
       Or else the actions done by one would give results that others reap.

129   You think there is no fault—these instants are a continuity!
       But we have earlier shown the defects of continua.
       The theory that the aggregates, or mind, are "self" is thus
            untenable;
       The world's end and associated questions were not discussed.

130   When yogis see there is no self, your theory thus implies
       That they must likewise see that there are no phenomena.
       But if you now refute a self that's permanent,
       Then for that very reason, self is not the mind or aggregates.

131   It follows from your theory that when yogis see there is no self,
       They fail to understand the final truth of form and other
            aggregates.
       They focus on them, "I" occurs, and so desire and all the rest
       Because the nature of this form they do not understand.

132   Now you may claim that Buddha said the aggregates compose the
            self;
       It's thus that you attempt to justify your view.
       But Buddha's words refute a self extraneous to the aggregates;
       In other sutras he explained that form is not the self.

133   Thus feeling, form, perception—these are not the self.
       Conditioning factors, consciousness are also not the self.
       In other sutras this has been explained.
       That aggregates compose the self, in brief, has never been
            proclaimed.

134 When the aggregates are said to be the self,
This means the aggregates together and not one by one.
And yet a mere assemblage is not "your protector,"
It cannot discipline or stand as witness, cannot be your self.

135 Were it not so, if we compare a chariot to the self,
The mere collection of a chariot's parts would constitute a
 chariot.
The sutra says that "self" *depends* upon the aggregates;
This shows their mere coincidence is not the self.

136 You say the self's their shape, configuration—
But shapes belong to form. So though you say the aggregates
Are self, this cannot mean the mental aggregates,
For they indeed are lacking any shape.

137 It makes no sense that grasped and grasper should be one,
For this would mean identity between the doer and the done.
And if you think that there's a deed without a doer of the deed,
This is not so; for where there is no agent, there can be no act.

138 Wherefore the Buddha has most clearly said
That self is based on earth and water,
Fire, wind, space, and consciousness—these six,
And also on the six supports of contact like the eyes.

139 He also said quite certainly that it is based
Upon the mind and mental factors. Thus from these the self is not
 distinct.
It is not they, nor yet the simple grouping of the same.
We grasp our ego independently of them.

140 Some think that when "no-self" is understood,
This means the refutation of a permanent, existent self.
But of our ego-clinging this could never be the ground.
How strange to say that understanding this suffices to uproot
 belief in "I."

141   For this is like a man who finds a snake's nest in his wall
      And overcomes his fright by saying, "It is not an elephant."
      A method such as this to cure one's dread of snakes—
      Alas, it's one sure way to be a laughingstock.

142   The self is not inherent in the aggregates,
      Nor aggregates inherent in the self. And why?
      It might be so if they were separate and distinct.
      But they are not distinct, and therefore this is but an idle notion.

143   The self cannot be said to own the aggregate of form.
      For self does not exist, thus ownership is void of sense.
      One owns a cow, in difference, or one's body, in identity.
      But self and form are neither same nor different.

144   Form is not the "I," and "I" is not a form possessor.
      There's no "I" in form, and form does not inhere in "I."
      Apply this now to all the other aggregates,
      And you will have the twenty views of "self."

145   To realize no-self is the vajra that destroys
      The mountain chain, the sense of "I." And when this goes,
      Its towering peaks will also fall—the twenty views that rise
      Upon the mighty range: the transitory composite, the "I."

146   Some say the self is indescribable:
      Not other than the aggregates nor yet the same;
      Not permanent nor changing, it is yet a real, substantial person,
      Cognized by sixfold consciousness. It is the base for clinging to
         the "I."

147   A "mind distinct from body" cannot be accounted inexpressible;
      A thing that is existent cannot be regarded as beyond expression.
      If one could show that self is an existent thing,
      It would be real, like mind, and not at all ineffable.

148   A pot, which in itself is not a self-sufficient entity,
      You say is indescribable apart from form and other features.

The self is also indescribable apart from aggregates;
Do not, therefore, regard it as inherently existent.

149   You do not think your consciousness is different from itself,
       But think it is distinct from form and other aggregates.
       In all existent things these aspects of distinction and identity are
           found,
       And so there is no self; it lacks the character of real existence.

150   Thus the basis for our clinging to an "I" is not a thing.
       And though not other than the aggregates, the self is not the
           aggregates themselves.
       It does not own the aggregates; the aggregates are not contained
           by it.
       Yet in dependence on the aggregates does self arise.

151   We cannot claim a chariot is other than its parts,
       Nor that it is their owner, nor identical with them.
       It is not in its parts; its parts are not contained in it.
       It's not the mere collection of the parts nor yet their shape.

152   Now if the chariot consisted of the mere collection of its parts,
       The scattered fragments likewise would comprise the chariot.
       But if there is no owner of the parts, there are no "parts,"
       And neither can the shape, or simple pattern, constitute it.

153   If the shape you mean is what was earlier in the parts,
       Supposedly remaining there when now the chariot is perceived,
       How is it that there is no chariot when the parts are disassembled?
       And even now there is no "chariot" present!

154   If within the chariot that's here and now assembled,
       The wheels and so forth have assumed a different shape,
       This fact would be perceived, but it is not.
       Therefore the shape alone is not the chariot.

155   Collections, you may say, are not real things.
       But if the chariot's shape is not the shape of gathered parts,

How can there be a shape—
Of something utterly unreal?

156   In accordance with your doctrine, you should know
      That on the basis of an unreal cause,
      Results of equal unreality arise,
      And so it is with all that comes to be.

157   Therefore, in respect of form and all the rest,
      It's wrong to claim that one identifies a thing in it.
      For forms and so forth (since there is no birth) have no existence.
      Things therefore do not subsist in shapes.

158   Thus this sevenfold reasoning reveals,
      In ultimate or worldly terms, that nothing is established.
      But if phenomena are left as found, unanalyzed,
      They are indeed imputed in dependence on their parts.

159   A thing made up of parts, themselves comprising parts,
      A chariot is regarded as a working entity.
      For living beings thus it is a means of transport.
      Do not undermine conventions that the world accepts!

160   How can a thing be said to be
      When sevenfold reasoning has discounted it?
      Finding nothing, yogis enter ultimate reality with ease.
      And yet the thing's existence, here and now, should be allowed.

161   If the chariot itself has no reality,
      There are no "chariot parts" because there is no "part possessor."
      The chariot burned, its parts are also burned;
      So too when fires of wisdom burn the owner of the parts, the parts
          themselves are also all consumed.

162   And thus the self—dependent on the aggregates,
      The elements, and the senses as they are in daily life—
      Is thought of as the owner of the same;
      These are the objects owned, the self their owner.

163   The self is not a real, existent thing, and thus it is not constant,
      And it is not inconstant, for it has no birth or ending.
      Attributes like permanence do not apply to it,
      And it is not, nor is it other than, the aggregates.

164   But linked to this, continuously and strongly, beings cling to "I,"
      And all that "I" possesses is conceived as "mine."
      This self will manifest empirically, the fruit of ignorance,
      As long as it's not subject to analysis.

165   Without a worker, there's no work performed,
      And likewise without "I" there is no "mine."
      Perceiving that both "I" and "mine" are void,
      The yogi will be utterly set free.

166   Vases, canvas, bucklers, armies, forests, garlands, trees,
      Houses, chariots, hostelries, and all such things
      That common people designate, dependent on their parts,
      Accept as such. For Buddha did not quarrel with the world!

167   Parts and part possessors, qualities and qualified, desire and those
          desiring,
      Defined and definition, fire and fuel—subjected, like a chariot,
      To sevenfold analysis are shown to be devoid of real existence.
      Yet, by worldly, everyday convention, they exist indeed.

168   If a thing produces an effect, it is indeed a cause.
      And if no fruit appears, there is no cause and no production.
      And as for the result, it's only if the cause exists that it comes into
          being.
      Tell me, therefore, which derives from which, and what precedes
          the other?

169   If you say the cause makes contact with the fruit that it produces,
      They share a single force, and cause and fruit are not distinct.
      But if they stand apart, a noncause does not differ from a cause.
      When these two cases are refuted, there's no third to take their
          place.

170   Well then, your cause produces no result, wherefore the fruit, so
          called, has no reality.
       And likewise, without fruit, a "cause" is quite unjustified.
       Both terms, effect and cause, resemble mere illusions.
       Therefore I'm not wrong in granting that the things of daily life exist!

171   But does our refutation, you object, make contact with the thing
          disproved,
       Or does it not? Are we not guilty of the selfsame fault?
       Indeed, when speaking thus, you say, we are ourselves
          confounded,
       Powerless to refute what we intend.

172   The outcome of our caviling, you say, applies therefore to us,
       And it is with absurdity that we deny existence of phenomena,
       And thus our view is not acceptable to Holy Beings.
       Devoid of any view, you say, we argue only to defeat our rivals!

173   That arguments refute their objects without touching them,
       Or the reverse—the faults involved in either of these claims
       Belong to those who hold to true existence. This is not our view,
       And therefore we are safe from such a consequence.

174   It's just as when the sun's eclipse is taking place,
       You see reflections of its changing shapes. To say the sun and its
          reflection
       Touch or do not touch indeed would be absurd.
       Such things arise dependently and on the level of convention.

175   Reflections are not real, but using them we smarten our
          appearance.
       In just the same way we should understand that arguments
       That have the power to cleanse the face of wisdom,
       Unlike your limping sophistries, engender realization of the goal.

176   But if the reasoning that proves our point were something truly real,
       And real also the point itself that should be understood,

Then arguments of contact and the rest indeed would have some
  truth.
But this is not the case. Your own fatigue is all you have achieved!

177   But we can demonstrate with easy cogency
       That all phenomena lack real, intrinsic being.
       The contrary indeed you cannot prove,
       So why ensnare the world in webs of faulty logic?

178   The extra refutation given above, devised for those
       Accepting contact and the rest, should now, once grasped, be set
         aside.
       The purpose of these arguments was not to give offense;
       But as we said, may our opponents thereby grow in wisdom.

179   The twofold view, the no-self of phenomena and persons,
       Was set forth to lead all wanderers to freedom.
       Our Teacher further classified and spoke of it
       In sundry ways to different kinds of beings.

180   And when he taught elaborately at length,
       He spoke of sixteen kinds of emptiness.
       When speaking briefly, he expounded four,
       And all of them the Mahayana teaches.

181   Since their very nature thus is emptiness,
       The eye is void of eye, the ear of ear,
       And likewise nose of nose and tongue of tongue.
       The mind and body too are thus defined.

182   Because they are not constant and do not disintegrate,
       The power of vision and the other senses
       Are without inherent nature.
       This is *inner emptiness*.

183   According to its very nature,
       Form is void of form.

Sound, smell, taste, and touch are also void,
And likewise all the workings of the mind.

184 That form and so forth have no real existence
Is classified as *outer emptiness.*
And that the outer and the inner have no real existence
Is designated *emptiness both out and in.*

185 That all things lack inherent being,
This is what the Sage described as emptiness.
And by the nature of this very emptiness,
Emptiness itself, he said, is also void.

186 This voidness of the so-called void
Is known as *emptiness of emptiness.*
It was set forth to counteract the thought
That emptiness is something real.

187 Space pervades all worlds
And all the beings that these worlds contain.
And as the Boundless Thoughts exemplify,
It is a great immensity in all directions.

188 That space itself is empty
Of its ten directions is the *voidness of immensity.*
It was set forth to counteract
Our clinging to immensity as truly real.

189 Since nirvana is the supreme goal,
It is the ultimate, beyond all suffering.
This being empty of itself is
Voidness of the ultimate.

190 Indeed to counter the conviction
That nirvana is a real, existent entity,
The Knower of the ultimate set forth
The voidness of the ultimate.

191 The three worlds, all arising from conditions,
Are said with certainty to be compounded.
That these are empty of themselves
Was taught as *emptiness of the compounded.*

192 And that which is devoid of birth and of abiding
And is without impermanence is qualified as uncompounded.
This being empty of itself
Is *voidness of the uncompounded.*

193 That which does not fall into extremes
Is said to be beyond extreme positions.
This in turn is empty of itself,
Referred to as the *voidness of beyond extremes.*

194 Without a first arising and a final end,
Samsaric wandering is qualified as endless and beginningless,
Wherein there is no ebb or flow,
Like things experienced in a dream.

195 Samsara's voidness of itself,
Is called the *emptiness of what
Is endless and beginningless,*
And this the shastra* has most clearly shown.

196 "To spurn" means to reject and cast aside;
As such it is most certainly defined.
And "not to spurn" means "not to throw away,"
And there is one thing that must never be rejected.

197 And what is not to be refused
Itself is empty of itself.
Wherefore its emptiness is called
The *emptiness of what should not be spurned.*

---

* The *Mulamadhayamaka-shastra.*

198   The essence of compounded and of uncompounded things
      Is not a thing invented
      By the Shravakas, Pratyekabuddhas,
      Bodhisattvas, or indeed the Buddhas.

199   And thus the essence of these things
      Is qualified as their essential nature.
      And this being empty of itself is
      Voidness of essential nature.

200   The eighteen *dhatus*, six sense powers,
      Six perceptions that arise therefrom,
      All things endowed with form, and things without a form,
      And all things uncompounded and compounded—

201   Are empty, every one, without exception,
      Empty of themselves.[53]
      The unreality of such as "being breakable"
      Is known as *voidness of defining attributes.*

202   Form has been defined as "that which can be broken."
      Feeling is defined as our experience.
      Perception apprehends specific character.
      Conditioning factors are what make and build.

203   The overall awareness of distinct phenomena
      Defines the character of consciousness.
      Suffering is the nature of the aggregates,
      While dhatus are compared to deadly snakes.

204   The sense fields, thus the Buddha said,
      Are gateways of production.
      And all that is produced dependently
      Displays the very nature of compoundedness.

205   Giving is the nature of transcendent generosity,
      And discipline is said to be an absence of affliction.

The character of patience is a freedom from annoyance,
And diligence a freedom from unwholesome action.

206 Concentration is defined as mental focus,
Wisdom as the absence of attachment:
And this is how we may define
The nature of the six perfections.

207 Samadhis, Boundless Thoughts,
And, like them, all absorptions without form—
He who knew them perfectly has said
Their character is undisturbed serenity.

208 The thirty-seven elements that lead us to enlightenment,
Their nature is to drive forth from samsara.
The character of emptiness
Is absence of a real, existent referent.

209 The absence of all attributes is peace.
And third (the absence of expectancy) has been defined as
    nonexistence
Of all suffering and ignorance. The perfect freedoms (eight
    in all)
Will extricate and disencumber us.

210 The ten strengths Buddha has defined
As what brings utter certainty,
While firmness, perfect and immutable, defines the nature
Of the Buddha's fourfold fearlessness.

211 His perfect knowledge, such as that conferred by power,
Is, by its nature, unconfined.
And "great love" is the name ascribed
To his achievement of the benefit of beings.

212 He perfectly protects all those who suffer—
This defines his great compassion;

His joy is marked by excellent rejoicing,
And unadulterated his impartiality.

213   The eighteen qualities,
      Distinctive attributes of buddhahood,
      Cannot be subtracted from the Buddha our Instructor;
      Therefore they are known as irremovable.

214   The wisdom of omniscience
      Is held to have the nature of direct perception.
      All other knowledge is considered less than this,
      For it is not regarded as direct perception.

215   The aspect of compoundedness,
      The character of uncompoundedness—
      Such features are devoid, are empty of themselves,
      And this is termed the voidness of defining attributes.

216   The present instant does not stay;
      The past and future have no being.
      Because these three cannot be pointed out,
      They are referred to as the "unobservable."

217   And the unobservable
      Itself is empty of itself.
      It has no permanence and yet does not disintegrate,
      And this is *voidness of the unobservable.*

218   Arising as it does from causes and conditions,
      A thing has no existence even as a composite.
      The composite is empty of the composite,
      And thus the *emptiness of nonthings* is defined.

219   In brief, the appellation "thing" is used
      In reference to five aggregates.
      But these are empty of themselves,
      And this is *emptiness of things.*

220   And, briefly, "nonthing" indicates
       An uncompounded thing.
       That this itself is empty of itself is known as
       Voidness of nonthings.

221   The nature of phenomena consists in their "nonentity."
       This is *emptiness of so-called nature.*
       This nature is indeed quite uncontrived
       And therefore "nature" is the name ascribed to it.

222   Whether Buddhas come or do not come
       Into the world, all things
       Are empty by their nature.
       And this is well described as their transcendent quality.

223   The *emptiness of this transcendent quality*
       Is also known as suchness, ultimate perfection.
       These twenty voidnesses have been proclaimed
       In scriptures of the Prajñaparamita.

224   And though illumined in their wisdom's light, the Bodhisattvas see
       As clearly as a *kyurura* that rests upon their palm
       The triple world as, from the first, unborn,
       In terms of truth conventional, they move into cessation.

225   And though their minds rest constantly therein,
       For those who drift, protectorless, they cultivate compassion.
       Those born from Buddha's speech and those halfway to
           buddhahood
       Are henceforth overshadowed by their wisdom.

226   And like the king of swans, ahead of lesser birds they soar,
       On broad white wings of relative and ultimate full spread.
       And on the strength of virtue's mighty wind they fly
       To gain the far and supreme shore, the oceanic qualities of Victory.

Here ends the sixth ground or stage in the cultivation of absolute bodhichitta.

Seven

FAR PROGRESSED

1   On *Far Progressed,* the Bodhisattvas
    Can at any instant enter and embrace cessation
    And gain the bright perfection of all skillful means.

Here ends the seventh ground or stage in the cultivation of absolute bodhichitta.

Eight

IMMOVABLE

1   That they may gain in merit, even greater than before,
    The Great Ones enter the *Immovable*, acquiring irreversibility.
    Their aspirations now are utterly immaculate,
    And from cessation they are roused by Buddhas.

2   Because, without desire, their minds are henceforth free from
        faults,
    Upon the eighth, impurities are stilled, together with their roots.
    But though defilements are no more, and nothing in the triple
        world surpasses them,
    The boundless, spacelike wealth of buddhahood lies still beyond
        their powers.

3   Samsara is now stopped, yet thanks to the ten powers that they
        have gained,
    They show themselves in various ways to those who wander in the
        world.

Here ends the eighth ground or stage in the cultivation of absolute bodhichitta.

Nine

PERFECT INTELLECT

1   Upon the ninth, not just the strengths, but all is pure and perfect,
    And likewise are acquired the spotless qualities of *Perfect Intellect.*

Here ends the ninth ground or stage in the cultivation of absolute bodhichitta.

Ten

CLOUD OF DHARMA

1   Upon the tenth ground is received supreme empowerment from all
      the Buddhas,
    And primal wisdom reaches its perfection.
    And from these Bodhisattvas, Dharma rain, like torrents from a
      water-laden cloud,
    Falls free and uncontrived, that wanderers may grow their crops of
      virtue.

Here ends the tenth ground or stage in the cultivation of absolute bodhichitta.

Eleven

THE ULTIMATE GROUND
OF BUDDHAHOOD

1   Upon the first ground Bodhisattvas see
    A hundred Buddhas, and they know their blessing.
    A hundred kalpas they can linger there
    And know what came before and what will follow after.

2   Wise, they enter and forsake a hundred concentrations;
    A hundred worlds they have the power to shake and to illumine;
    With miracles they ripen to maturity a hundred beings
    And journey to a hundred buddhafields.

3   The offspring of the Mighty One throw open wide a hundred doors
       of Dharma.
    In their bodies manifest a hundred other forms,
    Their beauty, wealth, and retinue reflected
    In the hundred Bodhisattvas thus revealed.

4   These are qualities the wise acquire upon the ground of *Perfect Joy*.
    Upon *Immaculate* the same arise, increased a thousandfold.
    And on the five succeeding grounds these qualities expand.
    Their qualities, at first, increase a hundred thousandfold,

5   And step by step again a thousandfold:
    A hundred million, then, and afterwards ten billion,

Then one trillion gained and after this
Ten million trillion—all such qualities now perfectly obtained.

6   And when residing on *Immovable*,
     The Bodhisattvas, now beyond conceptual mind,
     Have virtues many as the grains of dust
     That fill a billion worlds increased a hundred thousandfold.

7   And now on *Perfect Intellect*,
     All virtues mentioned earlier are theirs,
     Increased to equal all the grains of dust that fill
     Ten times a hundred thousand countless[54] billion worlds.

8   To say the least, the qualities of Bodhisattvas resting
     On the tenth ground lie beyond description.
     They equal all the grains of dust—
     Indeed a wordless quantity.

9   Such Bodhisattvas can, in every pore,
     Display the host of Bodhisattvas and unnumbered multitudes of
        Buddhas,
     And also gods and demigods and humankind besides—
     All these they can reveal at any time.

10   And thus because the moon shines brightest in a clear, unclouded
        sky,
     Again through striving on this ground, the ten strengths
        nurturing,
     They reach their highest aim in Akanishta, unsurpassed,
     The ultimate, unequaled qualities of peace.

11   Vessels may be different, but their space is one and undivided.
     Just so, phenomena are many, but their suchness is beyond all
        multiplicity.
     In understanding perfectly their single taste, such beings in their
        perfect wisdom
     Know all knowledge objects in a single instant.

12   But if, you may object, the final nature of phenomena is peace, the
        mind can never know it.
     Certainly, you say, when mind is not engaged,
        we cannot entertain the notion of a knowing subject.
     In total absence of a knowing mind, what knowledge can there be,
        for it is thus negated?
     And if there is no Knower, you will ask, who is it now who teaches
        others, saying: "It is thus"?

13   Suchness is unborn, and mind itself is also free from birth;
     And when the mind is tuned to this, it is as though it knows the
        ultimate reality.
     For since you say that consciousness cognizes when it takes the
        aspect of a thing,
     It's right for us to speak in such a way.

14   For by the power of the sambhogakaya, gained through merit,
     And likewise of its emanations, ultimate reality is shown;
     From space and sky and elsewhere it resounds,
     And thus may be perceived by worldly folk.

15   As when a sturdy potter plies his wheel
     And labors long and hard to get it turning well,
     It later spins without his further work,
     And pots are seen to be produced thereon.

16   It is the same for those who dwell
     Within the dharmakaya—all exertion ends.
     Yet through their special prayers and beings' merit,
     Deeds arise beyond imagining.

17   The tinder of phenomena is all consumed,
     And this is peace, the dharmakaya of the Conquerors.
     There is no origin and no cessation.
     The mind is stopped, the *kaya* manifests.

18   This peaceful kaya, radiant like the wish-fulfilling tree,
     Is like the wishing jewel that without forethought lavishes

The riches of the world on beings till they gain enlightenment.
It is perceived by those who are beyond conceptual construction.

19   The Buddhas can display at once within a single rupakaya,
     In concord with its cause, the births, abiding, and cessation
     Of their previous lives, in effortless display,
     Revealing them in clear and unimpaired distinction.

20   The buddhafields, the Buddhas dwelling there,
     Their bodies, actions, strengths, and powers;
     How were the Shravakas, how great their throng,
     And how the Bodhisattvas—this they can reveal.

21   They can display the Dharma that they taught, and how they
         were,
     And what they studied, what the works were that they did,
     The kind and quantity of offerings that they made:
     All this within their bodies they can clearly show.

22   Their discipline as well, their patience, effort, concentration,
     Wisdom—how they practiced them in earlier times,
     Without omission and in clearest detail,
     All this they show within a single pore.

23   And they can show how all the Buddhas of the past
     And those to come and those appearing now throughout the
         depths of space
     Set forth the Dharma with a clear and ringing voice, and how
     They live within the world and free all wandering beings from
         their pain.

24   And from the time when bodhichitta first appears in them,
         and till
     They gain the essence of enlightenment, their every deed they
         clearly show,
     As though it were their own, within a single instant and a single
         pore—
     And know them as a mirage, an illusion.

25   Likewise, all the actions of the Bodhisattvas of the triple time,
      And of Pratyekabuddhas and of noble Shravakas,
      As well as all the deeds of common folk,
      They show at once and in a single pore.

26   And by their merest wish, these pure, enlightened ones
      Can show the galaxies that fill the whole of space
      Within a single mote of dust, and show a mote as great as all the
          universe—
      Without the dust enlarging or the universe contracting.

27   Free from all discursive thought, a Buddha can display
      In every instant till the ending of existence
      Actions numberless in all their multiplicity,
      Countless as the dust grains in the world.

28   The strength to know what is correct and incorrect,
      The fully ripened consequence of action,
      The various aspirations of all beings,
      And all the dhatus in their great variety;

29   Likewise faculties, supreme and not supreme,
      The strength of knowing every different path,
      The perfect knowledge of samadhis,
      And also perfect freedoms, concentrations, and absorptions,

30   The strength of knowing past existences,
      And all the births and deaths of living beings,
      And the exhaustion of defilements:
      These comprise the ten strengths of the Buddhas.

31   That such-and-such a cause brings forth its certain fruit
      Is certainly correct, the Wise One has explained.
      The contrary, a host of incorrect beliefs that hinder knowledge,
      These he has rejected. This is his first strength.

32   Everything desired and undesired, and spotless action that
          contrasts with this—

All karmic deeds that ripen to their fruit, in infinite array,
With power and wisdom unconfined, a Buddha knows them all,
Past, present, and to come. This is his second strength.

33   Aspirations through the strength of craving and the rest,
Both low and high, and those between, and hidden inclinations
In their great variety: he knows for everyone, past, present, and to
      come.
In this his third strength does consist.

34   The Buddha, wise in all the dhatus' aspects and divisions,
Declared the nature of the eye, like all the rest, itself to be a
      dhatu.
The fourth strength of the perfect Buddha is his boundless
      knowledge,
Which penetrates and understands the different dhatus.

35   Sharp acumen in the mastery of mental states is called supreme,
And not supreme the lesser aptitudes, both moderate and dull.
Omniscience knows all this with neither grasping nor impediment,
      and all that is established
Through the interaction of the eyes and other senses. This is thus
      the fifth strength of the Buddha.

36   The paths that lead to buddhahood, and to the freedom
Of Pratyekabuddhas and of Shravakas,
And to the lives of beasts and pretas, gods and humankind, and all
      the realms of hell—
The sixth strength of the Buddha is to know them all without
      impediment.

37   The various samadhis of all yogis in unnumbered worlds,
The perfect freedoms, eight in all, and then, in step with these,
The various calm abidings and successive nine absorptions—
To know all these is Buddha's seventh strength.

38   To know his own past lives while once he dwelt in ignorance,
To know the lives of each and every living being numberless,

Their causes, country, dwelling place—
The eighth strength of the Buddha is to know all this.

39   The births and deaths of beings, each and every one,
      Who live within the world unto the very edge of space:
      To have this knowledge in its varied detail, pure, untrammeled,
          infinite—
      In this consists the ninth strength of the Buddha.

40   The tenth strength of the Buddha is to know unhindered,
          unconfined,
      That by the power of his omniscience,
      Defilements and their tendencies are instantly removed
      And that his followers arrest defilements through their wisdom.

41   It's not because there is no sky that birds turn back;
      It is because their strength has failed.
      And thus it is that hearers and the Buddha's heirs turn back
      From telling all the skylike, endless qualities of buddhahood.

42   And therefore how could such as I
      Discern and discourse on its properties?
      But since the Noble Nagarjuna has described them,
      I have briefly spoken, setting fear aside.

43   Profound is emptiness indeed,
      And vast indeed are all the other qualities.
      By understanding both profound and vast,
      It's thus that all these qualities are gained.

44   Although possessing the unchanging kaya, in the three worlds of
          existence you appear again;
      By means of magic forms you show your coming, birth, the peace
          of your enlightenment, you turn the Doctrine's wheel;
      And all who twist and whirl within the world, entangled in the
          string of their desire,
      You lead in your compassion to the state beyond all sorrow.

45   To dissipate the veils of ignorance—no other means is there than
         knowing suchness.
     Suchness of phenomena admits no fraction or division.
     The subject, mind, that knows it so is likewise undivided.
     And thus the Buddha taught us with a single, matchless vehicle.

46   This evil age compounds the plight of those who wander through
         the world,
     Unable thus to sound the great profundity of buddhahood.
     And so, though gone to bliss, with perfect knowledge and
         compassionate skill,
     You took a pledge, proclaiming thus: "These beings I will free."

47   And therefore like a mage who, to refresh the weariness of those
         who journey
     To an isle of jewels, does magically display a pleasant resting place,
     You set forth vehicles that soothe with peace the minds of some of
         your disciples;
     To those with trained, untrammeled minds you spoke quite
         differently.

48   O Buddha, gone to bliss, as many as the motes of dust contained
     In all the buddhafields, for just as many aeons
     Do you enter the enlightened state supreme and holy.
     But this, your secret, has not been revealed.

49   Victorious Lord, as long as worldly beings have not gone to
         supreme peace,
     As long as space itself does not disintegrate,
     What entry into supreme peace could be for you,
     Whom Wisdom has brought forth, Compassion nursed?

50   All those who feed on noxious food (the world obscured by
         ignorance)
     You make your dearest friends, with love more anguished than
     A mother feels whose dearest child has swallowed poisoned food,
     And thus you do not pass, Supreme Protector, into peace.

51   Beings ignorantly think that some things are, that some are not.
      And thus they suffer birth and death, the loss and getting of their
          loves and hates.
      They fall to evil destiny. This world is all the object of your
          tenderness.
      And therefore, Lord, in love, you turn from your Nirvana and your
          peace forsake.

52   This way of explanation I, the bhikshu Chandrakirti,
      Gathered from the *karikas* that teach the Middle Way,
      And here correctly I have set it down
      According to both scripture and instruction.

53   No scriptures but the *karikas* set forth
      This doctrine as it ought to be.
      The teaching here explained can nowhere else be found.
      O wise and learned ones, be sure of this!

54   But startled by the deep hue of the great and teeming waters of the
          mind of Nagarjuna,
      Some have shunned and kept their distance from this great
          tradition.
      Yet moistened by the dew, these stanzas opened like the buds of
          water lilies.
      Thus the hopes of Chandrakirti have been perfectly fulfilled.

55   It's by habituation to the suchness here described that beings come
          to grasp its fearful depths.
      But others fail, regardless of their learning.
      Seeing thus that all the other texts contrived by common minds are
          manifestos that propound the self,
      Abandon all delight in treatises that deviate and wander from the
          teaching given here.

56   May the merit I have gained through commenting the words of
          Master Nagarjuna grow in all directions to the limits of the
          sky!

And may the mind enshrouded by defilement's gloom
   be bright and shining like the autumn stars.
And taking thus the jewel upon the forehead of the cobra of the
   mind,
May all the world, through understanding suchness,
   swiftly journey to the state of blissful buddhahood.

Conclusion

The Author of the Treatise

The master who elucidated this profound teaching of emptiness and the vast teaching of the qualities of the path and fruit was Chandrakirti. He was utterly immersed in the truth of the supreme vehicle. Wisdom and compassion were inalienably his, and by milking the painting of a cow, he was able to dispel the inflexible conviction of beings that phenomena truly exist.

The Translator

This text was translated according to the tradition of Kashmir by the Indian abbot Tilaka Kalasha and the Tibetan translator, the monk Patsap Nyima Drak, when residing in the Hidden Jewel temple in the center of the Kashimiri city of Anuparna, or "Beyond Compare," during the reign of the king Shri Aryadeva. Subsequently, in the temple of Rasa Ramoche (Lhasa), a final version was established and corrected according to the eastern, Bengali, tradition by the Indian abbot Kanakavarman and the same translator Patsap Nyima Drak.

PART TWO

The Word of Chandra

THE NECKLACE
OF SPOTLESS CRYSTAL

A Commentary on the
Madhyamakavatara

Jamgön Mipham Rinpoche

Om svasti!
Wisdom's sun, resplendent with a thousand lights of boundless
    excellence,
Perceives reality devoid of thoughts, the cloudless sky of unborn
    dharmadhatu.
The mind beyond duality, the mother of all Aryas,
Has entered the profound, the Middle Way.
The lotus of the teaching of the supreme vehicle
Has opened in full flower—virtue, excellence, and fortune!
King of all the Shakyas, peerless Conqueror,
Your regents and your bodhisattva heirs,
Your chief disciples and the holders of your line—
May you prevail with universal victory!

May you who have perceived aright the crucial thought
Of Chandra and of Nagarjuna, noble and sublime,
Who taught and set it forth and thus may lead us
To the truth profound beyond all reference—Jampel Gyepa'i
    Dorje,[55] may you reign supreme!

Of the fourfold reasoning of realization,[56]
The first, which shows the single cause of all phenomena,
Is set forth here, a commentary upon the shastra
That elucidates the path of perfect reasoning.[57]

A Textual Outline of The Word of Chandra

PREAMBLE

I. THE MEANING OF THE TITLE

II. THE HOMAGE OF THE TRANSLATOR

III. THE TREATISE ITSELF
  A. The homage of the author
    1. The three causes of Bodhisattvas **(1)**
    2. In praise of great compassion
      a. In praise of compassion in a general sense **(2)**
      b. Homage to different kinds of great compassion
        i. Homage to compassion that has beings for its object **(3)**
        ii. Homage to compassion that has transience for its object
          and to compassion that is devoid of reference **(4)**
  B. The main body of the treatise

THE TEN GROUNDS OR STAGES OF REALIZATION

I. THE FIRST GROUND: PERFECT JOY
  A. A brief general description **(5)**
  B. A detailed examination of the qualities peculiar to the first
     ground
    1. The qualities that embellish the mind of the Bodhisattva
      a. A new and meaningful name
      b. The five additional qualities of lineage, elimination,
         realization, ability, and progression **(6, 7)**
      c. Birth in the lower realms is no longer possible

2. The qualities whereby Bodhisattvas outshine other
   beings **(8)**
3. The superior quality of the first ground
   a. The preeminence of the paramita of generosity on the first
      ground **(9)**
   b. In praise of generosity
      i. In praise of the generosity of ordinary people
      (1) Generosity is necessary for ordinary people **(10)**
      (2) The benefits of generosity
         (a) Generosity brings happiness in samsara **(11)**
         (b) Generosity leads to the bliss of nirvana **(12)**
      ii. In praise of the generosity of Bodhisattvas **(13)**
      iii. Concluding summary of praise
      iv. The respectful attitude of Bodhisattvas toward generosity
          thus praised
      (1) The extent to which they are devoted to generosity **(14)**
      (2) How they respectfully practice generosity **(15)**
   c. Different kinds of generosity **(16)**
C. Concluding summary of the first ground **(17)**

II. THE SECOND GROUND: IMMACULATE
  A. The definition of the second ground **(1)**
  B. The qualities of the second ground
    1. The preeminence and purity of discipline
    a. The explanation itself **(2)**
    b. Purity of discipline **(3)**
    2. In praise of pure discipline
    a. The eulogy itself
      i. Even ordinary people need to practice ethics
      (1) The defects arising from a lack of ethical discipline
         (a) Without discipline it is impossible to attain high
             rebirth **(4)**
         (b) Without discipline positive actions give only one
             fortunate result
         (c) Without discipline it is hard to escape the lower
             realms **(5)**
         (d) Ethical discipline as a remedy for all these ills **(6)**

(2) The benefits of being disciplined

  ii. Discipline is the foundation of all qualities **(7)**

 b. How Bodhisattvas abide in discipline **(8)**

 3. The different categories of the paramita of discipline **(9)**

C. Conclusion **(10)**

III. THE THIRD GROUND: LUMINOUS

A. The definition of the third ground **(1)**

B. The particular qualities of this ground

 1. The paramita of superior patience

 a. Patience is preeminent on the third ground **(2)**

 b. How to train in patience

  i. Meditation on patience on the level of ultimate truth **(3)**

  ii. Meditation on patience on the level of relative truth

 (1) The defects of anger

   (a) The futility and senselessness of anger **(4)**

   (b) It is senseless to make a beneficial situation harmful **(5)**

   (c) Anger is a heavy negativity **(6)**

   (d) Anger is the source of many disadvantages in this and
       future lives **(7)**

 (2) The benefits of patience **(8)**

 (3) Concluding summary on the defects of anger and the
     advantages of patience **(9)**

 c. The classification of patience **(10)**

 2. A description of the other qualities that manifest on this
    ground **(11)**

C. Conclusion: the qualities of this ground

 1. The common conclusion for the last three paramitas **(12)**

 2. Specific conclusion for the third ground **(13)**

IV. THE FOURTH GROUND: RADIANT

A. The excellence of diligence on the fourth ground **(1)**

B. The definition of this ground **(2)**

C. The particular qualities of elimination

V. THE FIFTH GROUND: HARD TO KEEP

A. The definition of the fifth ground **(1)**

B. The qualities of the fifth ground

VI. THE SIXTH GROUND: CLEARLY MANIFEST
  A. A brief explanation of the sixth ground from the standpoint of
     the wisdom that realizes emptiness **(1)**
  B. A detailed explanation of the sixth ground from the standpoint
     of emptiness, the domain or object of wisdom
    1. The greatness of emptiness **(2)**
    2. The exposition of this emptiness
      a. The manner in which emptiness is to be explained **(3)**
      b. Those to whom emptiness is to be explained
        i. The proper recipients of such an explanation **(4, 5)**
        ii. An encouragement to listen to the teachings on
            emptiness
        (1) The qualities associated with skilled means on the relative
            level will arise **(6, 7)**
        (2) The qualities of ultimate wisdom will arise
    3. The explanation of emptiness itself
      a. Establishing emptiness by rational demonstration
        i. Using reason to disprove the self of phenomena
        (1) Using reason to refute the theory of inherently real
            production
          (a) A refutation of the four theories of production from the
              standpoint of the two truths
          (i) A short exposition **(8)**
          (ii) A detailed explanation of the refutation of the four
               theories of production
            A. Refutation of self-production
              1. A refutation of this theory according to Buddhapalita and
                 Chandrakirti
                a. A refutation of self-production on the ultimate level
                  i. A refutation of production from a cause with which the
                     effect is identical
                    (1) Production accomplishes nothing
                    (2) Production is untenable
                    (3) Production is actually impossible; there is no point at
                        which it might occur **(9)**
                    (4) Seeds would be produced ad infinitum
                  ii. A refutation of the theory that causes and effects are
                      identical in nature

(1) *If causes and effects are identical in nature, they should not be observed at different moments*
   (a) *The identity of cause and effect contradicts the Samkhya admission that causes modulate and change into their effects*
   (b) *An identity of nature precludes differences of shape and so forth* **(10)**
(2) *The fact that causes and effects are observed at different moments disproves their identity of nature*
   (a) *The refutation itself*
   (b) *If cause and effect are of the same nature, it follows that both terms should be equally perceptible or otherwise in their different phases* **(11)**
b. *There is no such thing as self-production on the level of ordinary experience* **(12)**
c. *Recapitulation*
2. *A refutation following Nagarjuna's reasoning in the Mulamadhyamaka-karikas* **(13)**
B. *Refutation of other-production*
1. *A general refutation of the theory of other-production*
a. *A general refutation of other-production on the ultimate level*
i. *A refutation of other-production*
   (1) *A general refutation*
     (a) *A general refutation through revealing unwanted consequences of production in which cause and effect are considered to be inherently other* **(14)**
     (b) *Refutation of an objection*
      (i) *The objection* **(15)**
      (ii) *The refutation of the objection* **(16)**
   (2) *A specific refutation of the theory of production in which cause and effect are considered to be inherently other*
     (a) *The principal refutation by appeal to the chronological factor implicit in causality* **(17)**
     (b) *Refutation of an objection*
      (i) *The objection* **(18)**
      (ii) *The refutation of the objection* **(19)**
     (c) *A specific refutation of other-production in which cause and effect are regarded as simultaneous* **(20)**

*(3) A refutation by investigating the nature of an effect
    (according to the four ontological permutations)* **(21)**

*ii. An answer to the objection, based on the experience of
    ordinary people, regarding the refutation of other-
    production*

*(1) How ordinary people argue and try to dispose of this
    refutation* **(22)**

(2) An answer to this

*(a) Ordinary people affirm other-production, but they are
    unable to disprove its logical refutation*

*(i) A short outline of the two truths posited in relation to
    subject and object, distinguished as mistaken and
    unmistaken* **(23)**

*(ii) A detailed explanation of the two truths posited in
    relation to subject and object, distinguished as
    mistaken and unmistaken*

A. From the standpoint of the subject, the correctly
    perceiving consciousness, our refutation of other-
    production cannot be validly disproved by
    empirical experience

1. A discussion of valid cognition which investigates
    the relative truth

a. The difference between valid and invalid
    cognition **(24)**

b. How cognition evaluates its object

i. A general discussion of the difference between
    mistaken and unmistaken objects **(25)**

ii. A particular explanation showing how the
    mistaken kind of conceived object (self) cannot
    be established as truly existent for valid
    cognition on the conventional level **(26)**

2. Valid cognition on the conventional level is unable
    to invalidate valid cognition that investigates the
    ultimate level **(27)**

B. From the standpoint of the object, namely, the two
    truths, our refutation of other-production cannot
    be invalidated by empirical experience

1. The mistaken object, true on the relative level,
    explained by means of its etymology **(28)**

   2. The unmistaken object, true on the ultimate level,
      explained by an analogy **(29)**
   (iii) A concluding summary describing what can be
         invalidated by ordinary experience and what cannot
         be so invalidated
      A. Ordinary experience is unable to invalidate the
         ultimate truth when this is analyzed
         1. Ordinary experience cannot be taken as valid **(30)**
         2. Valid cognition cannot be called into question by
            invalid cognition **(31)**
      B. What is the only way in which empirical experience
         can invalidate our position?
   (b) Given that, even on the relative level, there is no such
       thing as naturally existent other-production, the
       opinion of ordinary beings cannot prevail against this
       refutation **(32)**
iii. The advantages of such a refutation **(33)**
b. There is no naturally existent other-production, even
   conventionally
i. A refutation of naturally existent other-production, even in
   the conventional sense
(1) The refutation itself
   (a) There is no such thing as naturally existent other-
       production, even conventionally. If there were such a
       thing, it would follow that the meditation of the Aryas
       would destroy phenomena **(34)**
   (b) Even conventionally, there is no naturally existent
       other-production. If there were, it would follow that
       conventional truth would resist analysis **(35)**
   (c) Even conventionally, there is no such thing as
       naturally existent other-production. If there were, it
       could not be disproved on the ultimate level **(36)**
(2) Refutation of an objection **(37, 38)**
ii. The advantages of this refutation
(1) It disproves the extremely subtle views of eternalism and
    nihilism
(2) It also demonstrates the connection between karmic
    cause and effect

*(a) A finished action is able to produce an effect even in
the absence of the alaya*

(i) A finished action is able to produce an effect **(39)**

(ii) A supporting example **(40)**

*(b) An answer to the objection regarding the assertion that
even if there is no alaya, a finished action can produce
an effect*

*(i) An answer to the objection that, in that case, results
would be produced ad infinitum*

A. Examples for the two kinds of object **(41)**

B. How effects of actions illustrated by the examples
are produced

1. Effects cannot be produced ad infinitum

2. Effects are not produced randomly **(42)**

*(ii) An answer to the objection that the above refutation
contradicts scripture, for the scriptures assert the
alaya*

A. Scriptures that speak of the alaya are not of
ultimate meaning and are to be interpreted **(43)**

B. An example **(44)**

2. *A specific refutation of the Chittamatra tenet*

a. *The Chittamatra position itself* **(45, 46, 47)**

b. *Refutation of the Chittamatra position*

i. *Refutation through reasoning*

*(1) Refutation of an inherently existent consciousness
devoid of outer objects*

*(a) Refutation of consciousness as such, devoid of outer
objects*

*(i) Refutations of the examples given of consciousness
devoid of outer objects*

A. Refutation of the dream example

1. An investigation of the example **(48)**

2. The refutation of the Chittamatra assertion

a. In fact the dream example is inadequate as a
demonstration of an inherently existent mind **(49)**

b. The example of dreaming is not enough to
demonstrate the unreality of an extramental
world in the waking state

i. The Chittamatra belief **(50)**

ii. Refutation of this belief **(51, 52)**

c. The dream example actually shows that all phenomena exist in an illusory manner **(53)**

B. A refutation of the example of black lines **(54, 55)**

(ii) A refutation of the example's supposed meaning, namely, that consciousness arises in the absence of an object thanks to the potential of latent tendencies in the mind

A. The Chittamatra position **(56)**

B. Refutation of the Chittamatra position

1. Brief rebuttal

2. Detailed refutation

a. There is no inherently existent potential associated with the present consciousness **(57)**

b. There is no inherently existent potential associated with the future consciousness

i. General refutation

ii. Refutation of an objection **(58)**

c. A refutation of an inherently existent potential associated with the past (moment of) consciousness

i. The refutation itself **(59)**

ii. Refutation of an objection

(1) An objection to the refutation **(60)**

(2) An answer to this objection **(61)**

(b) A refutation of the contention that inert objects manifest through the ripening of habitual propensities left latent in the consciousness

(i) The Chittamatra theory **(62, 63, 64)**

(ii) A refutation of this theory

A. The refutation itself

1. A refutation showing the theory's absurd consequence to the effect that if it is the mind manifesting in the aspect of an outer object (whereas there is no outer object), it follows that, while awake, the blind should also see **(65)**

2. A refutation of this theory by showing the

unwanted consequence of claiming that the
potential does not ripen during the waking state of
a blind man. The same should apply to the dream
state: nothing should appear **(66, 67)**

3. The sense organ, the object, and the sense
consciousness are all illusory

B. The other arguments adduced to show that
phenomena are just manifestations of the mind are
equally inconclusive

1. The thesis cannot be logically sustained **(68)**

2. Neither is the thesis supported by scriptures

3. The thesis is not supported by credible examples

a. The example of the yogi who, when meditating
on the ugliness of objects of desire, perceives
them as skeletons, is inadequate as a proof that
phenomena are but the manifestation of the
mind **(69, 70)**

b. The example of the perceptions in other samsaric
states is also inadequate as a proof of the Mind
Only position **(71)**

(iii) The concluding summary of the refutation

(2) A refutation of dependent reality considered as
inherently existent

(a) An inherently existent dependent reality is untenable

(i) A brief refutation consisting of an inquiry into whether
the theory of dependent reality is justified **(72)**

(ii) A detailed explanation of the refutation

A. A refutation of reflexive awareness as the valid
cognition that ascertains the existence of dependent
reality

1. A short refutation **(73)**

2. A detailed refutation using reasoning

a. Reflexive awareness cannot be established by
inference

i. The Chittamatra position

ii. A refutation of the Chittamatra reasoning

(1) Memory as a proof of reflexive awareness is
refuted simply because it is unsubstantiated

(2) Reflexive awareness is refuted because even if

its existence were admitted, memory would be
impossible
   (a) The refutation itself
     (i) An explanation of the reasoning employed
       in the refutation **(74)**
     (ii) This reasoning disposes of all other
       objections
   (b) According to the Prasangika tradition, the
      memory occurs even though there is no such
      thing as inherently existent reflexive
      awareness **(75)**
  b. There is no direct evidence for the existence of
    reflexive awareness **(76)**
 B. Since there is no valid cognition to prove its
   existence, the existence of dependent reality is
   untenable **(77)**
*(b) Dependent reality cannot be located in either of the
two truths* **(78)**
*(c) Only the system of Nagarjuna supplies a correct
understanding of the two truths* **(79)**
 *(i) Only the system of Nagarjuna is the authentic path for
those who wish for liberation*
 (ii) A demonstration of this
  A. Without a perfect assimilation of the correct
    teaching on the two truths, liberation is impossible
  B. Without a proper and complete understanding of
    the two truths, a realization of suchness is
    impossible **(80)**
*(d) The Chittamatra assertion of dependent reality is
not the same as the view of the Madhyamikas, who
accept ordinary experience as conventional reality*
(81, 82, 83)
ii. The meaning of the scriptures that teach Mind Only
 *(1) The sense of the teaching given in the Dashabhumika-
sutra*
 (a) What the scripture says **(84)**
 (b) Proof through coherence
  (i) Demonstration using scripture

       ii. Refutation by showing that if there were no cause, nothing
           would ever exist
         (1) It would be unnecessary to assemble causes in order to
            achieve results
         (2) Absence of cause implies nonexistence **(100)**
      b. A specific refutation of the doctrine that there is nothing
        beyond the present life
        i. There is no evidence to support the skepticism of the
          Charvakas with regard to life after death **(101)**
        ii. The falsity of the Charvaka view
         (1) The understanding of the Charvakas contradicts the
            ultimate status of things **(102)**
         (2) Disposal of the objection regarding the example used
            (103)
    (iii) Conclusion: the general message implied by the
       refutation of the four kinds of production **(104)**
  (b) Replies to the objections against the refutation of the
     four theories of production
  (i) The reply to the objection that if phenomena lack
     inherent existence by their very nature, this should be
     evident to everyone
    A. The cause or reason why the nature of phenomena is not
      perceived
     1. Why it is not perceived
     2. An illustration of this point **(105)**
    B. Showing that even this cause, namely, ignorance, is without
      inherent existence **(106)**
  (ii) An answer to the objection that if there were no ground
     of appearance, it would follow that nothing could be
     perceived on the conventional level
    A. The objection itself **(107)**
    B. A reply to this objection
     1. Examples demonstrating that the objection carries no
      weight
     a. Exposition **(108)**
     b. Further explanation
      i. The consequence of the earlier objection is that reflections
        and so forth should not be possible **(109)**

ii. This consequence shows that the objection is not conclusive
   (110)
   2. *There is no contradiction in the fact that phenomena appear*
      conventionally without being inherently produced
      a. *Inherently real production is not included in the two truths*
         i. *The actual teaching about the nonexistence of inherently*
            real production **(111)**
         ii. *The scriptures teach the nonexistence of inherently real*
             production **(112)**
      b. *Although phenomena are by nature unproduced, this does*
         not prevent their appearance **(113)**
(2) A reasoned demonstration that production is no more
   than dependent arising
   (a) Since phenomena are not produced in any of the four
      ways of inherently existent production, they are simply
      dependent arisings **(114)**
   (b) In praise of the argument of dependent arising, which
      vanquishes all false views **(115)**
(3) The result of analysis
   (a) A demonstration of the result of the analysis
    (i) The prevention of incorrect conceptions **(116)**
    (ii) The halting of thought processes is the outcome of
       analysis **(117)**
   (b) The need for the analysis that is productive of such a
      result
    (i) One must analyze because the Madhyamika
       investigation of the ultimate is without error **(118)**
    (ii) Analysis is needful, for it is productive of excellent
       qualities **(119)**
ii. Using reason to disprove the self of persons
 (1) Why is this necessary? **(120)**
 (2) A rational demonstration that there is no personal self
   (a) Refutation of the belief that the personal self is a
      concrete entity
    (i) A refutation of the belief that the self is different from
       the aggregates
     A. *The self as something different from the aggregates* **(121)**

      B. Refutation of the belief that the personal self is something
         different from the aggregates

       1. The self as a permanent entity cannot possibly exist

        a. General reasoning disproving the self as a permanent entity
          (122)

        b. This argument defeats all the various schools that say that
         the self is a permanent entity **(123)**

       2. The self is not different from the aggregates **(124, 125)**

   (ii) A refutation of the belief that the self is identical with
     the aggregates

    A. The belief that the self is identical with the aggregates **(126)**

    B. The refutation of the belief that the personal self is identical
      with the aggregates

      1. A general refutation

        a. A reasoned demonstration that the aggregates cannot be the
         referent of the notion of "I"

         i. A general refutation of the belief that the self and the
          aggregates are one and the same **(127)**

         ii. A specific refutation demonstrating the contradiction implicit
          in the belief that the self and the aggregates are identical

          (1) The contradiction implicit in this belief

           (a) The refutation itself by showing the unwanted
             consequences of this belief

            (i) The apprehension of the self would not be a mistaken
              conception

            (ii) The self would be a simple nonentity **(128)**

            (iii) It would be pointless to try to accomplish nirvana

            (iv) The karmic principle of cause and effect would be
              inadmissible

              A. The actual refutation

                1. Performed actions would have no effect

                2. One would encounter the effect of actions that one
                   had not performed

              B. The refutation of an objection **(129)**

           (b) Concluding summary of the refutation

          (2) The tenet that the self is identical with the aggregates
            contradicts scripture

*(3) The belief that the self is identical with the aggregates
contradicts reason*

*(a) A refutation by showing the absurd consequence that if
the aggregates were the referent of the notion of "I," it
would follow that on the realization of no-self, existent
phenomena should vanish*

(i) The refutation itself **(130)**

(ii) The refutation of an objection

*(b) A refutation by showing the absurd consequence that if
the aggregates existed, the self could never be refuted,
with the result that one could never overcome the
afflictions of craving and so forth* **(131)**

*b. An explanation of what the Buddha meant when he said in
the sutra that the aggregates were the referent of the notion
of "I"*

i. The sutra does not assert that the aggregates constitute the self

*(1) A statement of the belief that the sutra teaches that the
aggregates constitute the self* **(132)**

(2) A refutation of this assertion

*(a) The sense of the sutra is to be properly discerned from
the standpoint of the negation of an imputed,
permanent self* **(133)**

*(b) Even if the sutra is interpreted along the lines of the
Sammitiya assertion, it does not in fact support their
view*

*(i) If the aggregates were the self, this could only mean the
aggregates together, not individually* **(134)**

*(ii) If the self were the aggregates taken together, this too
would contradict the belief of the Sammitiyas*

A. How this is so

B. A refutation of the objection that the earlier assertion
is not false because the collection of parts and the
parts themselves share the same nature

1. A demonstration that this is not consistent with
the meaning of the sutras

a. The use of an analogy and the subject of the
analogy to disprove the assertion that the mere
gathering of the aggregates is the self

          i. If the mere gathering of the aggregates were the self, it would follow that the mere collection of the chariot's parts would constitute a chariot **(135)**

          ii. Just like the chariot referred to in the analogy, the self is conceptually imputed on the basis of the aggregates; thus the self is not the mere gathering of the aggregates

        b. Refutation of an objection **(136)**

     2. A demonstration that the Sammitiya assertion (that the gathering of the parts and the parts gathered share the same nature) is illogical

        a. The assertion is inherently contradictory **(137)**

        b. Refutation of an objection

  ii. The sutras say that the personal self is an imputation

    (1) The sutras say that the self is conceptually imputed in dependence on the aggregates, but not that the self is the aggregates **(138, 139)**

    (2) Even the innate apprehension of, and clinging, to the "I" does not seize upon the aggregates as being the self— whether on the general level, individually, or collectively

    (3) Tenets that aim at the realization of the nonexistence of the self without eradicating the referent of the innate ego-clinging do not achieve their aim

      (a) The teaching itself **(140)**

      (b) An example **(141)**

 2. Refutation of additional beliefs concerning the connection between the personal self and the aggregates

  a. Refutation of three additional beliefs

    i. Refutation of the idea that the aggregates and the self are related in the manner of a container and its contents **(142)**

    ii. Refutation of the idea that the self is the possessor of the aggregates **(143)**

  b. A concluding recapitulation

    i. A summary of the twenty views of the transitory composite **(144)**

    ii. These twenty views, inherent in the basic view of the transitory composite, are all conceptual imputations **(145)**

(iii) A refutation of the belief that the self is indescribable—
that it cannot be said to be either distinct from the
aggregates or identical with them
  A. *An exposition of the belief that the self is indescribable* **(146)**
  B. *A refutation of the Vatsiputriya position*
    1. *If the self really exists, it is expressible* **(147)**
    2. *If the self is inexpressible, it cannot be an existent thing* **(148)**
    3. *The self of the Vatsiputriyas lacks two properties common to
all things; it is therefore not a real entity* **(149)**
(b) The self is a mere dependent imputation
 (i) Even though the self has no existence according to the
sevenfold analysis, it is dependently imputed, just like a
chariot
  A. *The self is dependently imputed*
    1. *There is no self* **(150)**
    2. *Using the example of a chariot to disprove the self*
     a. *A general application of the chariot example* **(151)**
     b. *A specific application of the chariot example to the self*
      i. *The refutation of the belief that the chariot is the mere
collection of its parts* **(152)**
      ii. *A refutation of the belief that the mere shape of the
gathered parts constitutes the chariot*
      (1) *A refutation of the belief that the shape of the individual
parts is the chariot*
       (a) *A refutation of the belief that the mere shape of the
original parts, prior to the assembly of the chariot, is
the chariot* **(153)**
       (b) *A refutation of the belief that a new configuration of
parts—different from the shape of the original parts—is
the chariot* **(154)**
      (2) *The refutation of the belief that only the shape of the
assembled parts is the chariot*
       (a) *The refutation itself* **(155)**
       (b) *The opponent's belief accepts that empty effects arise
from empty causes*
        (i) *The general exposition* **(156)**
        (ii) *A more detailed explanation* **(157)**

B. *The benefits of understanding that the self is a mere imputation*
  1. *An explanation using the example of the chariot*
    a. *This reasoning does not undermine conventional reality but agrees with it*
      i. *When not subjected to the sevenfold reasoning, the chariot merely exists according to empirical consensus* **(158)**
      ii. *Dependently imputed conventional phenomena perform their functions, even though they are without real, inherent existence* **(159)**
    b. *If one understands that the self is a mere imputation, one will easily gain an understanding of ultimate reality*
      i. *The actual benefit of such an understanding—an easy grasp of the ultimate* **(160)**
      ii. *Dealing with doubts on this matter* **(161)**
  2. *The benefits of understanding that the self is a mere imputation, applying the example of a chariot to the self*
    a. *The self is in harmony with conventional experience even though it lacks inherent reality* **(162)**
    b. *The benefits with regard to the realization of ultimate reality*
      i. *By understanding that the self is no more than an imputation, one assimilates the view of the path that transcends eternalism and nihilism* **(163)**
      ii. *This understanding causes one to attain the fruit of complete freedom*
        (1) *Since the self, as the object of innate ego-clinging, is no more than a designation, it can be eradicated* **(164)**
        (2) *When the self is eradicated, the notion of "I" and "mine" will also cease to occur* **(165)**
        (3) *If "I" and "mine" are no more, liberation is possible*

(ii) An adaptation to phenomena in general of the arguments that demonstrate that both the chariot and the self are mere imputations
  A. *The reasoning applied to all "wholes" (pots, cloths, and so on) and their parts* **(166, 167)**
  B. *The reasoning that shows that the self is a mere imputation applied to cause and effect*
    1. *The actual reasoning*

THE QUALITIES OF THE TEN GROUNDS

I. AN EXPOSITION OF THE TWELVE GROUPS OF ONE HUNDRED QUALITIES THAT MANIFEST ON THE FIRST GROUND (1, 2, 3, 4)

II. THE ADAPTATION OF THESE QUALITIES TO THE FOLLOWING GROUNDS

  A. On the following six impure grounds, the number of qualities is multiplied **(5)**

  B. On the pure grounds, the number of qualities is compared to particles of dust
  1. The qualities of the eighth ground **(6)**
  2. The qualities of the ninth ground **(7)**
  3. The qualities of the tenth ground
    a. The multiplication of the twelve qualities **(8)**
    b. Other qualities **(9)**

THE ULTIMATE GROUND OF BUDDHAHOOD

I. THE ATTAINMENT OF BUDDHAHOOD

  A. How buddhahood is attained
  1. When buddhahood is attained **(10)**
  2. The place where buddhahood is attained
  3. The manner in which buddhahood is attained **(11)**

  B. An answer to objections
  1. The objections themselves
    a. It is inadmissible to say that the unborn nature is realized as an object **(12)**
    b. If the subject (the mind) and object (the unborn nature) are of a single taste, it follows that even when the unborn nature is understood, it cannot be taught to others
  2. An answer to the objections
    a. It is admissible to talk about the realization of the unborn nature as an object **(13)**
    b. Even though the subject and object are not distinct, teachings can be given
      i. Though the subject and object are not distinct, it is possible to expound the teachings **(14)**
      ii. An example **(15, 16)**

II. WHAT IS THE GOAL, NAMELY, BUDDHAHOOD?

  A. A description of the kayas, which are the basis
  1. The dharmakaya **(17)**

2. The sambhogakaya **(18)**
3. The kaya similar to its cause
  a. How Buddhas display all their activities within a single pore of their bodies **(19, 20, 21, 22)**
  b. They can display in a single pore of their bodies the activities of other Buddhas **(23, 24, 25)**
  c. The power of Buddhas to accomplish all that they wish
    i. With respect to space **(26)**
    ii. With respect to time **(27)**
B. The qualities based on the kayas
  1. An explanation of the ten strengths, which are the principal qualities of buddhahood
    a. A brief exposition **(28, 29, 30)**
    b. A detailed explanation **(31, 32, 33, 34, 35, 36, 37, 38, 39, 40)**
  2. The qualities of buddhahood are beyond telling
    a. It is impossible to describe all the Buddha's qualities **(41)**
    b. A brief description based on the scriptures **(42)**
  3. The benefits that result from knowing the qualities of buddhahood **(43)**
C. How, after achieving buddhahood, one may benefit others by means of nirmanakaya emanations
  1. The deeds of the Buddha our Teacher, the supreme nirmanakaya **(44)**
  2. The ultimate teaching of the Buddha is established as a single path
    a. Reasoned proof that ultimately there is only one path to buddhahood **(45)**
    b. The teaching that there are three paths is an expedient **(46, 47)**
  3. The Buddha our Teacher is beyond all limitation as concerns his perfect enlightenment and his sojourn in samsara
    a. With respect to the moment of his perfect enlightenment **(48)**
    b. With respect to the Buddha's sojourn in samsara
    i. A brief explanation **(49)**
    ii. A detailed explanation
    (1) The Buddha's unbounded compassion for beings **(50)**

(2) The Buddha never departs into nirvana because the
suffering of beings is endless **(51)**

CONCLUSION

I. THE CONCLUSION OF THE MAIN BODY OF THE TREATISE
A. How the text was composed
1. The composition of the text
a. On what it was based **(52)**
b. The shastra, thus composed, is indeed extraordinary **(53)**
2. Why this text was composed
a. Its purpose **(54)**
b. An injunction to uphold only this text **(55)**
B. The dedication of the merit accruing from the composition of
the text **(56)**

II. CONCLUSION OF THE TREATISE
A. The author of the treatise
B. The translator
C. Colophon to the commentary
D. Colophon of the Tibetan editors

PREAMBLE

CHANDRAKIRTI'S *Madhyamakavatara, The Introduction to the Middle Way,* is the king of all shastras elucidating the ultimate view of the second Buddha, the noble and glorious master Nagarjuna. In our presentation of it, we will discuss four topics: the meaning of the title, the homage of the translator, the treatise itself, and the conclusion.

I. THE MEANING OF THE TITLE

The Sanskrit name of the root text is *Madhyamakavatara nama* which, when rendered into Tibetan, is *dbu ma la 'jug pa zhes bya ba* (Introduction to the Middle Way). The expression "Middle Way" has two meanings. First, on the ultimate level, it refers to the *dharmadhatu,* the absolute madhyamika, reality beyond all concepts. Second, it refers to the scriptural madhyamika, that is, the texts introducing this ultimate reality. Here we are concerned with the scriptural madhyamika, which is itself subdivided into two compartments: the Buddha's teaching and the commentaries on the same. Once again, it is the latter that is of interest here, since we are dealing with a text that elucidates the meaning of the shastra of Nagarjuna known as the *Mulamadhyamaka-karikas,* the *Root Stanzas on the Middle Way.* It is an introduction that incorporates the profound and vast approaches. As to the profound approach, it presents the teachings of the scriptures of ultimate meaning together with Nagarjuna's own instructions. The latter, namely the *Mulamadhyamaka-karikas,* is the common ground of the Svatantrikas and Prasangikas, in relation to which their views are distinguished. In his commentary on this text, Chandrakirti emphasizes the ultimate truth in itself,* which lies beyond

---

* *rnam grangs min pa'i don dam.*

the reach of all assertion. He therefore adopts the extraordinary view of the Prasangikas. As for the vast approach, he explains the three levels of ordinary beings, the ten grounds or stages of realization of sublime beings on the path of learning, and the supreme level of the path of no more learning .

II. THE HOMAGE OF THE TRANSLATOR

The root text begins with the reverential invocation: "Homage to Mañjushri Kumara—tender, glorious, ever-youthful!" Mañjushri is called "tender," for he is free from the roughness of negativity, and he is "glorious" in being rich in the fruits of the twofold goal. He is "everyouthful" because, although the sire of all the Buddhas, he appears in the form of a Bodhisattva, the Buddha's offspring. Therefore, at the start of his labors, the translator pays homage with these words of salutation, using the formula appropriate to the ultimate teachings of the Abhidharma, to which the present discourse belongs.[58]

III. THE TREATISE ITSELF

The *Madhyamakavatara* falls also into three main sections: the homage of the author, the main body of the treatise, and the conclusion.

A. The homage of the author

Chandrakirti's expression of homage comprises two main items. First he identifies the three causes of bodhichitta and then he praises compassion, first generally and then in detail according to its classifications.

1. The three causes of Bodhisattvas

1   First of all, Chandrakirti mentions the Shravakas, who listen to the instructions of the Buddha, their perfect spiritual friend, and then proclaim them to others. He then mentions the Pratyekabuddhas, who in merit and wisdom are greater than the Shravakas and swifter to gain realization, but who are lower than the Buddhas and are therefore assigned an intermediate position. Shravakas and Pratyekabuddhas arise from the speech of the Mighty Sage, the Buddha himself. Buddhas in turn are said to be born from Bodhisattvas, referring to that special moment[59] when the latter, on the path of learning, enter into the possession of perfect purity. Now three factors are the cause of Bodhisattvas, the children of the Conqueror: first, the compassionate mind, the wish to protect all beings from suffering; second, the nondualistic mind, the wisdom that sees beyond the extremes of existence and nonexistence; and third, bodhichitta, the mind of enlightenment. As it is said in the *Ratnavali*:*

> *If we, ourselves and all the world,*
> *Should wish for unsurpassed enlightenment,*
> *Its basis is a bodhichitta*
> *Stable as the lord of mountains,*
> *Compassion reaching out to all directions,*
> *And a wisdom that transcends duality.*

2. In praise of great compassion
a. In praise of compassion in a general sense

2   Chandrakirti begins by praising great compassion generally; he then pays homage to specific kinds of compassion. Great compassion is declared to be important in the beginning, the middle, and the end of the path. At the outset, love, or rather compassion, is important as the germ of the abundant harvest of buddhahood. It is also important in the middle term, as a means of development, just as water is essential for the nurturing of crops. For it is thanks to their compassion that Bodhisattvas do not weaken in their resolve, even though confronted by beings infinite in number, evil in conduct, and devoid of gratitude. Finally, compassion is important at the end, for it ripens into the state of lasting happiness. Consequently, the venerable Chandrakirti declares that at the outset he will praise compassion.

b. Homage to different kinds of great compassion

He then proceeds to praise, first, compassion that has beings for its object; second, compassion that has transience for its object;† and third, compassion that is devoid of reference.‡

---

* That is, by Nagarjuna himself.
† *chos la dmigs pa'i snying rje.*
‡ *dmigs pa med pa'i snying rje.*

i. Homage to compassion that has beings for its object

3   At first, that is, before any notion of "mine" can arise, there is a clinging to "I," to the self that is assumed to exist. All that is considered to pertain to this self—one's eyes, for example—is in turn assumed to exist truly, and attachment to it is consequently engendered. It is due to this that beings wander helplessly in samsara, from the Peak of Existence down to the hell of Torment Unsurpassed, as though revolving on an irrigation wheel. Chandrakirti pays homage to compassion for such beings. The image of an irrigation wheel to describe the situation of living beings is appropriate in six ways. (1) Like buckets tied to the wheel with ropes, beings are bound tightly by the strings of their karma and defilements. (2) The driving force of consciousness is like a person turning the water wheel. (3) Samsara resembles a deep well, from the Peak of Existence to the hell of Torment Unsurpassed—a fathomless abyss, down which beings are constantly hurled. (4) Like the buckets fastened to the chain, beings fall down naturally into the lower realms, whereas they are led upward into higher states only with great effort. (5) The buckets on the chain are like the twelve links of dependent arising: the three of Ignorance, Craving, and Grasping, related to defilement, the two of Conditioning Factors and Becoming, related to karma, and the other seven, all of which are related to samsaric birth.[60] Of these three groups, it is impossible to say which is first, second, or third, for they follow one another uninterruptedly like a firebrand whirled in the air.[61] (6) Finally, the three kinds of suffering (the suffering of suffering, the suffering of change, and all-pervading suffering in the making) are like the waves that, day in and day out, ripple the water in the well, endlessly lapping against each other.[62]

ii. Homage to compassion that has transience for its object and to compassion that is devoid of reference

4   Wandering beings are like the reflection of the moon in water troubled by the wind. They do not stay the same even for an instant. Chandrakirti pays homage to compassion for them, compassion that sees that they are "fleeting," that is, transitory and by nature empty of inherent existence. When it is said that beings are like the moon reflected in limpid water rippled by a gentle breeze, the reflection and its watery support are alike in being, at every moment, impermanent and empty in their nature. With this understanding, Bodhisattvas are overwhelmed by a compassion that sees beings immersed in the ocean of the view of the transitory composite,* an ocean fed by the vast, dark rivers of ignorance. They perceive that in this ocean, agitated by the winds of discursive thought, the cause of so much harm, beings must confront the effects of their good and evil actions reflected in the ocean like the moon. Compassion that considers beings as disintegrating moment by moment is called compassion that has transience for its object. Compassion that focuses on beings devoid of inherent existence is called nonreferential compassion.

In short, the three kinds of compassion are: (1) the compassion that has as its object beings generally, in an unspecified sense; (2) compassion that has as its object beings in their impermanence; and (3) compassion that has as its object beings in their lack of true existence. It should be understood that these three kinds of compassion all have the same aspect, namely, the attitude of wishing that beings be free from suffering; they differ only as to their specific objects.

B. The main body of the treatise

The main body of the treatise discusses three main topics: the ten grounds or stages of realization, the qualities of the ten grounds, and the ultimate ground of buddhahood.

---

* Self-sense, or sense of "I."

THE TEN GROUNDS OR
STAGES OF REALIZATION

I. THE FIRST GROUND: PERFECT JOY

This chapter consists of an explanation followed by a concluding summary. The explanation itself comprises three main topics: the qualities that embellish the mind of the Bodhisattva on the first ground, the qualities of the Bodhisattva whereby other beings are eclipsed, and the superior qualities of the first ground.

A. A brief general description

Bodhisattvas, offspring of the Conqueror, see in their minds that beings are without inherent existence, and, overwhelmed by compassion, they yearn for their complete liberation. **5** Such Bodhisattvas, now on the first ground, make ten great aspirations of bodhichitta and hundreds of thousands of other prayers and countless wishes. They are all summarized in the Aspiration of Samantabhadra, which Bodhisattvas use to dedicate perfectly all their merit and wisdom devoid of dual appearance.* They dwell on the first ground, Perfect Joy, which is said to be the first level of the transmundane mind.

B. A detailed examination of the qualities peculiar to the first ground
1. The qualities that embellish the mind of the Bodhisattva

---

* *gnyis snang.*

a. A new and meaningful name

As soon as Bodhisattvas enter the first ground, they attain ultimate wisdom. They are therefore known as Bodhisattvas of the ultimate level, having become Superior or Noble Bodhisattvas.

b. The five additional qualities of lineage, elimination, realization, ability, and progression

6 (1) The first bodhisattva ground transcends the levels of ordinary beings, Shravakas, and Pratyekabuddhas. The Bodhisattvas who enter this ground become members of the family of the Tathagatas; they will never more stray to other paths, for their lineage is now irreversible. (2) The Bodhisattvas on this ground have a direct realization of the nonexistence of the self. This enables them to abandon the three fetters: the view of the transitory composite, the belief in the superiority of their ethical discipline, and doubt—together with all the obscurations eliminated on the path of seeing. (3) Because they have attained the sublime qualities of realization and have eliminated all defects, the Bodhisattvas experience an extraordinary happiness, which is why this ground is called Perfect Joy. (4) At the same time, the Bodhisattvas acquire one hundred and twelve powers, such as the miraculous ability to cause a hundred different worlds to tremble.[63] These are the qualities of their extraordinary, indeed sublime attainment. **7** Finally, (5) the Bodhisattvas' quality of progression means that they joyously proceed to the higher grounds, from first to second and so forth.

c. Birth in the lower realms is no longer possible

It is said that when Bodhisattvas reach the first ground, all paths whereby they might fall into the lower realms are closed. The realization of the level of "acceptance" on the path of joining,[64] in fact, does not furnish the complete conditions for prevention of lower birth, whereas on the first ground, the seed for such a birth is counteracted by antidotes and annihilated. Bodhisattvas who attain the first ground are now Aryas or Superiors, for they can never relapse into the states of ordinary beings. This ground of the Mahayana is said to correspond, by analogy, to the eighth Arya level of the Hinayana (that of "Stream Enterer abiding by the result"). This is according to a scheme[65] that counts the state of "Arhat abiding by the result" as the first level, and proceeds in reverse order through the level of "candidate for arhat-ship," and so on, to that of "Stream Enterer abiding by the result." On all these levels, all that is eliminated by the wisdom of seeing and so forth is abandoned, and all corresponding qualities of elimination and realization are gained. The eighth level is sometimes explained as refer-ring to the stage of "candidate for Stream Enterer."

2. The qualities whereby Bodhisattvas outshine other beings

8   With enlightenment as their aim, Bodhisattvas, while only on the first ground, overwhelm the Shravakas, born from the Buddha's speech, and eclipse the Pratyekabuddhas. They do this through the power of their merit accruing from relative bodhichitta and nonrefer-ential compassion; for compared with the Shravakas and Pratyekabud-dhas, the merit of Bodhisattvas is ever-increasing. It is on the seventh ground, called Far Progressed, that they outshine them also by their wisdom, their understanding of absolute bodhichitta.

3. The superior quality of the first ground
a. The preeminence of the paramita of generosity on the first ground

9   Of the ten paramitas, the causes of perfect buddhahood, that of gen-erosity is the most important for Bodhisattvas on the first ground. Even when they donate their own flesh, they are free from even the most sub-tle attachment and clinging to its existence. Consequently, not only do they have no regret, but they act with the keenest enthusiasm. On being witness to such deeds, ordinary people can infer what they cannot see, namely, that the Bodhisattva has attained the grounds of realization, in much the same way that fire can be inferred by the presence of smoke.

b. In praise of generosity
i. In praise of the generosity of ordinary people
(1) Generosity is necessary for ordinary people

10   Ordinary beings want only to be happy. But happiness, the cure of human sufferings like hunger and thirst, does not occur uncaused; it re-quires material sustenance. Knowing that such wealth is the karmic fruit of acts of generosity performed in the past, the Buddha praised it in his first teaching, even before ethical discipline and the rest. And he did so, furthermore, because generosity is easy to practice.

(2) The benefits of generosity
(a) Generosity brings happiness in samsara

11   Even for people whose faith and compassion are negligible, whose disposition is extremely rough and who bestir themselves only in their own interest, the getting of material satisfaction—in other words, a reprieve from their portion of sorrows—comes solely as the karmic result of generosity. Generosity is therefore the source and origin of samsaric happiness.

(b) Generosity leads to the bliss of nirvana

12   Moreover, even if they have no compassion, open-handed people will, as a result of their generosity, swiftly find themselves in the presence of superior beings. For it is in the nature of things that sublime beings appear in the vicinity of generous people. And the latter, on meeting them and receiving their teachings, turn their backs on samsara and meditate on the path. So doing, they completely sever the continuum of samsaric birth and death. On the basis of such encounters, they progress toward the peace of the Shravakas and Pratyekabuddhas.

ii. In praise of the generosity of Bodhisattvas

13   Thanks to their generosity, which satisfies all who ask, Bodhisattvas, who have promised to benefit beings immediately and ultimately, are quick to obtain happiness, the resultant effect of giving. That is why they constantly delight in it.

iii. Concluding summary of praise

For compassionate Bodhisattvas and for ordinary beings, Shravakas, and Pratyekabuddhas, who are imperfect in their compassion, the bliss of the higher realms and the ultimate goodness of enlightenment are the outcome of generous giving. Thus the teachings on generosity are of paramount importance.

iv. The respectful attitude of Bodhisattvas toward generosity thus praised
(1) The extent to which they are devoted to generosity

14   When they hear a beggar crying "Give!" or even when they think of such a thing—in other words, when the merest thought occurs to them that they might have the chance to practice generosity—Bodhisattvas experience a joy greater than that of Arhats entering the expanse of peace beyond suffering. Is there any need to speak of their happiness when they actually do give away everything—their possessions and even their physical organs—to satisfy the wants of those in need?

(2) How they respectfully practice generosity

15 Because they are so delighted by the practice of giving, Bodhisattvas have no thought for their own suffering; instead they try to remove that of others as quickly as they can. For they see or understand that the pain they felt (when as ordinary beings they had the flesh of their bodies cut and given away) is as nothing compared with the agony of beings in hell, whose suffering is a thousand times worse.

c. Different kinds of generosity

16 An act of generosity associated with the pure wisdom whereby one sees that neither act of giving, nor gift to be given, neither receiver nor giver* has any real existence is called a transmundane perfection, or paramita. The Sanskrit word *paramita* is a combination of the elements *para* and *ita*. *Para* takes the accusative termination *–am*, while *ita* assumes the visarga aspiration which is a sign of the nominative case: thus, *param + itah*. When combined, this gives *paramita*. The "m" termination and the visarga are not normally audible in a compounded form. However, since the second element begins with a vowel, the preceding nasalization is heard while the visarga remains mute.

Even when an act of generosity is not combined with wisdom, it can still be referred to as a paramita. For it has been said that if generosity is dedicated to complete enlightenment, it is certainly on the way to the far shore— "gone to the far shore" being the sense of the Tibetan words *pha rol tu phyin pa* and the Sanskrit *paramita*. The Tibetan term may be interpreted in two ways. In the first case, the "far shore" is understood in the sense of the Tibetan accusative,† indicative of movement toward a destination. In this case the term means "gone to the far shore," that is, buddhahood. According to this interpretation, perfect transcendent virtue is found only in the state of perfect buddha-

---

* *'khor gsum*, the three spheres, namely, the subject, the object, and the act itself.
† *las su bya ba*.

hood and indeed is that state. In the second case, *pha rol tu phyin pa* may be interpreted in an instrumental sense, in other words, referring to the means whereby buddhahood is attained. In this sense, transcendental virtues are found even on the path of learning.

In short, *para* or *pha rol* refers to the far shore, that is, the far shore of the ocean of samsara. This is buddhahood wherein the two veils are stripped away. By contrast, it is taught that when there is attachment to the three spheres, the generosity in question is referred to as a worldly paramita because it is still qualified by dualistic reference.

C. Concluding summary of the first ground
17 Just like the moon aloft in the sky, Bodhisattvas ride high in the wisdom of the first ground because the bodhichitta of the first ground is now an intrinsic part of their minds. Such Bodhisattvas are supremely holy beings, radiantly beautiful with the light of wisdom. Like the moon, the jeweled mandala of water crystal, the Bodhisattvas on the first ground of Perfect Joy eliminate through their wisdom the thick darkness of those obscurations that are removed on the path of seeing.[66] They overcome them and are completely free.

Here ends the first ground or stage in the cultivation of absolute bodhichitta.

II. THE SECOND GROUND: IMMACULATE
This section comprises three topics: the definition of the second ground, its qualities, and a concluding summary. Of these, the second topic contains three main items: the preeminence and purity of discipline, a eulogy of pure discipline, and the different categories of the paramita of discipline.

A. The definition of the second ground
1 From the point of view of defects to be abandoned, Bodhisattvas on the second ground possess perfect discipline. They have relinquished all disordered conduct, that is, all transgressions of the precepts—not only in the waking state, but also in their dreams. From the point of view of accomplishment, they possess pure qualities. For, since their physical, verbal, and mental behavior is untainted by even the slightest fault, they practice the sacred path of the ten virtues, forsaking the seven faults of body and speech and the three of mind that underlie them.

B. The qualities of the second ground
1. The preeminence and purity of discipline
a. The explanation itself

2   Although the tenfold virtuous path is followed also on the first ground, the second-ground Bodhisattvas are preeminent in their practice of it, for this is exceedingly pure and perfect. Like the autumn moon in a cloudless sky, their discipline is immaculate. And just as the cool light of the moon soothes away the torments of heat, discipline brings peace through the binding of the sense doors. At the same time, it sheds light like the moon's white radiance. This is the beauty of ethical discipline.

b. Purity of discipline

3   On the other hand, if a monk is extremely strict in his observance of the pratimoksha discipline but is at the same time complacent, thinking of it as a pure and really existing phenomenon, his discipline is actually impure. For this reason, Bodhisattvas always free themselves from the dualistic mental processes involved, first, in the forsaking of distorted discipline; second, in the antidotes to be used in such an enterprise; and third, with regard to the person who is the subject of such an abandoning.

2. In praise of pure discipline
a. The eulogy itself
i. Even ordinary people need to practice ethics
(1) The defects arising from a lack of ethical discipline
(a) Without discipline it is impossible to attain high rebirth

4   It is possible for wealth, the product of generosity, to manifest even in the lower realms. This happens because the "limbs" of discipline leading to higher realms have been broken and refers, for instance, to the wealth enjoyed by the *nagas* or minor *pretas* endowed with miraculous powers.[67]

(b) Without discipline positive actions give only one fortunate result

Beings in the lower states are improvident and fail to use their wealth in order to practice further generosity. They consequently exhaust the deposit of what they had accumulated and from which further benefits could be made to grow. Afterward, no further possessions are forthcoming, for there is no impulse from the past to bring them about. On the contrary, it is the product of past generosity that is consumed, as when people exhaust their capital by spending it.

(c) Without discipline it is hard to escape the lower realms

5   Like men and women at liberty in a pleasant environment, beings live freely in the happy circumstances of the divine and human realms. But if one does not grasp this opportunity in order to continue in this state, one will be like a once-powerful hero, bound hand and foot and thrown into an abyss. One will fall into the lower realms, all freedom lost, without a hope of ever emerging.

(d) Ethical discipline as a remedy for all these ills

6   This is why the Buddha spoke of generosity first and then of discipline.

(2) The benefits of being disciplined

Discipline is necessary because if the qualities of generosity are cultivated in the field of discipline, the resulting benefits, namely, an excellent body and a wealth of possessions, together with their cause, namely, generosity and so on, will continually increase.

ii. Discipline is the foundation of all qualities

7   The state of ordinary beings, of Shravakas born from the Buddha's speech, or of Pratyekabuddhas firmly established on their path, and likewise the attainments of the Bodhisattvas—namely, high status (in samsara) and the ultimate goodness (of enlightenment)—all have only one cause: discipline. Without discipline, none of these attainments can be gained. They have no other cause.

b. How Bodhisattvas abide in discipline

8   Just as the great ocean, the pure abode of the nagas, will always eject a corpse (casting it up onto the beach), and just as good and evil fortune are mutually exclusive, the great Bodhisattvas on the second ground, who are masters of discipline, are likewise said never to keep company with dissolute and disordered behavior, for their ethics are pure.

3. The different categories of the paramita of discipline

9   If one is still caught in the concepts of the three spheres—the real existence of an act, an object of abstention, and an agent who abstains—the discipline that one practices is called a worldly paramita. By contrast, a discipline combined with stainless wisdom, untainted by the belief in the true existence of the three spheres, is the transmundane paramita of discipline.

C. Conclusion

10   The Bodhisattvas who appear "within the moon of the second ground" are the glory and riches of the world even though they are beyond it. The second ground is called Immaculate because such Bodhisattvas are free from the defilement of indiscipline, and like the radiance of the autumn moon, they dispel the sorrow of beings.

> *Here ends the second ground or stage in the cultivation of absolute bodhichitta.*

III. THE THIRD GROUND: LUMINOUS

This section comprises three topics: the definition of the third ground, its particular qualities, and a concluding summary. The second topic contains two main items: the paramita of superior patience and a description of other qualities that manifest on this ground.

A. The definition of the third ground

1   The third ground is called Luminous because here the wisdom fire that burns up the tinder of phenomena glows with light and, in meditative equipoise, has the power to lay to rest all the conceptual constructs related to the perception of dual appearance. On this ground, there appears in the postmeditation experience of the Bodhisattva, the offspring of the Sugatas, a copper-colored glow as at dawn before the rising of the sun.[68]

B. The particular qualities of this ground
1. The paramita of superior patience
a. Patience is preeminent on the third ground

2   Bodhisattvas may, without any provocation on their part, fall victim to the anger of attackers who torture them, cutting their flesh and breaking their bones in lingering torments. But all such brutality serves only to increase the power of their great patience.

b. How to train in patience
i. Meditating on patience on the level of ultimate truth

3   Moreover, since the Bodhisattvas have realized the nonexistence of the self, they see that victim, tormentor, time, and manner—all such phenomena—are like a reflection in a mirror, whereupon their patience grows even greater.

ii. Meditating on patience on the level of relative truth
(1) The defects of anger
(a) The futility and senselessness of anger

4   If, when attacked, one gets angry at the aggressor, one should ask oneself: Is this doing anything to remove the harm already perpetrated? It is clear that revenge is both pointless with regard to the present life and counterproductive for the life to come. For the anger that is now indulged in will ripen into unwanted situations in future lives.

(b) It is senseless to make a beneficial situation harmful

5   It is said moreover that the damage inflicted exhausts the results of negative actions performed in the past. On the other hand, if one reacts angrily and attacks the aggressor in return, one's own suffering will be the only outcome. For anger serves only to create the cause, to plant the seed, of future sorrow. It is senseless to turn an essentially positive situation into something negative.

(c) Anger is a heavy negativity

6   Moreover, a single moment of anger experienced toward a Bodhisattva instantaneously destroys the merit accumulated by generosity and good discipline over a hundred kalpas. There is consequently no evil more devastating than anger and intolerance. To be more specific, if a Bodhisattva becomes angry against another Bodhisattva on the same level, the merit of a hundred kalpas is destroyed. But if one who is not a Bodhisattva gets angry at a Bodhisattva, it is certain that this destroys the merit of a thousand kalpas.[69] Even if they do not express their feelings in word and action, Bodhisattvas who become angry at other Bodhisattvas must "don the armor" for as many kalpas as they have experienced moments of anger.[70] For example, if Bodhisattvas who are able to progress swiftly from the great path of accumulation to the path of joining indulge themselves in anger against a Bodhisattva who has "received the prophecy," they will be prevented from taking this step for a number of kalpas equal to the moments of their anger.[71] They must begin their training from the beginning again.

(d) Anger is the source of many disadvantages in this and future lives
7 The mere upsurge of anger causes one's appearance to become ugly and leads to the antithesis of all that is wholesome. Anger destroys one's ability to act intelligently and to distinguish what is appropriate from what is inappropriate; it is a blinding force that shatters mental composure. The angry inability to tolerate situations is quick to hurl beings into the lower realms in their future lives. It is important to think of these defects and to cultivate patience.

(2) The benefits of patience
Patience counteracts the defects of anger described above and brings about the opposing qualities. **8** If you practice patience, you will have a beautiful form and be held in the affection of holy beings, and you will be able to discern skillfully between what is right and what is wrong. After death, you will be born in the human or celestial realms and experience no anger or any other negativity.

(3) Concluding summary on the defects of anger and the advantages of patience
9 Ordinary beings and Bodhisattvas, offspring of the Victorious Ones, should both be aware of the defects of anger and the advantages of cultivating patience. They must rid themselves of anger and constantly have recourse to the practice of patience, which is so much praised by sublime beings.

c. The classification of patience
10 If in the practice of patience and the dedication of it to the attainment of perfect buddhahood, the subject, object, and action are regarded as truly existent, the patience in question is considered a

worldly paramita. If, however, the same is practiced in a manner free from these three considerations, or spheres, it constitutes, as the Buddha himself said, the transcendental paramita of patience.

2. A description of the other qualities that manifest on this ground

11   While on the third ground, Bodhisattvas attain the four samadhis of the realm of form, the four formless absorptions, the four boundless qualities,* and the five kinds of preternatural knowledge. At the same time, they completely uproot the seeds of desire, anger, and ignorance, which are precisely the obscurations to be eliminated on this ground. It is due to their fearless acceptance of the profound nature of things that they obtain the above-mentioned qualities of elimination and realization. Such Bodhisattvas are at all times able to overcome the attachment experienced in the desire realm. The majority of them are born as "Indra" and they are able to draw their divine subjects out of the mud of desire.[72]

C. Conclusion: the qualities of this ground
1. The common conclusion for the last three paramitas

12   When Chandrakirti says "Generosity and so forth," he means to include both discipline and patience. The Buddha praised these three paramitas mainly for the sake of lay practitioners. They are also referred to as the accumulation of merit, and, when the fruit is attained, their expression is the Buddha's very form, for they are the source of the enlightened rupakaya.

2. Specific conclusion for the third ground

13   When the Bodhisattvas first reach the third ground, luminous like the sun, the mental darkness that had hitherto obstructed their attainment is utterly dispelled. Revealing their own brilliance, they then wish to overcome the darkness that prevents other beings from attaining this ground. Here, even though the Bodhisattvas, who now have the power to annihilate the gloom of wrong behavior, are as sharp and penetrating as the sun's rays, they are not irritated by the shortcom-

* *tshad med bzhi.*

ings of others. For their minds are softened by compassion and they abide in patience.

Here ends the third ground or stage in the cultivation of absolute bodhichitta.

IV. THE FOURTH GROUND: RADIANT
A. The excellence of diligence on the fourth ground
1 The qualities of birth in the upper realms of samsara and the attainment of the ultimate goodness of buddhahood follow in the wake of enthusiastic diligence. It is through diligence that the two accumulations of wisdom and merit are made. On the fourth ground, laziness is completely eliminated and diligence blazes ever more brightly. Therefore the fourth ground is called Radiant.

B. The definition of this ground
2 On this ground, the Bodhisattvas, offspring of the Sugata's mind, accustom themselves with increasing intensity to the thirty-seven elements leading to enlightenment. The light of wisdom deriving therefrom is even brighter than the copper-colored light experienced on the third ground. The fourth ground radiates with light, and this is the reason for its name.

C. The particular qualities of elimination
On this ground, the coarse view of self, which consists in regarding the self as a self-sufficient entity—together with the associated subtle view of self—is wholly eliminated, along with the view of the phenomenal self. This means that the seeds or tendencies toward a belief in these two selves have been destroyed.

Here ends the fourth ground or stage in the cultivation of absolute bodhichitta.

V. THE FIFTH GROUND: HARD TO KEEP
A. The definition of the fifth ground
1 The Bodhisattvas, now great beings, who dwell on the fifth ground, Hard to Keep,[73] cannot be overwhelmed or defeated by demonic forces.

B. The qualities of the fifth ground
On this ground, the paramita of concentration is preeminent. Consequently, the Bodhisattvas concerned are noble in name and excellent

in mind. They acquire great skill in the extremely subtle understanding of the nature of the two truths and the Four Noble Truths.

Here ends the fifth ground or stage in the cultivation of absolute bodhichitta.

VI. THE SIXTH GROUND: CLEARLY MANIFEST
A. A brief explanation of the sixth ground from the standpoint of the wisdom that realizes emptiness

1   On the sixth ground, Irreversibly Advancing,[74] Bodhisattvas abide in sublime evenness of mind. The power of their wisdom gives them a complete mastery of the two truths, and they perfectly assimilate the principle of dependent arising. In other words, they have a direct experience of the ultimate nature of phenomena, perceiving them to be unreal and "reflectionlike." Having, on the fifth ground, focused on the truth of the path, the Bodhisattvas on the sixth ground advance irreversibly to the actualization or attainment of the qualities of buddhahood. They can see the truth of all phenomena, namely, that they are completely subject to conditions, the mere play of interdependence. With this understanding, they abide in the supreme paramita of wisdom and thus attain cessation. This is not the same as the cessation experienced by the Shravakas and the Pratyekabuddhas, for this involves the arresting of the seven consciousnesses[75] and their attendant mental factors. By contrast, the cessation of the Bodhisattvas is said to be the utter absence of all extreme ontological constructs.

B. A detailed explanation of the sixth ground from the standpoint of emptiness, the domain or object of wisdom
1. The greatness of emptiness

2   Provided that he can see, a single man is easily able to lead a whole multitude of blind people to their desired destination. It is the same with the first five paramitas. Without the view, all such virtues are "sightless." But when they are taken up and informed by the perfection of wisdom, they lead to buddhahood, the fruit of the path, the level of Universal Light.[76]

2. The exposition of this emptiness
a. The manner in which emptiness is to be explained

How does a Bodhisattva on the sixth ground realize the nature of dependent arising? In his autocommentary, Chandrakirti declares that it is not within his power to answer such a question, since his eyes are covered by the cataracts of ignorance. Rather than asking him, he says, we should put the matter to someone who is actually abiding on the sixth ground or above. We should ask those in whom the balm of understanding has completely dissolved the scales of ignorance, and whose eyes of wisdom possess unclouded vision. We should, in other words, address ourselves to the Buddhas and Bodhisattvas—those who have actual realization of suchness!

To this it may be objected that since the Prajñaparamita sutras and the *Dashabhumika-sutra* both say that Bodhisattvas who practice the paramita of wisdom understand the meaning of dependent arising, it should be possible to answer this question on the basis of scriptural authority. But once again, Chandrakirti replies that the underlying meaning of the scriptures is difficult to discern with certainty and that, in any case, people like himself are unable to demonstrate suchness on their own authority, even when they have recourse to scripture.   3   He points out, however, that the noble Nagarjuna has composed shastras on the Madhyamika, which are authoritative and do explain suchness as this is understood by a sixth-ground Bodhisattva—and this not only by appeal to scripture but also by means of reasoned demonstration. Chandrakirti therefore concludes by saying that his own explanation will follow in the tradition of Nagarjuna, as this still existed at his time.

b. Those to whom emptiness is to be explained
i. The proper recipients of such an explanation
4   Even in the case of ordinary people, there are some who, on hearing authentic teachings on emptiness, experience an intense joy surging in their hearts. Their eyes fill with tears and their skin stands up in gooseflesh.   5   This is a sign that they have within them the seed of the thought-free wisdom of perfect enlightenment, the realization of emptiness. Such people are proper vessels for the teachings on the ultimate truth. They should be instructed because their efforts will be fruitful.

ii. An encouragement to listen to the teachings on emptiness
(1) The qualities associated with skillful means on the relative level will arise

Good qualities arise when people of this kind are instructed in the doctrine of emptiness. It is written in the *Bodhichittavivarana*:

> *When voidness of phenomena is understood,*
> *The wondrous law of karmic cause and fruit*
> *Shines forth as yet more wonderful,*
> *And though amazing is yet more astonishing.*

This means that if, trusting to the fact that phenomena are without inherent existence, a person gains a genuine conviction in the truth of the karmic process of cause and effect and takes an increasing delight in the practice of skillful means, he or she will discover the authentic view. If, on the other hand, this is not the case, the person in question is not a suitable vessel for the doctrine of emptiness, and the result will be as it is said:

> *A defect in the view of emptiness*
> *Will prove the bane of those of little wisdom.*

To the extent that one gains an understanding of emptiness, one will be convinced of the truth of the doctrine of karma, the principle of cause and effect.

6   Out of fear of falling, through the practice of nonvirtue, into the lower realms (with the result that the teachings on emptiness cannot be received and meditated upon), practitioners constantly observe pure ethics and prevent them from declining. Moreover, even though they may be born in higher realms, they must be generous in relation to the upper and lower fields, donating food, medicine, clothing, and so on.[77] For this constitutes the condition for listening to, and meditating upon, the view of emptiness. Understanding that the view, without compassion, will not result in the realization of buddhahood, they steep their minds in great compassion. Realizing that anger results in an evil appearance and birth in the lower realms, and knowing that through anger one is a source of grief to sublime beings, they also cultivate patience. And because the failure to dedicate virtue to the attainment of enlightenment will impede the ceaseless increment of merit, they pledge their discipline and so forth to the realization of the ultimate wisdom of emptiness, and to the liberation of beings in the full enlightenment of buddhahood.

7   Shravakas, Pratyekabuddhas, and ordinary beings are unable to set forth the true doctrine of emptiness. Therefore, the practitioner shows intense reverence for the great Bodhisattvas who possess this view.

(2) The qualities of ultimate wisdom will arise

One who is skilled in profound wisdom, indivisible from vast skillful means, will tread the paths of accumulation and joining and will gradually attain the ground of Perfect Joy. Anyone who wishes for such an accomplishment must attend to the profound path, which will be explained presently. As for the scriptures that set forth the pure and ultimate reality of phenomena, the *Dashabhumika-sutra* says: "One who passes from the fifth to the sixth ground does so by embracing the tenfold equality of phenomena."

All phenomena are equal in the sense that: (1) they are without attributes; (2) they are without a particular nature; (3) they cannot be produced; (4) they are unproduced; (5) they are empty; (6) they are utterly pure primordially; (7) they are beyond all conceptual constructs; (8) they are beyond acceptance and rejection; (9) they are like illusions, dreams, mirages, echoes, the moon reflected in water, reflections, and magical displays; and (10) they are neither real nor unreal.

(1) Although phenomena *seem* to have distinct attributes, these same attributes do not appear in the meditative equipoise of Superiors. (2) Neither do phenomena exist according to their characteristics. (3) Phenomena cannot be produced—coming into being at some subsequent moment. (4) Phenomena are unproduced. That is, no kind of production can be ascribed to them. (5) Phenomena are empty, for they have not been produced and they will not be produced. (6) Phenomena do not "acquire" the aforementioned characteristics when their nature is revealed by scripture and reasoning, for they are utterly pure from the very beginning. (7) Phenomena are beyond all conceptual constructs. In other words, dualistic mental processes, which ascribe reality to what are merely names, no longer operate with regard to them. (8) Phenomena are beyond the discrimination of acceptance and rejection, and (9) the seven similes listed above certainly succeed in

describing their nature. (10) No phenomenon can be said to be either inherently existent or nonexistent.

Of these ten points, only the third, related to nonorigination, can be established by reasoning and is the subject of the present commentary. An understanding of the other points is the result of realization alone.

There now follows an explanation of emptiness itself. This is divided into two parts: the establishment of emptiness by rational demonstration and the categories of emptiness thus established. The first part is further subdivided into a section on the use of reason to disprove the self of phenomena and a section on the use of reason to disprove the self of persons.

3. The explanation of emptiness itself
a. Establishing emptiness by rational demonstration
i. Using reason to disprove the self of phenomena
(1) Using reason to refute the theory of inherently real production
(a) A refutation of the four theories of production from the standpoint of the two truths
(i) A short exposition

8   Effects do not emerge from causes[78] with which they are substantially identical. And how could they emerge from causes from which they are intrinsically separate? They cannot. Neither can effects be produced from a combination of both *self-production* and *other-production*. And finally, how can effects arise uncaused? For if production actually takes place, it can only derive from one of the three possibilities just mentioned.

A discussion concerning true existence regarded as extraneous to phenomena

The *Sutralankara* gives an illustration of the procedure for proving or disproving something about a phenomenon commonly perceived by two interlocutors and that acts as the ground or basis for their debate. The text reads: "One applies correct reasoning not to the specifically logical subjects elaborated in the texts of philosophy, but to things that are common knowledge to everyone—the learned, as well as ordinary men, women, and children."[79]

For example, sound may be taken as a commonly perceived subject for discussion. When it is proved that sound is an impermanent phe-

nomenon, it seems as though one is eliminating the ascription of permanence (the object of refutation), distinct from the sound itself,
whereas it is understood that the sound itself is not being refuted. This
method of presenting a proposition (in which a threefold distinction is
made between the proposition to be proved; the subject, or locus, of the
proposition; and the reason or justification) has given rise to the contention "A pot is not empty of pot; it is empty of true existence." There is
nothing wrong with this logical procedure for presenting a thesis (just
now illustrated in reference to sound), and there is no need to call it into
question. But we are to consider that, when something ascribed to a
given subject is disproved and something about it, hitherto unproved, is
demonstrated, it may seem that the subject itself is somehow enlarged
(or modified). In reality, however, nothing in the subject changes. This is
discussed in the *Pramanavarttika*.

With regard to the object of refutation, one necessarily proceeds by
disproving the true existence of the pot (an object directly available to
common perception), as though this true existence were the pot's attribute. This is standard Madhyamika procedure, and indeed, there is no
other way of establishing that the pot lacks true existence. Let us take
sound as an example. When sound is made the subject of debate, whereas
Buddhists consider that the permanence of sound is not established,
non-Buddhists do the opposite and consider that the impermanence of
sound is not established.[80] Consequently (in order for the discussion to
get under way) the subject posited is simply sound, just as the ear perceives it—shorn of all the qualifications expressive of the beliefs of the
contestants: permanence in the case of non-Buddhists, impermanence in
the case of Buddhists. Commonly perceived by the interlocutors, independently of the notions they may have of it, the sound appears in the
same way for both parties. Purely from the point of view of sound itself,
however, permanent sound and sound that is neither permanent nor impermanent are impossibilities; they do not at all correspond to sound as
heard. For the sounds that we actually hear are, quite certainly, qualified
by impermanence. This situation is parallel to that of a pot, which some
believe to be truly existent while others do not. When it is pointed out to
someone who misguidedly believes that sound (i.e., the sound that we
commonly perceive) is permanent, that "Sound is impermanent because
it is fabricated," the conceived object,* namely, the supposed permanence
of sound, is refuted, while the reverse, the impermanence of sound, is established. When the permanence of sound is dismissed, however, the im-

* *zhen yul.*

pression is given that sound itself is not dismissed. But it should be noted that since there has never been any such thing as permanent sound, it is not permanence (as a feature of sound) that is now being disposed of, but rather the idea of *permanent sound* in its entirety. This is parallel to the case of the commonly perceived pot. As with the sound just mentioned, the pot itself is simply left without refutation, while the true existence that had been ascribed to it is eliminated. Here too, it is the conceived object, the pot's supposed true existence, that is refuted. However, when the conceived object—the pot's imaginary true existence—is refuted, it is the pot itself (the *truly existent pot*) that is refuted. For it is recognized that a truly existent pot, as imagined by someone believing in true existence, has never existed. Indeed, "truly existent pots" are purely fictitious; they are not at all the pots that are commonly experienced. The pots that are commonly experienced are devoid of true existence. This (and only this) is the way that the "truly existent pot" is refuted, while the commonly perceived pot is left untouched and unquestioned.

Now thinking that the pot that we commonly perceive is the pot that exists conventionally, some have asserted that absolutist reasoning does not refute the pot itself but only the pot's true existence. However, even granted that reasoning directed at the ultimate refutes not the pot but only a true existence extrinsic to the pot itself, it is impossible to demonstrate the latter's lack of true existence unless one can show that, on the ultimate level, the pot is unfindable and cannot be observed. Now if one investigates the conventional, commonly perceived pot with absolutist reasoning, nothing will be found or observed that is able to withstand analysis.[81] This unfindability of the pot is also called the pot's "nonexistence on the ultimate level," its "empty nature," and its "lack of a true existence able to withstand analysis." Aside from this, there is no other way to posit either true existence or the lack of true existence of phenomena.

Consequently, given that the argument of neither one nor many negates the conceived object, namely, the mistaken notion of true existence, it is admissible to say that when the true existence of the commonly perceived pot is disproved, the pot is shown to be without true existence. This procedure is similar to the one seen earlier whereby a permanence ascribed to sound is negated. All the great Madhyamika texts teach this method of proof, and it must be upheld. Aside from true existence, they speak of no other object for absolutist reasoning to refute. And no one would ever say the reverse, that the position of the Madhyamika texts is that the commonly perceived object is refuted while the true existence ascribed to it is not refuted.

Reflecting on this procedure, whereby the absence of true existence is proved without denying the phenomenon as commonly perceived, some people enunciate the following proposition: "The pot is not empty of pot; it is empty of true existence." They mean that phenomena are not, by their nature, empty of themselves. They are not self-empty.* For if phenomena are self-empty, these people say, their conventional existence is excluded. They therefore say that phenomena are empty of an extraneous factor, something other than themselves: they are empty of true existence. In so saying, they are maintaining that if phenomena are refuted in themselves, when examined with absolutist reasoning, they cannot be said to exist on the relative level. It is thus that, at heart, they are drawn to the view of the substantialist schools, which regard the two truths as mutually exclusive. That which is to be refuted by absolutist reasoning, they say, is something that, on the conventional level, does not exist. And even though such people claim to be maintaining the Madhyamika view, they are in fact propounding a newfangled theory of substantialism. They are in fact rejecting emptiness as taught in such scriptural passages as "Phenomena are empty and devoid of self," or "the eye is empty of eye," the meaning of which is that every phenomenal appearance is devoid of inherent existence. They say instead: "Phenomena are not empty of themselves; they are empty of true existence;" "the eye is not empty of eye; the eye is empty of true existence."

Let us examine these statements. These scholars may blithely say that it is correct to talk about things being empty of true existence, since there is no other emptiness apart from this. And we would agree that there is nothing to be added when phenomena are shown to be empty of true existence. But when, in their tenet system, they investigate the nature of phenomena, using reasoning directed at the ultimate, they fail to show that phenomena are *themselves* unfindable and are *themselves* empty. Consequently, when those who uphold this tradition say that "the eye is empty of true existence," this is nothing more than a verbal sophistry; they are not at all saying that the eye really is empty of true existence. On the contrary, what they actually mean is that the eye is not empty of eye. And this does not apply merely to the conventional level; for even when they examine phenomena on the ultimate level, they also say that they are not empty of themselves. If, however, one investigates on the ultimate level and discovers that the

* *rang stong.*

eye is not to be found, this can only mean that the eye *is* empty of eye. Nevertheless these scholars believe that reasoning directed at the ultimate does not, and should not, refute the eye itself, which is not empty. They consider that it is only the eye's true existence that is to be refuted.

If, when examining the commonly observed conventional eye using the argument of neither one nor many, such people fail to show that the eye is unfindable, this means that the eye is truly existent! If the eye is not empty of itself but truly exists, how can it be said to be empty of a true existence extraneous to itself? The fact that a pillar is empty of something extraneous to itself, such as a piece of cloth, can be established by valid reasoning on the relative level. There is no need to appeal to reasoning examining the ultimate level! But how could this possibly be the meaning of emptiness? If a pot is investigated with absolutist reasoning and is found not to be empty of itself, the result is that, however much you may say that the pot is empty of true existence, you are still confronted with it even after its true existence has been disposed of! Emptiness conceived thus, moreover, is an affirming negative. Conversely, if the pot is established as truly existing, how could it be empty of true existence? One is forced to the conclusion either that it exists truly or that it both truly exists and does not truly exist, which is impossible. Consequently, if, without negating the commonly perceived pot, it is established that it does not exist truly—in other words, if pots and all other phenomena are not wholly refuted in themselves—it must be explained that they exist purely on the relative level. But how could they be impervious to refutation on the ultimate level? If they are not so refuted, it follows that they are established as resisting absolutist analysis. In that case, they cannot be established as lacking in true existence.

All Madhyamikas are agreed that phenomena, as experienced empirically on the relative level, are not to be refuted. Emptiness and nonemptiness, as understood in the context of absolutist reasoning, are not the same thing as emptiness and nonemptiness on the conventional level. It is to existence and nonexistence on the ultimate level that the terms of non-emptiness and emptiness apply. And it should certainly be understood that on the ultimate level there is nothing that is not empty.

Our opponents say that, on the relative level, the pot is not empty of pot, because they think that if it were empty on the relative level, it would simply be nothing. Why then do they not go ahead and say that the pot is truly existent? Valid cognition operating on the relative level inevitably establishes the pot as a truly existing pot,[82] in the same way as it establishes the Three Jewels and the principle of karmic cause and effect as true realities. In short, these people have not the slightest comprehension of the united level of emptiness and dependently arising phenomena (in other words, the incontrovertible appearances of the relative truth, which are by nature empty and yet appear unobstructedly). They simply repeat their much cherished formula that phenomena are empty of true existence. They think that there is no other way of speaking about emptiness and indeed that there is no need for one. For otherwise, they believe, emptiness would be a nihilistic nothingness. But even if they do say that phenomena have no true existence, and hold this clearly in their minds, they are doing no more than dismissing the verbal ascription of true existence; they are in fact disqualified from correctly understanding what emptiness of true existence really means.

As for the way in which emptiness consists in the dependent arising of phenomena, declarations like "While having no true existence, phenomena appear on the relative level" or "The absence of true existence does not undermine the relative truth of appearances" are quite correct. And again, "emptiness of true existence," "nonexistence on the ultimate level," and "emptiness" are all undeniably synonymous terms. The people we are referring to do not consider that phenomena lack true existence in the sense of being empty by nature. They think that phenomena are devoid of a true existence that is extraneous to them—a true existence that has never been a part of phenomena. This kind of emptiness is called other-emptiness.* But this emptiness of a true existence, separate from phenomena that are not themselves empty, is unintelligible. Moreover, it cannot coincide with the dependent arising of such phenomena. This would be as absurd as saying that the "no-horns" of a rabbit are the horns of a yak. Our opponents say that such phenomena have their own nature and are not empty; and they label them as empty because they are lacking in a true existence considered as something other and separate from them. But even if it were possible to comprehend such a union (that is, that the "existent pot" somehow coincides with the "not truly existent pot"), such an understanding could in no way undermine, even slightly, the root of samsara. Such an approach gives no access to freedom from conceptual constructs; on the contrary, it renders it impossible. For it is by playing with words, by avidly adopting this method of explaining emptiness, that our opponents actually weaken its crucial significance. They succeed only in deceiving themselves.

* *gzhan stong.*

Furthermore, if it is established that the pot is empty of an extraneous true existence, something other than itself, by the same token it may be labeled as "not truly existent"—but only in the sense of a "nontrue existence" that is also extraneous to it. And even the emptiness that negates this extraneous object of refutation is necessarily established as no more than a property of the pot and is inadequate as a means of showing that the pot *itself* lacks true existence. This is like the position of the Vaisheshikas, according to whom a defined object and its defining characteristic[83] are separate entities. Therefore, if one says that the pot is not empty, it is impossible for it to lack true existence. To say that the pot is separate from its true existence is the same as saying that the pot is separate from its emptiness of true existence.

If, therefore, it is concluded that because sound on the relative level is empty of an extraneous permanence, sound in itself is not empty of sound, it necessarily follows that if sound's impermanence is something distinct from it, then sound in itself is not impermanent! This position may be contested, since sound is shown to be impermanent by the evidence of our senses. It is therefore false to declare otherwise, given that the identity of the sound and its permanence (that is, permanent sound) is validly disproved. Consequently it is a permanence, alien to the sound, that is refuted. To this we reply that since a permanent sound has always been an impossibility, this permanence cannot be posited as either identical with or extraneous to the sound. Such a permanence, after all, has no reality. And it is the dispelling of such a misconception that establishes that sound is impermanent.

The same argument may be applied to the previous question (of true existence). It can be said that phenomena that are nonexistent even on the relative level (a barren woman's son, truly existent things, and so on) differ from phenomena that do exist relatively. They are different not just nominally, but also according to a distinction that negates their sameness.* But in their nature they are not different. What has no existence on the conventional level has no conventional "nature." Is it then permissible to say that the pot's emptiness of a barren woman's son is an emptiness of something extraneous?[84] Furthermore, people who consider that a pot is truly existent *apprehend that very pot* as truly existent. They have no apprehension of some misconceived, illusory, truly existent pot separate from the pot. This being so, who is it that stands in need of an emptiness that is a negation of the pot's separate true existence, which in any case

---

* *gcig pa bkag pa'i tha dad.*

has no reality—ordinary people who have no grasp of Madhyamika, or yogis who understand it? Ordinary people have no need of it because they have no such misconception (of the pot having a true existence separate from itself). It is only when there is some doubt or ambiguity about it that the conceived object, the mistaken conception of true existence, must be eliminated. Yogis, for their part, have no need of such an emptiness either. For not even ordinary, unphilosophical people entertain such a misconception. To what end, therefore, do those who know the tenets enlarge on something purely imaginary and unsupported by reasoning? The thing to be dispelled is a misconception: the belief that the pot that undeniably appears exists inherently as it is perceived. The refutation of this conceived object is precisely the purpose of Madhyamika.

How then is this to be established? When the pot appearing to the senses is investigated with the argument of neither one nor many, not even the slightest fragment of it is found. This shows that the pot has no existence in absolute terms, in other words, that it lacks true existence. The Prajñaparamita sutras and the texts and commentaries of the Madhyamika do not at all propound the kind of reasoning that leaves phenomena unexamined on one side and refutes only their true existence distinct and separate from them. Such a position cannot be sustained by any rational argument. But those who uphold this theory say that "the pot is not empty of pot; it is empty of true existence." It is thus that they deviate from the teachings of the sutras and the shastras, which state that phenomena are empty of *themselves*. Such people claim that phenomena are empty of something alien to them, that they are empty of an extraneous true existence. But all this is just verbiage; it carries no comprehensible meaning. Wishing to underline this emptiness of true existence separate from the thing itself (an idea that is not to be found in the Madhyamika texts), they deny that phenomena are empty of themselves; and this is wrong. Therefore one should think well on it.

To cut a long story short, we should ask ourselves in whose interest it is that this doctrine is put forward—a teaching to the effect that relative phenomena are not empty of themselves but that their true existence (something alien to them) is nonexistent. People who believe that the pot is truly existent apprehend the pot itself as truly existent and certainly have no notion that it has a true existence extraneous to itself. Since they are innocent of this misconception, what need is there to explain to them a reasoning that negates it? This is like proving that the barren woman has no son. Skilled practitioners who have no apprehension of the pot's true existence have no need of such reasoning either.

To repeat, ordinary people—to say nothing of yogis—have no notion of the true existence of the pot as something separable from the pot itself.

Since, according to this way of thinking (whereby the pot is empty of an extraneous true existence), the pot appearing to the senses is not empty by its nature, this amounts to a belief that the pot is truly existent. But if this is investigated with reasoning directed at the ultimate, it will be discovered that the apprehension of the true existence of the pot is nothing but a failure to understand that phenomena themselves have no inherent existence. Conversely, if a phenomenon on the relative level is not empty of itself, this means that it is truly existent. In that case, how can it be empty of an extraneous true existence?

It will be objected, perhaps, that a pot is empty of an extraneous true existence—in the sense that it is empty of a truly existent pot—in the same way that it is empty of a truly existent cloth. But to establish this there is no need for reasoning directed at the ultimate, and therefore such an absence of true existence is not the object of this kind of reasoning. Or again, if the pot's emptiness of true existence is described as an other-emptiness, in the sense of a conventionally existent phenomenon being empty of something that is, even conventionally, nonexistent (like a rabbit being empty of horns), once again this does not require reasoning directed at the ultimate; it is established by valid cognition operating entirely on the conventional level. In this kind of refutation, the arguments of neither one nor many and so on have no place. How can a rabbit's horns be investigated by breaking them down into their constituent parts? How can the argument of dependent arising be applied to them? The idea of true existence considered as extraneous to the thing itself is attended by exactly the same difficulties. For how could a true existence of this kind be refuted by the kind of argument that negates the four theories of production?

In order to show that, though unfailing in their appearance on the phenomenal level, things do not exist in the way they seem, items such as pots are investigated (1) with the reasoning of neither one nor many (which breaks them down into parts); (2) with the reasoning that disproves the four theories of production (showing that, although objects seem to be produced, they have in fact no origin); (3) with the reasoning that refutes origination according to any of four alternatives; (4) with the reasoning that refutes the production of truly existent, or truly nonexistent, effects; and finally (5) with the reasoning of dependent arising.[85] Accordingly, if the pot is examined with the argument of neither one nor many, it will be discovered that even though it is undeniably apparent, it is not *found* in a manner corresponding to its appearance. Though it *seems* to be a product, if examined with the argument refuting the four theories of production, the pot in question cannot be established as inherently produced. Though it appears as dependent arising, this very dependent arising is also found to be in itself nonexistent. When examined, no phenomenon on the conventional level can withstand analysis, and this is what is called its lack of true existence. Conversely, if something is found to resist such an analysis, it is designated as truly existent. Thus, the object refuted by the kind of reasoning that establishes emptiness is precisely "truly existent phenomena." This reasoning demonstrates that emptiness, that is, the phenomenon's lack of inherent existence, and the phenomenon, as a dependently arising appearance, are not mutually exclusive. They refer to exactly the same reality. This very reasoning establishes emptiness: the absence of all conceptual constructs.

One should never say that conventionally existing phenomena are not refuted by reasoning directed at the ultimate, that they are not empty. If one does, the absence of true existence thus proved will amount to nothing more than mere words. Emptiness in the true sense will not be established in the slightest way. And one will end up proving that phenomena are truly existent, just as the substantialists believe. When those who adopt such an approach refute true existence, they do so using the argument of neither one nor many and so forth. However, even granted that they do not actually say that phenomena are truly existent, the fact is that, until they give up the assertion that phenomena are not empty of themselves but of something extraneous to them (that is, a separable true existence), they necessarily end up affirming that phenomena exist truly. This is the inescapable conclusion.

Although he expressed himself differently, the Lord Tsongkhapa arrived at a similar verdict when he classified the Svatantrikas as substantialists.

> "For," he said, "they do not refute the natural existence of phenomena,* but rather their true existence. This means that, for the Svatantrikas, relative phenomena exist by their own nature. Now in my tradition, phenomena like pots are not said to be empty of themselves but empty of true existence. Therefore when we refute a relative phenomenon—its production and so on—we always specify that we are talking about truly existent phenomena and truly exis-

---

* *rang bzhin gyis grub pa.*

tent production. Indeed, when logical analysis is applied, the inevitable conclusion is that if reasoning directed at the ultimate does not succeed in refuting the natural existence of phenomena on their own level, the result is that phenomena become truly existent. If the belief that conventional phenomena are empty of true existence but are not empty according to their characteristics is not refuted by reasoning directed at the ultimate, the result is that phenomena are truly existent. Therefore, even though the Svatantrikas do not actually say that things exist truly, nevertheless, because they do not refute them with reasoning directed at the ultimate, and because they assert that phenomena have an existence according to characteristics, they succeed, in effect, in proving the true existence of things, though this is not what they intend."

These are Je Rinpoche's own words. He admitted, nevertheless, that the Svatantrikas are Madhyamikas. Now to the objection that, in that case, the Svatantrikas are simultaneously substantialists and Madhyamikas, he might reply that he is not at fault. For though the Svatantrikas assert a natural existence of phenomena and do not refute it, this amounts only to a natural existence of phenomena on the conventional level. On the other hand, they correctly refute the true existence of phenomena and establish that they are empty. They are guilty of propounding a substantialist position only by virtue of an inconsistency implicit in their argument. But since they use the argument of neither one nor many to establish that the very nature of conventional phenomena cannot be found, they are, notwithstanding, Madhyamikas. In other words, Je Rinpoche is saying that if people conclude, by way of Madhyamika reasoning, that phenomena are lacking in true existence, they qualify as Madhyamikas, even if they express this true existence as something extraneous to the phenomena themselves. Be that as it may, a strong attachment to the idea that phenomena are lacking in a true existence that is (merely) ascribed to them leads such people to affirm that on the conventional level, phenomena are not empty from their own side (that is, empty of themselves). This in turn hinders a proper understanding of the union of dependent arising and emptiness, and because of this weakness in the Svatantrika method of investigation, their position is not actually different from that of the substantialists.

If one reflects about the way our opponents express themselves in their writings, one can see that if one does not deviate from the idea that all phenomena are empty of themselves, it is possible to achieve certainty that the emptiness of phenomena and the dependent arising of phenomena coincide. If absolutist reasoning is used and it is asserted that phenomena are empty of themselves (as expounded by the great Madhyamika masters), and if this is applied in meditation, a correct realization of emptiness will swiftly occur. But if one thinks that the statement "Phenomena are empty of themselves" negates the conventional level, and if one adjusts one's position accordingly, saying that "Phenomena are empty (only) of true existence," one may be very pleased with this formula, regarding it as an admirable solution, since while emptiness is retained, the conventional is not abandoned. However, the assertion "The eye is empty of true existence" carries the implication that an eye, thus qualified as empty of true existence, is itself established as *not* empty on the conventional level.

In propounding this very point—namely that "the eye is not empty on the conventional level; it is empty on the ultimate level," our opponents mean to summarize the entire teaching of the Madhyamika shastras to the effect that all phenomena are lacking in true existence and yet appear incontrovertibly as dependent arising. Then to underline even more clearly the import of these two statements, they add: "The eye is not empty of eye." But this is no improvement. After all, if the eye is not empty of eye on the ultimate level, nothing is gained by saying that it is empty of true existence. And if the eye is not empty of eye on the relative level, what is one to understand of a statement adding that it is empty of true existence?

The scriptural text "The eye is empty of true existence" means that the eye does not exist truly. It is the basis, the thing itself, that does not exist truly. It was never intended to imply that there is another eye apart from the eye that is empty of true existence. This is so because, when it is said that the eye is empty of true existence, this means that the eye *itself*, the basis of the qualification, is empty. Accordingly, when concrete phenomena are examined, the natural thrust of the statement that they lack true existence is that phenomena, which appear without existing truly, are illusionlike. This being so, a correct understanding of the absence of true existence does not lead to an emptiness that is just a nonaffirming negative, a mere nothingness. To the objection that, in that case, one arrives at an emptiness that is an affirming negative, we would reply: No. To establish that the eye is without true existence does not in any way imply its nonemptiness on the ultimate level. Once again, it may be objected that, in that case, there is no need for the expression "true existence." For if the eye is just empty of eye, why is it not said, without more ado, that the eye is empty? We would reply that, although it is not so expressed, the meaning of the expression "empty of true existence" is nevertheless this. And while this is indeed the meaning, if it had been baldly stated that "the eye is empty," the statement could be construed as meaning only that the eye cannot be found on the ultimate level. On the other hand, if one says that the eye is empty of true existence, the implication is that although the eye does not exist on the ultimate level, it is nevertheless "there" on the conventional level and that these two statements nevertheless involve no contradiction. But even though it is perfectly acceptable, as well as easily understandable, to say that the eye is empty of true existence, it is, however, wrong to claim that the eye is not empty by its nature but is empty of a true existence extraneous to itself. On the merely verbal level, of course, the expression (the eye is empty of a true existence) hangs together since the various aspects of the statement are verbally distinct (there is a basis of discussion, probandum, and so on). But if one reflects on the actual meaning of what one is saying, the statement is untenable. While being empty according to its nature, the eye undeniably appears on the conventional level. The eye's emptiness of itself is the ultimate reality, the true nature of that same eye that appears on the conventional level. As it is said in the *Madhyamakavatara*: "Since their very nature thus is emptiness, the eye is void of eye."*

If the eye is not empty according to its nature, it cannot be empty of true existence. For, in that case, the nature of the eye is not emptiness. Indeed, since an other-emptiness is not a self-emptiness, such an (extraneous) emptiness cannot be the nature of the thing itself. It is instead something wholly alien to it, in the same way as a nonexistent sky-lotus cannot exemplify the nature of a natural lotus grown in water. A phenomenon that is empty of an extraneous true existence is not the same as a phenomenon empty of itself, and no one, wise or foolish, would hold that it was. One must therefore affirm that the nature of all phenomena is emptiness: phenomena are empty of themselves. But as long as one says that phenomena are not empty of themselves, however much one may claim that they are empty of true existence, how can such an extraneous emptiness correspond to their true reality? For it is (already) being asserted that what is empty and what is not empty are two different things. A cow is not a pot. But who would ever say that the pot's nature is "noncow"? One might just as well say that the nonexistent sky-lotus or the barren woman's nonexistent child is the nature of the pot. Ordinary people would simply laugh. It is wholly impossible that this is what the Madhyamika masters are talking about.

---

* See *Madhaymakavatara*, VI, 181.

Since lack of true existence and emptiness are synonymous terms, what is wrong with saying that the lack of true existence is the *nature* of phenomena? For if the lack of true existence is not the nature of phenomena, this amounts to saying that emptiness is not the nature of phenomena.

The pot's lack of true existence is the name given to the pot's "emptiness nature." If, however, lack of true existence means that phenomena (regarded as not empty by nature) are empty of an extraneous true existence, the implication is that this lack of true existence is not the nature of phenomena. Although reality cannot be attributed to this extraneous factor, this same factor cannot coincide with the nature of the pot. Otherwise, the above consequence is inescapable, and the proposition "The pot is not empty of pot, it is empty of an extraneous true existence" necessarily establishes that the emptiness of true existence extraneous to the pot (which is not self-empty) is the pot's ultimate status.*

To sum up: the message of all the Madhyamika texts is that commonly perceived, conventional phenomena are established as being empty of true existence. Both the verbal formulas and their meaning are faultlessly defined therein. But if one goes on to add statements like "The eye is not empty of eye," a defect is introduced into the argument, and until it has been abandoned, it will actually hinder the establishment of the eye as being empty of true existence. Consequently it should never be said that phenomena are "other-empty," empty of an extraneous true existence, but not "self-empty," empty of themselves.

How should we define self-empty and other-empty? When, with reasoning directed at emptiness, one examines phenomena to see whether they are empty or not, if phenomena are found to be empty, they are self-empty. If they are not found to be empty of themselves, they are other-empty. There is no sense in adding that the pot is empty or not empty *on the relative level*. Because phenomena cannot be found by reasoning aiming at the ultimate level or, to put it another way, because phenomena are not observed on the ultimate level, they are empty. Such reasoning cannot find phenomena on the relative level either. As it is said in the root text, "And reasoning cannot uphold it even as conventional. What comes, then, of your theory of production?"† If one uses reasoning directed at the ultimate to examine phenomena, the latter will not be found or observed on either of the two levels of truth. But it goes without saying that people ordinarily experience phenomena on

---

* In other words, a blatant contradiction.
† See *Madhaymakavatara*, VI, 36.

the conventional, empirical level. As it is said in the text, "Phenomena are ultimately unborn, and yet relatively they are born indeed."*

From the substantialist point of view, it may be said that if something has no existence in the ultimate sense, it cannot exist conventionally or empirically. Conversely, if something exists and is available to experience on the relative level, it cannot be ultimately nonexistent. To this we reply that if whatever exists on the conventional level must exist in an ultimate sense, the substantialists ought to be able to find something that can withstand absolutist reasoning, showing that conventional phenomena are ultimately real. But if the things that are not found, when subjected to absolutist reasoning, have no existence on the conventional level, it follows, absurdly, that everything occurring empirically should be outside perception. If the substantialists could prove that the empirical were unperceived, it would follow that everything refuted by absolutist reasoning is also nonexistent on the conventional level. But even if this were tenable, how could the substantialists (and not only they, but all other worldly beings, human and divine) establish something that is able to withstand absolutist reasoning? It is impossible. Indeed, while there is nothing that is not refuted—nothing that can be found or observed—by reasoning directed at the ultimate, no one, divine or human, is able to disprove the fact that everything thus refuted appears, nevertheless, as conventional phenomena. As the perfect Buddha has proclaimed: "The nature of phenomena, appearing undeniably, is emptiness. They are not other than emptiness and yet they arise as the undeniable appearance of ordinary existence. Therefore, emptiness and dependently arising phenomena are inseparable." No one in the realms of gods and men can oppose or overturn this lion's roar on the path of reasoning. It is this path alone, as expounded in the texts of Madhyamika, that is to be upheld. If, however, one is unable to grasp the fact that emptiness and dependently arising phenomena do not exclude each other, and if on top of this, one adds words and expressions that merely reflect one's own understanding but do not appear in the sutras and commentaries, it may seem, for the time being, that one has found a good and easy expedient. However, all assertions that contradict the sutras and the great commentaries are inevitably defective. Consequently, if when explaining the Middle Way, one keeps to the manner in which it is expounded and commented on in the Madhyamika sutras and shastras, it is definite

* See *Madhyamakavatara*, VI, 93.

that one will gain, through rational means, a commensurate certainty and that unmistaken, authentic wisdom will take birth.

When substantialists and Madhyamikas debate on whether perceived objects exist truly or not, the discussion proceeds with propositions such as: "The subject, a pot, does not exist truly because it is not found by valid cognition investigating its ultimate, ontological status." A pot that is present and commonly perceived is thus negated as nonexistent. Its nonexistence on the ultimate level, in other words, its lack of true existence, is established. Insofar as it is posited as the subject of the syllogism, the pot is not, in itself, (verbally) negated—the object of the exercise being to disprove its nonexistence on the ultimate level, or lack of true existence. In this entirely verbal procedure, whereby the subject's true existence is refuted, the subject itself is not invalidated, and this is not a fault. Now one might, as a result, be led to conclude that phenomena are not at all refuted on the conventional level and that only their true existence is negated. It is, however, an aberration to think that the mere refutation of a true existence distinct from the phenomenon will lead to the realization of its emptiness.

When debating with substantialist thinkers, it is necessary to proceed with a syllogism, in the way just described. But why is it that nonexistence on the ultimate level means the lack of true existence? Arguments like that of neither one nor many show that phenomena, though commonly perceived, cannot be found. This is the sole purpose of such reasoning. And if absolutist arguments do not refute commonly perceived phenomena, there is certainly no other way of showing that phenomena are ultimately unreal—that they are without true existence. If it were otherwise, phenomena, commonly perceived, would indeed be ultimately real and possess true existence.

Therefore, in asserting that the object of refutation is true existence, one is referring to the fact that actual phenomena, commonly perceived, cannot be shown to withstand the kind of reasoning that investigates their ultimate status. Nothing apart from that can possibly be intended. Now, true existence (as understood by our opponents in the present context) does not occur on the conventional level, whereas things like pots do. Therefore, the two do not coincide. One is (of course) obliged to say such things as "the object of refutation is the true existence of the phenomenon." Nevertheless, while the conventionally existent thing as spoken of by our opponents is established through common experience, its true existence is not so established. And it is the latter that cannot withstand absolutist reasoning. But if something (in this case, the pot) can resist such reasoning, it is truly existent; if it cannot, it is not. Thus, apart from the pot itself, there is certainly no other object of refutation (a so-called truly existent pot distinct from the pot). True existence, distinct from the object that is said to possess it, is not the same as the actual true existence of the object itself. The refutation of it, therefore, cannot show that the object *itself* is without true existence. Such a refutation is no more than playing with words. And besides, the apprehension of the "truly existing object" as distinct from the object itself is certainly not part of the experience of ordinary folk. It is only verbally that one can distinguish the various aspects (subject, predicate, sign) of a thing. But in actual experience, it is impossible to divide a subject from its predicate. When denying the permanence of sound, one is not negating a permanence that has been separated off from the sound; it is rather the misconception of permanent sound that is dispelled. The same applies in the refutation of the true existence of a thing. Although, on the purely verbal level, it is possible to say that an object is empty of true existence (as though this were something separate from it), the purpose is to dispel the mistaken idea that the object is not empty in itself, that the object truly exists.

Thus a pot is empty by its nature. It is self-empty. How could it be other-empty? If an other-emptiness were intended, we would be faced with a complete divorce, like a pillar being empty of a cloth, or a cow's horns being empty of rabbit's horns. But this cannot be the meaning of emptiness. If things are not empty by their nature, neither can they be empty of true existence. Something that is not empty by its nature truly exists. This is the inescapable conclusion.

Now, if our opponents deny this, saying that the pot is established as empty of true existence, considered as something distinct from it, how do they substantiate their view? They will answer that it is proved that a phenomenon lacks true existence because it is found not to exist by absolutist reasoning; this very nonfinding of the object is called its lack of true existence. If the object is observed, they say, it cannot be "untrue." Since the object is observed on the conventional level, it cannot be established as lacking true existence. And isn't it a fact, they will ask us, that we both observe the phenomenon on the conventional level? Our reply to this is quite simply that to establish an object as lacking in true existence, even though it is "there," conventionally speaking, means that it is not found by reasoning investigating its ultimate status. And this is all it means. But they will object further that because the object is available on the conventional level, it can only be its true existence, distinct from it, that is refuted. Once again, we reply that if the pot's true existence is something separate from the pot itself, and if this true existence is to be investigated with arguments like that of neither one nor many—while the pot is left to one side uninvestigated—the question remains: given that the pot's true existence (as distinct from the pot) has, like the rabbit's horns, no reality on the relative level, how could arguments like that of neither one nor many be applied to it? There is no need for such arguments, just as there is no need to use absolutist arguments to prove that the conventionally nonexistent horns of a rabbit are indeed nonexistent. If, under the influence of words, one is drawn into negating a true existence that is supposedly separated from the object and merely ascribed to it, asserting that the pot is not empty of pot but only of its true existence, it is just as though one were trying to refute the horns of a rabbit. This will not eradicate in the slightest degree the conceived object, namely, one's misapprehension of commonly perceived phenomena as truly existent. For the fact is that people misconceive the "conventionally nonempty" pot as truly existent. But there is no one who would ever take for a truly existent pot something that is separate from the pot itself, something indeed that has never existed within the ambit of common perception.

This manner of expression (that phenomena are lacking in true existence) is to be found in all the great commentaries of India and Tibet, and we cannot refuse the formulas that they adopt. To think, however, that they mean that there is something left unrefuted by reasoning investigating the ultimate status of things, and to claim that the teaching "The eye is empty of eye" does not mean what it says, constitutes a deviation from the correct understanding of emptiness. If one has a clear grasp of the fact that the two expressions "The eye is empty of eye" and "The eye is empty of true existence" are not contradictory in meaning, there is no fault in saying that phenomena are empty of true existence. To say that something is empty of true existence will then enable one to understand that, on the ultimate level, the thing itself cannot be found.

As long as one of the four ontological positions (existence, nonexistence, both, and neither) is asserted, it is impossible to go beyond the conceptual mechanisms of reason. This is why (on the level of philosophical discourse) the two truths are distinguished, because without such a distinction there is no way to transcend the four ontological extremes, and one is necessarily propounding a position or theory. However, when one attains the realization of the freedom from all mental constructs (on the path of seeing) and one is free from all four extreme positions, the two truths are seen to be inseparable and there is no need to distinguish them. This, however, does not imply the taking up of a position in the earlier sense, in which the negation of one thing implies the assertion of its opposite or vice versa. Freedom from conceptual constructs is established without reference to the four ontological extremes. Otherwise, if one cannot abide by the literal sense of the "freedom from all assertions" as taught by Nagarjuna, one is obliged to say that freedom from all assertions refers only to true existence. But if ultimate reality can be adequately established or expressed only by the freedom from any assertion of true existence, it follows that "truly existent phenomena" must be negated in each of the four extremes. But it is impossible to say of a truly existent thing that it "exists, does not exist, both, or neither." One is obliged to say that the truly existent thing is nonexistent, but one cannot affirm the other three extremes. For is it possible to assert that the pot does not have true existence and that the pot does not *not* have true existence? If it were possible to explain how to refute the two, four, or eight extremes in reference only to true existence, the ploy might succeed. But as long as the absence of true existence in phenomena is not indivisibly united with the conventional existence of phenomena, the mere assertion that phenomena lack true existence cannot refute the extreme of nonexistence. This is proved simply by the force of logic, as our opponents themselves assert. And if the extreme of nonexistence is not refuted, how can they refute the other three extremes? That is something for them to think about!

(ii) **A detailed explanation of the refutation of the four theories of production**
   A. *Refutation of self-production*
   1. *A refutation of this theory according to Buddhapalita and Chandrakirti*
   a. *A refutation of self-production on the ultimate level*
   i. *A refutation of production from a cause with which the effect is identical*
   (1) *Production accomplishes nothing*
According to the Samkhya view, cause and effect are identical in nature. The effect, clearly manifest in the result phase, is said to be present, though latent, in the cause phase. But if an effect emerges from a cause that is the same as itself, its actual emergence serves no purpose; there is no need for it. For nothing new has been added to what was previously there;[86] the effect was already present at the time of the cause. (According to the Samkhyas) before the result arises, this very result must pre-

exist as the cause in order for itself to arise. But if it already exists, what need is there for it to arise again? The entity, the effect, that is already produced (being present in the cause phase) cannot be reproduced since it is by definition no longer potential (it is already actual). Since what is produced must by definition be present, produced effects must be present from the outset and should be produced without interruption. Alternatively, if they are not present, new things like plants can never eventuate.

(2) Production is untenable

Furthermore, when an entity is produced, it cannot be produced again, for its production is complete, like a child that has been born. And here the implication of the word "furthermore" is that not only does production (as explained in the Samkhya theory) serve no purpose, but it cannot be maintained.

(3) Production is actually impossible; there is no point at which it might occur

9   If it is claimed that something already existent can come into being again, this implies that seeds again arise out of themselves. There is consequently no point at which the germination of the plant with its stem can occur, for the shoot cannot emerge without the disappearance of the seed. On the other hand, given that the seed arises from itself and since the conditions for such production are never incomplete, there is no point at which the seed stage terminates, and therefore no point at which germination becomes possible.

(4) Seeds would be produced ad infinitum

It follows that the seed, already produced, must continue to produce itself endlessly till the end of the world, for there is nothing to stop or interrupt the process.[87]

ii. A refutation of the theory that causes and effects are identical in nature
(1) If causes and effects are identical in nature, they should not be observed at different moments
(a) The identity of cause and effect contradicts the Samkhya admission

that causes modulate and change into their effects

The Samkhyas see no fault in their theory, for they say that given the presence of water and the passage of time (conditions favorable to germination), the seeds eventually transform into a grassy meadow. The seeds themselves disappear and germination takes hold. Nevertheless, they say, the seed and the shoot are not different in nature; the effect does not arise from something other than itself. But how, Chandrakirti asks, can the seed be destroyed by an effect (the shoot) when the two are at all times of the same nature? It cannot, just as the shoot itself cannot be destroyed by the seed.

(b) An identity of nature precludes differences of shape and so forth

10 Another drawback in the Samkhya system is that it fails to account for the fact that cause and effect have different attributes, such as size and shape, length or roundness; or colors, whether green or yellow; taste, such as sweetness; the power to cure such things as sickness; and possibilities of transformation, as in the case of *arura*, which turns sweet due to the effect of milk, and so on. All such attributes, which distinguish the shoot from the productive cause or seed, should be reduced to nothing if cause and effect are identical. The Samkhyas think, however, that the (observable) differences, and the destruction of the seed by the sprout, are simply modulations taking place within a single entity. For them, consequently, no absurdity is involved in saying that the seed is destroyed by something identical to itself, or in maintaining that seed and shoot are not different. But the Samkhyas consider that the seed and shoot have inherent existence; and it should be understood that it is illogical to say that different changes occur in a single inherently existent entity.[88]

(2) The fact that causes and effects are observed at different moments disproves their identity of nature

(a) The refutation itself

It may be urged that the seed phase is abandoned and another phase is assumed, with the result that the seed becomes the shoot. Even though they are found at different moments, they are of a single nature. The answer to this is that if the preceding entity of the seed is eliminated and something different from it—namely, the condition of the shoot—eventuates, how can the seed be said to *become* the shoot? For the two terms are related to each other as destroyer and destroyed.

(b) If cause and effect are of the same nature, it follows that both terms should be equally perceptible or otherwise in their different phases

11   Furthermore, if the seed and shoot are not different in nature on the level of ordinary experience, it follows that when the seed is not perceived, during the shoot phase, the shoot itself should also be invisible. And conversely, if the seed and shoot are identical, when the shoot is perceived, the seed should be perceived at the same time. If the two terms are the same in nature, they cannot be different in aspect, one appearing to the sense consciousness and the other not appearing. Thus the Samkhya position is untenable.

In conclusion, the Samkhyas say that since the accidental conditions of seed and shoot are expressions of a single prakriti, which is uniform in nature, it follows that causes, conditions, and results all share the same nature (or substance). The evolutions of cause and result are indeed mutually distinct, yet these evolutions all partake of a single nature. It should be understood, however, that if the Madhyamika critique is applied to it, the theory of self-production is invalidated. It is unacceptable to attribute different changes to a single inherently existing entity.

b. There is no such thing as self-production on the level of ordinary experience

12   Since it is a matter of ordinary experience that when the resultant plant appears, the causal seed is no longer to be found, ordinary people certainly do not regard causes and results as identical.

c. Recapitulation

In conclusion, the theory that phenomena are self-produced is shown, when subjected to criticism, to have no validity—either on the ultimate level or on the relative level of empirical experience.

2. A refutation following Nagarjuna's reasoning in the Mulamadhyamaka-karikas

13   The theory of self-production implies the identity of produced effects and productive causes, for example, the child that is begotten and the father who begets, or the identity of objects of actions and agents, like wood and fire, pot and potter. But the fact is that they are not identical, and therefore the theory of self-production should not be countenanced. It entails unwanted consequences as is demonstrated at length in the *Mulamadhyamaka-karikas* of Nagarjuna.

   B. Refutation of other-production
   1. A general refutation of the theory of other-production
   a. A general refutation of other-production on the ultimate level
   i. A refutation of other-production
   (1) A general refutation
   (a) A general refutation through revealing unwanted consequences of
      production in which cause and effect are considered to be inherently
      other

14   If it is possible for an inherently existent effect to derive from an inherently existent cause other than itself, it follows that a flame could give rise to darkness (which is what it normally dispels). In addition, everything (cause or noncause) could produce anything (whether its usual effect or something else). The reason is that, if this view is correct, what normally does not produce an effect is placed on the same level as what normally does produce one. For both are inherently other than the effect. The unwanted consequence here is not just a matter of the empirical experience of a seed producing a shoot. It implies, rather, that if the two terms, cause and effect, are inherently other, existing independently from their own side, it follows, most importantly, that they cannot be set in a causal relation to each other, and that cause and noncause are placed on an equal footing. The difference between the rice shoot and the rice seed is as great as the difference between the rice shoot and fire, coal, or barley seeds: they all have the same status. There is no difference between them; they are all the same in being other. There cannot be a relationship of dependence between two items that are inherently other, for they are of equal weight and validity. Such a relationship in this case has no meaning. If seed and shoot exist inherently, they are necessarily both already produced and existent in and of themselves. It cannot be otherwise. Consequently, if a perfectly complete and existent entity is said to arise from another perfectly complete and existent entity, it follows that anything can arise from anything, for a relationship of causality is excluded. This is because two inherent existents cannot coincide and be one, and two already existent things possessed of entirely equal status cannot be said to be linked together in a relationship of cause and effect—which would be void of meaning and purpose. According to this argument, our opponent might just as well say that all extraneous phenomena are causally related with each other.

(b) Refutation of an objection
(i) The objection
15   It may be objected that, even if cause and effect are extraneous to each other, it does not follow that anything can arise from anything. Since a certain thing can incontrovertibly produce its effect—even though this effect is an inherently existent other—one can definitely say that the outcome is the effect of that cause. And that which is able to produce the effect, even though it is an inherently existent other, is the cause of the effect. Accordingly, although there is a division between cause and effect, which are separate items, they nevertheless belong to a single continuum in that an ensuing entity only arises, after its kind, from the appropriate foregoing entity. Rice shoots (as a matter of fact) can never spring from barley seeds.[89] This is how the proponents of this theory substantiate their position.

(ii) The refutation of the objection
16   Given that barley, lotus blossoms, *kimshuka* flowers, and so forth are all regarded as other (different from rice), nobody thinks that they are producers of rice shoots, that they have the potential to be so, that they belong to the same continuum, or that they are of like kind. But in exactly the same four ways, the rice seed too cannot be regarded as a cause of the rice shoot, for it is inherently other. Since there is not the slightest difference between the rice and barley seeds and so forth, in that both are inherently other than rice shoots, there are no grounds whatever for saying that one of them is the cause of the rice shoot and the other is not.

(2) A specific refutation of the theory of production in which cause and effect are considered to be inherently other

(a) The principal refutation by appeal to the chronological factor implicit in causality

17   The shoot and the seed do not exist simultaneously. But if the shoot is not present, how can the seed be posited as *being other* than the shoot?[90] Moreover, if an inherently existent entity arises from another inherently existent entity, production can only happen when the two coexistent terms meet. But given that a meeting of this kind is precluded, in the chronological sequence demanded by a causal relationship, how can production take place between what are two wholly extraneous entities? Therefore no production can take place between a shoot and a seed regarded as inherently other. Consequently, the theory of other-production should be rejected. To designate Maitreya and Upagupta as being in a relation of dissimilarity is to imply their coexistence. In the same way, if the seed and shoot are established as being by nature other, they must occur simultaneously and as different things. It is only thus that one can speak of otherness. To do so in any other way is just meaningless verbiage.

(b) The refutation of an objection
(i) The objection

18   Even so, this response may be countered with the following objection. The situation is like the rod on a pair of weighing scales. Its extremities can be seen to rise and fall simultaneously. It is the same with a cause and its effect. In proportion as the latter arises, the former subsides. They thus occur in the same moment.

(ii) The refutation of the objection

The answer to this refutes the opponent's objection, his arguments, and the idea that even though the effect does not exist, it is nevertheless in the process of being produced.

It is quite all right to say, in the terms of the analogy given, that the arms of the weighing scales move up and down at the same time. However, since in point of fact the seed and the shoot do not occur at the same moment, the analogy is inappropriate. While the movement of the arms of the scales may be said to be simultaneous, this is not the case with seed and shoot. The proposed analogy is out of place.   **19**   The reason for this is that, while the effect, namely, the shoot, is emerging, its full appearance remains a future event; it is not happening now. Conversely, while the seed is in the process of subsiding, it is still not fully destroyed and continues to exist in the present. In short, as long as there is a seed, the shoot is a future event. And when the shoot is produced, the seed has already ceased and no longer exists. Thus the two entities never coincide simultaneously. How is it possible, therefore, to compare the seed and shoot to a pair of scales? They are not at all similar.

There is a further defect in the argument. It might be argued that although the shoot does not exist, it is nevertheless in the process of being produced. But this is also a fallacy. It is senseless to affirm production when there is no actor,[91] for example, an existent shoot.

But is it not the case, the opponent will ask, that the example of the scales appears in the *Salistamba-sutra*? For here it says: "As with the upward and downward movement of a pair of scales, in just the moment that the seed ceases, the shoot appears." It is surely wrong, therefore, to reject the idea that the seed and shoot can be compared with a pair of scales. Chandrakirti's answer to this is that he does indeed accept the truth of the quotation. However, the purpose of the scripture is not to affirm "other-production"[92] or production according to characteristics.* In refuting the theory of production, Chandrakirti is contesting the notion of an inherently existent production. He is not questioning the simple fact of life that shoots arise from seeds. In the sutra, the Buddha had in mind only the experiential fact that the production of the effect is simultaneous with the cessation of the cause. He was not saying that *inherently existent†* causes and effects arise and subside simultaneously. In the first case, the simultaneity of the process does not necessarily imply that the cause and effect are simultaneous. By contrast, in the second case, the simultaneity of the process does involve the simultaneity of the cause and effect.[93]

(c) A specific refutation of other-production in which cause and effect are regarded as simultaneous

20   Having accepted that other-production is not admissible when cause and effect are chronologically differentiated as earlier and later, the opponent might still object that it is nevertheless tenable if cause and effect occur simultaneously. But this is not admissible either. If a

---

* *rang gi mtshan nyid kyis skye ba.*
† *ngo bos grub pa.*

resultant consciousness is simultaneous with what stimulates it (for example, the visual faculty, the form, and concomitant mental factors of perception and feeling), it must already exist—for it is other than its cause and simultaneous with it. What need is there for it to arise anew? None at all.[94] It may again be suggested that the effect is not present at the time of the cause, but we have already exposed the failings of such a proposition when discussing the idea that cause and effect are chronologically separate.

(3) A refutation by investigating the nature of an effect (according to the four ontological permutations)

21   If a cause gives rise to an effect that is other than itself, we should examine whether, on that account, the effect is inherently existent, inherently nonexistent, both, or neither. If the effect inherently exists as such, what need is there of a cause? Being already produced, its existence is complete—as an effect. No "new arising" is possible. If the effect is inherently nonexistent, what can the cause bring forth? Such a cause would be like the cause of a rabbit's horns. If the effect is both inherently existent and nonexistent, again, how can the cause produce it? It is impossible for both existence and nonexistence to coincide in a single entity. Finally, if the effect neither exists nor does not exist, once again, what could the cause possibly produce? Such an effect, which would be neither existent nor nonexistent, is wholly impossible.

ii. An answer to the objection, based on the experience of ordinary people, regarding the refutation of other-production

(1) How ordinary people argue and try to dispose of this refutation

22   It may be objected that ordinary people, relying on the "normal" point of view, regard everyday experience as trustworthy and valid. Because this is so convincing, they exclaim: "Your attempts to disprove other-production by logic are completely pointless! You can't deny it; it's self-evident!" That there is a difference between causes and effects, the opponent says, is indeed the experience of ordinary people. And since it is obvious, it has no need of proof.

(2) An answer to this

(a) Ordinary people affirm other-production, but they are unable to disprove its logical refutation

(i) A short outline of the two truths posited in relation to subject and object, distinguished as mistaken and unmistaken

People without a correct understanding of the meaning of the scriptures fall victim to the primordial habit of clinging to true existence. They believe firmly in the reality of things. They are unfamiliar with the fact that phenomena are without inherent existence, and they are grounded entirely in the baneful misapprehensions of everyday life. Unless they are constantly reminded of the way phenomena arise, they are quite incapable of overcoming the harmful, unexamined assumptions of mundane existence. It is necessary to spell out to such people what can and what cannot be invalidated by worldly experience. As a preliminary to this, it is important to expound the doctrine of the two truths and how these are distinguished.

23 The Buddhas, who have an unmistaken knowledge of the nature of the two truths, proclaim that all things, outer and inner, as they are perceived by two kinds of subject (deluded consciousness on the one hand and perfectly pure wisdom on the other), possess a twin identity. This double identity (i.e., the two truths) is the conclusion of correct reasoning; it has no reality on the level of being.[95] They say that the object perceived by authentic primordial wisdom is ultimate reality, whereas the object of deluded perception is the relative truth.

The ultimate truth in itself and the approximate ultimate truth

The two truths are two distinct isolates* of a single reality. Their one shared nature resides in the inseparability of appearance and emptiness. This is validly ascertained by the analysis of the two truths. What appears is empty. If emptiness were different from appearance, phenomena would not be empty. Consequently the two are not separate. This nature, which is established as the indivisibility of appearance and emptiness, is the ultimate truth in itself;† it cannot in any way be described and is the object of individual self-reflexive awareness. This ultimate truth is referred to as the dharmadhatu, the *tathagatagarbha*, and so on. It is the ultimate nature of phenomena and is different from the approximate ultimate truth,‡ as is shown by the following points. With reference to emptiness, in the sense of the approximate ultimate truth, when the four

---

* *ldog pa.*
† *rnam grangs min pa'i don dam.*
‡ *rnam grangs pa'i don dam.*

ontological extremes are being disproved, the extreme position that phenomena are inherently existent must be refuted by revealing their lack of true existence. Conversely, the extreme position that phenomena are nonexistent is disproved by demonstrating their existence on the relative level. Therefore, the four extremes cannot be refuted by an exclusive appeal to the ultimate nature of phenomena. Ultimate reality, qualified as a nonaffirming negative, is able to refute the extreme of existence. But given that the refutation of the extreme of nonexistence involves an appeal to relative truth, ultimate reality, from its own side, constitutes an ontological extreme (nonexistence). And such an extreme kind of emptiness cannot be regarded as *dharmata*, the ultimate nature of things.

Moreover, when the two truths are differentiated, if they are considered to coincide (and this is said to refute the four extremes), either their natures are distinct and do not merge, like the designs in a brocade, or else they are undivided. If they are undivided, their union is established as ultimate reality; but in that case, the dharmadhatu expresses itself in appearance and is not simply an emptiness devoid of phenomena. If there is a difference in nature, the single nature of the two truths is discounted, for the two are in that case mutually exclusive. Just as all objects of knowledge have two aspects, one permanent and one impermanent (the object's self-isolate being, of necessity, permanent)* the ultimate truth in itself has likewise two aspects, and of these its uncompounded nature[96] is necessarily the permanent one. It is said in the *Panchakrama*: "When the two truths blend together perfectly, they are said to be united." Accordingly, when one realizes that the two truths are indivisible, they are said to mingle. In fact, their indivisibility is primordial. Because phenomena have one taste or nature, their appearance and their emptiness cannot be separated as two distinct entities. Phenomena that are empty appearances cannot but be complete and perfect within a single essence,[97] and for this reason they do not abide in the extreme of uncompoundedness (in the sense of nothingness). The appearance aspect of a phenomenon does not refer to something that is not empty; it does not refer to an instantaneous, compounded phenomenon.[98] All phenomena have the same taste; they are empty. Once again, this emptiness is not a sort of lesser, circumscribed emptiness.† Emptiness is beyond any kind of assertion; it is indivisible from appearance. It is an emptiness that is *supreme in all aspects.*‡

---

* *rang ldog.*
† *nyi tshe ba'i stong pa,* emptiness as the object of the mind, emptiness that is defined merely as an absence of origin, and so on.
‡ *rnam kun mchog ldan.* This emptiness corresponds to the qualities of buddhahood.

On the level of approximate ultimate truth, the extreme positions of existence and nonexistence are to be refuted as we have just described. But how is one to refute the other two extremes, namely, those of both existence and nonexistence, and neither existence nor nonexistence? There is no need to attach the notion of true existence to the extreme of both existence and nonexistence, since on the empirical level there is nothing that is both inherently existent and inherently nonexistent. According to the manner of refuting the ontological extremes (on the level of approximate ultimate truth), in which the two truths are not blended together, the two truths together (juxtaposed) constitute the third extreme of both existence and nonexistence, and one is forced to admit that the united level of the single nature of the two truths is simultaneously existence and nonexistence. Were it otherwise, the union of the two truths would not invalidate the third extreme of both existence and nonexistence, for the two truths would not be united in one. This is illustrated by the fact that the nonexistence of a cloth in an existent pillar does not contradict the pillar's extreme of existence. In order for it to do this, the pillar would have to be both an existent pillar and a nonexistent cloth.

If the view is held that existence and nonexistence cannot share a single nature—that is, that something both existing and nonexisting could never be an object of knowledge—it follows that the two truths are also contradictory and therefore without a single nature—that appearance and emptiness are also without a single nature and are antagonistic. In that case, emptiness and dependently arising phenomena are as alien from each other as fire and water. It is incorrect to deny that phenomena are both existent and nonexistent or that they are neither existent nor nonexistent. In the case of any established basis or phenomenon, to deny that something is both (that is, existent and nonexistent) amounts to saying that it is neither (that is, neither existent nor nonexistent). If it is not neither, it must be both, and once again, something that is neither existent nor nonexistent cannot be known.

Those who maintain that it is illogical to say that things neither exist nor do not exist[99] ascribe true existence to the four ontological extremes, as if it were an attribute. They then ask: "What need is there to refute the four extremes? It is sufficient to refute only their true existence. Merely by refuting this, the four extremes are disposed of."

But, in that case, what are we to do with all the teachings (of Nagarjuna) about emptiness and dependent arising? The statement of our opponents amounts to saying that once the true existence of the four extremes has been removed, the mental apprehension* of the same, as well as the four extremes themselves, are both features of ultimate reality. However, the dharmadhatu in itself† obliterates all four extremes at a single stroke. There is no need to predicate true existence of them, for the dharmadhatu transcends the entire fabric of conception. How could a pot and its "pot nature"—in other words, an ordinary, everyday thing on the one hand and a permanent phenomenon on the other—be identical? All the key points that effectively demolish the assertions of our opponents are in fact present in the single nature of the two truths. The ultimate truth in itself is alone said to be the ultimate, while everything that can be cognized, spoken of, and manipulated on the conventional level is said to be the relative. But I do not think that this implies a distinction that negates the oneness of the two truths. For everything on the relative level—all conventional things—have in fact no existence. According to the approximate ultimate truth, the two truths are the distinct isolates or aspects of the same nature.[100] But all the wisdom teachings of the Mahayana—for example, "There is no multiplicity of dharmadhatus in the one and only dharmadhatu," "The three times are not to be ascribed to the dharmadhatu," "All phenomena are, in the dharmadhatu, of a single taste," and so forth—point to the ultimate truth in itself. How could they accord with the approximate ultimate? As far as the latter is concerned, there *are* different dharmadhatus, which can be ascribed to the three times; and the ultimate nature of individual phenomena is of a lesser, limited kind. The dictum "The emptiness of one thing is emptiness of all" is understood, in the context of the approximate ultimate truth, to mean: "The impermanence of one thing is the impermanence of all" and "The existence of one thing means the existence of all," and so forth. These statements bear a merely formal resemblance to the foregoing one and are reminiscent of the teaching of the Jainas to the effect that all objects of knowledge are indeterminate. The teaching that the realization of the ultimate nature of one thing is the realization of the ultimate nature of all is in accord with the ultimate truth in itself. But the approximate ultimate is not the ultimate in itself; it is only the gateway to it.

(ii) A detailed explanation of the two truths posited in relation to subject and object, distinguished as mistaken and unmistaken

---

* *'dzin stang*, lit. way of apprehension, i.e., mental image, object appearing in the mind, *blo'i yul*.

† *rnam grangs min pa'i chos dbyings*.

A. From the standpoint of the subject, the correctly perceiving
   consciousness, our refutation of other-production cannot be
   validly disproved by empirical experience
   1. A discussion of valid cognition which investigates the relative
      truth
      a. The difference between valid and invalid cognition

24 The differentiation of the two truths is found in knowledge objects and, in addition to this, a twofold division is also made on the
level of the subject, namely, the deluded consciousness. The distinction in the latter case is made according to whether perception is unmistaken, owing to (the presence of) clear faculties unimpaired by
accidental causes of illusion, or mistaken, owing to the effect of impaired faculties. When compared with the perception of healthy faculties, the perception of faculties impaired by an accidental abnormality
is regarded as mistaken.

   b. How cognition evaluates its object
      i. A general discussion of the difference between mistaken and
         unmistaken objects

25 Just as the subject, namely, the perceiving consciousness, is
twofold, its objects are also. Things apprehended by the six senses, unimpaired by anything that causes illusion and perceived by the generality of
people in the ordinary run of events, are true or unmistaken on the level
of empirical experience (but only on this level). Everything else—everything apprehended by senses that misperceive because of some defect—is
regarded as mistaken within this same context. Some of the sense faculties have the cause of illusion within themselves. This is the case with
cataracts, or jaundice, or the ingestion of hallucinogenic substances.
Other causes of mistaken perception are found in outer circumstances,
as with a mirror, or the fact of shouting in a cave, or of being on a white
plain in the light of the summer sun. These conditions respectively produce perceptions of reflections, echoes, and mirages of water. In like
manner, a magician can produce apparitions by means of incantations,
magic potions, and so forth. Appearances that arise through the alter-
ation of the mental sense-organ[101] through the effect of magic spells and
drugs, the propositions of false theories, and sleep (which gives rise to
dreams)—all such objects, the product of hallucinatory situations, are regarded as mistaken also in the realm of ordinary experience.

The valid establishment of phenomena

In an inquiry directed at the ultimate level, it will be found that both Ishvara, the creator, and a pot existing on the conventional level are merely the imputations (the reifications) of thought. They are on an equal footing in that neither is found to exist by its own nature. In other words, they are the same in being nonexistent. However, nonexistence on the ultimate level does not amount to nonexistence on the conventional level. Conventional phenomena are established by valid cognition; therefore, how could phenomena like pots be regarded as nonexistent? To say that they are nonexistent would be to discount the entire range of conventional existence and to affirm that there is nothing. This would amount to a nihilist view, with the result that nothing at all would remain that could be posited as validly existent, nonexistent, both, or neither, on the conventional level.

If, despite the fact that they have no "entity" conventionally, phenomena are *validly established* by the force of mental imputation,* it follows that Buddhist and non-Buddhist tenets are on a level in being neither correct nor incorrect (since there is, in that case, no objective criterion of truth or falsehood), and all distinctions of virtue and vice, cause and effect, good and bad, and the notion of (rational) moral choices would dissolve into chaos. Therefore, the Prasangika tradition does not say that phenomena are validly established by the force of mental imputation. When, on the conventional level, conceptual imputation corresponds to the object, the phenomenon in question is necessarily regarded as validly established (or established through valid cognition). When the imputation does not correspond with the object, the phenomenon is not validly established. But there is absolutely no way to distinguish between "correspondence" and "noncorrespondence" without reference to the relative thing in itself. Given, therefore, that the subject is regarded as valid or invalid according to whether the way of apprehension corresponds to relative phenomena or otherwise, the object itself must be established as valid, or discounted as invalid, according to whether the consciousness is unmistaken or not. If, however, relative phenomena are merely the imputations of thought, they have no "entity." It is therefore worth reflecting: How can you speak of valid or invalid cognition at the same time as entertaining the notion of validly or invalidly established objects?[102]

---

* *rtog pas brtags pa'i tshad grub.*

By contrast, what appears to the undamaged sense powers is regarded as conventional, beyond which it is impossible to assert a further validly established conventional reality.[103] If there is no ground of imputation on the conventional level and if things are no more than conceptual imputations, they are all like a rabbit's horns, nonexistent. How, therefore, can they be validly established? On the other hand, if there is a ground or basis of imputation, namely, phenomena arising in interdependence, the latter do exist conventionally; they are not mere imputations. Furthermore, if mere conceptual imputation is made equivalent to conventional existence, it absurdly follows that anything can become anything. Poison could become medicine, virtue could become sin, and fire could become water. Thus valid cognition would be the same as invalid cognition. But this is not the case; therefore, mere imputation and relative phenomena are not equivalents, and it must be asserted that on the conventional level, there are objects that appear to the unimpaired senses.

> ii. A particular explanation showing how the mistaken kind of
> conceived object (self) cannot be established as truly existent
> for valid cognition on the conventional level

26   Sunk in the sleep of ignorance and failing to recognize ultimate reality, the non-Buddhist (Samkhya) philosophers assert in their texts, and with the seemingly rational arguments of their tenets, the existence of *purusha*, and the three *gunas*. In addition, people in general are misled when they see illusions and mirages and think that they are seeing real horses, real oxen, and real water. But such phenomena have no reality within the scope of ordinary conventional experience, still less on the ultimate level.[104] No phenomena of this kind can be substantiated by conventional valid cognition. These theoreticians aspire to perfection, but they are like a man climbing a tree who lets go of the lower branch before he has grasped the higher one. The result is that they fall into the abyss of wrong views.

> 2. Valid cognition on the conventional level is unable to
> invalidate valid cognition that investigates the ultimate level

Why is it that valid cognition on the conventional level is unable to invalidate the stainless reasoning that investigates the ultimate truth? The refutation of the doctrine of other-production is not something based on ordinary consciousness. It derives from the insight of sublime beings.   **27**   The illusion of black lines seen by people suffering

from cataracts has no validity compared with the experience of someone with healthy eyes. In the same way, the consciousness of someone
who has not realized stainless wisdom has no validity compared with
the perception of one who has.

     B. From the standpoint of the object, namely, the two truths, our
        refutation of other-production cannot be invalidated by
        empirical experience
     1. The mistaken object, true on the relative level, explained by
        means of its etymology

28   The nature or ultimate reality of phenomena is hidden from us
because of ignorance. This nature is misapprehended and not perceived as it really is; and this erroneous perception is called the all-
concealing or relative level, because it covers or obscures the ultimate
reality or status of phenomena. (Relative) phenomena, contrived by ignorance, do appear as true to the individual who is aware of them, and
this is why the Buddha referred to them as all-concealing or relative
truth.* Sublime beings, on the other hand—Shravakas and Pratyekabuddhas who attain arhatship, and Bodhisattvas—have dispelled, in
some measure and according to their different levels, the ignorance of
apprehending phenomena as truly existent. The contrived appearances
that occur in the postmeditation of the three kinds of superior beings,
who see everything as illusion, are "relative," that is to say the "bare relative." They are not, in this case, relative truths because sublime beings
do not in the slightest way assent to their reality. It is therefore ignorance that acts as the condition on account of which the nature of
things is misapprehended. To what is contrived through ignorance,
the name of *relative* and *truth* is given as defined in the root verse. The
Tibetan perfective particle "- *o*" expresses the affirmation that, aside
from the unfailing experience of phenomena in the way they appear,
there is not the slightest need for any additional relative or all-concealing truth. There is simply nothing else. One may experience fire as
warm, water as wet, happiness as the result of positive action, suffering
as the outcome of negative action, liberation as the fruit of the realization of no-self, samsara as the product of self-clinging, illness as coming from the ingestion of poison, recovery through the taking of

---

* *kun rdzob bden pa.*

medicine, and so forth. In the same way, the pains of Torment Unsurpassed may be experienced, but they are none other than *seeming to experience*—the perception of sensations arising from the contact of the body with fire. The same is true of the bliss of Brahma and so on up to the total liberation of sublime beings. All such common perceptions, though perceived, are nothing but the designations (imputations) of thought. And they are all equal in that none of them is inherently existent.

Now, although something is "only" the ascription of thought, it is admissible to say that it is validly cognized in the direct perception of the senses, owing to the fact that appearance actually occurs. If one finds that such an appearance is somehow insufficient and that what so appears necessarily entails existence from its own side, such a thing would be truly existent, and this is impossible. The karmas accumulated by the mind appear to the mind, and these "mere assumptions" (mere conceptions) of the mind (phenomena assumed as truly existent) are relative (i.e., all-concealing) phenomena. If they were not so, they would inevitably exist on the ultimate level. In the last analysis, the mere imputations of thought are all that there is on the relative level; nothing else is found. Consequently, phenomena are defined as conceptual designations. How does the mind create such designations? The mind apprehends the characteristics of phenomena and assumes that they exist truly, thinking thoughts such as "This is a pillar; this is a vase; this is happiness; this is suffering," or else, "This is permanent, that is impermanent; this is compounded, that is uncompounded." In so doing, the mind identifies and reifies* phenomena. From the point of view of such a mind, phenomena are not equal. They are divided up dualistically into apprehended object and apprehending subject. On the other hand, in the sphere of absolute suchness, which is nonreferential equality, phenomena cannot be characterized as real or unreal, permanent or impermanent. For it is the cessation of all references. How could phenomena be apprehended as "without true existence"? This is why it is said: "Outside thought, there is nothing that can be posited as such-and-such." In short, if phenomena were anything more than mere "all-concealers" (conventionalities) imputed by thought, they would be truly existent.

Ultimate truth is not a conceptual imputation; it cannot be grasped by thought. How could conceptualizations occur in a situation in which

* *dmigs par byed*: i.e., it "finds" something.

all characteristics totally subside? Conceptually imputed phenomena appear incontrovertibly, but being mere designations, they cannot actually be found as such. They can be referred to only on the conventional level and by the conceptual mind. The nonconceptual mind does not indeed apprehend and cling to anything, but this is not to say that it does not encounter dependently arising appearances. For the Aryas bring their prayers of aspiration to perfection, bring beings to maturation, and make the buddhafields manifest*—all in the manner of an illusion.

As will be considered later, "Dense ignorance enshrouds the world as though by massing clouds, and due to this, phenomena are misperceived."†

> 2. The unmistaken object, true on the ultimate level, explained by an analogy

29   Someone suffering from cataracts might think that he sees black lines on a plate held in his hand. On the other hand, a person with healthy sight looking at the same plate will see nothing, and this should be understood as analogous to the realization of suchness (that is, that to perceive suchness is to be free from misapprehension).

> (iii) *A concluding summary describing what can be invalidated by ordinary experience and what cannot be so invalidated*
>> A. Ordinary experience is unable to invalidate the ultimate truth when this is analyzed
>> 1. Ordinary experience cannot be taken as valid

30   If, when investigating suchness, ordinary perception constituted valid cognition, it would follow that ultimate reality would be a matter of empirical, ordinary experience. In that case, what need would there be for suchness to be revealed by superior beings? It would be superfluous, along with their path of discipline and the threefold wisdom of hearing, reflection, and meditation. For this reason, when investigating the ultimate, the experience of the ordinary and naïve should not be regarded as valid.

---

* *rdzogs smin sbyang gsum.*
† See *Madhyamakavatara*, VI, 104.

2. Valid cognition cannot be called into question by invalid
cognition

31   When the ultimate is investigated, ordinary experience is without
validity. It is therefore unable to disprove statements about the ultimate level.

B. What is the only way in which empirical experience can
invalidate our position?

On the other hand, the phenomena of ordinary experience are accepted by the common consensus, and if we try to deny them and
point out their inner contradictions, we find ourselves refuted by
everyday life. For example, suppose someone comes to us and com-
plains that he has been robbed. "What have you lost?" we ask. "A vase,"
the man might reply. If at this point we inform him that a vase is not a
thing but only a knowledge object no different from a vase in a dream,
all that will happen is that the person will get angry. In a similar vein,
it is possible, speaking from the standpoint of the perception of a superior being, to affirm that the vase does not exist, that things such as
vases and harvests are without origination. One may be able to prove
logically that phenomena are without concrete existence or origin, but
as long as one is grounded in empirical experience, all such assertions
(about the unreality of phenomena and so on) will be refuted by direct
and valid ordinary experience, for all such phenomena are established
by the general consensus.[105]

(b) Given that, even on the relative level, there is no such thing as natu-
rally existent other-production, the opinion of ordinary beings can-*
not prevail against this refutation

32   In the ordinary run of things, a man who deposited his seed in
the womb of his wife will point to his baby and say: "I have fathered
this child." In other circumstances, he might say of a tree: "I planted
this tree." It is evident that people identify effects with causes, and it
is therefore clear that other-production (implying a complete divorce between inherently existent cause and inherently existent effect) has no validity even on the level of ordinary experience. If the

---

* *rang bzhin gyis gzhan skye.*

contrary were true, it would be nonsense to say: "I have fathered this child" or "I planted this tree"—because only the causes, namely the semen and the sapling, were deposited, whereas their two respective effects were not present from the first moment. Therefore, since no normal person says that the seed and the shoot, the cause and effect, are two utterly divorced, inherently existent items, it is said that there is no such thing as other-production even on the relative level.[106]

iii. The advantages of such a refutation

If cause and effect are inherently existent separate entities, a seed cannot be the cause of a shoot because when the shoot supervenes, the continuum of the seed is cut off and there is no connection between the two. The presence of a shoot can do nothing in the way of maintaining the continuity of a seed—any more than a cow can contribute to the prolongation of the horse's continuum when the horse has expired. On the other hand, if cause and effect are a single inherently existent entity, even when the shoot has come into being, it follows that the seed, being permanent, still persists and does not cease. Our own position, however, is without these defects of ontological nihilism or eternalism. This is the advantage of holding that no production occurs according to any of the four possible ways, but that there is only dependent arising.   **33**   Accordingly, because shoot and seed are not considered to be inherently existent entities extraneous to each other, when the shoot emerges, we escape the difficulty involved in the previous assertion that the seed is destroyed and that there is an interruption in the continuum of the same likeness.* And because seed and shoot are not regarded as a single, truly existent identity, we also escape the unwanted consequence that the seed is permanent, in other words, that it does not transform into the shoot but continues to exist alongside it.

b. There is no naturally existent other-production, even conventionally
i. A refutation of naturally existent other-production, even in the conventional sense
(1) The refutation itself

---

* *rigs 'dra rgyun chad pa.*

*(a) There is no such thing as naturally existent other-production, even
conventionally. If there were such a thing, it would follow that the
meditation of the Aryas would destroy phenomena*

The difference between the Svatantrikas and the Prasangikas consists
in the fact that the former consider that, at the level of the unmistaken
relative truth, phenomena exist according to their characteristics. The
Prasangikas, for their part, refrain from such an assertion. If it is asserted that phenomena exist according to their characteristics on the
relative level, a division is created between the two truths. They turn
into two ontological extremes (of existence and nonexistence), and
emptiness and dependent arising do not blend into a single taste. This
is why in the extraordinary tradition of the Prasangikas, such a teaching is refuted. In this connection, the general arguments as explained
above and in the sequel, and especially the three sovereign methods of
reasoning, are extremely important. It is only with their help that one
is able to grasp the crucial differences between the Svatantrikas and
Prasangikas.[107]

Now, with regard to the refutation itself, if phenomena possess even
the slightest existence according to their characteristics on the relative
level (whereas in the meditation of superior beings they have no existence at all), it follows that such phenomena have existence prior to
such meditation and subsequently collapse. In other words, the meditation does away with things[108] and renders them empty like a hammer
smashing a pot. Thus the unacceptable consequence is that the meditation of superior beings would bring about the destruction of phenomena. In the same way, if phenomena have even the slightest
existence on the relative level, they must be possessed of existence also
in the ultimate sense. But if they do not exist on the ultimate level, they
cannot be established on the relative level either.

34   If form, feeling, and all other phenomena were produced through
causes and conditions existing according to their characteristics, it
would follow that when emptiness is realized directly, and phenomena
are seen to be without inherent existence, these same phenomena
would actually be destroyed by wisdom. But it is nonsense to say that
emptiness brings about the annihilation of phenomena. Therefore,
from the very beginning, phenomena have no existence according to
their characteristics.

What is refuted by absolutist reasoning?

The Svatantrikas say that the pot is not empty of pot, but of true existence. They say also that if absolutist reasoning finds no pot, this means that the pot has no existence on the ultimate level although the pot is not empty of itself on the relative level. This, however, is incorrect. The Svatantrikas are unable to show that there is a difference between a pot that is supposedly found by absolutist reasoning and a truly existent pot that is not so found. They are unable to demonstrate that the difference implied in these two formulations has some basis in fact.

They may put forward the following objection: "When it is said that the subject under discussion, namely, the pot, does not exist because it does not appear to valid cognition,[109] this constitutes a refutation of the true existence of the pot. It is this, they say, that is eliminated as the object of refutation; it is this that is removed from the basis of refutation, namely, the pot itself, to which it had been ascribed. For the pot that has existence conventionally is different from the truly existent pot, which has no existence conventionally. Therefore, they continue, there is no need for other arguments concerning the unfindability of a truly existent pot in addition to absolutist arguments, in the course of which no pot is found. There is no need for further evidence: the unfindability of the pot simply means that the pot does not *truly* exist, not that it does not exist at all. With regard to the terms cited in the debate, although the argument refutes the pot as nonexistent, in fact this means only that the pot is refuted as being truly existent.

To this we reply that if the pot is refuted as truly existent, this means that the pot itself is also refuted on the ultimate level. It is hard to see the difference implied in the kind of statements that our opponents unavoidably make, such as "The pot does not exist on the ultimate level; it exists on the conventional level," and "The pot has no inherent existence; it exists without inherent existence," and so on. There is nothing wrong, therefore, in saying that the pot is empty of pot and is consequently self-empty. Although it may appear that when the pot is refuted its conventional existence is negated, in point of fact it is its own *inherent* existence that is refuted. Our opponents assert a sort of self-emptiness, but this is just wishful thinking on their part and does not correspond to self-emptiness in itself (that is, the lack of inherent existence). Neither can it be regarded as the refutation of the true existence of phenomena.

Our opponents' affirmation that the pot itself is not to be investigated with absolutist arguments (because this would entail the nonexistence of

the pot on the relative level) is just the same as saying that in the case of
the colored rope that is empty of snake, the snake does not exist but the
rope exists, or rather that, in a place that is empty of pots, there are untrue pots. This manner of establishing the emptiness of phenomena,
whereby they are regarded as empty not of themselves but of something
else, results in clinging to the conventional existence of phenomena as
such, with the result that there is no way to prevent craving, aversion,
and so forth from arising. Of what possible use could this be for those
training on the path? The Svatantrikas insist that phenomena lack true
existence, but they do not refute phenomena existing according to their
characteristics. This means that, of necessity, they apply the same notion of true existence to the process of arising and cessation, saying:
"There is no truly existent arising of a pot, but there is a conventional
arising of a pot. There is no truly existent cessation of a pot, but there is
a relative cessation of a pot." Though they accept that their object of
refutation, namely, truly existent production and so on, has no existence, nevertheless all such things, like pots and their attributes (their
production, cessation, abiding, and impermanence) exist conventionally, according to their characteristics. And since for them such things
exist according to their characteristics, they inevitably cling to them as
such. This stimulates in turn the innate conceived object, in other
words the "I," considered as a true reality. This is why the afflictions,
like desire or anger, cannot be counteracted. If the characteristics of
conventional phenomena are not empty of existence, they are inherently existent. It may seem perfectly all right to *say* that the true existence of phenomena is refuted, but the result is that one ends up
asserting (unconsciously perhaps) the opposite, namely, that phenomena existing according to their characteristics are truly existent. On this
point, the logical conclusion to which one arrives by the (three kinds of)
Prasangika reasoning*—to the effect that the Svatantrika affirmation
that phenomena exist according to their characteristics amounts to the
affirmation of their true existence—is therefore applicable also to our
opponents.[110]

The Svatantrikas will object that if one denies that phenomena have
existence according to their characteristics at the relative level, this
amounts to saying that relative phenomena do not exist at all. Production on the conventional level, they say, is conventional production in
the ordinary sense of the word, specifically characterized production—
and if this were not the case, phenomena would be completely nonex-

* See note 107.

istent. We answer that absolutist reasoning does indeed refute a truly existent production. But this is not to imply that it fails to refute conventional production. It is impossible that what cannot be found on the ultimate level by such investigation should still be findable on the conventional level. There is no such thing as ordinary, conventional, specifically characterized production; and since ordinary beings never themselves apprehend any other kind of production, there is no need of absolutist reasoning to refute it. This notion that the specifically characterized production of conventional phenomena exists as it appears is none other than the apprehension of, and clinging to, the phenomenal self. On the ultimate level, however, such a thing cannot be found. When one uses absolutist reasoning to investigate production, no such production is found from the point of view of either of the two truths. It is inadmissible to assert that conventional, specifically characterized production is not disproved.

> (b) *Even conventionally, there is no naturally existent other-production. If there were, it would follow that conventional truth would resist analysis.*

35   If the view is advanced that, on the conventional level, production *must* occur from extraneous causes, our answer is that the only things one perceives are conditioned mere appearances.* If one tries to estimate which of the four theories of production applies to them, one will discover that there is only unborn suchness; no locus of arising, cessation, and so on can be found. Therefore, conventional phenomena, experienced as real on the empirical level, are not to be analyzed and their mode of production is not to be investigated. For if they are analyzed, they will be found to be nonexistent.[111]

In that case, it might be objected, conventional phenomena must surely cease to exist. But if it is only by absolutist reasoning that production and so forth is not found, why should the existence of conventionalities be disrupted? As Chandrakirti says: "And you should know that, in our view and from the very first, phenomena are ultimately unborn, and yet relatively they are born indeed."† No one can deny the fact that in ordinary experience, something like production does occur—through the interplay of dependent arising. It is as Lord Buddha said: "You argue with the world, but I do not."[112] As long as they are

---

* *rkyen nyid 'di pa tsam.*
† See *Madhyamakavatara*, VI, 93.

not investigated and subjected to analysis, phenomena are seen to arise in ordinary experience. On the other hand, if absolutist reasoning is applied, nothing is found to arise according to any of the four possible theories of production; no conventional arising is found. It is therefore said that when one is discussing conventional truth[113] one should refrain from analyzing it. One should simply accept that things appear as they do, without examining them. If, on the other hand, one investigates conventionalities and comes to the conclusion that such phenomena *are* produced, affirming that this is *not* what is to be refuted, but rather their *truly existent production*, it remains to be explained how the absence of true production means the same thing as the absence of production. Since conventional production exists, there is production. This being so, there is cessation. If arising and cessation exist according to their characteristics, they are impermanent. It is impossible to establish emptiness in this way—that is, an emptiness qualified by the absence of arising and cessation, and superior to the kind of emptiness defined by the Shravakas. If one does not refute all such things as "self," "other," afflictions, karma, suffering, and all the rest, simply to *say* that they lack true existence will not remove a single conceptual construct! If one investigates the ultimate mode of things (which is superior to their merely relative and conventional mode) with absolutist arguments, and finds nothing new to understand, it is pointless to teach an emptiness of extraneous "true existence." For nonexistence on the conventional level has already been demonstrated by reasoning at this same level.

Further discussion concerning true existence considered as extraneous to phenomena

In short, the statement that phenomena are without true existence should bring one to the understanding that in ultimate truth they do not exist. Nevertheless, it is appropriate to add to this that the fact that phenomena do not exist on the ultimate plane does not necessarily mean that they are not "there" on the conventional level. No one, myself or anyone else, can find fault with such a way of speaking. However, in the midst of their excogitations, our opponents understand that the object of refutation is not conventional phenomena themselves but something extraneous to them. They say that the pot is empty of something different from the pot itself (that is, its true existence). They fail to grasp that the scriptural statement "A man is empty of man" is an assertion made by reasoning on the ultimate level. In other words, they understand it in a completely newfangled way, to the effect that if a man is empty of man, he is nothing on the conventional level. The conclusion at which they arrive, therefore—namely, that a man is not empty of himself but of a true existence extraneous to him—strikes them as a highly satisfactory solution. This, however, drives a wedge between the two truths; and conventional phenomena, existing according to their characteristics, end up by not being empty. Indeed, they become truly existent. Failing to understand this crucial point, our opponents *say* that phenomena lack true existence, but all the time they are whispering to themselves: "How can things *really* lack true existence?" Chandrakirti said that the Svatantrikas were content with tenets that are only verbally coherent. The very same criticism applies here to our opponents.

The latter will defend themselves with the following argument. Emotional and cognitive obscurations arise on account of the dualistic experience of the perceiving self and the perceived phenomenon. If we wish to eliminate these obscurations, we must eliminate our clinging to the personal and phenomenal selves, by understanding, through investigation, that the very objects of this clinging, the personal and phenomenal selves, have themselves no existence. Now, the mere apprehension of the personal and phenomenal selves does not in itself constitute a clinging to these selves. It is because one apprehends oneself and phenomena as *truly existent* that obscurations arise. Shantideva himself said: "True existence is to be eliminated." He did not say that self and phenomena are to be eliminated. Indeed, if the person and the phenomenon were in themselves (totally) denied, one would arrive at mere nothingness, the view of the nihilists.

Our reply to this is that "truly existent" is a term applied to the person and phenomenon when they are not considered to be empty of themselves. Consequently, emptiness and lack of true existence are synonyms and express the same crucial point. By contrast, our opponents say that the personal and phenomenal selves are not empty of themselves but rather that they are empty of true existence. But when sentient beings point to their five aggregates, which are present on the conventional level, they think: "This is me." This surely is what we call innate self-clinging. The *Pramanavarttika* says:

"May joy be mine, may suffering
Not come to me"—this wish,
This thought that thinks, "I am,"
Defines the innate self of living beings.

In the same way, the cognition "This is a pot" is the apprehension of the reality of the pot. Simply by apprehending something as existing as such, the personal and phenomenal selves are conceived. This mere thought therefore is enough to trigger the arising of defilements, for karma to be accumulated, and for suffering to be experienced. Therefore, if this thought is not removed, what advantage is there in refuting a truly existent self, which is somehow distinct from the innate sense of self, and which is incapable of generating afflictions and accumulating karma? For, like a rabbit's horns, it does not exist, even conventionally.

In the same way, with respect to the twenty kinds of emptiness, the mere fact of perceiving the six inner sense powers of sight and so forth, and the six outer sense fields, and everything else, as existing in their own right gives rise to clinging to them—one assumes their true existence.

The apprehension of phenomena as existing as such prevents their being established as empty. And if they are established as being *not* empty, simply to know about the twenty kinds of emptiness (of outer sense fields, inner sense powers, and so forth) does not suffice to eliminate clinging to the inner senses and the rest as being real and existent in their own right. And this renders meaningless all the teachings on the twenty kinds of emptiness, which were set forth specifically to remove the apprehension of the inner senses, outer objects, the union of these two, immensity, emptiness, and so on, as truly existent realities. An emptiness of true existence, considered separate from the thing to which it refers, is powerless to remove the apprehension of phenomena as inherently existing. As it is said: "As long as one apprehends and clings to the aggregates, one clings to 'I.'" Therefore, if the five aggregates of empirical experience are not empty of themselves, this means that it is impossible ever to avert our apprehension and clinging to them, for they are established by direct perception. And since this same direct perception proves that the apprehension of the five aggregates is what produces ego-clinging in the first place, it would follow that ego-clinging can never be averted.[114]

Our opponents in this debate may think that their position is sound, to the effect that the five aggregates are empty of an extraneous true existence. But we would comment that it is precisely in relation to the five aggregates (when not considered to be empty of themselves) that ego-clinging is produced. And even if the aggregates *were* empty of an extraneous true existence, simply to be aware of this could never in the slightest degree counteract the way the aggregates are apprehended and clung to. To know that the pot is empty of being a cloth (that is, to know that it is not a cloth) does nothing to help us see that the pot is by nature empty of itself.

In fine, if the statement "The five aggregates are by nature empty of themselves" is regarded as meaning that they are empty of true existence, there is nothing wrong in saying that phenomena are lacking in true existence. But if one sees a difference between these two propositions, and believes that the aggregates are empty not of themselves but of true existence, then no matter how much one reflects on such an emptiness, one will never put an end to one's clinging to the aggregates. It is with an excessive literalism that our opponents have interpreted the three elements of the syllogism: "The subject, pot, is empty of true existence because there are neither one nor many truly existent pots." They feel compelled to interpret this as meaning that the pot is empty of a true existence that is somehow separate from it. They do not consider that it means the same as "The subject, pot, is empty because it is not found by analysis investigating its ultimate status." They believe that the emptiness of the pot is the pot's emptiness of true existence, which is then regarded as an attribute detachable from the pot itself—with the result that the pot and its emptiness become two distinct things. This in turn means that the conceived object, namely, the misconception of the pot as truly existent, cannot be removed. And indeed, to understand the assertion "The nature of the pot is emptiness" as implying that the pot's nature somehow inheres in the pot as a reality distinct from the pot itself would mean that one could say that fire is separable from its fiery nature, its own heat! True, such a way of speaking, which hangs together only verbally but is wide of the mark as far as the meaning is concerned, is occasionally adopted when emptiness is being investigated. However, far from being a help in the direct realization of emptiness, it creates numerous obstacles to the attainment of this goal. In the immediate term, such a formula might appear to be a key point in the understanding of emptiness. But if one concentrates and reflects, one will see that to espouse a merely verbal formula that does nothing to reduce one's clinging to the supposed reality of things will not bring about liberation. On the other hand, if one *sees* what is meant by emptiness, one is free. This is precisely why emptiness was taught: to bring beings to liberation. It was not set forth simply to give people something to argue about!

The five aggregates are undeniably present. But when they are subjected to a close analysis down to infinitesimal particles, one may, as a result of such an investigation, conclude that they do not amount in fact to a discrete, bulky object. On the contrary, they then appear as multiple and impermanent. The inherent existence of the indivisible particle may be a matter of uncertainty. However, when one sees that it is impossible to regard the five aggregates, whether together or individually, as discrete entities, one will not identify with such multiple and impermanent elements. For this would involve the faulty consequence that the self is likewise multiple and ephemeral. One inevitably comes to the conclusion that the self or "I" is no more than an imputation dependent on the aggregates, and not an entity existing in its own right. Such an understanding is able to subvert ego-clinging and is indispensable even for the Shravakas. And the Shravakas certainly do not say: "These coarse aggregates are not empty of themselves; they are empty of true existence. Their multiplicity is not empty in itself; it is empty of true existence. Impermanent aggregates are not empty from their own side, but only of true existence." This is not the position of the Shravakas, who do not ascribe an extraneous emptiness to the aggregates. They nevertheless realize that the self does not exist. If they were to make such an ascription, the result would be truly existent, gross aggregates (either the group of five taken together, or each one individually), or a gross collection of the six kinds of consciousness, or even a gross mental entity—none of which would be empty in itself. Not being empty, they would constitute a real basis for the imputation of self. There would indeed be a self, which would be the object of ego-clinging, and it would be quite impossible to invalidate it by reasoning. Such a gross object would be single, discrete, and enduring. For in being regarded as *not* empty, it would necessarily be one; and far from being instantaneous, it would be permanent. But since, as a matter of fact, it is divisible and can be separated into parts and instants, it is evident that the object is indeed a multiplicity that is merely labeled as permanent and singular. The supposedly permanent, singular thing cannot but be empty by nature. If now this is called emptiness of true existence, such an estimate concords perfectly with our own view.[115] But in the view of our opponents, "this single, permanent thing is not empty by its nature; it is empty of true existence." In other words, emptiness by nature and emptiness of true existence are not regarded as synonymous. But for as long as phenomena are regarded as not empty of themselves, there is no advantage in saying that they are empty of something else.

If, instead of saying that the aggregates are empty of actual discreteness (because they are multiple), one says only that they are empty of a truly existent discreteness;[116] and if, instead of saying that they are empty of actual permanence (in being momentary), one says only that they are empty of a truly existing permanence; and if one talks about truly existing aggregates (as distinct from the aggregates themselves), one is referring to something that cannot possibly occur in the world of conventional reality. No one experiences the aggregates in this way, so it cannot be this that stimulates ego-clinging. For this reason, there is no need to refute such permanent, discrete aggregates.

No advantage is to be derived from the explanatory method just described, which defines phenomena as empty not of themselves but only of an extraneous true existence. On the contrary, such an explanation is a hindrance. For as long as we consider that phenomena are not empty of themselves, it is impossible to prevent ourselves from apprehending them as real—however much we may say that they are empty of a true existence that is in fact different from them. Not only does such a formula fail to improve on the understanding that phenomenal appearances on the relative level are self-empty, it actually worsens the situation. With regard to the way that conventionalities appear, the five aggregates are undeniably present. They appear as multiple and changing, whereas their contraries (discrete and permanent aggregates) do not appear. Therefore, it is on the basis of their conventional mode of appearance that analysis shows them to be empty of their nature—empty of themselves. There is indeed no way to understand the ultimate in isolation from the conventional. Therefore, because of the way conventional phenomena present themselves—appearing while never at any time existing inherently—they are said, of necessity, to be self-empty.

One may complain that it is not permissible to refer to this as emptiness, that emptiness means emptiness of true existence, and that relative phenomena are not self-empty. But this statement is no improvement on the previous one. On the contrary, a true existence of things, separate from the things themselves, does not form part of normal experience, and no one makes such an assumption. It is a mere figment of the imagination, and to prove that things are empty of such a figment is completely pointless. The only thing that people ever apprehend is the empirical object itself, and there is no way to apprehend the object's true existence apart from it. If the object—a pot, for instance—is not empty from its own side, the object itself is not established as an illusion, even if it were empty of a true existence separate from itself. In just the same way, the illusory character of the rope itself is not demonstrated by the mere fact that it turns out not to be a snake. Thus the relative and ultimate do not exclude each other; and it should be understood that it is precisely due to their own nature (emptiness) that conventional phenomena are able to appear.

In brief, all sentient beings fix on the phenomena of conventional existence, the aggregates and the rest, and regard them as having their own nature or reality. They consider them truly existent in an ultimate sense, in just the same way, in other words, that they appear. It is due to this that they experience chains of dualistic thoughts, which arise with regard to themselves and other things, in inner and outer experience. This is what makes beings wander in samsara. As a solution to this predicament, therefore, the teachings of the three vehicles speak of three kinds of nirvana. The result of the Shravaka vehicle is actualized through the elimination of the emotional obscurations—an elimination that is produced by the realization of the personal no-self. This brings liberation from the sufferings of samsara. The result of the Pratyekabuddha vehicle is actualized by realizing the no-self of the person and also of phenomena belonging to the aggregate of form. Finally, the nonabiding nirvana, which is the fruit of the Bodhisattva vehicle, is attained by means of the wisdom that realizes the no-self both of persons and of phenomena, through the elimination of the emotional and cognitive obscurations. If, in the case of any phenomenon, one comes to the conclusion that the object apprehended has no reality, one's clinging to it will be undermined. And indeed without such an understanding, clinging will never be overcome. As Aryadeva has said:

> When you see that things lack true reality,
> The germ of all existence will be halted.

As we have just explained above, with regard to the realization of noself, the objects that are examined with absolutist reasoning and established as empty are the generality of phenomena existing on the conventional level. (Imaginary) things that do not exist on the conventional level—a rabbit's horns and the like—do not require such a refutation, since ordinary people do not generate self-clinging in relation to them. Therefore, when the argument of neither one nor many is used to investigate whether or not a pot exists according to its characteristics, one finds that it cannot resist such an analysis. Consequently, one is forced to conclude that the pot is empty of itself. The object of refutation by such reasoning is the pot itself. The pot has to be shown to be unfindable or nonobserved, and as long as it is not established as being unfindable, it cannot be shown to lack true existence.

Ordinary people see the actual pot. They apprehend it as truly existent, whereas in fact it is only the occasion for the misperception of true existence. They do not focus on a true existence ascribed to the pot and then conclude that the pot really exists. True existence is not an object of direct perception to the eye or any other sense consciousness; it is nothing but an illusory figment, a mental imputation. By contrast, the objects of refutation by absolutist reasoning are conventionally existing phenomena, and they, pots and suchlike, appear as they do through the power of dependent origination. They undeniably appear. If then one examines the status of the objects that are manifest to the senses and asks whether they have a real existence in themselves, one can investigate them using the four ultimate reasonings of the Madhyamika tradition. And one will find that while conventionalities like pots and so on appear to us, they and their constituents, down to the tiniest infinitesimal particles, are unable to withstand analysis. This means not that they are empty of some extraneous true existence—other-empty—but that, by their very nature, they abide in emptiness, the emptiness of being primordially unborn and unobservable. This is the emptiness that we need to establish. Phenomena that are empty from their own side are said to lack inherent identity. They are so designated because, when they are investigated by absolutist reasoning, it is precisely this that is not found. Again, when we say that something lacks inherent nature, it is because we cannot find and identify this nature. Phenomena are likewise said to be without attributes, beyond expectation.[117] They are said to be impossible to define, empty, without self, beyond the extremes of samsara and nirvana, spacelike, and so on. All this is the same as saying that they lack true existence. By contrast, if, on being subjected to absolutist analysis, a thing were found to resist such an investigation, it would necessarily be established as truly existent. But no phenomenon, compounded or uncompounded, is found to resist such analysis. Phenomena are therefore said to lack true existence.

To affirm, as certain modern Dharma teachers do, that a thing is not empty from its own side but is empty of an extraneous true existence, is the same as saying that it is other-empty. Therefore, since pots and the

like are not empty from their own side, it follows that no conventionally existent thing can be shown to be empty. Nothing can be shown, in
itself, to be without inherent identity. These philosophers, in other
words, do not use absolutist arguments to refute conventionally existent phenomena. On the contrary, they refute true existence—which actually has no conventional reality. When they say that they are using
absolutist reasoning to refute phenomena, all that they are doing is
sticking "true existence" onto phenomena and making a show of refuting that!

Generally speaking, of course, there is no harm in pointedly referring
to the true existence of things. Such a procedure occasionally facilitates
one's understanding, as in the present case when phenomena, empty by
their nature, are said to lack true existence. But if the verbal expression
is not understood in this sense, and instead it is imagined that true existence is being refuted somehow separately from the object referred to,
it is clear that clinging to the reality of the object will in no way be arrested. The whole point of establishing that things are empty will be
lost, and the ultimate reality of phenomena will turn out to be no more
than a nonaffirming negative—denying the true existence of phenomena as something extraneous. This will effectively prevent the realization that emptiness and dependently arising phenomena are one and
the same thing. And freedom from conceptual construction will be rendered impossible owing to the fact that the actual *concept* of a nonaffirming negative will not have been overcome. Some people may well
assert that they are free from the duality of subject and object and that
their meditative equipoise is free of perceptions.* But even if they habituate themselves for a hundred kalpas to such an emptiness, refuting
true existence as something separated from the things to which it is ascribed, they will never be able to rid themselves of dual appearance—
perception that subject and object are separate.

The absolutist reasoning found in the Madhyamika texts is able to
dismantle the assumption of the reality of phenomena. This is precisely
what the arguments of our opponents fail to do. Their only object of
refutation is so-called true existence, and that is all that they disprove.
And for minds reasoning in this way, the chance to realize emptiness
beyond all conceptual extremes is still very remote. For their position
contradicts the very meaning of the authentic Madhyamika and is the
occasion of a hundred inconsistencies.

---

* *snang med.*

The empty nature of phenomena, their unborn, ultimate reality, may be grasped thanks to arguments like that of neither one nor many. This argument shows that phenomena cannot withstand analysis, with the result that they are described as lacking true existence. This is the correct way to understand the lack of true existence. Our opponents, however, say that even though phenomena cannot resist analysis directed at the ultimate, this does not prove that they are empty, only that they are empty of true existence. But if they say that the object of refutation is an extraneous true existence, and the probandum is its emptiness; if they say that nonobservability, namely, the emptiness of phenomena themselves, is not to be established but only the nonobservability, or emptiness, of their true existence; and finally, if they need to investigate with the argument of neither one nor many only the true existence of phenomena, as distinct from phenomena themselves, the question is: How do they do it? How can they possibly investigate with absolutist reasoning a so-called true existence separate from the phenomenon itself, which is no more than a verbal label, as unreal as a rabbit's horns?

Our opponents say that when a rope is mistaken for a snake, the locus of the misperception of the snake is the rope itself. The mind that apprehends the snake in the rope, so to speak, takes the rope itself for a snake; it does not apprehend the snake anywhere else than in the rope. When the rope is investigated to see whether or not it is a snake, and when the understanding is gained that there is no snake, the rope remains; and this rope is empty of the extraneous object, namely, the snake. But the mind that apprehends the rope as a snake never, at any time, saw a snake, but only the rope that it misperceived. When investigating the mistake, one necessarily examines the rope and discovers that there is no snake. And our opponents say that just as the rope is empty of something different from itself (namely, snakeness), and just as it is not empty from its own side (of ropeness), the same applies to pots. Pots and other objects are empty of a true existence that is distinct from them.

We reply to this by saying that if phenomena like pots are not empty from their own side, parallel with the rope in the example, this means that even though it is not actually said that pots and suchlike are truly existent, nevertheless, in saying that they are not empty from their own side, our opponents are in fact affirming their true existence. This being so, they must also be asserting that such phenomena do in fact withstand absolutist arguments and are findable. As Chandrakirti has said, the unwanted consequence for such a philosophical position is that conventional truth is found to resist logical investigation. If phenomena are established as truly existent by their nature, they cannot be empty of a true existence extraneous to them. How could they be? It is senseless to say that they are!

Our opponents, however, say that just as one can disprove the presence of the snake in the rope, one can also disprove the rope by analyzing it down to its finest fibers. Only the name will remain, but the rope itself will not be found. And the same can be done to the rope's fibers and again to the particles that make up the fibers. Nevertheless, the consciousness that apprehends the rope and the rope itself (the object of consciousness) are not mistaken or deluded on the conventional level. Consequently, when establishing that the rope is empty, one must ascribe to the rope the character of true existence. But when establishing the nonexistence of the snake in the rope, there is no need to ascribe true existence to the snake. In the same way, when refuting the pot, if one does not specify that one is refuting only a truly existent pot, the conventional thing is itself negated.[118] Our reply to this is that, generally speaking, we also say that true existence is to be negated and that inherent identity, inherent existence, and the status of nonemptiness are all the object of our refutation. But if one fails to establish that the conventionally existent phenomenon is *itself* unobservable, unfindable, and so on, there is no way to refute its inherent identity. And if it is established as unfindable, by the same token it is established as lacking true existence. Thus when, with absolutist arguments, one dismantles the rope, its fibers, and so forth, dividing them into smaller and smaller parts, the gross object, the rope itself, cannot remain established on the conventional level either. The rope itself is necessarily shown to be no more than a conceptual designation. Were it not so, it would be impossible to disprove its true existence. On the other hand, if it is shown to be just a concept, its real existence and identity are exploded. It therefore makes no sense to say that the pot is not empty by its nature.

Of course the objection is made that if phenomena are denied on the conventional level, the resulting view amounts to a species of ontological nihilism. That is why it is important to say that it is only true existence that is refuted—not the conventional thing itself. To this we reply that something is said to be refuted when it is not found by absolutist reasoning. It is a silly mistake to think that the reality of conventionalities is refuted by reasoning operating only on the conventional level. Our opponents say that when something is not found or observed by investigation directed at the ultimate, this means that it is wholly inexistent (absent) on the relative level as well. But in that case, they are implying that there should be something on the conventional level that withstands ultimate analysis. But this is not possible. If it were, the thing in question would be truly existent and we should find ourselves with a truly existing conventionality.* It is established for both ourselves and others that conventional phenomena cannot withstand such investigation. Our opponents' opinion that what cannot withstand absolutist analysis is necessarily nonexistent on the conventional level is a reflection of their mistaken belief that the two truths are mutually exclusive. Therefore, if they say that what is not found by absolutist reasoning is of necessity nonexistent on the relative level, it follows that (if they are to retain the relative truth) there must be something that withstands absolutist analysis. But this is impossible. Given, therefore, that absolutist reasoning cannot establish, and does not find, phenomena like pots, origination, and so on, what is gained by simply saying that truly existent phenomena are to be denied, while conventional phenomena themselves are left unrefuted? Absolutist reasoning certainly does not just refute true existence while leaving conventionalities alone. When conventional phenomena are examined, they are not found. Therefore things like pots and suchlike are established on the relative level as the mere imputations of thought, dependent on the coming together of their constituent parts.

On the other hand, how can our opponents claim that nothing appears to the undamaged senses, apart from the "truly existent" phenomenon? A truly existent pot (as distinct from an actual pot) cannot, we insist, be an object of the senses, and it cannot be refuted by analytical dissection. It is not this that is shown to be unproduced by virtue of the arguments that refute the four theories of production. The entity that is dissected into parts and shown to be without inherent identity is the conventionally existent pot itself. That which is shown to be unproduced is the shoot itself that sprouts from the seed on the level of conventionality. What these arguments demonstrate is that it is conventional phenomena themselves that are unobservable and unproduced. Therefore one can *say* that these inherently identityless phenomena lack true existence; one can *say* that their production and cessation lack true existence. But when absolutist reasoning is invoked, it is unnecessary to qualify the investigation as being of a truly existing phenomenon—a truly existing production—while at the same time failing to inquire whether the conventional object *itself* exists or

---

* That is, a contradiction in terms.

does not exist, and whether it is produced or unproduced. It is enough to investigate conventional phenomena and their production themselves, without qualifying them as truly existent. The ground of investigation for the absolutist reasoning that investigates the existence or nonexistence, the production or nonproduction, of phenomena (in other words, the probandum that is to be demonstrated as empty) is conventional phenomena pure and simple. It is not "truly existent phenomena." If conventional phenomena are shown by absolutist reasoning to be unable to withstand analysis, these same phenomena are established as being without intrinsic identity and true existence. It is quite redundant to say that it is only the truly existent pot and truly existent production that do not exist. If conventional phenomena were found to resist analysis, they would be established as truly produced and truly existent. But as they are not so, they are by the same token shown to be lacking in true existence and true production. This is tantamount to a refutation of true existence, and conventionalities are thus shown to be without it. In other words, what absolutist reasoning disproves is precisely conventionally existing pots, production, and so forth—not "truly existing pots" and "truly existing production." For the latter have no reality on the conventional level and are not therefore something to be investigated by arguments like that of neither one nor many. It is pointless to say that an extraneous true existence is shown not to resist analysis and is therefore refuted, for such a true existence cannot be the object of such an inquiry. Of course, once again, there is nothing wrong in *saying* that true existence is refuted. But just as true existence cannot withstand analysis and is thus shown to be empty, in the same way phenomena, such as pots and production, cannot withstand analysis and are also shown to be empty.

But why do our opponents say that phenomena are not empty? They may reply that, in their view, phenomena resist analysis and that only their true existence is refuted—meaning that the conventional is not refuted. For if true existence is not refuted as a *separate* adjunct to phenomena, they say, it follows that the conventional is obliterated by absolutist analysis. But (we answer) the situation here is not to be compared with the refutation by conventional analysis of something that, on the conventional level, has no existence.* On the contrary, absolutist reasoning refutes phenomena as nonobservable in absolute terms. This is what this kind of reasoning is for. If phenomena are not refuted, their putative inherent identity and true existence are not denied. By saying

---

* For example, a rabbit's horns or a four-sided triangle.

in stanza 36 that "reasoning cannot uphold it even as conventional," Chandrakirti is affirming that there is no production according to either of the two truths. If a pot is investigated by absolutist reasoning, it is shown to be empty precisely because it is ultimately unfindable and unobservable. On the conventional level, no really existent thing can be found even to the slightest degree.

(c) *Even conventionally, there is no such thing as naturally existent other-production. If there were, it could not be disproved on the ultimate level*

36 When an analysis is made on the ultimate level, no rational account can be given of production, whether in terms of effects being the same as or different from their causes. From the point of view of this kind of analysis, production is not even conventionally possible. What valid cognition can therefore support the opponent's belief in naturally existent production? It is impossible.

(2) Refutation of an objection

One may object that if, with regard to conventional phenomena, production according to its characteristics were not accounted for in either of the two truths, this would mean that form and suchlike would have absolutely no existence, and our eyes could not perceive them. If they could, then indeed a rabbit's horns ought also to be visible too, since in that case, actual (visible) horns and a rabbit's horns would be on a level! **37** The answer to this is that if a cause is unable to produce its effect, empty or illusory things like reflections and echoes could not be produced through the coming together of certain conditions, which are themselves devoid of inherent existence (mirrors and so on). Such phenomena would not be experienced, but, as a matter of fact, they are experienced and are universally accepted as illusions. A reflection is illusory (empty) but empirically experienced (producing a consciousness that resembles it in aspect). **38** In the same way, even though phenomena are empty in that they do not exist in their own right, they are not thereby prevented from appearing. Though they are empty, one is vividly conscious of their appearance. The corresponding direct perception occurs. The fact that an object without inherent existence is able to produce an effect—that is, the fact that, though empty, it is able to appear and be perceived[119]—illustrates broadly how empty phenomena are able to manifest. Whatever appears in a reflection is void, but the fact that it is so does not stop it from having an effect (the stimulation of a corresponding consciousness). And this shows *mutatis mutandis* that it is logically acceptable to say that, like reflections, which are not just nothing, phenomena appear even though they are empty.

ii. The advantages of this refutation
(1) It disproves the extremely subtle views of eternalism and nihilism

As the root verse says, "And since inherent nature is in neither truth, phenomena are neither nothing nor unchanging entities." No need then to mention the ultimate truth. Even on the level of relative truth, we do not say that phenomena have some sort of "natural existence."* Thus even the subtle extremes of eternalism and nihilism, in relation to the two truths, are negated. On the other hand, if phenomena were to exist naturally on the relative level, then neither eternalism nor nihilism on that same level could be disproved. Therefore, since phenomena are without such relative existence, we are free of even the subtlest trace of eternalism or nihilism related to the relative.

(2) It also demonstrates the connection between karmic cause and effect
(a) A finished action is able to produce an effect even in the absence of the alaya
(i) A finished action is able to produce an effect

39   In themselves, actions, being devoid of inherent existence, are without inherent cessation. Therefore, although there is no such thing as the *alaya* to provide the intervening link between action and effect of action, an act that is over and done with can in fact bring forth a result. In some cases, as the text says: "Indeed, some acts may be completed long ago, but you should know that they will bear their fruit." The Chittamatrins give a rational account of the karmic law of cause and effect by introducing the notion of the alaya. The Sautrantikas do the same with their theory of a mental continuum, while the Vaibhashikas invoke their idea of "obtention"[120] and the principle of karmic indelibility. The theories of these schools do not hold together. For those who believe that actions and effects possess inherent

---

* *rang bzhin gyis yod pa.*

reality, an action that is over and done with cannot produce effects. They are therefore obliged to speculate about a medium in which actions are supposed to leave imprints of some kind, or about some sort of continuum that links causes with their effects—without which karma could not function. But from our point of view, neither action nor effect has inherent existence; they arise in interdependence. And we do not investigate whether the cause and its effect meet or do not meet, whether there is a space between them or not. It is like looking into mirror: there is a face and there is the reflection of a face—something has simply arisen in dependence on a cause. Nevertheless, if you inquire whether the cause and its effect contact each other, you will never be able to devise an acceptable explanation of how the seed is the cause of the shoot. The child of a barren woman cannot die—for the simple reason that it has never been born. Conversely, if something ceases, this can only be because it has previously been produced. Therefore, because the action itself is not inherently produced, it has no inherent cessation either. If the cessation of an action, in the sense of its being completed and finished, has no inherent reality, this cannot invalidate the production of an effect.

Disintegration as a positive entity

In the scriptures one finds the words "Because of aging and death there is birth." And it is also said that disintegration itself is productive of a result. For as long as there is no cessation, there is no arising. If disintegration is done away with, no generation is possible: "*A thing and a nonthing are both compounded phenomena.*" However, if all these texts are cited (out of context) as support for the theory of disintegration as a positive entity,* Nagarjuna will be found guilty of immediately contradicting himself. For he said (in the same place) that "*nirvana is an uncompounded phenomenon.*" (If the proponents of this doctrine are right) he should not have done so, because nirvana is a cessation brought about through the exhaustion, that is, the disintegration, of the obscurations and is, besides, the result of the path of learning.

Furthermore, since sorrow is produced both by the death of a child (in the case of a parent) and by childlessness (in the case of a barren

* *zhig pa dngos po.*

woman), it follows—if this doctrine is correct—that the nonexistence (of the dead child) and the childlessness of the barren woman are both existent things while the child itself is nonexistent. This is absurd. Moreover, since emptiness arises as the interdependence of cause and effect, it becomes a positive entity, in other words, an affirming negative. Therefore "disintegration as a positive entity," as expounded in this tradition, is an affirming negative. Thus our opponents' position in this matter completely contradicts their other assertion that emptiness is a nonaffirming negative. Something that does not disintegrate, for example, a pot that is not broken—in that it is "undisintegrated"—is a present, functioning item. It must therefore be a positive existent. But if this is so, it follows that its disintegration cannot also be a positive entity, for (as we have just said) it is the "undisintegrated" item that is the functioning thing. Therefore disintegration cannot be a positive entity, just as a nonexistent pot is not a thing. The nonexistence of an "undisintegrated thing" is not a positive "something." This is simply the reverse of what has just been said (that an undisintegrated thing is an existent thing).

Two successive negations are understood as applying to a thing, and a single negation, applying to a nonthing, is the contrary of such a double negative. This is like three successive negations.[121] Consequently, if the disintegration and the nondisintegration of something are both said to be real entities, it follows that the two negatives (a single negative and a double negative) are not contraries—in other words, that the existence of something and its nonexistence are not opposites. They do not cancel each other out. Furthermore, owing to a complete failure to respect the correct meaning of words, the proper significance of "existence" and "nonexistence" has been entirely muddled.

In addition, it also follows that a cause could never be reduced to nothing, since (according to this theory) a disintegrated cause and an undisintegrated cause are equal in being positive entities. This is necessarily so since it is impossible to have a cause that is neither "disintegrated" nor "undisintegrated." If both cessation and noncessation are positive entities, it follows that they are not mutually exclusive opposites, for they are causally related and each is a (discrete, functioning) entity. Now, if an existent thing and its contrary (that is, that same thing but now regarded as nonexistent) are not mutually exclusive, it follows that permanence and impermanence are not opposites. And, to change the terms, the same applies to disintegration and nondisintegration, permanence and impermanence, past and future. It follows that every thing is permanent, for it would be impossible ever to have a nonexistent thing that is precisely the reverse of the existent thing.

Some say that since darkness arises from the extinguishing of a light, the light's extinction is a positive, functioning entity. Such a theory necessarily amounts to saying that the light is the indirect cause of darkness because if there is no light, there can be no extinction, and if there is no extinction of light, there can be no darkness. It follows that in the space between the cosmic continents, there is no darkness, for there was never any light there to be extinguished! Of course, they may say that "extinction of light" means the same as "nonexistent light." But then it would follow that the child of the barren woman died, for it is nonexistent. And since, when one's horse dies, one is obliged to walk, it follows that a horseless beggar need never walk, for his horse has never died. Ha ha! Very amusing!

The foundation of our habitual tendencies is the sense of "I." This is a continuum designated in dependence on the continuum of consciousness. Thus, even though we observe this "I," it lacks inherent existence. As Master Nagarjuna has said:

> No fruit will ever come from seeds
> Destroyed or undestroyed.
> And you have said that all arising
> Is but the play of mere illusion.

(ii)   A supporting example

40   As it is explained in the *Bhavasamkranti-sutra*, when an ordinary, foolish man sees an attractive woman in his dream, he desires her. And he will feel desire even when he wakes up and the woman has disappeared. Just so, actions that are devoid of inherent existence, and are now over and done with, can produce effects in the future.

(b)   An answer to the objection regarding the assertion that even if there is no alaya, a finished action can produce an effect
(i)   An answer to the objection that, in that case, results would be produced ad infinitum

A. Examples for the two kinds of object

The objection to the above statement runs as follows. Something that lacks "naturally existent production"* cannot have a "naturally existent cessation."† If the Madhyamikas say, nevertheless, that such an action is productive of an effect, the question is: Why should it not continue, once it has produced its effect, to produce effects to infinity? Logically, this should be possible, since it is evident that the action just mentioned is not discontinued due to the cessation. Such is the objection, and our opponents may go on to complain that this means that ripened and unripened karmic effects are on a level in being equally unreal.

Taking the second point first, although ripened and unripened karmic effects are equal in being both unreal, they differ in that one is functional‡ and the other is not.   **41**   All illusory objects, such as a rabbit's horns and black lines, are on an equal footing in being devoid of inherent existence. Nevertheless, a person suffering from an ocular defect might see black lines but will not see just anything, for example, rabbit horns or the children of a barren woman.

B. How effects of actions illustrated by the examples are produced

1. Effects cannot be produced ad infinitum

In just the same way, it should be understood that although all actions are equal in being devoid of an inherently real cessation, nevertheless, an action that has not yet produced its effect will do so, while an action that has produced its effect will not continue to give effects. An illusory object, like the black lines just mentioned, produces a consciousness in aspect similar to itself (that is, a consciousness of black lines) but no other kind of consciousness. In the same way, a phenomenon that is without inherent existence also produces an effect. Given that there is a coherence between this produced effect and its cause, and that what arises cannot be just anything, this illustrates broadly how the karmic mechanism, devoid of inherent existence, functions. For as long as there are black lines, a consciousness in their aspect is generated.[122]

---

* *rang bzhin gyis ma skyes.*
† *rang bzhin gyis zad pa med pa.*
‡ *don byed nus pa.*

2. Effects are not produced randomly

42 In the same way, although virtue and nonvirtue are without inherent existence, it may be observed that happiness and suffering are
the ripened effects of virtuous and nonvirtuous actions respectively. It
is certain that there is nothing confused or haphazard in the process
of karmic cause and effect. And just as someone with healthy eyes does
not see black lines and so forth, a wise person who sees that both
virtue and nonvirtue are without inherent existence will attain freedom.[123] Some people try to analyze the functioning of the karmic law
and try to explain logically *why* certain actions give certain effects.
When they fail to do so, there is the danger that they might go completely astray and conclude that the karmic principle in itself is absurd. Consequently, in view of the fact that the karmic principle
cannot be proved on the basis of limited human experience,[124] the
Buddha said that karma was inconceivable and discouraged attempts
to investigate it. For it is indeed difficult to penetrate such a profound
topic.[125]

(ii) An answer to the objection that the above refutation contradicts scripture, for the scriptures assert the alaya
A. Scriptures that speak of the alaya are not of ultimate meaning and are to be interpreted

It may be objected that the above statements contradict scripture,
which says that the alaya exists. **43**   However, passages like those in
the *Lankavatara-sutra*, which assert that the alaya, or rather the *alayavijñana*, is the matrix of all potential phenomena—just like the sections
of the Abhidharma that teach that the person exists or that the aggregates exist—are all texts of provisional meaning. They were taught as
expedients, in order to instruct those who are incapable of grasping
the extremely profound teachings on the ultimate nature of phenomena, namely, their lack of true existence.

B. An example

44 For example, the Buddha had completely overcome the tendency
of seeing the transitory composite of aggregates as constituting a self
and had therefore transcended all notion of "I" and "mine." Nevertheless, in order to be intelligible to ordinary people, he said things like "I
am saying this to you," and he referred to himself and his body, his

hands, and so forth. In the same way, even though phenomena are indeed without inherent existence, the Buddha spoke to his disciples on a provisional basis, alluding to things as though they existed.

2. A specific refutation of the Chittamatra tenet
a. The Chittamatra position itself

45   The Chittamatrins[126] say that sixth-ground Bodhisattvas see neither substances separate from the mind (for they are the ripening of inner propensities), nor a subject that apprehends or conceives such objects. For they fully realize that, on the ultimate level, the three worlds are nothing but consciousness. They therefore dwell in the wisdom that is empty of the dualistic experience of perceived object and perceiving subject. Such Bodhisattvas realize the ultimate, which they understand as the mind alone, devoid of duality. For them, there is no other ultimate reality.

If there are no outer objects, however, how is it that a consciousness can arise in their aspect? When asked this question, the Chittamatrins reply that   **46**   both outer and inner phenomena manifest like waves appearing on the sea moved by the wind. All negative impulses such as desire, and all positive impulses like faith, experienced in the past, have deposited a potential within the so-called alayavijñana, the "seed of all." It is from the ripening of this potential that consciousness—and only consciousness—arises. This is the so-called impure dependent reality. Naïve realism, on the other hand, believes that perceived objects and perceiving subjects exist separately from each other.

Theists say things like "Just as the spider is the cause of the cobweb, and the water crystal brings forth water, and the bud is the cause of the shoot, in the same way, God is the cause of beings." And exactly like the theists saying that God is the creator of beings, the Chittamatrins, with their belief in the alaya, say that consciousness is the basis of all perceived phenomena. The only difference between God and the alaya is that the former is supposed to be immutable while the latter is said to fluctuate.

47   Therefore, the essence of dependent reality[127] (which is possessed of inherent existence) is the basis or cause of the conceptual framework whereby the false imputations of "real" phenomena occur; and these are apprehended according to the dichotomy of subject and object. The Chittamatra doctrine states that dependent reality has three particular features. (1) It manifests from the mind's own latent tendencies, in the absence of outer objects. (2) It exists inherently. (3) On the ultimate level, as understood by the Chittamatrins, it is inconceivable and inexpressible. To use the example of the rope-snake, if there were no rope, the illusion of the snake would be impossible. In the same way, without a ground for appearance, appearances are ruled out. Thus the cause and basis of false imputation (the mistaken perception of "mind stuff" as outer objects) is impure dependent reality. This, they say, is what binds us in samsara. It is also this that makes liberation possible.

> b. *Refutation of the Chittamatra position*
> i. *Refutation through reasoning*
> (1) *Refutation of an inherently existent consciousness devoid of outer objects*
> (a) *Refutation of consciousness as such, devoid of outer objects*
> (i) *Refutations of the examples given of consciousness devoid of outer objects*
> > A. Refutation of the dream example
> > 1. An investigation of the example

48   In the debate, Chandrakirti asks the Chittamatrins for an example of an inherently existent consciousness that is devoid of a (separate) outer object. And the instance given is that of dreaming. A person may lie asleep in a tiny room and dream about wild elephants. Obviously, no elephant is present (there is only the mind, devoid of object). However, this example, says Chandrakirti, requires investigation.

> > 2. The refutation of the Chittamatra assertion
> > a. In fact the dream example is inadequate as a demonstration of an inherently existent mind

From the Madhyamika point of view, in the absence of external referents, consciousness cannot be produced in the aspect of such referents.[128] The Madhyamikas say that there is no inherently real cognitive subject, just as there is no real elephant as an object. In other words, the example given by the Chittamatrins is inadequate.[129]

49   The Chittamatrins continue their argument as follows. If, when dreaming, the consciousness is not real (more real than the dream visions), it follows that on waking, it would be impossible to recall one's dreams. But as a matter of fact, one does remember them, and this shows that the mind is real. To this, the Madhyamikas reply that in that case the object of the dream should be just as real as the dreaming consciousness. For if, having woken up, one remembers and thinks: "I dreamed about such and such a thing," this thing must have the same degree of existence as the subject, namely, the dreaming consciousness.[130]

> b. The example of dreaming is not enough to demonstrate the unreality of an extramental world in the waking state
>   i. The Chittamatra belief

50 In answer to this, the Chittamatrins elaborate their theory. They say that since the visual sense power is not operative during sleep, there is no corresponding visual consciousness. Therefore there cannot actually be any extramental shapes and colors* as objects of perception. The mental consciousness remains, however, and this, altered or affected by the state of sleep, manifests in the form of outer objects. These various aspects of the mental consciousness are taken to be extramental phenomena. And what happens in the waking state, the Chittamatrins say, is exactly the same as what happens when the mind is dreaming.

> ii. Refutation of this belief

51 Chandrakirti replies that if, in a dream, as the Chittamatrins say, extramental phenomena are unproduced, the same is also true of the mental consciousness itself. It too is devoid of inherent production (reality). For just as in a dream no visual sense power is operative, and just as there is no real object of the visual sense, in the same way there is no real consciousness arising therefrom. In other words, the three elements—object seen, operative sense power, and seeing consciousness—are all equally unreal. **52** As the words "and the rest" of the root text indicate, all other objects, sense powers, and consciousnesses (ear, nose, tongue, body, and mind) are equally unproduced. And, says Chandrakirti, just as the three elements mentioned (object, sense, and consciousness) are equally unreal in the dreaming state, the same applies to

---

* *gzugs kyi skye mched.*

the waking state as well. Phenomena like sense objects, sense organs, and consciousness are all unreal. There is no such thing as an inherently existent consciousness; there is no such thing as a real object of experience; and there is no such thing as a real sense faculty to act as the dominant condition.

c. The dream example actually shows that all phenomena exist in an illusory manner

53   For as long as one has not been roused from the sleep of ignorance, when one wakes from ordinary sleep, these three points of reference persist. And while one is asleep these three likewise occur in dreams. But just as these three elements of the dream vanish when one wakes up, in the same way, when one awakens from, or dispels, the slumber of ignorance and recognizes the dharmadhatu, these three aspects of object, sense power, and consciousness also disappear. It is just like waking from a dream.

B.   A refutation of the example of black lines

54   The mind of someone afflicted with a visual ailment (as the dominant condition) may think he sees black lines floating before his eyes. As far as the mind of that person is concerned, both the object and consciousness are true. He actually sees black lines. But for someone whose vision is good and normal, both the object and the corresponding consciousness are false, for he does not perceive them.

55   It might be objected, of course, that although there are no black lines present, there is nevertheless a consciousness that sees them. The answer to this is that, in that case, even people with healthy sight, when looking at the same place as the invalid, should see black lines also. But this is not the case, which shows that the consciousness perceiving the black lines is not inherently existent.[131] On this point, Rendawa remarks that the example of the dream consciousness illustrates delusion, while the example of the eye disease illustrates the deluded senses and sense consciousnesses.

(ii)   A refutation of the example's supposed meaning, namely, that consciousness arises in the absence of an object thanks to the potential of latent tendencies in the mind

A. The Chittamatra position

56 The Chittamatrins elaborate their theory yet further by saying that the reason people with healthy eyesight do not see black lines is that the mental potential for their seeing them is not ripening. This is why they see nothing. It is not because there are no black lines as a visual object that they do not see them.

B. Refutation of the Chittamatra position
1. Brief rebuttal

The claim that even though the object is absent (due to the absence of mental potential) the subject, or consciousness, exists is still not proven. For if there is such a thing as a mental potential, it must be asked whether it is associated with the present, future, or past moment of consciousness. If the potential is connected with the present consciousness, there are two possible scenarios. In the first case, with regard to the twin aspects of "possessor of potential" and "potential itself," the term "consciousness of potential" (meaning "potential consciousness") expresses a genitive relation of the same essence.[132] In other words, the two elements cannot be dissociated. But on the other hand, the "potential consciousness" cannot be the actual potential itself. If it were, the effect would not have a cause different from itself; or it would be like a seed still existing, undestroyed, even after the shoot has appeared. In the second case, if the consciousness arises from the potential, the relation between the two terms is ablative, expressing origination.[133] It is, however, impossible for consciousness to arise from a potential that is simultaneous with itself, since in that case cause and effect would actually coincide. Finally, since the future consciousness is not present, it is absurd to claim that this potential is the potential of such a consciousness—for the latter does not as yet exist.

2. Detailed refutation
a. There is no inherently existent potential associated with the present consciousness

57 It is impossible for the present moment of consciousness to contain its own potential, for this implies that cause and effect are simultaneous, which is absurd.

b. There is no inherently existent potential associated with the
future consciousness

i. General refutation

The potential cannot be associated (in a relation of the same essence)
with a future consciousness, which by definition has not yet been produced. For if there is no future consciousness as a specific entity, it
makes no sense to speak of a potential for it. If it were possible to
speak of the potential of a thing when the thing itself does not exist, it
would make equal sense to say that there is a potential for the child of
a barren woman.

ii. Refutation of an objection

The opponent may observe that, in ordinary life, people can and do say
things like "Cook a meal" or "Weave a cloth with this yarn." Also, in
The Root Stanzas on the Middle Way, the passage "Three enter the womb:
a Chakravartin and the two spontaneously manifested (a Buddha and a
Pratyekabuddha)" is interpreted as referring to *causes*—the elements that
enter the womb and will become the Chakravartin and so on. **58** In
the same way, since the future consciousness will manifest, it may be
objected, it is legitimate to refer to that which will produce it as being
its *potential*.

In actual fact, it is not admissible. The potential in question is not existent in the present, and therefore, in its absence, there can be no consciousness manifesting as its effect. Of course, one might reply that one
can talk about a potential with regard to a future consciousness (yet to
arise) and say that the consciousness arises from this potential. Therefore the consciousness is posited in relation to the potential, and the
two prove (the existence of) each other. But this is false. They cannot
demonstrate each other's *existence*. For one term to be proved in dependence on another term, the latter must be demonstrated before the former. If one term is not shown to be existent first, the other cannot be so
demonstrated either. The result is that neither is shown to exist.[134] Mutually dependent phenomena, like shortness and length, the locations of
here and there, and so forth, are mere imputations. They have no inherent reality—as has been said by those who possess supreme knowledge.

c. A refutation of an inherently existent potential associated with
the past (moment of) consciousness

i. The refutation itself

59   The Chittamatrins say that a future consciousness arises through the ripening of a potential present in a consciousness that has elapsed—to which we reply that, in that case, the potential of a consciousness has given rise to a consciousness that is completely extraneous and alien to it. Indeed, according to Chittamatra theory, the interconnected continuity consists of a succession of instants that are separate and distinct by nature. And the Chittamatrins assert that the distinct and separate instants (precedent and subsequent) have a real existence according to their characteristics. But the unwanted consequence of such a contention is a breakdown of causal coherence, for anything could arise from anything (whether it be an extraneous cause or not).[135]

ii. Refutation of an objection
(1) An objection to the refutation

60   Chandrakirti's opponent will say that the mind stream is a continuum of instants that are intrinsically distinct and that, in addition, the continuity, which of course implies past and future instants, is itself a single reality. And this, they say, will save their position.

(2) An answer to this objection

Chandrakirti's reply to this is that it is impossible to show that distinct and separate instants come together to form a single continuum. It is in fact unacceptable to say that separate items, occurring in a temporal sequence of past and future, constitute a single, undivided continuity. **61**   Just as the specific characters of two people, Maitreya and Upagupta, cannot be ascribed to a single mind (being two separate and distinct persons), the same applies to other phenomena that are also different from each other according to their peculiar characteristics. They too are unable to make a single continuum, for they are just as separate, by virtue of their specific features.

(b) A refutation of the contention that inert objects manifest through the ripening of habitual propensities left latent in the consciousness
(i) The Chittamatra theory

62   The Chittamatrins say that a visual consciousness occurring in a precedent moment deposits in the alaya the potential (or tendency) for the manifestation of a subsequent moment of visual consciousness. As soon as this potential ripens, the visual consciousness occurs. The seamless, uninterrupted manifestation of these instants of potential (on which the arising of the visual consciousness is based) is what ordinary people, victims of ignorance, call the material* visual power. But in reality, there is no visual sense power distinct from consciousness. The same applies also for all the other material sense organs, of hearing and so forth.   **63**   Ordinary people understand that perceptions of the five objects of sense (forms, sounds, and so on) arise through the operation of the five sense organs. They fail to realize that there are no extramental objects—patches of color, for instance. Whatever appears does so through the ripening of the corresponding seed or propensity within the beginningless continuum of consciousness. The Chittamatrins say, therefore, that what ordinary people take to be an outside world is in fact the mind's projection.   **64**   This, they say, can be illustrated by the process of dreaming. The things seen in dreams are not extramental objects. On the contrary, it is when the potential for the respective experience ripens that the corresponding consciousness manifests in due form, sound and so forth. Exactly the same thing happens in the waking state: there are no outer phenomena; there is only the mind.

> (ii) *A refutation of this theory*
>   A. The refutation itself
>   1. A refutation showing the theory's absurd consequence to the effect that if it is the mind manifesting in the aspect of an outer object (whereas there is no outer object), it follows that, while awake, the blind should also see

65   The Madhyamikas reject this notion as false. If it is true that, in the waking state, the mental cognition of something—the color blue, for example—can manifest from its own propensity, as it does when one is dreaming (that is, in the complete absence of a functioning sense power), how is it that a blind man, even when awake and lacking the visual sense power, cannot see like someone who is not blind? Both the dreaming man and the waking blind man are on a level, in that both are deprived of a functioning sense power. For indeed, if an inherently existent consciousness can be produced in the absence of outer

---

* *gzugs can.*

objects, the very distinction between the dreaming and waking states is abolished.

In reply to this, the Chittamatrins will say that the reason a waking blind man does not see things (as a dreamer might) is not due to the absence of the sense power, but because the potential for the mental consciousness (latent in the mind) has not ripened. By contrast, if a dreamer sees something, this is because the potential is ripening in his sleep, while in the waking state (of a blind man) it does not.

To this we would say that if the visual power is in fact the potential and if, when this potential has not yet ripened, nothing appears, the same should apply also in dreams. Nothing should appear, due to the fact there is no visual power present (and therefore no ripening of the potential).

> 2. A refutation of this theory by showing the unwanted
> consequence of claiming that the potential does not ripen
> during the waking state of a blind man. The same should apply
> to the dream state: nothing should appear

66 If the Chittamatrins simply declare, dogmatically and without proof, that the potential of the sixth consciousness ripens in a dream but not in the waking state of a blind man, why should not Chandrakirti simply affirm the opposite, to the effect that just as the potential of the sixth consciousness of a blind man does not ripen while in the waking state, it does not do so either in the case of a man with healthy eyes who is asleep and dreaming?

67 Just as the lack of eyes, in the case of a waking blind man, does not prompt the ripening of the potential for the perception of objects, by the same token, neither in the case of a dreaming man should sleep occasion such a ripening, namely, the experience of seeing things. If, during sleep, and in the absence of a functioning visual sense, the potential for "seeing" forms is able to ripen, there is no reason why the same potential should not ripen in the experience of a blind man during the day. For both men are similar in that neither has a functioning visual sense. If the Chittamatrins say that outer objects only appear due to the unfolding of this potential and have nothing to do with the visual sense, then just as eyelessness in a waking blind man cannot be said to be the cause of his seeing objects, the same applies to a dreaming man for whom sleep has suspended his visual power so that he is as though eyeless: sleep likewise cannot be the cause of the appearance of objects.[136]

Form is, for the Chittamatrins, consciousness appearing as form, and eyesight is nothing but consciousness. This being so, if eyesight and the thing seen are false, while the consciousness alone is true, the form (the object seen) is deceptive both in the dreaming state and in the waking state. Likewise no visual sense is operative, either in the waking state of the blind man or in the sleeping state of the dreamer. Since consciousness is always present, the Chittamatrins say that the functioning of the visual power is suspended by sleep, but the appearance of objects and the consciousness are not impaired.[137]

3. The sense organ, the object, and the sense consciousness are all illusory

As it has just been explained, since neither external objects nor sense powers exist in dreams, there cannot be just consciousness (existing in isolation). And it must be accepted that just as in the waking state, objects (such as forms) and the sense of sight and so on, in the dream state, are the causes of, or the occasion for, the false mental consciousness,[138] namely, the subject.

B. The other arguments adduced to show that phenomena are just manifestations of the mind are equally inconclusive
1. The thesis cannot be logically sustained

68   When it is pointed out that object, sense power, and consciousness are without true existence, the Chittamatrins reply that though the outer object has no real existence, the mind itself does. Consciousness in the waking state is empty of an object in the same way as consciousness in the dream state. They say also that, in the waking state, the object is illusory, precisely insofar as it is an object, just as the object experienced in a dream. And they say too that without a dependent reality, there could be no such thing as samsara and nirvana, for there would be no basis for it; it would be as fictitious as a turtle's feathers. But whatever response they may give to the Madhyamikas, their assertions are for the latter no more than mere hypotheses and are wholly unsubstantiated. They are suppositions (asserted dogmatically) that are yet to be proved. This being so, there can be no further debate with the Chittamatrins.[139]

2. Neither is the thesis supported by scriptures

Furthermore, no passage can be found in the scriptures where the perfect Buddha taught that phenomena (of any kind) are really existent. The *Lankavatara-sutra* says:

> *There are no real existents and there is no mind;*
> *There is no alaya; there are no things.*
> *But childish beings, like the lifeless dead,*
> *Philosophize with empty sophistry.*

The Chittamatrins may well claim that this same sutra teaches that dependent reality is empty of a distinct substance, namely, imputed reality. But it is to be observed that the Buddha said: "O you so greatly learned, emptiness understood as the subtraction of something from something else is indeed a lower kind of emptiness." One cannot say, for instance, that the ox does not exist because it lacks "horseness." How could emptiness mean the absence of something from an inherently existent thing? It is impossible.

The purpose of absolutist reasoning [continued]

In general, when one is establishing emptiness by reasoning, one does not use absolutist arguments to refute what can be disproved by ordinary reasoning operating on the relative level. No normal person believes in the reality of what is commonly held to be purely imaginary (a rabbit's horns, for instance, or the offspring of a barren woman). It is therefore unnecessary, in addition, to prove their ultimate nonexistence or lack of true existence with absolutist arguments. The non-Buddhist misconception of an eternal *prakriti* is to be disproved on the relative level. It can of course be refuted by means of the (absolutist) argument of neither one nor many, although in that case, the refutation is applied on the conventional level.[140] Phenomena, which undeniably manifest on the relative level, are apprehended by ordinary people as really existing by their nature and in a manner corresponding to the way in which they appear. With the help of examples drawn from empirical experience (for instance, the hallucinatory elephant, which looks exactly like a real elephant but does not exist and function like one), absolutist reasoning can validly demonstrate that what appears as really existent, due to the interplay of dependent arising, does not in fact exist in the way that it appears. The very thing that absolutist reasoning does not encounter as resisting analysis—in other words, the very thing that cannot be found or referred to as an object—is precisely the so-called conventional phenomenon. Such phenomena are shown to be unable to withstand absolutist reasoning. They are empty by their nature. They have no ultimate existence and are devoid of reality. In other words, we have a variety of expressions, but they are all synonymous. There is no difference between them, and they all come down to the same thing.

When establishing emptiness, some people may find that it is not sufficient to say that while objects like pots have no existence on the level of ultimate reality or suchness, they exist in empirical experience as a worldly convention. They may feel that it is necessary, when proving emptiness, to say that "the pot is empty not of the pot itself, but only of true existence," in other words, that the pot is not empty of its own nature but of a true existence distinct from it. Nothing, however, is gained by such an assertion. In fact it introduces a defect in the argument which I understand to be as follows.

If an object—the pot—is not empty from its own side, the consequence is that it resists investigation by absolutist reasoning. If it does so, this must mean that it is not empty and not empty of true existence. For absolutist arguments can only show whether phenomena are empty or not, nothing else. If one says that phenomena are not empty, one is necessarily saying that they resist the analysis of absolutist investigation. Otherwise, even though absolutist reasoning does not establish true existence, it would be possible to say that the true existence of phenomena is not empty of true existence, and thus true existence would not be empty of itself.

Of course, some might answer that the pot exists conventionally but that the truly existent pot does not so exist, being empty of itself. But what proof can be put forward to show that the truly existent pot is lacking in conventional existence? If the argument used is that of neither one nor many, and if this argument is used to investigate the pot— mentally dissecting it down to its elementary particles—no "pot" can be found. Why not say, therefore, that the pot is empty of itself? And conversely if the pot is not empty of itself, then our opponents must produce other arguments to refute its true existence, arguments that do not demonstrate its unfindability by dissecting it down to its particles. What is unfindable by absolutist reasoning is precisely that which can be said to be "without true existence," or "empty by its nature," or "nonexistent on the ultimate level." This is discussed in the text *lta ba'i rtsod yig pha lam*. Here it is said that when a phenomenon does not resist analysis, it is a mistake not to say that it is lacking in true existence. For the "lack of true existence" and the "inability to withstand analysis" are one and the same thing. If they do not mean the same thing, the question is whether or not the pot's emptiness of true existence is to be established by the argument of neither one nor many. If it is so established, and if, for our opponent, this argument establishes the pot as something able to withstand analysis, it is incumbent upon our opponent to produce another argument whereby true existence, as something distinct from the pot itself, can be disproved as being itself incapable of withstanding analysis. If a pot were established as resisting analysis, it would be truly existent and it would be impossible for anyone to destroy it. And no one can deny that if the pot is unable to withstand analysis, it is empty by its nature. Ordinary people are deluded in considering that the apprehended pot is really existent. But if one wants to demonstrate the falseness of this apprehension of real existence, what other means is there apart from an analysis that uses absolutist reasoning and that investigates until it is demonstrated that the object is unfindable? If the (deluded) apprehension is not refuted and one maintains that the pot is not empty of pot, what method, what argument can refute the true existence of the pot, separate from the pot itself? In fact, the refutation of such a true existence is wholly unnecessary since no ordinary people apprehend the true existence of the pot as separate from the pot itself. Therefore, I ask you, for whose benefit is it being refuted?

3. The thesis is not supported by credible examples
a. The example of the yogi who, when meditating on the ugliness of objects of desire, perceives them as skeletons, is inadequate as a proof that phenomena are but the manifestation of the mind

69 A yogi who, in accordance with the instructions of his master, has become adept in the meditation on repulsive objects[141] will see the ground covered with skeletons. As an example, this is inadequate as a means of showing that the mind alone exists and that there is no extramental world. For in that situation, all three factors: the object, the sense power, *and* the consciousness itself are all understood to be without origin (that is, without real existence). This concentration does not refer to reality at all; it is just an imaginary figment, for it is taught in the sutras that such a concentration is not an ultimate reality but only a visualization.   **70**   If the situation were otherwise, the skeletons—in other words, the subjective experience of the yogi—would be visible to everyone, just like a theatrical performance, which is generally perceptible to everyone. When the yogi perceives an object as a skeleton, this same object should appear as such to anyone else who looks at it. The vision of the yogi should be as generally available as a patch of color and so forth. These skeletons, however, are not false; through the power of concentration, they do actually appear. This point requires careful analysis.

      b. **The example of the perceptions in other samsaric states is also inadequate as a proof of the Mind Only position**

71   With regard to the root text "Like one who suffers from an eye disease" (and who as a result sees black lines), Chandrakirti comments that black lines are seen due to the influence of an eye disease and that it is sufficient to understand the perceptions of beings in other states of existence in a similar way. As for the meaning of the second line: "A preta will perceive a river as a stream of pus," the *theg bsdus* says:

> *Pretas, stooping beasts, and humankind,*
> *The gods also, perceive a single thing*
> *In different ways according to their realm.*
> *Therefore the thing itself is not considered real.*

Phenomena as validly established by direct sense experience alone

"Water" is perceived by the pretas as pus, by fishes as a dwelling place, by humans as water, and by the gods of the absorption of Infinite Space as space itself. Because phenomena are, in the final analysis, empty, their (present) character cannot be substantiated by rational means. They are merely the deposit of mental habituation.[142] For this reason, the objects of the outer world cannot be validly established logically. This can be illustrated by the fact that fire (which for us is hot) is perceived by certain organisms as cool. This points to the important fact that because outer objects are the deposit of our mental propensities, they cannot be established as independent entities in their own right.

It might be objected that if this were so, it would make havoc of the causal process.[143] To this we would reply, however, that if one examines dependently arising phenomena, which incontrovertibly appear and are validly established by our senses, it will be found that, due to different causal connections, it is perfectly possible for a "single thing" to appear in different ways. Again, this is illustrated by fire, which we can establish validly as being hot, but which to certain organisms might appear as something cool. In the same way, what is deadly poison for us might turn out to be beneficial for a peacock. Thus the individual entity water may also appear in different ways. And likewise, thanks to the power of certain concentrations, it is possible to walk through fire without being burned and by virtue of certain mantras, fire may prove not to be hot, and so forth.[144] Thanks to karma, concentration, mantra, and miraculous powers, a single thing may appear in a variety of ways. Such manifestations are undeniable and are in fact possible precisely because the external object, the thing that seems real, has no true existence on its own account. Through the various gatherings of causes and conditions, it manifests in different ways, and its undeniable appearance may be analyzed according to the three principles of rational examination with regard to its characteristic nature or evidence, efficient function, and dependence.[145]

This being so, whereas in the general run of things, a negative action is the cause of suffering, it might be asked whether negativity could sometimes produce happiness, as for instance in the case of people for whom to inflict harm is a tenet of their religion. And if a negative action can generate happiness, it follows that the law of karma is not incontrovertible. The answer to this is that an evil action, such as killing, is regarded as negative from the standpoint of its efficient function, that is, because it is productive of suffering. Such an action, when fully ripened, produces suffering for the mind (of the agent), and for this reason, even if one believes that it is virtue and that its fruit will be happiness, this will never be the case. In the same way, however much one *tells* oneself that fire is cold, the fire one experiences will not cease to be hot. One could object here that there are times when fire is not hot, as in the case of the organisms mentioned above. Our answer is that if one tries to kill someone and fails to do so, one will not get the fully ripened fruit of suffering, just as if the fire is not lit, one cannot be burned by it. But if, on the other hand, the person is killed, the evil consequence of such an act cannot be averted. Therefore, killing should be recognized as such, and to claim that it gives a good result is simply a wrong view, for a wholesome result can never come from it.

Furthermore, when a Bodhisattva's body is being mutilated, to him the pain is experienced as bliss, whereas he perceives worldly happiness as misery. And whatever other conditions he goes through, his feelings will likewise depend on his mind. It is in the very mind that the feelings of happiness and pleasure, suffering and pain actually occur, and this is what we call being happy or unhappy. Thus pleasure and suffering are never confused. It is in the same way that actions inspired by the three poisons are said to be negative, while those that are performed with an attitude free of these poisons are positive. This is not a matter of convention or of simply considering that certain actions are virtuous and some are unvirtuous. This is why there is never any confusion as to the effects of good and evil actions.[146] The pleasure that one experiences after eating the meat of an animal that one has killed or the satisfaction one feels at the destruction of one's enemy are but fleeting attendant circumstances. But these experiences are not in fact the fully ripened effect of such actions. By contrast, the principle of cause and effect implicit in positive and negative actions is inescapable, while the secondary circumstantial effects depend on the presence of attendant conditions. Since there is no certainty in the way that happiness and suffering occur, the three laws of reasoned investigation (evidence, efficacy, and dependence) cannot stand in isolation, and the fault of their application's being too broad does not arise.

In that case, it might be objected, since reasoning is incapable of providing us with certainty, no confidence should be placed in it. But this does not follow. The argument from evidence or the characteristic nature of things is based on phenomena themselves as they appear due to the coincidence of certain conditions. The argument from efficacy refers to the causes of such phenomena. The argument from dependence refers to their dependence on causes,[147] while the argument of valid proof comprises the logical means whereby the conclusion is correctly established. This is just how it is; it can never be different. Therefore, for as long as an object perceived in common by a multiplicity of observers has for them (by and large) the same features of humidity, color, shape, and so forth, the object is posited as ordinary water, and it can be further assessed (on this basis) as to whether, for example, it is clean or dirty. For human beings, water, pus, and molten metal seem separate and quite distinct entities. For pretas, on the other hand, water appears as pus or molten metal. If, leaving aside the question which of

these different perceptions is true, one says that there is no difference
between them, in that they are mere perceptions arising through habitual propensities, this will involve the faulty conclusion that a commonly observed object—a cow, for instance—is something completely
indeterminate. Finally, if appearances related to our habitual tendencies are examined, all the objects (water and so forth) that one perceives
will be found to be without true existence. From that point of view, all
appearances are indeed the same. But this does not contradict the fact
that the appearing aspect of phenomena can be validly cognized. Whatever a given being perceives, that very thing is undeniably established
for that being. A validly established conventional phenomenon is no
more than this. On the other hand, even given that pretas perceive all
water (that is, all that we perceive as water) as pus on a temporary basis,
the perception of water is not completely out of the question for them.
It is in fact possible.[148] In general, whatever appears on the conventional
level—water, pus, and so on—is indeed undeniably experienced on the
conventional level. Phenomena are validly established by experience.*
They cannot, however, withstand analysis; they have no real existence.

One may object that if phenomena are established by experience, it
follows that the experience of a white conch shell as white and the experience of a white conch shell as yellow are of equal validity.[149] By the
same token, thought and the absence of thought, delusion and the absence of delusion are all on a level. To this we reply that phenomena are
valid or otherwise depending on the stability, or the reverse, of habitual
tendencies.[150] In the final analysis, the fact that external objects have no
real existence, that they are no more than appearances arising according
to habitual tendencies, is demonstrated by the evidence of phenomena.
This is definitely established in the *theg bsdus* in the passage: "Since, with
regard to one thing, there are different mental perceptions . . ." The
texts† in which outer phenomena are spoken of as though they were
truly existent are in agreement with what beings, for the time being, perceive. But these are said to exist in the manner of the horses and oxen
that one might see in a dream. If these same phenomena are examined
again and again, one finds that in the last analysis, phenomena are dependent arisings, that is, dependent on our habitual tendencies. And
this is the essential message of the Buddhist doctrine. As the text says, it
is because of the mind that innumerable worlds, animate and inanimate,

---

* *myong ba'i tshad grub tu song.*
† For example, the texts of Abhidharma.

together with all migrating beings without exception, arise by virtue of the karmic process. If the mind is eliminated, karma is also.

It is the mind, therefore, that binds us to existence. Liberation happens when the mind is free—which shows that it cannot be simply bestowed on us by the gods like Ishvara. It is due to the strength of habit that some beings perceive fire as hot, some perceive it as cool; some, like fire gods, perceive it as a dwelling place; others, like humans, as something that burns. Likewise, at a given moment, the power of mantra can make fire cool or suspend the deadly effects of poison. This is only a temporary, dependently arising situation. But if one investigates deeply, one will find that, as the text says: "The whole array of the universe and beings arises through the action of karma. It is a product of the mind. Karma and defiled emotions are thought." To gain liberation from samsara it is necessary to reverse discursive thought. When this is halted, the ultimate is realized. Now thought is the mind's natural expression, and this is due to its dualistic apprehension of, and clinging to, phenomena in all their variety.

(iii) The concluding summary of the refutation
In brief, it should be understood that just as there are no phenomena, or knowledge objects, as such, neither is the mind that perceives them an inherently existent entity.

(2) A refutation of dependent reality considered as inherently existent
(a) An inherently existent dependent reality is untenable
(i) A brief refutation consisting of an inquiry into whether the theory of dependent reality is justified

72   Let us suppose that there is such a thing as dependent reality, devoid of both subject and object—something existing on the ultimate level and empty of the subject-object duality implicit in perception. Who or what could know of its existence? And it would indeed be completely absurd to claim existence for something that is wholly unknown!

(ii) A detailed explanation of the refutation
   A. A refutation of reflexive awareness as the valid cognition that ascertains the existence of dependent reality
   1. A short refutation

73   The idea of dependent reality experiencing itself is a contradiction; there is no proof for it. This is illustrated by the examples of the sword, lamp, eyes, fingers, and acrobat.* There is nothing aside from it to prove its existence, and to claim that something is self-proving is absurd.

2. A detailed refutation using reasoning
a. Reflexive awareness cannot be established by inference
i. The Chittamatra position

According to the Chittamatrins, the existence of reflexive awareness is proved by the fact that the consciousness, as the subject, has a memory of its own earlier experiences. For in recalling the experience, the object is remembered and the experiencing subject is also recalled.[151] If, in yesterday's experience, the mind were aware only of its object and not aware of itself, there would be no seer of yesterday's mental state, the subject of the experience. In that case, how could today's mind remember that it had such-and-such experience yesterday?[152] The situation is like the experience of seeing one's own eyes, as in a mirror. If my eyes are not seen *by me*, it would be impossible to have the recollection "My eyes are shaped like this."[153] Thus, for the Chittamatrins, the existence of reflexive awareness is proved, and the evidence for it is the recollection of the experiencing subject. The Chittamatrins add to this that the experiencing subject must be either a self-knowing or an other-knowing mind. However, if the experiencing subject were the other-knowing consciousness, we should find ourselves (in any experience of knowing) with an infinite regress, because every moment of consciousness would require a subsequent one to ascertain it. The consequence of this would be that the other-knowing mind could never experience its object. For the earlier moment of consciousness is constantly becoming the object of a later consciousness. Therefore, the Chittamatrins say the mind reflexively observes itself and nothing else.[154]

ii. A refutation of the Chittamatra reasoning
(1) Memory as a proof of reflexive awareness is refuted simply because it is unsubstantiated

In order to prove what in fact remains unproved, namely, an inherently existent reflexive awareness, the Chittamatrins advance their argument of recollection. But this is like trying to prove the impermanence of

---

* The sword cannot cut itself, and so on.

sound by pointing to the actual object of perception.[155] In point of fact, since it is not itself established, memory cannot serve as evidence to prove the inherent existence of reflexive awareness. For it has not been shown that memory is a real, independent entity existing according to its characteristics. In itself, it has no existence. And even in worldly, conventional terms, there is no proof that memory has reflexive awareness as its source. Where there is no fire, there is no smoke: no cause, no effect. And in the present instance, we cannot cite reflexive awareness as a cause of memory, since it is precisely reflexive awareness that we are trying to establish, and therefore it cannot be adduced as evidence.[156] Likewise, the fact that one encounters fire and water does not constitute proof of the existence of the fire crystal and the water crystal; they could just as easily be produced by rain and tinder.[157] Likewise, since memory may (for all we know) arise even in the absence of reflexive awareness, memory is not an unmistaken proof for the existence of reflexive awareness.

> (2) Reflexive awareness is refuted because even if its existence
>   were admitted, memory would be impossible
> (a) The refutation itself
> (i) An explanation of the reasoning employed in the refutation

74   Now, since consciousness does, as a matter of fact, experience both its object and itself, there is of course such a thing as reflexive awareness. But even if we do concede this, it is still incorrect (for them) to say that subsequent memory remembers both the past moment of consciousness and the cognized object. For according to the Chittamatrins, the past experience and the present recollection are different, inherently existent entities. The situation is no different from the fact that the past moments of reflexive awareness and the object-experience in Maitreya's mind cannot be known by Upagupta, who has no experience of Maitreya's former state.[158]

> (ii) This reasoning disposes of all other objections

The reason given, namely, that the moments are alien and extraneous to each other, in fact destroys all claims about the possibility of memory as a distinct, separate entity, such as the assertions of a single continuum and causal relationship.

(b) According to the Prasangika tradition, memory occurs even
    though there is no such thing as inherently existent reflexive
    awareness

75   At this point, the Chittamatrins might well ask how the
Prasangikas explain memory. According to the Prasangika tradition,
the present recollecting consciousness is not considered to be an inherently existent consciousness defined as something extraneous to the
past conscious experience. Therefore, when people recall something
with the thought "I saw it yesterday," the remembered object, now past,
and the recollecting subject are not categorized as extrinsic and alien to
each other. The Prasangikas simply go along with empirical experience.[159] However, if an analysis is made of the recalled object and the experiencing consciousness, both are found to be without true existence.

The next question is whether the Prasangika tradition ascribes a
conventional existence to reflexive awareness and the alaya. When discussing conventional reality, the Prasangikas do not, as a matter of
fact, employ such terms, with the result that they do not affirm their
existence. This is not necessarily to deny the conventional existence of
reflexive awareness and the alaya, for if they were nonexistent (if their
existence were impossible) then, like permanent sound, they would inevitably be disproved in the course of conventional analysis. The
Prasangikas accept, simply on the strength of experience, that the
mind is what knows. It is like a lamp shedding light and a sword cutting. In knowing its object, the mind is self-knowing. This is sufficient
for the Prasangikas—it is enough to observe that the six consciousnesses are aware of objects and time. There is no need for them to talk
about reflexive awareness. It is indeed well established that in order for
it to be seen, the lamplight does not need something else to illuminate
it. On the other hand, it is not (inherently) self-illuminating (there is
no need for it to be self-illuminating) because the darkness does not
darken it. To say that the mind is self-knowing, in this sense, is like
saying that darkness is self-obscuring or that a sword is self-cutting.
All this refers to analysis directed at the ultimate status of things. But
when it comes to the reflexive awareness as a conventional label, the
Prasangikas do not of course refute it. Indeed, it would be impossible
to do so. There is no need to object to what is just a name corresponding to the facts of experience!

b. There is no direct evidence for the existence of reflexive awareness

76   If therefore there is no such thing as reflexive awareness,[160] who or what can know of dependent reality? In any given activity, the agent (for example, a woodcutter), the object (wood), and act itself (the action of cutting) are three distinct items; they are not a single thing. Accordingly, to speak of awareness as self-experiencing is unacceptable. This point is reminiscent of the discussion in which partless particles are shown to have parts. If the particles have no parts, it would be impossible for extended, gross objects, like pots, ever to manifest.[161] In the same way, reflexive awareness[162] cannot arise as knowing subject and the known object. If, on the other hand, these occur, this shows that they are not a single, undifferentiated reality.

B.   Since there is no valid cognition to prove its existence, the existence of dependent reality is untenable

77   Now, the Chittamatrins may persist in their position and insist on the existence of dependent reality, despite the fact that it is said to be by nature unborn and unknown by any form of valid cognition. But how, in that case, could the Chittamatrins deny the existence of a childless woman's son, given that he is on an equal footing with their dependent reality? Chandrakirti asks the Chittamatrins what the childless woman's son has done to upset them. Why should they not apply the same argument to him and say that he exists—that his existence does not need to be proved by valid cognition, that he is conceptually ungraspable and inexpressible and is the object of the wisdom of the Aryas?

(b) Dependent reality cannot be located in either of the two truths

78   Now, if dependent reality is not proved, and not even the slightest degree of existence can be ascribed to it, how can we account for the existence of relative phenomena? If they have no cause, it surely follows that they do not exist. The Chittamatrins say that phenomena are imputations and that the cause of these is dependent reality. But since there is no proof whatever of the existence of dependent reality as a cause, the ultimate truth (which they assert to be the final nature of dependent reality) is undermined. Consequently, conventional reality is also undermined, being left without a cause. Indeed it is because they are so attached to the idea that their dependent reality has substantial, real existence that, by denying on the relative level the causal sequences implicit in such activities as going somewhere or making something, or the experiences of feelings prompted by external objects and so on, the Chittamatrins fly in the face of the facts of ordinary life.

> *(c) Only the system of Nagarjuna supplies a correct understanding of the*
>   *two truths*
> *(i) Only the system of Nagarjuna is the authentic path for those who*
>   *wish for liberation*

79   Aside from the path of the master Nagarjuna, who has distinguished the two truths without error, there is no other means of attaining the peace of nirvana.

> *(ii) A demonstration of this*
>   A. Without a perfect assimilation of the correct teaching on the
>   two truths, liberation is impossible

Great nirvana arises from an unmistaken understanding of the two truths. The proponents of systems other than that of Nagarjuna have an imperfect understanding of the relative and ultimate. Consequently, until they abandon their system and embrace the view of Nagarjuna, they will not attain liberation.

> B. Without a proper and complete understanding of the two
>   truths, a realization of suchness is impossible

80   The correct formulation of the relative truth is the means of realizing the ultimate truth, and conversely, the ultimate truth depends on the understanding of the relative. The ultimate is in fact the true nature of the relative. If there were no relative, the ultimate would be entirely impossible, for the ultimate cannot be reached if the relative is removed. Thus the two are interdependent and can never be dissociated. How then is the ultimate to be realized? As has been explained, a correct understanding of the ultimate truth comes as a result of skillful means (the relative truth). A person who does not understand the difference between the relative truth as a means and the ultimate truth as an end will fall into confusion and wander into error. In Chandrakirti's tradition, dependent arising and emptiness mean the same thing. Whatever appears is empty. It is superfluous to add that it is only "truly existent" phenomena that are empty. The reason for saying this is that some people assert that when one specifies that only ultimately or truly existent phenomena are empty, this implies that phenomena themselves retain something that is not refuted by analytical investigation. But what could possibly remain of an appearance that is empty of all conceptual constructs? Yet to say that there is nothing left does not amount to a nihilistic view. In fact, emptiness and appearance have a single taste; they perfectly coincide. As emptiness is, from the very beginning, the nature of empirical phenomena, it is pointless to ascribe to the latter a separate true existence so that (after this is refuted) they remain untouched. For appearance and emptiness are inseparable. If you remove appearance, you will not have emptiness remaining on one side, for emptiness is the very nature of dependent arising. And if you remove emptiness, appearance becomes impossible; it would be like fire without its heat. What we call the ultimate truth is but the absence of inherent existence in phenomenal appearance; what we call the relative is appearance itself, arising through interdependence. When one clearly understands the mutual inseparability of these two aspects, one will no longer indulge in theoretical assertions. All one does is to set forth the reasoning whereby the true nature of phenomena may be recognized. By contrast, our opponents may think that dependently arising phenomena are refuted by absolutist reasoning; they therefore try to maintain that they have existence on the relative level. But this shows that they have failed to recognize that dependent arising and emptiness are one and the same. They think that emptiness eliminates dependently arising phenomena.

> (d) *The Chittamatra assertion of dependent reality is not the same as the view of the Madhyamikas, who accept ordinary experience as conventional reality*

At this point, the Chittamatrins may say to the Madhyamikas: "You have rejected our position. Now it's our turn to debate with you! Indeed, if you, who are so proud of your skill in defeating others, reject the inherent existence of dependent reality, saying that it cannot be rationally substantiated, we for our part will disprove your own account of relative, empirical phenomena. For your position is equally untenable, given your refutation of both self-production and other-production."[163] To this the Madhyamikas might reply that since the conceived

object of the Chittamatra view—namely, a truly existing dependent reality—is as harmful as poison, they should not be attacked for rejecting
it. To refute it is indeed a worthy and highly meritorious thing to do.

The Chittamatrins complain that the Madhyamikas refrain from
using reasoning to assert even the slightest degree of existence, yet here
they are saying that the common experience of worldly people has a
conventional existence. But this existence, the Chittamatrins say, cannot be logically substantiated, and therefore the Madhyamika claim is
false. The Madhyamikas reply that to say that ordinary experience exists is not the same as saying that it exists inherently. All they mean is
that it exists—occurs—in the perceptions of ordinary people. How is
this comparable to making a theoretical statement about an autonomously existent dependent reality? If the Chittamatrins are able
to disprove empirical experience and show that there is no such thing,
let them debate with ordinary people and inform them that there is no
such thing as an extramental world! If they succeed in bringing them
to the cessation of such empirical extramental events, similar to the experience of the Arhats as they enter into peace, they will certainly have
won the argument!

The Chittamatrins complain that the Madhyamikas say that all existents must be subjected to analysis like that of the reasoning that refutes the four theories of production. On the other hand, the
Madhyamikas also accept (that is, they do not refute) the phenomena
of empirical existence, even though the four arguments just mentioned do not support them. Why, the Chittamatrins ask, do the Madhyamikas not go the whole way and deny the existence of empirical
phenomena? The answer is that to accept phenomena on the level of
common experience is not the same as saying that they truly and completely exist.

81 Unlike the Chittamatrins, who hold that dependent reality is a
real entity, existing autonomously, the Madhyamikas refrain from
making claims even about the relative. What then is their position? It is
that, for the sake of attaining the goal, namely, the realization of suchness, they adopt the perspective of ordinary people. They accept relative
phenomena even though these are without inherent existence—for the
simple reason that they are the data of everyday experience.

All such conventional parlance is not just for the sake of others (that is, non-Prasangikas).[164] The Prasangikas themselves also refer to the empirical data of conventional truth. They speak about the path, fruit, and so forth, thereby subscribing to the common consensus—a consensus that, it should be understood, refers to phenomenal appearance, the product of interdependence and an undeniable part of commonly shared experience. The Prasangika Madhyamikas take phenomena just as they appear, without analyzing them, for in any case common perceptions cannot be negated. That is why it is said that, on the level of empirical experience, Madhyamikas refrain from philosophizing about the nature of phenomena.

82   If, in empirical experience, no relative phenomena occurred (as is the case for the Arhats, who have transcended the remainder of the relative truth—that is, the body—and entered the peace of nirvana, and for whom the aggregates no longer exist), the Madhyamikas would never entertain the notion of phenomena in the worldly sense. But this is not the case. Phenomena do appear. Consequently, the Madhyamikas cannot deny them on the level of common experience.   **83**   The Madhyamikas say that since the Chittamatrins affirm that the facts of ordinary experience do not invalidate their theory, and that, *even on the relative level*, the phenomena of common experience are nonexistent, it is unnecessary for them to adopt a complicated position. They should just tell people that the things they experience in everyday life are nonexistent. Let them debate their view with ordinary people! The Madhyamikas, says Chandrakirti, will follow the victorious party, the stronger of the two!

ii. The meaning of the scriptures that teach Mind Only
(1) The sense of the teaching given in the Dashabhumika-sutra
(a) What the scripture says

The Chittamatrins counter this last statement by saying that the Prasangikas may accept the reality of relative phenomena because they are afraid of being refuted by ordinary people—despite the fact that ordinary people are unable to supply any valid proof. For their part, they adhere to the doctrine of Mind Only because they are afraid of being contradicted by the word of scripture. For indeed, in the *Dashabhumika-sutra*, the Buddha does say: "For so I consider: the three worlds are but the mind."

84 The Madhyamikas respond by saying that the Chittamatrins have misunderstood the real import of the scripture. On the sixth ground, Clearly Manifest, Bodhisattvas are indeed said to be advancing irreversibly toward the dharmadhatu and to fix their attention on the omniscient wisdom of buddhahood. In so doing, they are said to understand that the three worlds of existence are only consciousness or mind. Their understanding thus contradicts the notion of an inherently existent, eternal Self as the creator of the universe. It is therefore said that in the period of postmeditation, such Bodhisattvas understand that the creator of the three worlds is just the mind, the mind alone. If the context of this passage is examined, it will be found that it is only after showing that dependently arising phenomena are devoid of a creator, that suffering is devoid of an experiencer, and that it is through clinging to the notion of an active agent that karma exists (for without an agent, there is no karma), that the Buddha proclaims: "For so I consider: the three worlds are but the mind. The twelve links of existence that were discerned and set forth by the Tathagata are grounded in the mind alone." Consequently, the Prasangikas understand that these words are intended as a (specific) refutation of the idea of an eternal Self as an agent of creation.[165]

(b) Proof through coherence
(i) Demonstration using scripture
A. The sutra that proves this

85 As a means of enhancing the acuity of wise Bodhisattvas, who are able to realize ultimate reality, the Omniscient Buddha stated in the *Lankavatara-sutra* that when he said (in the *Dashabhumika-sutra*) that there is only mind, he did so to counter the false views, enormous like mountains, of those outside the Dharma who believe that there is a personal self existing within their own continua, or who believe in prakriti or some other kind of universal creator. These are his diamond words, and they clarify his intended meaning.

> *The person, the continuum, the aggregates,*
> *Conditions, likewise, and atomic particles,*
> *Prakriti, Ishvara—creators such as these*
> *Are all, I do proclaim, the mind alone.*

He thus declared that all such entities, from the individual self to the divine Ishvara, are not, as is supposed, creators. The creator is the mind alone.

B. A clear explanation of the Buddha's teaching

86   Non-Buddhist teachers of different denominations teach in their respective scriptures the existence of creative principles like the self, prakriti, Ishvara, and so on. But the Conqueror has found no evidence for their existence and therefore has taught that there is no creator of the world other than the mind alone.

(ii) A reasoned proof
A. The words "alone" or "only" do not imply the negation of extramental objects; they indicate only that the mind is the main factor

87   When one speaks of "One who blossomed into Suchness," the reference is to a Buddha (*sangs rgyas*), in other words, to one who "blossoms" (*rgyas*) but is also purified (*sangs*). Even if the first syllable (of *sangs rgyas*) is missing, its meaning is there and has to be explained. In the same way, of the two factors (mind and extramental forms) the mind is the more important; and this is what the Buddha was stressing in the *Dashabhumika-sutra* when he said that the three worlds are the mind only, omitting the qualification "as the main thing." But he is not, in this sutra, negating the reality of form; that is not the sutra's meaning.

B. The proof of the above contention
1. It is a mistake to interpret the words "only" and "alone" as a negation of an extramental world

88   The Chittamatrins claim that the Buddha, in the *Dashabhumika-sutra*, denied the existence of material forms (an external world), for he understood that the three worlds of existence are the stuff of an inherently existent mind. But if that were so, why did he say, in the very same sutra, that mind or consciousness is the product of ignorance and the conditioning factors of karma? He said that due to ignorance, there are the conditioning factors of karma; due to karma there is consciousness, and so on. He taught that consciousness arises through the (twelve) links of interdependent production, whether in forward or reverse order.[166] He never said that consciousness is a thing endowed with independent existence. If this was his meaning, why did he say that when there is ignorance and the conditioning factors of karma, consciousness arises, and that when these two factors are not present, consciousness does not occur? For indeed, something that exists inherently does not arise in dependence on causes and conditions. Our Teacher is free from error; he does not contradict himself. It is therefore certain that the Chittamatra interpretation of the scriptures is inaccurate.

> 2. It makes sense to regard the words "only" and "alone" as
> indicating the mind as the main factor
> a. The mind is the main factor

89   The minds of beings accumulate individual karmas,[167] and these account for the variety of animate life. The mind is thus the principal factor. In addition, there is the common karma that individual minds share and that brings forth different inanimate environments, from the mandala of the wind to the Fair Palace of the Akanishta buddhafield. As the scripture says:

> *As shown by those who, through their karma's power,*
> *Take birth upon the hills of night,*[168]
> *The mind, caught in the hells or higher realms,*
> *Perceives upon the trees sharp blades or precious gems.*

Thus the Knower of the World has said that beings take birth according to the karma they have accumulated. If there is no mind, there is no karma, for the latter depends upon the former.

> b. Nothing is as important as the mind

90   The *Dashabhumika-sutra* does indeed say that there is form (an extramental world). But, unlike the mind, this is not the creator of things. Thus form as creator, separate from the mind, is negated, but the existence of form is not denied.

> (iii) *Conclusion of the reasoned exposition*

91   Ordinary people experience the five aggregates as real. On the other hand, for a yogi who in meditation actualizes the ultimate primordial wisdom, the object of his quest, none of the five aggregates exist.

92 Therefore, if form does not exist, it is a mistake to think that mind exists. Logical reasoning shows that neither is real. Both reasoning and scripture demonstrate that the mind and extramental objects are the same in being equally nonexistent on the ultimate level and equally existent on the relative level. Consequently, if mind is thought to exist, form should not be dismissed as nonexistent, for both occur in empirical experience. In the scriptures too, the Buddha either denied the five aggregates or affirmed them. In the Prajñaparamita sutras, he negated the inherent existence of all five aggregates when he said that form is empty of form and so forth. By contrast, in the Abhidharma he affirmed that all five aggregates exist, saying that they are endowed with specific and general characteristics.

93 The theory of the Chittamatrins flies in the face of the two truths. Their really existent dependent reality is untenable and has been logically disproved. The two truths should therefore be understood correctly, in the manner previously explained. Although on the ultimate level, phenomena are primordially without origination and are unproduced, nevertheless on the conventional level of empirical experience, they are indeed produced.

In this connection, one authority deviates from the specifically Prasangika way of establishing emptiness, which exposes the crucially inappropriate way in which the Svatantrikas, in order to avoid having to refute existence according to characteristics, specify that they refute only true existence. In certain other of his commentaries, he describes himself as a Prasangika and yet does not forsake the Svatantrika method. What could be the reason for such a stance? If the Svatantrika and Prasangika approaches are not clearly distinguished, there are occasions when there appears to be no difference between them; at other times they seem to diverge sharply. There is no way to set one over the other, and the mind is entangled in confusion, owing to which it is difficult for certain knowledge or conviction to arise. On the other hand, once one has understood that the crucial point lies in the examination of whether phenomena are empty *by their nature*, and if in this way one succeeds in proving emptiness, one's understanding will be correct and one will achieve certainty.

When this conviction has been gained, one may ponder the terminology of the texts that establish emptiness, to the effect, for instance, that the two kinds of self are the object of refutation but that conventional phenomena are not disproved. And one will find that in fact there is no conflict; they all come down to the same thing. What then is the point of all this wrangling, rigidly espousing, and debating back and forth tenet systems that are in fact only different ways of saying the same thing? It is all a question of timing, of making different statements appropriate to different moments. On some occasions one proves emptiness with absolutist reasoning; on other occasions, phenomena are established with conventional arguments. And I think it would be a good thing if it were recognized that both these approaches are in fact able to establish the same wisdom.[169]

(2) An explanation of the teaching given in the Lankavatara-sutra
(a) The Lankavatara-sutra belongs to the sutras of expedient meaning

94   It is stated in the *Lankavatara-sutra*:

> *Apparent things, external to the mind, do not exist;*
> *They are the mind, in various forms, appearing to itself.*
> *Bodies, goods, locations—all such things*
> *Are but the mind alone, I do affirm.*

In this sutra the Buddha thus proclaimed that external, nonmental appearances have no existence; it is the mind alone that appears as manifold external appearance. The underlying sense of this teaching is that, because people have a strong attachment to objects, the Buddha, in order to counteract this defilement occasioned by external phenomena, began by declaring provisionally that such things have no existence. This is an expedient teaching, for it is said that teachings expounded in a manner commensurate with the abilities of the hearers are teachings of provisional sense. If beings with a strong attachment to form were taught the profound Prajñaparamita sutras, they would be incapable of implementing them. Therefore, in order to help them overcome their attachment to phenomena, the Buddha negated external forms and spoke, for the time being, as though the mind itself existed.

(b) The definite proof of this
(i) Showing with the Buddha's words and reasoning that the
      Lankavatara-sutra belongs to the sutras of expedient meaning

95   The Buddha's teaching that the mind alone exists is an expedient. This can be demonstrated logically but also by appeal to the Buddha's own words, as recorded even in the *Lankavatara-sutra* itself. For here he says:

> According to the ailments of an ailing man,
> The doctor will apply his doctoring.
> And likewise Buddha, for the sake of living beings,
> Has said indeed that mind alone is true.

Remedies are administered to invalids on an individual basis: not for the doctor's sake, but according to the needs of the patients and the kinds of diseases they are suffering from. In the same way, we should understand from the above quotation that the teaching on "mind only" was not an expression of what the Buddha, in his wisdom, had realized on his own account; it was set forth with reference to the minds of his hearers and what they were capable of understanding. This quotation from the *Lankavatara-sutra* makes it clear, moreover, that other sutras of a similar type, for example, the *Sandhinirmochana-sutra*, in which the doctrine of the three natures and the existence of dependent reality are expounded, also belong to the class of sutras of expedient meaning.

(ii) The implied teaching of the Buddha's words

96   All the Buddhas have said that once the nonexistence of an extramental object of knowledge has been demonstrated, it is an easy matter to disprove the inherent existence of the knowing consciousness. For subject and object exist only in relation to each other. Consequently, when the object of knowledge is seen to be nonexistent, it follows logically that the knowing mind is also disproved. In other words, when there is a realization of the nonexistence of the "known," there will come a realization (either through one's own efforts or through the gentle promptings of others) of the nonexistence also of the "knower." This is a specific method for penetrating the meaning of noself. Accordingly, objects of knowledge were negated first.[170]

(iii) An injunction to the effect that we need to understand which sutras
belong to the expedient meaning and which belong to the ultimate
meaning

97 It is thus that the Buddha's words may have either an expedient or an ultimate meaning. Equipped with an understanding of how he bestowed his teachings, it is important to recognize that the sutras, the subject of which is not ultimate reality, were set forth to lead beings on the path. These are the scriptures of the expedient meaning. By contrast, sutras that discourse about emptiness are scriptures of ultimate meaning.

C. Refutation of production from both self and other
1. Production from both self and other has already been refuted by the foregoing arguments

According to the Jainas, a pot manifests from a ball of clay, the potter's wheel and spindle, water, and the potter himself. Since the clay pot retains the nature of clay and is produced from it, it is self-produced, produced from itself. Insofar as it is produced through the action of the potter and so on (items that are different from the clay), it is other-produced, produced from extraneous causes. The pot is thus produced from both self and other. What is true for outer phenomena is true also of the inner workings of the mind. The individual man Maitreya may be said to comprise nine elements: (1) his life principle, in other words, his personality and his self; (2) inanimate factors such as the sense organs; (3) his virtuous actions that bring forth high birth in samsara and the ultimate goodness of liberation; (4) the reverse of this, namely, his negative actions; (5) his defiled emotions; (6) his vows whereby indiscipline is checked; (7) his happiness; (8) his suffering—all of which originate in (9) his consciousness and are the cause of future conscious states. Given that Maitreya's present incarnation arises on the basis of his previous lives, he is self-produced, for Maitreya and his life are not two different things. But since Maitreya was born from his father and mother, his virtuous and nonvirtuous actions, defiled emotions, and so on, all of which are other than himself, he arises from extraneous causes also; he is other-produced. The Jainas say therefore that their position overcomes the difficulties of self-production and other-production when these are taken in isolation.

98   However, the theory of production from both self and other, propounded by the Jainas, is also untenable because the faults already
shown to be implicit in both kinds of production are equally present in
this new position.

2. Production from both self and other is untenable

There is no such thing as production from both self and other, either
on the empirical level or on the ultimate level. This kind of production
is not established for the simple reason that self-production and other-
production, taken individually, cannot themselves be established. One
sesame seed can produce oil; therefore many sesame seeds can produce
oil also. On the other hand, no grain of sand can produce oil, therefore
many grains are equally incapable of doing so.[171]

D. Refutation of uncaused production
1. The theory of uncaused production

The Charvakas affirm that phenomena arise by themselves, uncaused.[172] But if effects depend on no cause, it follows that anything
can arise at any time from anything, irrespective of suitability either of
time or of cause—for it implies that phenomena arise by themselves
without depending on anything at all.[173]   **99**   The Charvaka theory,
that everything arises uncaused in random spontaneity, involves numerous consequences.

2. Refutation of uncaused production
a. General refutation
i. Refutation of uncaused production by showing that if there are
(uncaused) effects, these should exist constantly
(1) Effects must be constant

It follows that things should occur constantly because, being without
a cause, they are independent of time.

(2) Effects should arise from anything

If there is no such thing as causality, all relationships of dependence
are annihilated and everything should be able to arise from anything.

ii. Refutation by showing that if there were no cause, nothing would
ever exist

*(1) It would be unnecessary to assemble causes in order to achieve
results*

The idea of uncaused production contradicts empirical experience. For
if there were no such thing as causality, people would not go to so
much trouble to assemble a host of different elements in order to obtain certain results. For such elements could not be expected to produce
the desired effects, while effects for their part would arise spontaneously, unprompted.

(2) Absence of cause implies nonexistence

100   If beings do not themselves constitute the cause, there would
in turn be no effect, namely, a world experienced empirically. Phenomena would be like the sky-lotus; they could never be detected;
everything would be beyond experience.[174] Yet, as a matter of fact, the
reverse is true. The world appears bright and clear, and therefore its
appearance should be understood to arise from causes, in the same
way that a consciousness in the aspect of blue arises in connection
with something blue.

> *b. A specific refutation of the doctrine that there is nothing beyond the
> present life*
> *i. There is no evidence to support the skepticism of the Charvakas with
> regard to life after death*

The Charvakas say that there are four realities: earth, air, fire, and
water. These are the cause of all living beings, in the sense that everything—including such things as lotuses and pomegranates, and animals like peacocks and other birds—is but the maturation of these
physical elements. Even the mind, which experiences such phenomena, is itself no more than the product of these same elements. Just
as the admixture of certain substances produces the intoxicating
fermentation of beer, which has the power to overcome with drunk-
enness, in the same way, the last stage in the ripening of the physical
constituents in the developing fetus is consciousness, which is able
to be aware of objects. Consequently, the Charvakas say, empirical
entities, both mental and extramental, arise from the elements
alone. There is no such thing, therefore, as past and future existences.[175] The only reality is what we can see, here and now, in this
present life.

Aside from the experience of our senses,
And this our present being, there is nothing more.
Whate'er the learned have to say,
Good woman, 'tis the false trail of a wolf.

So saying, the Charvakas declare their acceptance only of direct perception, not inference, as a source of valid knowledge. When asked why they do not believe in past and future existences, they reply that such states are not directly perceived by the senses; there is no evidence for them. But the question is this: Is the nonperception of past and future existences a direct perception or not? If they answer positively, we reply that if the nonexistence of past and future lives is directly perceived, it follows that even a nonexistent thing is directly perceived. And since it is directly perceived, it follows also that this nonexistent thing becomes existent.[176] In that case, since nonexistence is now without its contrary, existence also becomes nonexistent. And if there are no existent things and no nonexistent things, the Charvaka beliefs as to the existence of elements and the nonexistence of past and future lives are equally invalidated.[177]

If, on the other hand, the Charvakas reply that the nonexistence of past and future lives is not a matter of direct perception, on what grounds are they able to decide that they do not exist?[178]

101 What reasons, Chandrakirti asks, are given in their texts that lead the Charvakas to think that the earth and the other elements are the causes of sentient life? That which is the object of their own minds, namely, the earth and other elements, cannot be the cause of those same minds. In this present life, when mental obscurations are very dense, one can only perceive gross material objects. It is impossible to cognize extremely subtle objects, such as existences beyond the present life, for these are perceptible only to those gifted with divine sight.[179] This being so, it is a mistake to place one's trust in people whose vision is obscured. They are like people with bad eyes who see hallucinations like black lines and a double moon.

ii. *The falsity of the Charvaka view*
(1) *The understanding of the Charvakas contradicts the ultimate status*
    of things

The Charvakas consider that the world consists of nothing more than the four elements. There is nothing that transmigrates from a previous life into the present life and from this life to a future life. **102** One should be aware, however, that when the Charvakas deny existence beyond the world, they understand the nature of phenomena amiss. Their nihilistic view is based upon and correlated with the physical body of the person. When Chandrakirti says: "It's just as when you say the elements are all that is," he is referring to the fact that the Charvakas' mistaken belief in the true existence of the elements reveals that their view is based on a misunderstanding of the nature of the physical body and other knowledge objects. He means that such an understanding is incompatible with the ultimate status of phenomena.

Why is it wrong to deny existence beyond the world? It is wrong because the nihilistic view that makes such a denial is coordinated with, and based upon, the physical body. The affirmation that there is nothing before or after the present life is rooted in the body and the person possessing it—a view that will persist for as long as one is convinced that there is nothing beyond this world and remains prejudiced against such a possibility.

The Charvakas claim that the elements are truly existent, but they base their assertion on their belief in the reality of the present physical body. This question may be approached in two ways. One concerns an understanding of the nature of the elements; the other refers to the denial of postmortem existence. Given that it is the second point that constitutes the Charvaka thesis, Chandrakirti approaches it by citing the first as an illustration, with the words: "It's just as when you say the elements are all that is." The Charvakas say that it is right to think that the elements exist and that therefore the objection implied by Chandrakirti in the example is not established. On the contrary, however, it *is* established, for the elements are unborn. In the same way, to deny the possibility of omniscience, to propound the existence of things, to say (nihilistically) that there is absolutely nothing, to assert the existence of Ishvara or the indivisible instants of consciousness and of matter, to advocate the theory of *svabhavavada*, the natural existence of things, and all the rest—all such theses should be regarded as incorrect. It is said that, if suitably adapted, stanza 102 refutes them all. For example: "For when you say there is no perfect buddhahood, the nature of phenomena you understand amiss. Your view is based upon, coordinated with, the body you possess. It's just as when you say the elements are all that is."

It may be objected that we too are vulnerable to the same kind of consequence. But this is not true since no example can be cited and used against us. Once again, we can adapt the root verse to our own purposes and say: "For when we say that there are past and future lives, our understanding of the nature of phenomena is correct. Our view is based upon, and correlated with, the body we possess. It's just as when we say the self does not exist." Likewise, we can say: "When we say that there is omniscience, our understanding of the nature of phenomena is correct. Our view is based upon, and correlated with, the body we possess. It's just as when we say the self does not exist." And similarly for all phenomena.

In their negation of future lives, the Charvakas have a wrong idea of the nature of phenomena. They believe that future lives are nonexistent, and the basis of their nihilistic view is this body, which they take to be truly existent like the rest of the surrounding world. Focusing on their present body as their referent, they say that this same body does not survive death and that these elements are all that there is. For, they observe, the elements exist in the present and nowhere else. By contrast, our assertion of postmortem existence is of a wholly different order.[180] On the other hand, the Charvakas' assertion that the nonexistent elements exist is based on a wrong appraisal; the same is true when they deny that there is anything after death. The Charvakas are mistaken in their understanding of the nature of phenomena, for their nihilistic view is based upon, and coordinated with, the body.

Since it is correct to deny the existence of the nonexistent self, it follows that the Buddhists who believe that there are lives after death are not mistaken, because their view that the self is nonexistent is based upon, and is also coordinated with, the body. Furthermore, it follows that the Charvakas' appraisal of knowledge objects is not a correct view, because it is the mind that is the basis of the eternalist or nihilist view. Similarly, when the followers of Ishvara affirm the reality of phenomena, they misunderstand the nature of knowledge objects, and so on.

(2) Disposal of the objection regarding the example used

103 As already explained, the elements are without inherent existence. This was demonstrated, in a general manner, in the course of the foregoing discussion about production (from self, from other, from both, and from no cause). In view of this, how could true existence be ascribed to the elements?

(iii) Conclusion: the general message implied by the refutation of the four kinds of production

104   If phenomena exist inherently, they must be produced through one or other of the four ways. But since there is no such production, phenomena are not produced. They do not come into being out of themselves, from something other than themselves, nor from a combination of these terms, nor do they arise independently of causes. Therefore phenomena have no intrinsic existence.

(b) Replies to the objections against the refutation of the four theories of production

(i) The reply to the objection that if phenomena lack inherent existence by their very nature, this should be evident to everyone

A. The cause or reason why the nature of phenomena is not perceived

1. Why it is not perceived

Given that the absence of inherent existence is the very nature of phenomena, some people will ask: "How can the nature of phenomena be imperceptible, if we directly perceive things like color, which are supposedly unproduced?" The answer to this is that features such as the color blue are only perceived by those whose minds are clouded by ignorance. These things in fact have no intrinsic existence, and those who are free of ignorance do not perceive them as such. By contrast, the experience of ordinary people is thickly obscured by ignorance, like the sky overcast by black rain clouds. Ignorance veils the nature of phenomena, which are, as a result, misperceived as though they existed inherently.

2. An illustration of this point

105   Some people, due to a defect of sight, have the impression of black lines before their eyes, or else they see double (two moons, for example, instead of one). Others may perceive illusory objects caused, for instance, by the iridescence of a peacock's plumage or by swarming bees, although they are not really there.[181] In the same way, to the untutored perception of ordinary people, and on account of their ignorance, the actual nature of existence is not evident. What appears to them instead is wholly unreal: such things as colors and the whole variety of compounded phenomena.

B. Showing that even this cause, namely, ignorance, is without inherent existence

Now, it may be thought that the phenomena of outer and inner experience arise from a cause, namely, the ignorance just referred to. But this is not so.   **106**   To think that it is in dependence on ignorance that conditioning karma arises, and that if there were no ignorance there would be no karma, is undoubtedly nothing but a delusion of the uninformed (who believe that this factor, ignorance, is real and must be eliminated).

It is because of our ignorance that we fail to perceive the *nature* of phenomena, and this nature becomes evident precisely when ignorance is dispelled. As an everyday illustration of this, the visual perception of hallucinations indicates a malfunctioning of the eyes, as in the case of cataracts, and is regarded as something to be rectified. Similarly, the Shravakas and Pratyekabuddhas think that if there is ignorance there is karma and that if ignorance is removed, karma will also cease. Ignorance is therefore regarded as a real entity to be destroyed. This view, however, betrays an imperfect understanding of the true nature of phenomena. Those who are expert in the Madhyamika* understand the Buddha's words "Because there is ignorance there are conditioning factors" to mean that conditioning factors are without inherent existence, and this they regard as the meaning of dependent arising. The sunlight of their accurate understanding completely dispels the stygian gloom of ignorance. They do not accumulate the conditioning factors of karma and are thus freed from samsara. The Madhyamikas have fully assimilated the doctrine of emptiness, in which there is nothing to refute and nothing to assert. For they understand that, in the very moment in which deluded appearances manifest—as the result of their cause, namely, ignorance—these same phenomena are without inherent existence. This is liberation. This is why the root verse says that they do not consider that the cause of appearance is something to be eliminated. The sunlight of their

---

* *mkhas pa dbu ma pa.*

intelligence gives a complete view of the ultimate status of things and dispels the thick darkness implied in the assumption of true existence. Those who are wise realize emptiness. They understand that all things—cause and effect, defilements to be abandoned, and also the antidotes to these same defilements—are empty of inherent existence. It is thus that the wise gain freedom. One should not understand that the attainment of liberation comes through the exhaustion of ignorance.

(ii) **An answer to the objection that if there were no ground of appearance, it would follow that nothing could be perceived on the conventional level**
　A. The objection itself
107　The objection runs as follows. If forms and other phenomena have no real existence in an ultimate sense, they are like the son of a childless woman: it is impossible for them to have existence on the conventional level. Therefore (because they appear), phenomena must have real, inherent existence.

　B. A reply to this objection
　1. Examples demonstrating that the objection carries no weight
　a. Exposition
108　Our reply to this is that when a person's eyes are not functioning normally, because of some malady or owing to the effect of hallucinogenic substances and so forth, they may perceive things like black lines, elephants, and so forth. These are figments, on the same level as a barren woman's child in being equally unborn. So, if it is impossible for something unborn to appear, the proponents of real existence should now be able to disprove those who are perceiving the nonexistent lines. They should ask them why, if they can see the unborn black lines, they cannot also see the rabbit's horns and the barren woman's son. Having done so, they should apply the same procedure to the eye disease of ignorance and prove wrong those the eyes of whose minds are similarly infected. The opponent may argue that what does not exist cannot appear. Our reply is that even though phenomena have no ultimate existence, it is still logically possible for them to appear. This can be seen in the example of the black lines and so forth. Although they are like the barren woman's son in being nonexistent, the fact is that while the barren woman's son is not perceived, the black lines are.

Consequently, it cannot be said that to be unborn or nonexistent precludes appearance, for some phenomena are perceived even though
they have no origin (existence).[182]

There is a further possible objection from the proponents of true existence or those who tend to this position. If, they may say, one realizes
that phenomena cannot be "found" and are beyond acceptance and rejection,[183] how is it possible to practice generosity with a view to helping others and so on? After all, if one is to practice virtue and avoid
evil, a distinction is necessarily made between what is to be undertaken
and what is to be avoided.

Such a question indicates a complete misunderstanding of the ultimate reality of phenomena. This is the state of great equality, in which
no thing is found—a state beyond acceptance and rejection. But why
should an understanding of this involve the denial of phenomena that
appear merely on the level of relative truth? Even though samsara and
nirvana, acceptance and rejection, adopting and repudiating, appear as
distinct phenomena, their nonreferential ultimate reality, which belongs to neither extreme of samsara nor nirvana, never stirs from the
state of perfect equality. If one realizes this ultimate reality, one (automatically) experiences, like the Buddhas and Bodhisattvas, a great compassion for all who have not realized it. Although one correctly
discriminates between the practice of virtue and the avoidance of evil,
there is no need to consider that what is to be accepted or repudiated
(or indeed any other point of reference) has an ultimate existence. On
the other hand, the fact that none of this is found to exist on the ultimate level does not mean that it is equally nonexistent on the conventional level. These two levels are not antagonistic. What is not found on
the ultimate level is, precisely, conventional phenomena. Without such
conventionalities, there would be no such thing as ultimate reality.
Thus for those who realize that a phenomenon and its ultimate nature
are not in contradiction, there manifests a love and compassion that
are nonreferential. This is the authentic path of the Mahayana. If the
absence of reference on the ultimate level and the presence of reference
on the conventional level were abolished in favor of one level only (that
is, if one or other of the twin aspects were missing), the two truths, distinguished on the basis of phenomena and their nature, would cease.
Either the two levels would be equally observable, in which case it
would be impossible for phenomena *not* to be found, with the result

that the ultimate truth would be abolished, or both levels would be equally unobservable, that is, nonexistent, with the result that there would be only the ultimate truth and nothing at all would appear. Thus, even though these two levels do not actually exist as two, they appear as two. This twofold aspect, namely, that the two levels do not exist as two (separate realities) but appear to be so observed, implies no contradiction. This then is how the two truths are differentiated. This profound doctrine, arising from the wisdom of the Buddha, is the perfect and genuine path. It is unknown in non-Buddhist teachings.

Beginners, in the early stages, who think of the two truths as contradictory and who are unable to refute phenomena on the ultimate level, consider that the refutation of the true existence of things is the ultimate and absolute truth. This is where their reasoning brings them. Finding that the existence and the nonexistence of phenomena completely diverge, they conclude that ultimate reality is a nonaffirming negative, which negates a particular instance of unreality, namely, the true existence of phenomena. They exclusively refute this true existence of things (something that is not found in either of the two truths) and claim that it is only correct to say that "a pot exists on the conventional level but does not exist on the ultimate level." However, the following question may be asked of them. If a pot has no ultimate existence, it can also be described as unfound in an ultimate sense. In that case, the absence of a separate true existence is not equivalent to nonexistence on the ultimate level. What therefore is one to do with this true existence of a pot, separate from the pot itself? Since it is nonexistent on the conventional level, there is no finding it. And since it is asserted that no conventional existents can be said to be unfindable, but rather that they can be found or observed, it must also be admitted that on the ultimate level the pot is found. What is found on the conventional level is indeed established for all sides of the debate, but at the present moment, we are investigating the ultimate. Therefore our opponents are obliged to assert that there is a pot found on the ultimate level. Thus the pot of our opponents really does have an ultimate existence. Since the true existence of a pot belongs to neither of the two truths, once the truly existent pot has been refuted, one is left with a "pot that does not truly exist." An emptiness of this kind, which is an affirming negative, is not at all emptiness as it should be properly understood. Phenomena that are not empty are truly existent. Now emptiness is beyond all attributes, whether of existence or nonexistence. If it is made the object of assertion and reference, it may be referred to as being included in the two truths. Therefore, if the pot is designated as possessing two distinct attributes—meaning, on the one hand, that it has the characteristics of an existing pot and, on the other, that it is empty of true existence (as being a nonexistent pot), such a path is unable to lead one out of attachment to the three worlds. How can one be freed from attachment thereby? How can nonconceptual wisdom arise? How can the perception of dual appearance ever subside? Even if such an emptiness were realized, it would be incapable of producing such qualities.

How could the realization that the yak's horns are empty of rabbit's horns be the same as the profound realization of the absence of contradiction between the two truths, which is indeed the preserve of the Aryas? Ordinary people are perfectly aware that the yak's horns are empty of rabbit's horns. But this is not at all what is meant when it is said that the two truths are not contradictory. How could this even be a matter of doubt?

b. Further explanation
i. The consequence of the earlier objection is that reflections and so forth should not be possible

109   It is possible to see a house in a dream, the vision of a castle in the clouds, a mirage of water, the impression of a man or woman, a face reflected in a mirror; it is possible to hear an echo and see a magical display, even though they are all without origin and therefore nonexistent. They are all the same in being unreal; nevertheless they are perceived even by the proponents of real existence (who believe things exist because they appear). But how is it that they perceive them? It ought not to be possible since, according to their argument, the things in question should be as imperceptible as the child of a barren woman.

ii. This consequence shows that the objection is not conclusive

110   On the ultimate level, reflections and so forth are without origin.[184] But this does not mean that, like the child of a barren woman, they cannot appear on the level of empirical experience. Thus the objection of the opponent carries no weight.

> 2. *There is no contradiction in the fact that phenomena appear*
>   *conventionally without being inherently produced*
> a. *Inherently real production is not included in the two truths*
> i. *The actual teaching about the nonexistence of inherently real*
>   *production*

111 Of its very nature, the child of a barren woman is unproduced
on the ultimate level and also on the conventional level of empirical
experience.[185] The same is true of forms and the rest; they are not inherently produced on either the conventional or the ultimate level.
When one says "of its very nature," one is referring to the nature of
conventionally existent things like pots and phenomena such as production. If this nature were understood to be only the nature of "truly
existent" phenomena, then the example given in the statement "Phenomena are unborn by their nature, like a barren woman's child"
would be inapplicable because such a child is never born and is by definition nonexistent.

It may be objected that, in that case, so-called ultimate truth is a nihilistic blankness, the negation of all conventional experience. For if
the existence of conventional phenomena is not asserted, it is necessarily denied.

Our reply to this is that if, by "the negation of all conventional experience," the opponent means an emptiness that is a pure nonentity
as when wood is burned up in a fire, then this does indeed mean the
end of conventional appearances. But conventional phenomena, such
as pots, regardless of whether they are analyzed, are, by their nature,
empty. Despite the fact that they are empty, these conventional phenomena manifest constantly and without interruption, by virtue of dependent arising. If we now investigate whether or not conventional
phenomena exist *as such*; if we examine them, mentally dissecting, for
example, a pot into its component parts, the neck, belly, and so on,
down to infinitely small particles, nothing is found as an inherently existing thing—either on the level of the pot itself or even on the level of
its parts and particles. Nevertheless, the appearance of the actual pot
does not cease. Thus it is clear that conventional phenomena still appear, even though they are empty of a self-nature. And this appearance
does not contradict, or militate against, the ultimate (empty) condition of these same phenomena. Thus the nature of conventional
phenomena is made clear. But if these conventional appearances, es-

tablished by direct perception, are left completely unrefuted, it follows that when they are examined with absolutist reasoning, one arrives, on the one hand, at an emptiness of an extraneous object of refutation and, on the other, at conventional things that are not refuted by absolutist reasoning—in other words, phenomenal appearances, like pots, which are therefore not empty from their own side. This is like saying that the pot is empty of cloth or that cow's horns are empty of rabbit's horns.[186] To say that the mere juxtaposition of two completely extraneous items (like a black thread and a white thread twisted together in a string) constitutes the united level of emptiness and dependent arising—to explain emptiness in this way—really is an amazing achievement. Not even Nagarjuna and Chandrakirti thought of it! However, meditating in this way will not bring an end to one's clinging to the reality of outer and inner phenomena. It is therefore preferable to go for the meaning of the tenet rather than getting stuck with its literal expression. For it is the meaning that helps one on the path to liberation. But of course, people have the right to think whatever they want!

Even though no Madhyamika will say that it is completely wrong to use the term "truly existent" phenomena or that it is completely wrong to say that the object of refutation is true existence (for on many occasions to speak thus is an aid to understanding), the formulation "A pot is not empty of pot; it is empty of true existence" comes down to saying that conventional phenomena are not empty from their own side; they are empty of true existence, which is extraneous to them. When referring to true existence in a purely nominal fashion, as when one constructs the syllogism "The subject, pot, does not exist truly . . . ," even though one considers that the pot, as the basis of emptiness, is empty of the object of refutation, namely, true existence, the resulting formulation is the same kind of statement as "The rabbit's horns do not exist, because they are not found by valid cognition." Due to the verbal differentiation between subject, probandum, and reason, one is actually confronted with a subject, and this seems to imply that the emptiness in question is extraneous to the subject. This in itself is not a problem.[187] If, however, one interprets this as meaning that the Madhyamika arguments fail to establish that conventional phenomena are empty of *themselves*, a great many important mistakes will ensue, as we have previously shown.

These points are not being mentioned just for the sake of controversy.

People who are really trying to understand emptiness should be aware of their importance. And although I have alluded to it here only in passing, it is a point of crucial importance.

ii. *The scriptures teach the nonexistence of inherently real production*

According to the sutra: "When the Bodhisattva Sarvaviranavishkambhin expounded the Dharma, he exclaimed: 'You, Lord Buddha, have taught that all phenomena are primordially peaceful. They are unborn and naturally nirvana."

112 Thus the perfect Buddha proclaimed that phenomena are primordially peace: naturally unborn and naturally nirvana. There has never been such a thing as inherently existent production.

b. *Although phenomena are by nature unproduced, this does not prevent their appearance*

113 The proponents of real existence, the Vaibhashikas, Sautrantikas, and others, say in their traditions that empirically experienced objects like pots, forests, and so on have no existence in ultimate reality.[188] In a similar vein, the Madhyamikas say that things do not exist on the ultimate level, although they do have empirical existence on the relative level. Thus it does not follow that they are nonexistent in the same way as a barren woman's child, which cannot be perceived. The Vaibhashikas might object to this comparison, saying that in their view, the pot's ground of imputation is the eight kinds of particle[189] and that these exist. To this the Madhyamikas would say that since the appearing pot is manifestly not these eight kinds of particle, these particles have no relevance to the pot itself. And in any case, when these particles are analyzed, they cannot be established as really existing either. But since (the substantialists will again protest) there is a ground or basis of arising, their theory does not accord with the view of the Madhyamikas. Once again, the latter disagree. The substantialists are unable to prove that this ground is really existent, for the reality of the indivisible particle cannot be logically sustained.

With regard to the above, perfect understanding consists in the confidence that emptiness manifests as dependently arising phenomena. It consists in the certainty that (and this is the crucial point) appearance and emptiness are united. This is something that should be strenuously examined.

Existence and nonexistence do not (in this sense) exclude each other. In the case of any given object or base, there is no contradiction in its both being and not being—its existence on the relative level and its nonexistence on the ultimate level. No one can deny that pots and so forth appear or exist on the conventional level. But when these same things are examined with reasoning in order to establish their ultimate status, not even an atom can be found to have intrinsic existence. Again there is no contradiction, and no one can deny what is simply the case by the sheer nature of things. People who assert emptiness, but in a way that shows that they do not understand it in the way just described, believe that it is impossible, without contradiction, to prove that conventional existence and ultimate nonexistence coincide in the same thing. They believe that they are mutually exclusive, that they are opposites and cannot simultaneously occur in the same basis, and that the pot's existence and the pot's (nonexistent) true existence are separate.

Of course, existence and nonexistence, as found by the operation of conventional reasoning, are indeed opposites. A pot exists, for example, whereas the rabbit's horns do not. But this is a wholly different question. By contrast, there is no opposition between the existence of a thing on the conventional level and the nonexistence of the same thing on the ultimate level. Both can be predicated of the same basis without contradiction. If the reverse were true, it would follow that whatever does not exist ultimately does not exist conventionally, and whatever exists conventionally would not be nonexistent ultimately. And if this were the case, reasoning directed at the ultimate would be able to take as its object of refutation—and prove its nonexistence—only what has no existence conventionally, like a rabbit's horns. Aside from that, it would be impossible to demonstrate even one conventionally existent phenomenon as unfindable (nonexistent) on the ultimate level. That being so, the two truths would be in stark opposition to each other.

However, the object that absolutist reasoning proves to be unfindable is the entire aggregate of dependently arising, conventional phenomena, appearing incontrovertibly. Objects like the rabbit's horns or the child of a barren woman, which do not exist on the conventional level, are already disproved by conventional reasoning. Their unreality never needs to be established by reasoning directed at the ultimate. If they were examined from that perspective, nothing new would be demonstrated, which shows that they are not the proper object for an analysis of that kind.

If conventionally existent phenomena, like pots, are investigated using techniques like the argument of neither one nor many, not even an atom is discovered or found to exist. Phenomena are established on the strength of conventional reasoning, which is why no one can prove that they exist, or find them, on the ultimate level. This shows that ultimately they have no existence. On the other hand, though not existing on the ultimate level, their unfailing appearance, dependently arising, on the conventional plane cannot be denied. There is no sort of logic that could possibly prove their nonexistence conventionally or their existence ultimately. No one in the world, not even the gods, can refute this, for it is established by the strength of phenomena themselves. This is not a mere theory, put forward for the sake of controversy. What appears is empty; what is empty appears. And this fact is described as the noncontradictory coincidence of appearance and emptiness.

The notion that phenomena are not empty in themselves but are empty of something that is extraneous to them is no different from the ordinary, everyday understanding of emptiness.[190] But what has this got to do with the experience of the yogi who has realized the ultimate? How could emptiness of something extraneous, as suggested in propositions like "The pot exists and there is no cloth in it" (that is, it is empty of being a cloth) or "The cow's horn exists and there is no rabbit horn in it" be the equivalent of the emptiness of phenomena existing conventionally? The fact that there is a pot and there is no cloth, or the fact that there is a cow's horn and not a rabbit's horn, is entirely and exclusively established by conventional investigation alone. How indeed could the pot's being empty of a cloth be established by an investigation into the ultimate status of phenomena? For such an investigation shows that on the ultimate level, the pot cannot be found at all, and it is precisely this unfindability of the pot that is referred to as its lack of true existence. If the pot is found, it cannot be shown to lack true existence, and, conversely, if the pot's lack of true existence is proved, this should be understood in the sense that the pot itself has no ultimate reality. How could these two instances (the pot that is found and the pot that does not exist truly) be identified as existence and nonexistence on the ultimate level? If true existence is discounted on the relative level and through the operation of relative cognition, of what use is an investigation aimed at the ultimate status, given that the task has been performed by an examination on the conventional level? There is no need for it. And if the absence of true existence cannot be established without an absolutist investigation, and if such an investigation does not succeed in establishing the nonexistence of the pot, it follows that the (truly existent) pot cannot be refuted. On the other hand, if the pot is established as nonexistent, this means that it is empty in an absolute and ultimate sense—how can true existence be negated separately from the pot? Absolutist reasoning finds there is no pot on the ultimate level; neither can it find one on the conventional level. Just as an examination on the conventional level proves that there is no such thing as a rabbit's horns, when an investigation is made by means of absolutist reasoning, all phenomena are shown to be primordially unborn. Being unborn, they are unceasing. And just as they are understood to be forever unoriginated, they are not even found or born on the relative level. For if they were found, they could not be unborn. Consequently, in the postmeditation period, as experienced by a sixth-ground Bodhisattva, phenomena, wherein appearance and emptiness are united, are illusionlike. In ultimate terms, they are like space, beyond the extremes of existence and nonexistence. All conventionally existing phenomena are empty by their nature. Though empty, they nevertheless appear, and thus their appearance and emptiness are indivisibly united. They manifest in the four modes of emptiness.[191] The fact that appearance and emptiness are joined in union is revealed by phenomena themselves. Conventionalities (that is, dependently arising appearances) are shown by absolutist analysis to be empty of intrinsic existence. Conventionally, phenomena themselves, which *appear* to have their own self-nature, are not established by such an analysis. But although on the ultimate level they are without self-nature, if investigation is laid aside and phenomena are left unanalyzed, their appearance is undeniable. It is thus that their emptiness and appearance are shown to coincide.

However, a conventionally existent pot, regarded as not empty of its own self-nature, and a truly existent pot regarded as a separate entity (which does not exist conventionally and of which the pot is empty) are two entirely different things. The latter is empty; the former is not empty. This is quite different from a pot that is "empty but apparent" and that "appears although empty." As an example of the union of appearance and emptiness, the assertion that appearances are not empty by their nature but are empty of an extraneous true existence goes no farther than the mere juxtaposition of the appearance of cow's horns with the emptiness of rabbit's horns! If this were a correct appraisal of the situation, it would be impossible to apply the four modes of emptiness to phenomena like pots. Even if one *could* apply these four modes to a truly existent thing, since a *truly existent thing* is not an actual object, it cannot appear. Therefore, since the truly existent thing is never encountered, its so-called emptiness is actually the extreme of nothingness, in complete isolation from appearance, while the so-called appearance is just appearance by itself separated off from emptiness. This means that phenomena are not *by their nature* beyond existence and nonexistence, with the result that one is forced to rely on an emptiness that is extraneous to them. By the same token, since conventional phenomena do not, by their nature, transcend the extremes of permanence and nothingness, whatever appears falls to the side of permanent existence (eternalism). Once again one is forced to rely on a kind of emptiness that is extraneous to such appearance, but which is expected, nevertheless, to remove the extreme of permanent existence. Emptiness left by itself cannot but fall into the extreme of nothingness (nihilism), with the result that one must inevitably rely on conventional phenomena as being something separate from it. As an account of the absence of conceptual constructs, this is very odd. Just as there is no link between the dead Devadatta and the living Maitreya, how could the emptiness of an extraneous factor be of any relevance to something different from it that is not empty? Some people might say: "Since the pot is by nature without true existence, how could it be other than empty?" Of course, this is all very well. But if, while being without true existence, the pot is not itself empty, a wedge is driven between the lack of true existence and emptiness, and they do not mean the same thing.

(2) **A reasoned demonstration that production is no more than dependent arising**

(a) Since phenomena are not produced in any of the four ways of
    inherently existent production, they are simply dependent arisings

114   First of all, as has already been explained, since phenomena, outer
and inner, are not produced uncaused, nor are they produced through
divine creation nor by evolution through time from atoms, prakriti, purusha, Vishnu, and so forth (since it has been shown that they are produced—inherently—neither from themselves nor from something other
than themselves, nor from both), they arise merely as effects deriving
from causes and conditions.

But how, it may be asked, can one be certain that conditioning factors and so forth arise interdependently, due to ignorance, and that in
dependence on the seed, the shoot manifests? The answer to this is as
follows. Those who believe in substantial reality may, when something
is produced from a cause other than itself, believe that this is a case of
dependent arising. They may think like this, but they misunderstand.[192]
A thing is a dependent arising because it is not produced through any
of the four possible ways. If it were so produced, it would not be a dependent arising. Dependent arising is the complete antithesis and negation of production by any of the four ways. To understand this is of the
highest importance.

No phenomenon is denied or invalidated by the fact of being empty;
it is empty in the very moment of its appearance. If, before investigation,
it is not empty but becomes so only when the investigation is made (like
a pot smashed by a hammer), it would never be possible for a phenomenon to appear. In their appearing phenomena are empty; and in their
emptiness phenomena appear. One should be quite confident of this.

(b) In praise of the argument of dependent arising, which
    vanquishes all false views

115   Since phenomena arise in dependence on conditions, as expressed
in the formula "On this basis, that arises," it is impossible to hold the
false view to the effect that things are produced either from themselves or
from extraneous causes and so on; one cannot assert either existence or
nonexistence, eternalism or nihilism. It is thus that the argument of dependent origination cuts through the webs of incorrect, extreme views.

(3) The result of the analysis
(a) A demonstration of the result of the analysis

(i) The prevention of incorrect conceptions

116   The entertaining of ideas that give credence to the four theories of production is possible because one believes that phenomena have inherent existence. Analysis shows, however, that phenomena do not exist in this manner. When this knowledge is perfectly assimilated, such wrong-headed ideas will no more occur, just as there can be no fire when there is no more wood.

(ii) The halting of thought processes is the outcome of analysis

117   Being ignorant of the real nature of things as explained earlier, ordinary people are trapped in their thoughts, grasping at things as either existent or nonexistent. On the other hand, Aryas, or yogis residing on the grounds of realization, who have completely assimilated the knowledge of ultimate reality, are free from such false ways of thinking. This is how they attain liberation. For when all the objects to which conceptuality clings, as being existent or nonexistent, are disproved, discursive thinking comes to an end. Such, so the sublime scholars have declared in their shastras on the Madhyamika, is the fruit of investigation. It is as when the healing salve is applied to the eyes: distorted vision is rectified.

(b) The need for the analysis that is productive of such a result
(i) One must analyze because the Madhyamika investigation of the ultimate is without error

118   The sublime authors of the shastras on the Madhyamika have made very extensive use of reasoning and analysis. This was not through an addiction to debate or the mere wish to get the better of their opponents. They did so in order to set forth ultimate reality correctly and in a manner such that beings could completely internalize the authentic view and thus gain freedom. They are not to be blamed if the perfect analysis of ultimate reality necessarily demonstrates the hollowness of discordant views, for it is in the nature of things that darkness is dispelled by light.

(ii) Analysis is needful, for it is productive of excellent qualities

When the meaning of the Madhyamika writings has been grasped, this understanding cannot be appropriated as one's *own view* with words like "This is my position." For if this happens, one clings to one's view as supreme* and experiences aversion to contrary opinions. And this thought of attachment and aversion is still a thought that apprehends its referent as being truly existent.[193] When, however, there is the realization that nothing exists inherently, all thought (all ordinary mental activity) comes to an end. How could there be partiality with regard to one's own or another's side? Clinging or partiality is thought, and at this point, it is precisely this that vanishes.

119   Clinging to one's own view and displeasure at the views of others are thoughts that fetter us. And these same thoughts have no inherent existence. When attachment to one's own side and aversion toward that of others has been undermined by reasoned analysis, one quickly comes to the realization of what is "really the case." One comes to a state of freedom, for nothing has been established as "one's own position."

ii. Using reason to disprove the self of persons
Those who wish for liberation must first disprove the personal self by the application of reasoning.

(1) Why is this necessary?
120   Craving and the other defilements, the sufferings of birth, sickness, old age, and death, all arise because of the view of the transitory composite, the belief in "I" and "mine" as inherently existing realities. Having clearly seen this, and having perfectly understood that the belief in "I" is grounded in the personal self (namely, the object of ego-apprehension and clinging), those who wish for liberation must disprove the existence of such a self. For if the self is not disproved, if it is not shown to be inexistent, belief in and clinging to the "I" cannot be dismantled. As long as this conceived object (the self) is considered to be something real, apprehension of and clinging to the "I" will continue to operate. On the other hand, if the self is shown to be nonexistent, ego-apprehension and clinging will naturally subside.

The apprehension of true existence is considered to be a defiled emotion,† as indeed are all other kinds of ignorance. Such a designation, however, does not in itself mean that when a distinction is made between the

---

* *lta ba mchog 'dzin.*
† *nyon mongs.*

cognitive and emotional obscurations, ignorance is to be classified as the latter. True, "the tendency to ignorance"* is designated as defiled emotion, as also are ignorance and unwholesome thought processes. But if, in addition, they are designated as "emotional obscurations," there will be nothing left for the term "cognitive obscurations" to describe. This is why the defiled emotions deriving from the view of the transitory composite (the main factor preventing liberation) are said to be emotional obscurations, while the afflictions deriving from the apprehension of the three conceptual spheres (subject, object, and action) are referred to as cognitive obscurations and are the main factor that impedes omniscience.

(2) A rational demonstration that there is no personal self
(a) Refutation of the belief that the personal self is a concrete entity
(i) A refutation of the belief that the self is different from the
      aggregates
      A. *The self as something different from the aggregates*
According to the theory of the Samkhyas, all knowledge objects are accounted for in terms of twenty-five principles. The original nature, they say, is nonmanifest. The great principle (*mahat* or intellect) and the other six principles (thus making seven all together) constitute "nature as manifest," and the series of sixteen further principles are also manifest. Purusha† (the self) on the other hand is said to be neither the original nature (which is nonmanifest), nor the manifest. Prakriti (the original nature)‡ possesses three attributes or *gunas*. These are: *rajas*, characterized by movement and activity; *tamas*, characterized by inertia and darkness; and *sattva*, characterized by lightness and clarity. When these three attributes are in perfect equilibrium, without one of them being predominant, this constitutes prakriti,[194] the cause of everything. Prakriti is the nature of all things and is immutable. From this nature arises *mahat*, the great principle§ or intellect.[195] From this derive the outer objects of sense and the inner reflection of purusha, which allow the latter to unite with its object. From the great principle arises *ahamkara*, individua-

* *ma rig bag chags kyi sa.*
† *skyes bu (shes rig gi skyes bu).*
‡ *gtso bo.*
§ *chen po.*

tion or "self-sense."* This in turn is threefold (following the gunas): (1) ahamkara that is subject to change (*rajasa*), (2) ahamkara that is luminous (*sattvika*), and (3) ahamkara that is dark (*tamasa*). From the first of these (ahamkara in its rajasa aspect) derive the five subtle or simple elements (*tanmatra*),† such as the principle of form, and from these arise the five gross elements.[196] The five so-called gross elements‡ are said to depend on the subtle or simple elements taken alone, like form, or on their combination.[197] From ahamkara in its luminous (sattvika) aspect manifest the eleven organs of sense: the five of perception, such as sight, and the five motor organs (the voice, hands, legs, anus, and genitals), to which is added the mental organ that shares the nature of the two preceding groups. Ahamkara in its dark or tamasa aspect plays an ancillary role to the other two aspects.[198] To sum up: purusha is neither manifest nor the original nature; prakriti is not manifest but is the original nature; the group of five elements and the eleven organs (sixteen in all) is not the original nature but is manifest; and finally the sevenfold group of ahamkara, the great principle (mahat), and the five subtle elements (tanmatras) partake of the original nature while being at the same time manifest.

Prakriti and purusha are eternal realities. It is said that eternal liberation or *moksha* occurs when the modifications of prakriti subside and purusha remains alone, separate and isolated from objects.

The Samkhya view is very similar to that of a subschool of Chittamatra that denies the reality of the mental image.§ Prakriti, in this case, corresponds to the alaya, while purusha is like the mental consciousness that permeates the expanse of alaya.   **121**   The Tirthikas, that is, the non-Buddhist Samkhyas, consider that the self or purusha, as the experiencer or "consumer" of the manifestations of prakriti (pleasure, pain, and so on), is a permanent entity. It is not, however, the creator of these manifestations. It is itself devoid of gunas, namely, rajas, tamas, and sattva; it is inactive, neither contracting nor extending, and is immobile, for it is all-pervading. Minor variations on this theme of the self have given rise to a whole spectrum of non-Buddhist traditions. The Vaisheshikas, for example, say that the self possesses nine

---

* *nga rgyal.*
† *de tsam lnga.*
‡ *'byung ba lnga.*
§ *sems tsam rnam rdzun pa.*

characteristics, that it is active (expanding and contracting), and that, whereas there is a variety of physical bodies, the self is one.

B. Refutation of the belief that the personal self is something different from the aggregates
1. The self as a permanent entity cannot possibly exist
a. General reasoning disproving the self as a permanent entity

122 The self as propounded by non-Buddhist schools of thought has no existence at all; it is as unborn as a barren woman's child. Being unborn, it cannot of course act as the basis for the innate self-clinging of ordinary experience. Not only does it not constitute the basis for ego-clinging on the ultimate level, it has no existence even on the level of conventional reality. Something unborn is like the child of a childless woman; it does not at all exist. For what has never come into being previously cannot possibly exist here and now. It is impossible to ascribe existence to what has never arisen.

b. This argument defeats all the various schools that say that the self is a permanent entity

123 The characteristics of the self, as expounded in the non-Buddhist treatises of the Vaisheshikas and others (which differ somewhat from those described in Samkhya texts) are disproved by the very argument of "no origin" that they themselves advance. If the basis (in this case the self) has no existence, its characteristics likewise have no existence.

2. The self is not different from the aggregates

124 This is why there can be no self existing separately from the aggregates. If there were, it would be possible to apprehend it independently of the aggregates, whereas in fact this never happens. Indeed, ordinary people do not at all think that their sense of identity is rooted in an unborn self different and separate from the aggregates. For although the notion of "I" occurs to them, as of course it does, they have no knowledge or apprehension of such a self imputed apart from the aggregates. If there were such an unborn self, separate from the aggregates, as the basis of the sense of "I," then ego-clinging, which is the apprehension of self, should occur in reference to it and through knowledge of it. But this is not the case. There is no self so characterized; it is no more than a conceptual figment.

The innate clinging to self, therefore, does not refer to such an imputed entity but simply to the mere sense of "I." For if there is no object, there is no subject. If there is no imputed self separate from the aggregates, there can be no clinging to it—it cannot be clung to. Thus the basis of innate ego-apprehension and clinging is simply the sense of "I," something to which we have grown accustomed from beginningless time and that has always remained an unexamined assumption. And it is clear that such an "I" cannot be described as unborn. **125** Beings who are born as animals and who spend many kalpas in such bodies are quite without the propensities resulting from habituation to the doctrines given in the texts just referred to. Nevertheless, it is clear that even such profoundly nescient beings have self-clinging, though they have never seen (or heard of) such an unborn and permanent self. Therefore, there is no self extraneous to the aggregates.

(ii) A refutation of the belief that the self is identical with the aggregates

A. The belief that the self is identical with the aggregates

The Lord said: "O monks! Those monks or ascetics who refer to themselves, with the thought of 'I,' are in fact referring only to the five aggregates that maintain their existence in the world." One branch of the Sammitiya school interprets the words of the Buddha as meaning that the notion of the personal self has the five aggregates as its referent. Another branch of the same school thinks that the personal self consists of the mind (the mental aggregate) alone. For the Buddha said:

> You are yourselves your own protector;
> Who else is there to be your guardian?
> If you are wise and discipline yourselves
> You will indeed attain to higher birth.

And the sutra says:

> It is well to discipline the mind;
> The mind subdued is harbinger of joy.

Gorampa says that all who believe in a substantially existing personal self are alike in believing that this same self coincides with the referent for the view of the transitory composite (the notion of "I"). However, for those who consider that the personal self enjoys a conceptually imputed existence (that is, up to and including the Svatantrikas), the referent of the notion of "I" and the actual self are not the same. For even though the referent of the view of the transitory composite is the aggregates, the latter are not considered to constitute the personal self.

126 Because the personal self, then, does not exist separate from the aggregates, the Sammitiyas say that the referent for the notion of the self is the aggregates alone. As we have seen, some of the Sammitiyas think that this means all five aggregates, others that only the mind is concerned.

> B. *The refutation of the belief that the personal self is identical with the aggregates*
> 1. *A general refutation*
> a. *A reasoned demonstration that the aggregates cannot be the referent of the notion of "I"*
> i. *A general refutation of the belief that the self and the aggregates are one and the same*

127 The aggregates are fivefold and the mind itself is categorized into six kinds of consciousness. It is also a "multiplicity" in being a stream of conscious instants. If therefore the aggregates and the self were equivalent, the latter would also be a multiplicity. Now, although this consequence cannot apply in the case of a multiplicity that has but a single nature, nevertheless the statement that the self and the aggregates are *one* implies that there is absolutely no difference between them. Therefore, even though this is not what the Sammitiyas start out by saying, and even though there is, ostensibly, nothing wrong in speaking of a single nature with many aspects (provided of course that real existence is not ascribed to them), the fact that the Sammitiyas do regard both the self and the aggregates as really existent forces them to the logical conclusion that self and aggregates are identical and indivisible, and this entails the absurd consequence that there are many selves.

> ii. *A specific refutation demonstrating the contradiction implicit in the belief that the self and the aggregates are identical*

(1) The contradiction implicit in this belief

(a) The refutation itself by showing the unwanted consequences of this belief

(i) The apprehension of the self would not be a mistaken conception

Given that the aggregates have real substantial existence, the self too must be substantial. In that case, it should be possible to see it—just as one can perceive things like colors and so on. The self would not be a simple misconception. On the other hand, the Sammitiyas do not claim an unmistaken reality for the self.

(ii) The self would be a simple nonentity

128 Given, moreover, that the Sammitiyas consider that, at nirvana, the continuity of the aggregates is severed, it would follow that when nirvana is attained, the self too is completely extinguished. But this is not what the Sammitiyas say. On the contrary, they believe that the complete extinction of the self implies a nihilist view.

(iii) It would be pointless to try to accomplish nirvana

If the self and the aggregates are identical in nature, it follows that even before nirvana, the former is as momentary as the latter, arising and disintegrating at every moment. In that case, it would have been absurd of the Buddha to have said: "I remember my past life as Mandhata."

(iv) The karmic principle of cause and effect would be inadmissible

    A. The actual refutation

      1. Performed actions would have no effect

If the self is momentary, arising and disintegrating at every moment, it follows that actions have no agent and can bring forth no results.

      2. One would encounter the effect of actions that one had not performed

And indeed, if such actions did bear fruit, it follows that one could encounter the effects of actions accumulated by entities other than oneself. In other words, the effects of actions could be experienced by one who did not perform them. But, again, this is not what the Sammitiyas believe and is inadmissible.

B. The refutation of an objection

129   The Sammitiyas may respond to this with the claim that they are not at fault because, even though past and future moments are indeed extraneous to each other, in actual fact they constitute a single continuum. To this Chandrakirti retorts that he has already explained the difficulties entailed by continua, as when, for example, he examined the case of Maitreya and Upagupta.

(b) Concluding summary of the refutation

Therefore, the five aggregates taken together, or the mind taken by itself, cannot constitute the personal self.

(2) The tenet that the self is identical with the aggregates contradicts scripture

The foregoing assertion is clear also from the scriptures, because as a matter of fact the Buddha refrained from saying that the world has an end. This refers to the fourteen topics that the Buddha declined to discuss. Four concerned the question of whether or not the world has an end; four concerned the question of whether or not the world is eternal; four were about the existence or nonexistence of the Tathagata after death; and two concerned the question of whether the body and "living being" are the same or different. The questions about the world actually revolve around the question of the self. And the question about the living being also pertains to that of the self. Consequently, if the aggregates constituted the self, the Buddha should definitely have responded, saying that since the aggregates are impermanent, the world too is impermanent, and since the aggregates cease to exist in nirvana, the world has an end, and that the Tathagata is nonexistent after death. The Sammitiyas accept these scriptures, and in addition they assert that the aggregates and so forth are impermanent.

(3) The belief that the self is identical with the aggregates contradicts reason

(a) A refutation by showing the absurd consequence that if the aggregates were the referent of the notion of "I," it would follow that on the realization of no-self, existent phenomena should vanish

(i) The refutation itself

130   It follows from the above-stated belief to the effect that the aggregates, or mind alone, constitute the personal self that, when yogis see that the self has no existence, they necessarily understand that things (that is, their aggregates) are also lacking in existence, for the self and aggregates are identical. This, however, is not what the Sammitiyas assert. Because phenomena appear and are perceived, the Sammitiyas say that they exist. If, however, the referent of the notion of self is not the mere experience of "I," imputed on the basis of the aggregates, but is rather the aggregates *themselves*, there is no alternative but to say that the aggregates are the self. It is important to see this.

(ii) The refutation of an objection

Having applied the term "self" to the aggregates, as being the basis that links the karmic cause with its fruit, one cannot go on to say that in the realization of no-self, the self referred to is only the entity imputed by non-Buddhist philosophies—purusha, for example. One cannot simply apply the word "self" to whatever one wishes. Of course, one might object that when "no-self" is realized, it is only an (imputed) permanent self that is denied. But in that case, given that this self is supposedly permanent, it is evident that it cannot be the same as the mind or aggregates, which are in constant flux. Therefore, the aggregates are not the self.

(b) A refutation by showing the absurd consequence that if the aggregates existed, the self could never be refuted, with the result that one could never overcome the afflictions of craving and so forth

131   According to the Sammitiya tenet, when yogis realize the nonexistence of the permanent self, they understand only that there is no permanent self in the aggregates (form and so forth). They do not, however, realize the ultimate status (emptiness) of these same aggregates. But since attachment arises when form and the other sense objects are experienced, and given that this permanent self is not the experiencer of form, it follows that even when belief in it is eliminated, desire remains. Even though there is no cuckoo on the flower, it is impossible to eliminate the desire to taste the sweet nectar of the flower.[199] Now, the subject of experience is said to be simply the mere

"I"—not some imputed permanent self. Indeed, it is on the assumption that form and so forth exist, and in relation to these same phenomena, that the thought "I" emerges; and, on the basis of this ego-apprehension and clinging, the afflictions of desire and the rest occur. This happens simply because the true nature of form (the object of reference) has not been realized. And for as long as the desirable thing is not averted, the desire for it is not averted either.[200] When tasting the sweetness of honey, no one thinks that he is doing it to make his inner self or purusha happy.

> b. An explanation of what the Buddha meant when he said in the sutra
>   that the aggregates were the referent of the notion of "I"
> i.   The sutra does not assert that the aggregates constitute the self
> (1) A statement of the belief that the sutras teach that the aggregates
>   constitute the self

132   It may be objected that the Buddha himself taught in the sutra that the aggregates are the self. "O monks!" he said, "Those monks or ascetics who refer to themselves with the thought of 'I' are in fact referring only to the five aggregates that maintain their existence in the world." The belief that the aggregates constitute the self is therefore justified.

> (2) A refutation of this assertion
> (a) The sense of the sutra is to be properly discerned from the standpoint
>   of the negation of an imputed, permanent self

The text referred to is in fact refuting the existence of an imputed self extraneous to the aggregates. It does not teach that the aggregates constitute the self. For indeed, other sutras specifically deny that form and so forth are the self.   133   They say that neither form, nor feeling, nor perception, nor conditioning factors, nor even consciousness is the self. In short, this sutra does not teach that the aggregates constitute the self.

> (b) Even if the sutra is interpreted along the lines of the Sammitiya asser-
>   tion, it does not in fact support their view
> (i) If the aggregates were the self, this could only mean the aggregates
>   together, not individually

134   When it is said that the aggregates are the self, all of them together are necessarily intended, and not individual aggregates. The

same thing applies to the word "forest." The entire gathering is intended, not just the individual trees. On the other hand, whereas only individual trees can be said to function, as firewood and so on, a forest has no more than an imputed existence.[201] It does not have a real existence; it cannot be used for firewood or for anything else.

(ii) If the self were the aggregates taken together, this too would contradict the belief of the Sammitiyas
A. How this is so

The Buddha said: "You are your own protector" and so on. But, as we have said, a mere gathering of items has no real existence;[202] it cannot therefore act as a protector, trainer, or witness. Since a gathering cannot experience and lacks real, substantial existence,* the collection of aggregates is not the self.

B. A refutation of the objection that the earlier assertion is not false because the collection of parts and the parts themselves share the same nature
1. A demonstration that this is not consistent with the meaning of the sutras
a. The use of an analogy and the subject of the analogy to disprove the assertion that the mere gathering of the aggregates is the self
####### i. If the mere gathering of the aggregates were the self, it would follow that the mere collection of the chariot's parts would constitute a chariot

The objection may be urged that, because a collection is not different in nature from the collected parts that constitute it, it is permissible to say that one (by which is meant the collection of the five aggregates) is oneself one's own protector and so forth.

135 Chandrakirti answers that if the collection of the parts and the collected parts are identical, it follows that the chariot and its separate, unassembled chariot parts are also the same. Here, he is referring to the parallel, found in the scriptures, between the self and a chariot.

---

* *rdzas su med pa.*

O demon mind of mine, this thought of "I"
Is nothing but the product of imagination.
This conditioned thing is void indeed,
And living beings do not dwell in it.

But just as on the basis of its parts,
One may identify a chariot,
According to convention we may speak
Of beings in dependence on the aggregates.

ii. Just like the chariot referred to in the analogy, the self is
conceptually imputed on the basis of the aggregates; thus the
self is not the mere gathering of the aggregates

It is said in one of the sutras that the self is imputed *in dependence* on
the gathering of the aggregates. This is why the mere gathering of the
aggregates does not, in itself, constitute the self. The self is only a conceptual imputation, drawn up in dependence on them. The relation
between the aggregates and the self resembles the relationship between
the elements and the things arising from them. Because a dependent
arising is such *in relation* to "its parts," it follows that it is not identical
with the gathering of those same parts—if it were, it would mean that
the elements *were* the thing they form.[203]

b. Refutation of an objection

It is possible to object here that although the self is not the mere collection of the aggregates, nevertheless, when these same aggregates are
brought together, a special shape or arrangement is created. Accordingly, it is wrong to deny the presence of the assembled parts (the aggregates) in the whole gathering (the self). Since the gathering includes
everything (the objection continues), it does not, of course, suffice to
say that the gathering (the self) just consists of the aggregates with no
further ado; it consists of their specific arrangement or "shape."

136   In answer to this, Chandrakirti points out that since shape or
arrangement inheres in material forms, such as chariots, it may perhaps be possible to designate the form aggregate as the self, for this
does possess shape. But the same cannot be done to a gathering made
up of the four mental aggregates—which together are called the "name

aggregate," because these (feeling, perception, conditioning factors, and consciousness) are without shape.

  2. A demonstration that the Sammitiya assertion (that the
     gathering of the parts and the parts gathered share the same
     nature) is illogical
  a. The assertion is inherently contradictory

137   There cannot be an identity of the possessor or "grasper" (the self), and the possessed or "grasped at" (the aggregates), because the agent and the object of action would in that case be the same, which is impossible.

  b. Refutation of an objection

It might be objected that even though the agent, or self, does not exist, there is an object of action. But this is untrue. In the absence of an agent, it makes no sense to speak about an action. All such interdependent pairs should be similarly examined.

  ii. *The sutras say that the personal self is an imputation*
  (1) *The sutras say that the self is conceptually imputed in dependence*
       on the aggregates, but not that the self is the aggregates

138   In the *Pitaputrasamagama-sutra*, the Buddha said: "Great King! The individual person is the union of the six elements, the six bases of contact, and the eighteen movements of the mind."[204] It is thus that he unambiguously taught that the self is contingent on the six elements (earth, air, fire, water, space, and consciousness) and on the six bases of sense contact, such as the visual organ.   **139**   He declared too that the phenomena of mind and mental factors are taken as the basis for self-labeling. Consequently, the self is not different from the six elements, but neither does it consist of the six elements, whether individually or all together. The elements and so forth cannot therefore constitute the self.

  (2) *Even the innate apprehension of, and clinging to, the "I" does not*
       seize upon the aggregates as being the self—whether on the general
       level, individually, or collectively

The reason for this is that, from beginningless time, our ego-clinging does not actually refer to the aggregates and the rest (the elements, sense organs, *dhatus*, and so forth), whether generally, individually, or collectively.[205]

(3) Tenets that aim at the realization of the nonexistence of the self without eradicating the referent of innate ego-clinging do not achieve their aim

(a) The teaching itself

140   Some people say that when a yogi realizes the nonexistence of the self, he overthrows only the permanent self.[206] But since a permanent self cannot even be considered as the referent or basis of innate ego-clinging, it is astonishing to be told that merely to realize the nonexistence of such a self is sufficient to uproot inborn ego-clinging, which has been operative from time without beginning. As a matter of fact, the putative eternal, permanent self and innate ego-clinging are completely unconnected.

(b) An example

141   To assert the above is to be like someone who discovers a nest of snakes in the wall of his house and thinks that by telling himself that there are no elephants there, he can overcome his fright as well as remove the danger of the snakes! Alas, those who understand can only laugh at such an idiot. For indeed, snakes and an elephant are completely different objects of reference.

Furthermore, just as ego-clinging cannot be removed simply by knowing that there is no such thing as a permanent self, the same is true of the mere refutation of true existence. If one leaves vivid phenomenal appearances as they are and is content simply with the refutation of their true existence, considered as something extraneous to the phenomena themselves, the innate apprehension of the conceived object, namely, a truly existent pot, is not eradicated. The remaining object, which we continue to think of as a pot, for example, will still act as the basis of desire and aversion, of help and harm. Such an inferior kind of emptiness avails us little. In Nagarjuna's tradition, emptiness is not something to be sought in separation from the dependently arising phenomena that appear to us. When, therefore, it is said that the pot is empty of the pot, this does not mean that the pot does not (or cannot) appear. It means that it is empty *in its very appearing*. When this same pot is examined and analyzed, it disintegrates into a state beyond expression and reference. This is the actual Prasangika tradition. If the pot is not empty of pot, then its intrinsic characteristics—its bulbous shape and so forth—must exist on the conventional level. How could it be otherwise? If these characteristics exist, and if those who propound this theory claim that their existence is different from existence according to their characteristics (of the Svatantrikas), the question is how? It may be answered by saying that these conventional characteristics withstand analysis. But if so, it is incumbent upon those who make this assertion to explain the difference between "existence according to characteristics" and "true existence." The Svatantrikas are substantialists. If those who advocate the above theory claim to be Prasangikas, they must explain how they disprove the phenomenal self, over and above the argument of neither one nor many, which, when examining the ultimate status of phenomena, finds nothing. Let them explain, and we shall (finally) understand how they are superior to the Svatantrikas!

2. *Refutation of additional beliefs concerning the connection between the personal self and the aggregates*
a. *Refutation of three additional beliefs*
i. *Refutation of the idea that the aggregates and the self are related in the manner of a container and its contents*

142   The aggregates do not constitute an inherently existent basis for the self. The reverse is also true: the self is not an inherently existent basis for the aggregates either. If, indeed, the self and aggregates were distinct entities, then it would be admissible to think of them as being related in the manner of a really existent container and its contents, like juniper berries placed on a metal tray. But since they are not different entities, to think that they are so related is just an idle dream.

ii. *Refutation of the idea that the self is the possessor of the aggregates*

143   The self cannot be the possessor of the body, the form aggregate. The self has no existence, and thus it is nonsensical to talk about its possessing something—just as it makes no sense to discuss the physique of a childless woman's son. If the self and aggregates are different entities, the possession of the one by the other resembles the relationship between Devadatta and his cow. If they are not different, they are like Devadatta and his body. But the self and aggregates are neither the same nor different.

b. A concluding recapitulation
i. A summary of the twenty views of the transitory composite

144   The statements "Form is not the 'I'" and " 'I' is not a form possessor,"[207] once again, indicate that the aggregates and the self are not related to each other in the manner of a container and its contents. They mean that the one cannot possess the other. To say then that "there is no 'I' in form" and that "form is not the dwelling place of 'I'" means that the two are mutually dependent. These four points are also to be applied to the other four aggregates, which are also void, so that, all together, there are twenty ways of viewing the self.

ii. These twenty views, inherent in the basic view of the transitory composite, are all conceptual imputations

145   Belief in the self is like a mountain, but it is destroyed by vajra-like wisdom, the realization that the self has no existence. Pulverizing the innate apprehension of, and clinging to, the self or "I," it destroys, so to speak, the twenty views of the imputed self that are like so many peaks rising on the gigantic mountain range of the fundamental view of the transitory composite.[208]

(iii) A refutation of the belief that the self is indescribable—that it cannot be said to be either distinct from the aggregates or identical with them

A. An exposition of the belief that the self is indescribable

146   The Vatsiputriyas, a subschool of the Buddhist Sammitiya school, consider that the self cannot be said to be the same as or different from the aggregates. It cannot be said to be either permanent or impermanent. All such descriptions are, according to them, inadmissible. They say that the person is an existing substance,* and despite the fact that the self cannot be qualified in the ways just mentioned, it nevertheless underpins the karmic process. They say too that this self is known to the six kinds of consciousness and that it is the referent or basis of innate ego-clinging.[209]

But which consciousness, as subject, actually apprehends this self?

---

* *rdzas yod.*

If the self is the object of one or other of the six consciousnesses, it is necessarily the exclusive preserve of that apprehending consciousness. And it must be apprehended, for it cannot be said to exist as object if it is not detected by a conscious subject. In fact, the Vatsiputriyas say that the self is not distinct from the five aggregates and that it is known by all six consciousnesses. With regard to this second point, they say that the self is the object of the manifold of the senses, just like any other physical thing, such as milk, which is tangible at the same time as possessing color, taste, and smell. Some say that the self is the object of the sixth (mental) consciousness alone. But this is incorrect, for the person is never apprehended in its own nature; it is detected only as the object of the six senses.[210]

B. A refutation of the Vatsiputriya position
1. If the self really exists, it is expressible

147   When the mind is said to be other than the body, it is understood to be a distinct "something." In other words, it is not inexpressible. A thing that exists cannot be regarded as inexpressible; on the contrary, it may be variously described. If the self is proved to be an existent entity, it is certainly not inexpressible, for it is an established reality like the mind itself.

2. If the self is inexpressible, it cannot be an existent thing

148   The Vatsiputriyas accept that an object like a pot does not exist as a self-sufficient entity. They therefore say that, aside from describing its ground of labeling (for example, form), it is impossible to say whether the pot is identical with, or different from, this same ground. By the same token, apart from giving a description of the aggregates as the ground of imputation, it is impossible to say whether they are the same as the self or different. This being so, the self should not be regarded as existent in and of itself; it should not be thought of as a real entity.

3. The self of the Vatsiputriyas lacks two properties common to all things; it is therefore not a real entity

149   The Vatsiputriyas do not regard consciousness as something different from itself but as an existing entity different from the other aggregates such as form. Indeed, all things may be considered in these two ways—of identity and difference. But since the self, according to the Vatsiputriyas, is lacking precisely in these two qualities, characteristic of all real things, it cannot be regarded as existent. Something that has no heat cannot be fire.

(b) The self is a mere dependent imputation
(i) Even though the self has no existence according to the sevenfold analysis, it is dependently imputed, just like a chariot
A. *The self is dependently imputed*
1. *There is no self*

150   If one considers the question properly, the basis of ego-clinging is not a substantial entity. It cannot be so because what passes for an individual entity is not real. Again, if one examines the matter, the self is neither different from the aggregates, nor is it the aggregates themselves, whether individually or in combination. The self is not the foundation of (or the container for) the aggregates, nor does the self possess the aggregates. It "exists" only in dependence on them.

2. *Using the example of a chariot to disprove the self*
a. *A general application of the chariot example*

151   The nonexistence of the self can be explained by using the example of a chariot. First of all, (1) the chariot cannot be said to be different from its parts, its wheels and so on, which constitute its ground of labeling, because the chariot does not exist independently from them. A chariot is thus not different from its parts. But neither, on the other hand, is it (2) the same as its parts, for it is not present in them individually. (3) Again, the chariot does not "possess" its parts for the simple reason (given above) that it is neither the same as nor different from them.[211] (4) The chariot is not based on (contained in) its parts, nor (5) are the parts based on it, because the chariot and its parts are not extraneous or alien to each other. (6) The chariot is not the mere collection of its parts, nor (7) is it the shape or arrangement that these assume.

b. *A specific application of the chariot example to the self*
i. *The refutation of the belief that the chariot is the mere collection of its parts*

152   If the mere collection of the parts were the chariot,[212] this same collection (the shaft and so forth) should still be the chariot even after dismantlement. But this is not the case. Even if all the chariot parts are gathered together (in a heap), one would not refer to them as a chariot. An opponent might object that, in view of this, the chariot must consist in the actual arrangement or shape of the "chariot collection." In other words, the chariot does not exist while the parts are not assembled, but when they are assembled, there is a certain resultant shape or configuration and this is the chariot. In answer to this, it must be pointed out that since there is no possessor of the parts, namely, a chariot, it is impossible to speak of "chariot parts." For the shape of the chariot consists of its parts, and the chariot is the possessor of the parts.[213] Therefore since our opponents say that there is no "part possessor,"[214] it makes no sense for them to say that the mere shape, the arrangement, of the collection is the chariot. The word "neither" indicates that the mere gathering of parts is likewise untenable as the chariot.

> ii. *A refutation of the belief that the mere shape of the gathered parts constitutes the chariot*
> (1) *A refutation of the belief that the shape of the individual parts is the chariot*
> (a) *A refutation of the belief that the mere shape of the original parts, prior to the assembly of the chariot, is the chariot*

If it is thought that the chariot is constituted by shape alone, the question is: does this refer to the shape of the parts individually (that is, before assembly), or to the shape of them when gathered? If the first of these alternatives is intended, are we talking about their original shape before they are put together or about a new shape that arises subsequently? **153** If the opponent says that the chariot is in the original shape of the individual parts, it follows that the chariot is present in each and every part, like the wheels, even before the chariot is constructed and becomes recognizable! But, just as there is no chariot present in the separate parts, how can there be a chariot present in them when the parts are assembled?

> (b) *A refutation of the belief that a new configuration of parts—different from the shape of the original parts—is the chariot*

154 If, in the course of assembly, the parts take on a special shape and lose their old configuration, it follows that now, when the chariot is constructed, its parts (wheels and so on) should have a shape different from the one they had previously. Such a transformation would necessarily be perceptible. But since this is not the case,[215] it is unacceptable to say that the mere shape of the parts constitutes the chariot.[216]

(2) The refutation of the belief that only the shape of the assembled parts is the chariot

(a) The refutation itself

155   The opponent may claim that the particular shape of the collected assembly of individual ingredients is the chariot. On the other hand, this same opponent denies real (substantial) existence to collections; and since the chariot shape does not correspond to the shape of its substantially existent parts, juxtaposed in the assembly, but only to the overall arrangement, how is one to explain that the chariot is a perceptible shape based on an unreal, insubstantial collection that is wholly lacking in real existence?[217] A chariot is just an imputation, occurring in dependence on the collection of its parts. It is neither its individual parts nor is it simply their collection. Indeed, if the chariot *were* the particular shape of the assembled parts, then in answer to the question "What is this the shape of?" it is evident that the referent cannot be the chariot's shaft, nails, wheels, spokes, hub, rim, and so on, since the chariot's shape had no previous existence (prior to assembly). Moreover, because the chariot shape had no previous existence in the individual parts but arose simply in dependence on the assemblage of its parts, this shows that the basis of the shape is not just the assemblage, cut off from constituent parts. Finally, the mere shape cannot be the chariot because the chariot's shape is the chariot's attribute. Indeed one speaks of the shape *of* the chariot.

(b) The opponent's belief accepts that empty effects arise from empty causes

(i) The general exposition

156   In his argument, the opponent says that based on an imputed collection, itself devoid of true existence, there arises a shape, which, being also an imputation, has no real existence. It is exactly in this way that, based on a cause that has no real existence (ignorance, let's say, or a seed), effects arise, which themselves are also without reality (conditioning factors deriving from ignorance, and a plant from a seed). The opponent should understand that all phenomena arise in this way. There is no need for a substantial, really existent ground of appearance. Unreal effects arise from unreal causes.

(ii) A more detailed explanation

157   The analysis performed using the example of a chariot demonstrates that it is also inappropriate to identify and name real, substantial forms composed of the eight kinds of particle (pots and so on).[218] It may be objected that a pot has its ground of labeling, its form, and so on. But form is also unproduced; it has no real existence either. For this reason it is also said that the self and things like pots cannot even inhere in the shape or configuration of a material object.

B.   The benefits of understanding that the self is a mere imputation
1.   An explanation using the example of the chariot
a.   This reasoning does not undermine conventional reality but agrees with it
i.   When not subjected to the sevenfold reasoning, the chariot merely exists according to empirical consensus

158   If one uses this sevenfold reasoning to look for and examine phenomena like chariots—with regard to their reality on either the ultimate or relative level—it is impossible to establish their existence. However, for as long as, within the ambit of empirical experience, such things are not subjected to this kind of scrutiny, their existence is certainly imputed in dependence on their constituent parts. And one says, for instance: "This is a chariot."

ii.   Dependently imputed conventional phenomena perform their functions, even though they are without real, inherent existence

159   A chariot thus imputed on the conventional level is possessed of parts, and these in turn are also possessed of parts. People qualify this same chariot as mobile, in reference to its revolving wheels, and as a vehicle, in reference to the function it performs in transporting goods. All such qualifications, qua imputations, are perfectly acceptable. But if the object thus designated as a chariot is investigated from the point of view of its inherent existence, nothing will be found. Consequently, the chariot has no real existence. Even so, one

302 THE WORD OF CHANDRA

should not fly in the face of ordinary empirical experience and deny the existence of a "possessor of parts" existing distinctly from the parts themselves.[219] The so-called self is dependent upon the aggregates, but if, in conventional parlance, one denies that the self is what holds, or is the owner of, the aggregates, and denies that it is distinct from them, one will in practice be at fault, however much one may reason the case. All the conventional realities of empirical experience—parts and wholes, "my mind," and so on—which are dependent on the merely imputed self, should be left as they are. Otherwise it will be impossible to discuss even such commonplace things as a chariot's shape or one's own mind.

> b. *If one understands that the self is a mere imputation, one will easily gain an understanding of ultimate reality*
> i. *The actual benefit of such an understanding—an easy grasp of the ultimate*

160 How can a chariot, shown by the sevenfold analysis to be completely unreal, be said to exist? The yogi finds no trace of it. For if it did exist, it would necessarily exist in one of the seven ways (that the analysis has disproved). And one who realizes that the chariot has no existence will gain an easy understanding of ultimate reality. Still, it is important to understand that in the Madhyamika tradition, it is also said that as long as the chariot's existence is not subjected to investigation, it exists.

> ii. *Dealing with doubts on this matter*

161 There may be some hesitation here; and one might think that even though the collection as a whole (the part possessor) is not real, the parts are, and that although the "chariot" does not exist, its constituents do. But Chandrakirti's answer is that if the chariot does not exist, there is no whole to which the parts belong, and therefore there are no parts either. It is because we think we see a chariot that we perceive its constituents as "chariot parts." But if we do not identify (or recognize) the chariot as such, we will not regard its ingredients as "parts of a chariot." When, as in the example given in the root text, the chariot is burned, its parts disappear. In the same way, when the fires of wisdom burn away the chariot (a whole composed of parts), we will no longer find even its parts. For the chariot and the chariot parts exist in mutual dependence. It is as the proverb says: "Don't look for yarn in a burned cloth!"

2. *The benefits of understanding that the self is a mere imputation, applying the example of a chariot to the self*
a. *The self is in harmony with conventional experience even though it lacks inherent reality*

162   When a chariot is designated in dependence on its wheels and so on, the chariot is the "part possessor," and the wheels and other components are the "parts possessed." In just the same way, when the self is imputed in dependence on the relatively true phenomena of empirical existence—the five aggregates, the sense powers, the six elements, and the six consciousnesses—the self is regarded as the possessor of the aggregates and so forth. It can be said likewise that the five aggregates are the object of possession, while the self is the agent thereof.

b. *The benefits with regard to the realization of ultimate reality*
i. *By understanding that the self is no more than an imputation, one assimilates the view of the path that transcends eternalism and nihilism*

163   Since the self is a mere designation and is not a truly existing entity, it is not stable and immutable (in the sense that it is the same as it was in the past and will remain unmodified in the future). If the self were immutable, it would necessarily be a permanent entity, distinct from the aggregates. This is not the case. On the other hand, since it is not the same as the aggregates, it is not subject to change; it is not produced or destroyed as the aggregates are. Thus the self neither comes into being, nor does it cease to exist. The self is not permanent, nor is it impermanent; it is not both permanent and impermanent, nor is it neither of these things. It is not the same as the aggregates, and so it is not impermanent or mutable; it is not different from the aggregates, and thus it is not permanent or immutable either.

ii. *This understanding causes one to attain the fruit of complete freedom*
(1) *Since the self, as the object of innate ego-clinging, is no more than a designation, it can be eradicated*

164   Since the self is found to be nonexistent when it is subjected to the sevenfold analysis, we might well ask: "Well, what is it that we are clinging to?" The answer is that, fixating on the imagined self (as the basis or ground), beings constantly apprehend and cling to an "I"; and they apprehend as "mine" whatever is connected to it as a property.[220] This self of everyday experience is the manifestation of ignorance; it appears as long as it is not examined. It does not exist in and of itself. And the fact that it is no more than a designation means that it can be dissolved.

(2) When the self is eradicated, the notion of "I" and "mine" will also cease to occur

165   Just as there can be no object of action without an agent, no pot without a potter, in the same way, without the "I" as the possessor, there can be no notion of "mine."

(3) If "I" and "mine" are no more, liberation is possible

Yogis perceive that "I" and "mine" are empty of inherent existence and, by continuously habituating themselves to this by meditation, they free themselves completely from the chains of samsara. Moreover, if one understands that "I" and "mine" have no real existence, one will gain conviction that phenomena are mere conceptual designations. This is something that should be well examined!

(ii) **An adaptation to phenomena in general of the arguments that demonstrate that both the chariot and the self are mere imputations**

A. *The reasoning applied to all "wholes" (pots, cloths, and so on) and their parts*

166   We should understand that all things, designated in dependence on their parts (pots, cloth, bucklers, armies, forests, garlands, trees, houses, inns, carriages—even little carts only big enough to hold three measures of tea)—all are like the chariot, and we should (on the relative level) refrain from analyzing what ordinary people simply designate and reify. For the Buddha said: "People may argue with me, but I do not argue with them." It was in this way that he taught that phenomena exist in empirical experience. He did not argue with it.

167   Whenever mutually dependent objects—whether fragments (like potsherds) and wholes (like pots); qualities, like the color white, and the thing thus qualified, like the conch; passion and its basis, namely, the passionate person; the bulbous, vaselike shape and the vase thus characterized; firewood to be burned and the fire that burns it—when all these things are examined in the same way that a chariot is analyzed according to the sevenfold method, all are found to be non-existent. Nevertheless, when all investigation as to their ultimate status is laid aside, these dependent arisings occur and exist in the empirical experience of the world.

B. *The reasoning that shows that the self is a mere imputation applied to cause and effect*

1. *The actual reasoning*

a. *The refutation consisting of the question whether the cause or effect comes first, assuming that both are inherently existent*

168   If something is seen to produce an effect, it is indeed a productive cause. Conversely, if no effect is produced, there is no producer and no production. On the other hand, if there is a cause, an effect must be produced. However, if cause and effect were to exist in their own right and not in mutual dependence, the question is: What effect arises from what cause, and which of the two is prior? It cannot be the cause, since there would, in that very instant, be no effect in relation to which the cause could be so posited. Therefore it is impossible to establish the cause as existent. On the other hand, the effect cannot come first either, for it would have no cause in relation to which it could be established as an effect.[221]

b. *The refutation consisting of the question whether the effect is produced by being in contact with the cause or otherwise*

169   If, according to the opponent, the cause is said to produce, as an effect, what it touches, the productive cause and the produced effect are not distinct from each other.[222] As long as there is a gap between them, even if only on the atomic level, they are not touching. By contrast, if there is no space between them, they are like the water of a river and the water of the sea: they "share a single power" (they are not different).[223] By contrast, if they are different, they are not in contact—wherefore nothing is achieved. It would be like having the seed and fruit completely separate, one on one side, the other on the other, and there would be no criterion for distinguishing between the proper cause of something and its opposite, that is, something that is not the cause. And when the two sides of a dichotomy (in this case, contact and separation) are refuted, there is no third alternative.

c. A demonstration that if the cause is nonexistent, the effect is likewise—and vice versa

170   Neither of the alternatives (the cause contacting the effect or otherwise) is admissible. Therefore, the cause, as defined by the opponent, cannot be productive of an effect. Thus the so-called effect does not exist. Now if there is no effect, there is no reason for the cause, being now bereft, to be defined as such. Therefore, there is no cause either.

d. This consequence, however, does not apply to the Madhyamika position

For the Madhyamikas, however, neither cause nor effect is considered to be truly existent; they are like illusions. The Madhyamikas are thus unaffected by the difficulty just mentioned. It is rather like the four battalions of a king's army fighting a battle in the palm of a magician's hand.* This would be impossible if they were really existent. A single soldier could not fit on the magician's hand, let alone a whole army! But since they are mere insubstantial apparitions, without true existence, everything fits together, though the hand does not get bigger nor the army smaller. To say that an army cannot fit on a human hand is not an objection. In the same way, as long as phenomena are not analyzed, they do indeed exist in empirical experience.

2. The elimination of the objection that the Madhyamikas are vulnerable to the same unwanted consequence
a. A statement of the objections
i. Objection No. 1: the difficulties involved in the contact or separation of cause and effect apply also to the Madhyamikas

171   At this point, the opponent objects and demands to know how this affects the refutation argued by the Madhyamikas. After all, he says, does this refutation achieve its purpose by making contact with its object or without doing so? Do not the same difficulties mentioned earlier apply also to the Prasangikas? Indeed, the opponent objects, the argument about contact is self-defeating, for it means that the Madhyamikas are unable to refute what they intend.

---

* Or, perhaps, on a television screen.

ii. Objection No. 2: such a consequence does not constitute an authentic argument

172 "What sort of fallacious reasoning is this," the opponent cries, "the consequence of which applies equally to the Madhyamikas (when they say that, if there is no contact between cause and effect, there can be no production)?" For the opponent is adamant that production is possible (without contact). He might argue, for example, that there is no need for a magnet to have contact with a piece of iron. If the latter is placed at an appropriate distance, the magnet will attract it, but not wood or paper. In the same way, even though the eyes are not in direct contact with their object, they can detect the object placed at an appropriate distance. It is thus, the opponent says, that causes can produce their proper effects without touching them. Therefore the Madhyamika denial of the existence of phenomena is absurd and is to be rejected.

iii. Objection No. 3: the Madhyamikas do nothing but attack the position of others without offering any assertion of their own

And finally, the opponent says, the Madhyamikas have nothing to say for themselves. All they do is attack the views of others and try to demolish them.

b. Answers to the objections
i. An answer to the first objection
(1) A short demonstration that the objection applies not to the Madhyamikas but only to their opponents

173 The fault involved in asserting that the refutation negates the object of refutation without touching or being in contact with it is entailed only by those who assert true existence of phenomena and say that they exist inherently. The Madhyamikas, on the other hand, do not hold such a position and are thus untouched by the unwanted consequence. Since, according to Madhyamika teaching, neither the object nor the agent of refutation is accounted a real existent, no *real* refutation takes place, irrespective of whether the agent and object are in contact or otherwise. In one of the sutras, the Buddha was asked: "Do you think that the Unborn can be attained by means of what is born (that is, produced or compounded) or what is not born?" He replied that neither of these two alternatives was valid. "Surely," he said, "there is nothing to attain and no realization." And by this he meant that although both realization and thing attained exist (relatively), they do not do so in and of themselves. Attainment and realization have existence in conventional, empirical experience, just as the four kinds of Shravakas,[224] the Pratyekabuddhas, and Bodhisattvas exist in conventional experience, but they do not exist on the ultimate level.

(2) A detailed, reasoned explanation
(a) An example
(i) A general demonstration using the example of a reflection
174　For instance, during an eclipse, one can see the different shapes of the sun reflected on the water or on a shiny surface. But it would be absurd to ask whether the reflection arises by being in contact with the sun. The reflection occurs *in dependence on* the sun, and merely on the conventional level.

(ii) A particular explanation of the example showing that even though one's countenance reflected in a mirror lacks the reality of one's actual face, the reflection is nonetheless useful as an effective tool for tidying one's appearance
175　When one looks in a mirror, the reflection is not one's real face, but thanks to it one can groom oneself. And in the same way that a reflected image is effective, Madhyamika reasoning has the power to cleanse the face of wisdom, removing the stains of ignorance and unwholesome mental processes. It should be understood that Madhyamika reasoning, unlike nonsensical theorizing as to whether causes are or are not in contact with their effects, brings forth the realization of the goal, the realization that phenomena are without true existence.

(b) Showing the true meaning of the example
176　If the reasoning of the Madhyamikas, adduced to prove a point, had a real existence, and if the probandum itself were also truly existent, objections about causes contacting or not contacting their results would indeed be relevant. But this is not the case, and therefore the opponents are just tiring themselves out by making futile accusations. The vision of someone suffering from cataracts has no validity compared with what a person with healthy eyes can see. This is simply how

it is. This response should be understood to apply also to the examples given of eyes and the magnet.*

> (c) *Concluding summary: whatever the opponents of the Madhyamikas may say, they are unable to invalidate those for whom nothing exists inherently*

177 By using the examples of illusions and dreams and so on, all of which are acceptable to their opponents, Madhyamika thinkers are very effective in the way they can demonstrate, in simple terms, that phenomena have no intrinsic reality. By contrast, no one will have an easy time in convincing the Madhyamikas of the reverse! Ordinary people already put themselves to so much trouble, imprisoned as they are in the cocoon of their own thoughts. Why entangle them even more in webs of philosophical speculation?[225] This is something that one should rather avoid.

> ii. *Answers to the remaining two objections were already explained above*

178 First of all, in addition to the arguments disproving the two kinds of self (for example, the argument concerning the emptiness of phenomena), it is important to grasp the reasoning previously explained, the aim of which is to refute the two further objections (of stanza 172). This is intended as a riposte to those who consider that causes contact their effects or otherwise. But once understood, such reasoning should be laid aside. The purpose of the debate is not merely to engage in polemic. As was said earlier, the language of such arguments entangles people in webs of speculation. Madhyamika reasoning is intended simply as a corrective to the opponent's misunderstanding.

b. The categories of emptiness established by reasoning
i. A short explanation of the categories of emptiness
179 The nonexistence (that is, the lack of inherent existence) of the self was set forth as a means to liberate wandering beings. This nonexistence has two aspects: the nonexistence of the self of phenomena and the nonexistence of the self of the person.

---

* See commentary to stanza 172.

Do the Shravakas realize the no-self of phenomena?

In his autocommentary, Chandrakirti says: "The nonexistence of the personal self was taught for the sake of the Shravakas and Pratyekabuddhas. By contrast, the nonexistence of *both* the phenomenal and the personal self was set forth to enable Bodhisattvas to attain the wisdom of omniscience. It is true that the Shravakas and the Pratyekabuddhas understand dependent arising, the mere conditionedness of phenomena, but they do not meditate on the complete nonexistence of the phenomenal self. They concentrate instead on the complete nonexistence of the personal self as a means to eliminate the emotional afflictions experienced in the three worlds of samsara."

The omniscient Longchen Rabjam speaks to the same effect and in similar terms. The Shravakas and Pratyekabuddhas are also said not to possess a *complete* understanding of the emptiness of the phenomenal self. However, since the emotional afflictions of samsara cannot be eliminated without realizing the nonexistence of the self (for without this there is no way to rid oneself of the innate notion of "I," the transitory composite), and since, in a certain way, there being no difference between the personal no-self and the phenomenal no-self,[226] it is said that the Shravakas and Pratyekabuddhas realize the nonexistence of the phenomenal self. It is rather as when someone drinks a mouthful of seawater, one cannot deny that he is drinking "the sea."[227] Given that this is so, one might wonder why, when the personal no-self is realized, the nonexistence of the self of other phenomena is not recognized also. In fact, this is a matter of proclivity and interest, and it depends also on the completeness of intrinsic and extrinsic conditions, namely, the presence of compassion as well as the availability of a teacher of the Mahayana. The Shravakas and Pratyekabuddhas emphasize only the elimination of emotional defilement. They cleave to their own position and do not strive very much in the vast activities of the Bodhisattvas. Therefore, of necessity, they do not fully realize the nonexistence of the phenomenal self. Their karmic fortune does not, for the time being, allow them to realize it. If the nonexistence of the two kinds of self were necessarily realized simultaneously, it would follow that when the Shravakas realized that a pot was a mere conceptual designation, they would also realize that the indivisible particle and moment of consciousness were but conceptual designations. By the same token, the Chittamatrins would realize that if the percept has no real existence, the same must also apply to the perceiver. And for that matter, why should not the Svatantrikas also realize, by virtue of reasoning directed at the ultimate, that phenomena are lacking in natural existence on their own level in the conventional truth as well?* Furthermore, if emptiness is recognized as a nonaffirming negative, why should one not realize that emptiness coincides with dependently arising phenomena? Indeed, why should one not immediately embrace the Mahayana and become a Prasangika?

If all the conditions of the path are not present, beings remain in samsara for endless kalpas before gaining realization. And even if they do engage correctly in the practice of the Mahayana, realization is still not obtained until measureless kalpas have elapsed. This being so, how is it possible for the Shravakas and Pratyekabuddhas to gain such a realization after so short a period as three lifetimes? It is certain that the Shravakas and Pratyekabuddhas abide for ten thousand kalpas in the expanse of cessation, but at length they enter the Mahayana and definitely realize emptiness.

The nonexistence of the personal self amounts merely to a nonaffirming negative. It is not emptiness of everything (emptiness included). If all is empty, emptiness cannot be understood as a nonaffirming negative, for emptiness is beyond the thirty-two misconceptions.[228] Now, if it is true that the Shravakas and Pratyekabuddhas do not obtain the fruit of their paths without the (full) realization of emptiness, it stands to reason that the Madhyamika must be the common path of all three vehicles. But in that case, the unwanted consequence follows that the Mahayana is not an uncommon path. It also follows that, even if one were to realize the emptiness of the uncontrived mind in the Mantrayana middle way of the *Guhyasamaja*, if this is not associated with compassion and the accumulation of merit, it would correspond to (no more than) the obtention of the fruit of the Shravaka and Pratyekabuddha. What answer can be given to such a contention?

The *Pundarika-sutra* gives the reason (which shows that there is but one single final vehicle) by saying that if one realizes the state of equality of all phenomena, buddhahood is achieved. Both Nagarjuna and Aryadeva have given reasoned demonstrations of this. So the question is: Do the Shravakas and Pratyekabuddhas realize the equality of all phenomena, or do they not? If they do, they are Buddhas. And if they do not realize it, then it is incumbent upon our opponents to explain why they do not realize it. If the ultimate reality of phenomena is their

---

* *rang bzhin gyis ma grub.*

lack of true existence,* how, I ask you, can the realization of this be the same as the realization of the equality of all phenomena? And when ultimate reality—the union or equality of the two truths—is realized, how could the mere fruit of the Shravakas be all that is obtained? If it is possible for some Madhyamikas to become Shravakas, some to become Pratyekabuddhas, and some to gain buddhahood, it follows that the Prajñaparamita is not the extraordinary mother of the Buddhas. If the realization of ultimate reality does not definitely imply that one becomes Buddha, the only possible conclusion is that the extraordinary causes of buddhahood are (no more than) compassion and the accumulation of merit. And it follows that the seven grounds of realization (of the ten posited from the standpoint of absolute bodhichitta) are common also to the Shravakas and the Pratyekabuddhas.

Our opponents may object that this contradicts the fact that the ten grounds are explained as being exclusively the path of Arya Bodhisattvas. Are these grounds, they ask, gained through accumulation of merit or not?

But if they are gained merely through the accumulation of merit, it follows that even though the Shravakas and Pratyekabuddhas realize the equality of all phenomena, they still do not attain enlightenment. To say this, however, contradicts the *Pundarika-sutra*. Furthermore, if the Prajñaparamita, the realization of the evenness of samsara and nirvana, is the extraordinary cause of buddhahood, a nirvana that transcends both extremes of existence and of peace, the question is: Do the Shravakas and Pratyekabuddhas possess it or do they not? If they do, what is the difference between the realization of the Shravakas and that of the Bodhisattvas? Do first-ground Bodhisattvas realize the equality of the existence and peace from the point of view of ultimate reality or don't they? If they do not have this realization, how can they perfectly realize the sixteen kinds of emptiness? As long as one fails to realize that the compounded and uncompounded, samsara and nirvana, are without inherent existence, one cannot realize the sixteen kinds of emptiness.

This is a point of great importance. If, despite realizing the equality of samsara and nirvana, one is drawn, nevertheless, only to the extreme of nirvana,[229] surely this means that one does not have a realization of the equality of all things. If one had such a realization and were still drawn exclusively toward nirvana, the reasoning that establishes that

---

* In the sense of *med dgags* or *rnam grangs pa'i don dam*.

there is only one final vehicle leading to buddhahood, via the realization of evenness, would be overthrown. It would follow too that even if one were to realize the luminosity of the uncontrived nature of the mind (empty of all attributes), together with immutable bliss, one could still fall into the extreme position of the Shravakas and Pratyeka-buddhas. The union of the two truths, the dharmadhatu, the great equality of all things, does not, by its very nature, involve the rejection of samsara. Neither does it abide in the extreme of peace, for it is endowed with enlightened activities. Dharmadhatu is inseparable from great compassion, free of all references. How could someone fall into the extreme of peace, if he or she realized the great equality of all things? If such a thing were possible, the Aryas of the Mahayana and even those who actualize the luminosity of the Mantrayana would be caught in the extreme position of a one-sided nirvana. On the other hand, if the realization of the emptiness of true existence* puts a stop to the extreme of existence, why should not the realization of the union of the two truths destroy the extreme of peace? If one escapes from falling into samsara precisely through the realization that the latter does not exist inherently, how could it be possible to fall into nirvana (a one-sided peace) when one realizes that this same nirvana has no intrinsic reality? If one can still fall into a one-sided peace, it should still be possible to fall into the extreme of samsara. For if, despite having a realization that samsara and nirvana are without inherent existence, one can still fall into nirvana, there is no reason why one should not fall equally into samsara. If the realization that phenomena are empty of inherent existence does not serve to avert the extremes of existence and peace, and if the extreme of peace is averted solely by compassion, then even if one realizes emptiness and is without dismay and fear of samsara, it is still possible to fall into it!

Given also that one does not have compassion without focusing on the attributes of existence and peace, one needs to develop compassion by focusing on the attributes of samsara. This means that when one realizes emptiness, one would be without compassion. In fact the reverse is true: when emptiness is realized, the mind naturally takes delight in the benefit of others. Noble Bodhisattvas, who have realized the ultimate truth, feel no attachment to their bodies or possessions. They have in mind only the welfare of others, and thus they perfect the six paramitas. All this occurs though the realization of ultimate reality on

---

* *rnam grangs pa'i don dam.*

the first and subsequent grounds. Bodhisattvas realize emptiness, and compassion spontaneously arises; it arises effortless by virtue of realizing evenness, the union of the two truths. How indeed could Bodhisattvas ever abandon the welfare of others?

The Buddha further distinguished many different aspects of no-self, in a manner adapted to different types of disciples. **180** How so? When expounding the Prajñaparamita in a detailed and elaborate way, he spoke of sixteen kinds of emptiness, and when teaching in a more concise manner, he spoke of four. All these teachings are said to belong to the Mahayana, for in them the nonexistence of the phenomenal self is perfectly expounded.

ii. A detailed explanation
(1) A detailed categorization into sixteen kinds of emptiness
(a) An explanation of the first group of four kinds of emptiness
(i) Inner emptiness
181 Since the eye has no inherent existence, eye is empty of eye; and the same applies, *mutatis mutandis,* for the ears, nose, tongue, body, and mind.
182 As they have no inherent existence, the six senses, such as sight, are not permanent, ultimately existent entities. Neither are they impermanent, in the sense that, after subsisting for a short while, they disintegrate. They are thus neither permanent nor impermanent. The lack of inherent existence with regard to the six senses is regarded as inner emptiness, or "emptiness within." All six senses are thus empty.

Extraneous true existence [continued]

When it is said that the eye is empty of eye, the thing that is empty is *the eye itself.* But what is it empty of? Again, it is the *eye* of which it is empty. The eye is empty of itself. If it is said that the eye is not empty of eye but is empty of an extraneous attribute such as a true appearance of an eye, this is not at all the meaning of emptiness. As Chandrakirti says in his own autocommentary: "The expression 'The eye is empty of eye' (and so on for all other phenomena) expresses the nature of emptiness. Emptiness does not mean the absence of something from something else, as when one says that the eye is devoid of an inner agent or of the duality of the subject and object of perception."

Nowadays, however, some people are saying: "The eye is not empty of eye; it is empty of true existence." But what does this mean? This so-called true existence can only refer either to the true existence of the eye or to the true existence of something other than the eye. But that something other than the eye does not truly exist *as the eye* is obvious to any normal person. So there is no point in asserting the absence of such a true existence. If there is another eye, superimposed on the actual eye but established as not truly existent, and if this other eye is removed, what are we to say about the remaining "real" eye that is presumably not empty? Our opponents may assert that it is the mere appearance of the eye. But if that is so, we are left with an "eye appearance" that is truly existent! It has the same nature as a truly existent eye. When a chariot is burned, everything disappears (including the appearance of a chariot). In the same way, when the truly existent eye has been removed, its appearance must disappear too. To claim that there is something remaining—a nonempty eye—is ridiculous nonsense. Our opponents may object that if the eye were completely nonexistent, it would be impossible for it to appear. But the fact is that because our opponents do not believe in the union of dependently arising appearance and its self-emptiness, they are obliged to say that in a single eye there is a truly existent eye that is empty and another eye that is not empty. If, therefore, they dismiss the truly existent eye but leave the other eye intact without disproving it, the latter assumes the status of something that truly exists. On the other hand, if the truly existent eye and the "non-truly existent eye" are one and the same, when one is disproved, the other is also. But if they *are* different, of what use is it to disprove only the truly existent eye? Our opponents say that reasoning can never invalidate the consciousness that apprehends the eye. But in that case, the refutation of true existence has absolutely no effect on the "nonempty" eye, namely, the eye's appearance.* If it did, it would of course disprove this same eye as being empty. The eye's emptiness of itself does not at all invalidate the eye's appearance. Indeed the Madhyamika teaching asserts that phenomena, despite being empty, do nevertheless appear. The proponents of the other, utterly foolish, theory are passionately attached to words, but not to their meaning. Their idea is something at which the learned merely smile, rejecting it at first glance, as indeed they should.

---

* That is, the thing that is apprehended.

(ii) Outer emptiness

183 As the nature of form is emptiness, form is empty of form. It is neither permanent nor impermanent, and so on. The same applies to sound, smell, taste, touch, and all mental phenomena.

184 The fact that form and so on are without inherent existence is considered to be emptiness of external phenomena, or "outer emptiness."

(iii) Emptiness both out and in

Since the five inner supports[230] of the five sense organs included within the consciousness are not included within the senses, they are both outside and within. Chandrakirti says in the autocommentary: "The lack of inherent existence of both outer and inner phenomena is 'emptiness both out and in.'"

(iv) Emptiness of emptiness

185 The Buddha, the perfect Sage, has declared that emptiness is the absence of inherent existence in both compounded and noncompounded phenomena. This emptiness is itself regarded as being empty of emptiness.   **186** Emptiness of so-called emptiness is the "emptiness of emptiness." This was taught in order to overcome clinging to the notion that emptiness truly exists. As it was said:

> To vanquish our discursive mind,
> You taught ambrosia of voidness.
> But those who cling to emptiness
> You have reproved.

(b) An explanation of the second group of four kinds of emptiness
(i) Emptiness of immensity

187 Since space, encompassed by the directions east, west, and so on, pervades all beings and all universal world systems, and because it is infinite, as illustrated by the meditation on boundless love, which fills the whole of space on every side, it is a limitless immensity.   **188** The fact that space, in all the ten directions, is empty of itself as such is referred to as the emptiness of immensity. It was set forth in order to counter the Vaibhashika belief in a permanent and really existent space or infinite immensity.

(ii) Emptiness of the ultimate

189 Nirvana is the supreme goal of beings; thus the ultimate objective is cessation beyond suffering, the dharmakaya. The dharmakaya, empty of itself, is emptiness of the ultimate. **190** This was taught in order to dissipate the belief of the Shravakas that cessation, or nirvana, is a really existing phenomenon. Knowing the ultimate to be the dharmakaya, the Buddha taught the emptiness of the ultimate.

(iii) Emptiness of the compounded

191 Since they arise from causes and conditions, the three worlds are certainly said to be compounded. The fact that the three worlds are empty of themselves is said to be emptiness of the compounded.

(iv) Emptiness of the uncompounded

192 Phenomena, which have no arising, no abiding, and no cessation, are uncompounded. The fact that they are empty of themselves is called "emptiness of the uncompounded." This is designed to avert any clinging to emptiness: the belief of the Vaibhashikas and other Shravakas that the cessation of nirvana really exists, and the belief that the uncompounded is permanent.

(c) An explanation of the third group of four kinds of emptiness
(i) Emptiness of "what is beyond extremes"

193 What does not fall into the extremes of eternalism and nihilism is said to be "beyond extremes." The fact that this is empty of itself is said to be emptiness of "what is beyond extreme positions." This kind of emptiness was taught in order to counteract clinging to the Madhyamika path as something real.

(ii) Emptiness of "what is endless and beginningless"

194 Samsara, which is beginningless (in the sense that it cannot be said to have arisen at a certain moment) and endless (in the sense that there will be no moment when it will no longer occur) is also devoid of a middle term. This means that it has no duration dependent on the two terms just mentioned. Thus samsara is said to be without a beginning or end. It is also without duration. In samsara, there is no (real) going (from one life to a later life) and no coming (from an earlier life to the present life)—all is but a dreamlike appearance. **195** Samsara empty of samsara is therefore called "emptiness of what is without a beginning or an end." This is stated in the great shastra on the *Prajña-paramita-sutra* (the *Mulamadhyamaka-karikas*), in order to dispel all clinging to samsara as to something really existent.

(iii) Emptiness of "what should not be spurned"
196   In the autocommentary the terms "ultimate" and "nirvana" are treated as synonyms, and the term "undiscarded" simply refers to what is not to be rejected or spurned. "To discard" means to cast away or forsake. "Not to discard" means to retain and not to relinquish. And what is not to be spurned is the Mahayana.   **197**   This same Mahayana, not to be discarded, is empty of itself. As this same emptiness is the nature of the Mahayana, it is known as the "emptiness of what is not to be spurned." This was taught in order to eliminate attachment to virtue—regarded as a real thing to be practiced.

(iv) Emptiness of essential nature*
198   The ultimate essence of compounded and uncompounded phenomena in themselves is not something fabricated or made up by the Buddha's disciples (the Shravakas, Pratyekabuddhas, and Bodhisattvas) or by the Tathagatas themselves. All they did was to point out clearly what is in fact the case.   **199**   The ultimate essence of all compounded and uncompounded phenomena is called their "nature." This nature is also empty of itself, on account of which we speak of the emptiness of the essential nature. Why is it necessary to understand this? It was set forth in order to combat the belief in the true existence of the emptiness of emptiness (which is itself proved by reasoning), and in order to counteract the clinging that might arise when one asks whether the nature of phenomena really exists as the foundation of all things—given that it has not been contrived by anyone.

(d) An explanation of the fourth group of four kinds of emptiness
(i) Emptiness of all phenomena
200   The eighteen dhatus—namely, the six inner senses like the visual organ and the six outer objects like form, together with the six dhatus of consciousness, such as the visual consciousness—are respectively the

* *rang bzhin.*

support, the supported, and the object. These, along with the six kinds of sense contact, such as that which is related to the visual sense organ, together with the six kinds of perception that arise therefrom, in addition to whatever is endowed with form or otherwise, and finally everything that is compounded and uncompounded—all these phenomena are empty of themselves. **201** This is the "emptiness of all phenomena."

(ii) Emptiness of defining attributes
A. Exposition
There is no such thing as a truly existent defining characteristic (starting from the breakable—the definition of form—right up to omniscience). All this refers to the "emptiness of the defining attributes" of phenomena. This is not necessarily a reference to the meaning-isolates of phenomena but rather to their specific character.[231]

B. A further explanation
1. The defining attributes of phenomena on the level of the ground
202 Form is defined as what is breakable. Feeling is the experience of pleasure or pain or the sensation of indeterminate neutrality. Perception means the cognizance of phenomenal characteristics outer and inner.[232] Conditioning factors are themselves compounded things: causes and conditions that bring into being, or produce, other things. **203** The definition of consciousness is the overall awareness of individual objects like form. The specific characteristic of the five aggregates that maintain existence in samsara is the suffering that is implicit in them. The dhatus for their part are like venomous snakes, for they project us into samsara and keep us there. **204** The sense fields (the ayatanas: the inner senses and their outer objects) give rise to the "main mind" and its mental factors, and these are suffering. They are, the Buddha said, the open door to the production of suffering. Finally, dependent arising is defined as the conjunction of causes and conditions.

2. The defining attributes of phenomena on the level of the path
205 The attitude of giving one's body and possessions and the roots of one's merit—entirely and without attachment—is the paramita of generosity. Discipline is a state of being untroubled by the worry or

anxiety arising from defiled emotion and a lack of self-control. The definition of patience is the absence of anger, while diligence is defined as the pleasure and interest one takes in wholesome activities devoid of negativity. **206** Concentration is the focusing of the mind on wholesome objects or the maintaining of it in a state of absorption. Finally, wisdom is the absence of attachment produced by the belief in the true existence of things. These are said to be the defining characteristics of the six paramitas.

207 Possessing perfect knowledge of the four levels of samadhi, the four boundless thoughts (love and so on), and the four absorptions of the formless realm (such as the absorption of Infinite Space), the Buddha declared that these states are undisturbed by anger. For these levels of experience are attained only when anger is eliminated. **208** The thirty-seven elements leading to enlightenment (the four close mindfulnesses and so on) are defined as the factors that cause beings to emerge decisively from samsara into a state of freedom. The first door of perfect liberation, namely, emptiness, is the nonexistence of a truly existent referent (that is, the lack of inherent existence in phenomena). **209** The second door, namely, the absence of attributes, is defined as the "pacification" (that is, the dissipation) of conceptually ascribed phenomenal characteristics. The third door, the absence of all expectancy, is defined as the absence of suffering and ignorance. For when it is understood that suffering is a conditioned phenomenon, it is clear that suffering as such does not exist. Neither does ignorance, namely, the assumption of the true existence of suffering. Thus no expectancy is entertained with regard to conditioned things or situations. The third door of perfect liberation is sometimes defined differently. Some say that if one recognizes conditioned things as suffering, one relinquishes all expectancy in their regard, and being free also of the ignorance of considering nirvana to be a truly existing reality, one has no expectancy of this either. However, the subject of the three doors of perfect liberation (regarded as the ultimate object) is ultimate wisdom itself. If they were considered as suffering, their status would necessarily be conventional; it could not be ultimate. The eight perfect freedoms,[233] such as "form beholding form," are defined as what gives rise to the perfect freedom from obscuration in relation to a certain level of absorption.

3. *The defining attributes of phenomena on the level of the fruit*

210   The ten strengths (which will be explained later) are characterized, the Buddha said, by utter certainty. The four fearlessnesses, whereby the Buddha proclaims his complete and perfect enlightenment, are invulnerable to attack and cannot deviate into something else. It is their nature to be perfectly steadfast.   **211**   The fourfold perfect knowledge (to be explained later) of the words of the teachings, their meaning, the manner of enunciation (in different languages), and the knowledge bestowed by intelligence and ability, all of which pervade and embrace every object of knowledge, are defined as uninterruptible or inexhaustible. The Buddha's great love accomplishes the immediate and ultimate welfare of beings.   **212**   His great compassion extends as a perfect protection to suffering beings. His great joy is defined as perfect. (Rendawa comments that the object of this joy is the happiness of beings.) Finally, the Buddha's great equanimity is defined as being unstained by attachment or aversion.   **213**   The eighteen distinctive qualities attributed to a Buddha (such as the fact that his physical conduct is faultless) can never be impaired by delusion. They are therefore defined as irremovable.   **214**   The wisdom of omniscience is defined as the direct perception of all objects of knowledge in their every aspect. All other kinds of knowledge are of a lesser kind and are indirect in that they do not possess every aspect of direct perception.[234]

C. *Concluding summary*

215   In short, the characteristics of both compounded and uncompounded phenomena are empty of themselves. This is emptiness of defining attributes.

(iii) Emptiness of the "unobservable"

216   The present instant of time does not remain; it is not here in the next moment. The past and future have no existence: the former has gone, the latter is not yet born. The fact that these three aspects of time cannot be found (or pointed out) is referred to as their unobservability, that is, their emptiness.   **217**   This unobservability is devoid of intrinsic nature. It has no constancy or permanence; neither is it transient or impermanent. This is emptiness of the "unobservable."

(iv) Emptiness of "nonthings"

218 Since they arise from causes and conditions, things do not exist inherently as composites. Emptiness of being composite is what is meant by the emptiness of nonthings. Some authorities consider that "composite" actually refers to the collection or assembly. But Chandrakirti's autocommentary specifies that: "A composite manifests from an assembly. And because the composite arises from causes and conditions, it has no real existence." Interpreting this stanza in the light of the autocommentary, it is clear that what manifests from conditions is not really existent and is therefore called "nonthing." This is said to be self-empty. The terms "essential nature," "emptiness," "ultimate truth," "ground, path, and fruit," "nonthing," "beyond extremes," "unobservable," and "not to be discarded" are all synonymous and are employed according to the way this nature is apprehended.

(2) An abridged classification into four kinds of emptiness
(a) The four kinds of emptiness
(i) Emptiness of things*

219 In short, the term "thing" refers to the five aggregates. The fact that these are self-empty is set forth as "emptiness of things."

(ii) Emptiness of "nonthings"†

220 Once again, and to state the matter briefly, "nonthings" refers to uncompounded phenomena like space. These, empty of themselves, give rise to the expression "emptiness of nonthings."

(iii) Emptiness of the nature itself‡

221 The nature of phenomena is without intrinsic being. The emptiness of this so-called nature is glossed as "the nature that is empty of the nature." Why "nature"? Because it is not at all an invented category or figment, thought up by the Shravakas, for example.

---

* *dngos po stong pa.*
† *dngos med stong pa.*
‡ *rang gi ngo bos stong pa.* This is similar to emptiness of emptiness.

(iv) Emptiness of the transcendent quality*

222 Regardless of whether the Buddhas appear or not, the nature of phenomena is emptiness. This fact is also referred to as their transcendent quality. **223** The expressions "perfectly pure ultimate" and "thatness" are synonyms for this emptiness of the transcendent quality. The expression "transcendent quality" is used to describe the emptiness nature of all phenomena. In the autocommentary, it is explained thus: "The transcendent quality is beyond ordinary perception; it is something ordinary people do not recognize and is realized only by sublime wisdom." In other words, it is called transcendent precisely because it transcends samsara. This transcendent quality is empty of itself and thus one speaks of the emptiness of the transcendent quality.

These four kinds of emptiness are a summary of the other sixteen. The first two emptinesses embrace the emptiness of all phenomena and so forth, while the third includes the emptiness of the essential nature of things and so on. Finally, the fourth includes the emptiness of the ultimate nature and the rest. The third kind of emptiness negates all things, and the fourth disproves their transcendent quality. There is indeed no other object of refutation aside from the inherent nature of things. The way in which these two latter emptinesses are apprehended is mostly the same. The first emptiness is parallel with the ground and the second with the path. The various kinds of emptiness are simply distinguished from the point of view of the basis of emptiness, namely, phenomena.²³⁵

(b) Concluding summary of the twenty emptinesses

These twenty kinds of emptiness are described in the *Prajñaparamita-sutra*, the mother of all the Buddhas.

C. Concluding description of the sixth ground by stating its qualities

224 Bodhisattvas, the light of whose wisdom, as the outcome of perfect analysis, demonstrates the ultimate truth as clearly and unobscured as a fresh kyurura fruit resting on their palms,²³⁶ understand that the three worlds are primordially unborn. And even though on the ultimate level there is nothing to enter and no one who enters, yet,

---

* *gzhan gyi ngo bos stong pa.*

in terms of conventional truth, they enter into cessation, that is, absorption.

225 The fact that the minds of Bodhisattvas rest constantly in cessation means that they are always in a state of perfect equipoise. Whatever they do, their minds are never far from ultimate reality. And if one were to ask whether their being in cessation means that they turn away from beings, the answer is no. In proportion as their sublime minds have the capacity for cessation, their qualities on the relative level shine forth even more. Therefore, Bodhisattvas have compassion for defenseless beings. Nevertheless, the meditative equipoise of Bodhisattvas is still included within samsara, but later, on the seventh ground, their wisdom will outshine that of the Shravakas, born from the Buddha's speech, as also the Pratyekabuddhas (those "halfway to buddhahood").

226 The sixth-ground Bodhisattvas are like the king of the swans. Their broad, white wings—the relative and ultimate truths (the vast activities and the profound view respectively)—are fully developed, enabling them to soar ahead of lesser birds, namely, ordinary beings to be trained. And on the strong winds of virtue, they fly to the far shore of the ocean, the inexhaustible, endless qualities of buddhahood.

Here ends the sixth ground or stage in the cultivation of absolute bodhichitta.

VII. THE SEVENTH GROUND: FAR PROGRESSED

1 The Bodhisattvas on this ground are able to enter and emerge from cessation (absorption) at each and every instant. Nevertheless, they cannot yet be said to have attained true cessation. It is on this ground also that they master the powerful paramita of skillful means. The *Bodhisattvabhumi-shastra* specifies that there are two sets of six skillful means. With the first set of six, Bodhisattvas accomplish the qualities of buddhahood. Accordingly, Bodhisattvas (1) consider all beings with compassion; (2) they have a perfect knowledge of the nature "as it is" of all compounded phenomena; (3) they yearn for wisdom unsurpassed; (4) they do not turn away from and forsake samsaric beings; (5) they remain in samsara but with minds that are undefiled; and (6) they have great strength of diligence. Thanks to the second group of six skillful means, Bodhisattvas bring beings to maturation. (1) They cause even the slight virtue of beings to be productive of limitless results; (2) they likewise accomplish positive actions on a grand scale with only slight effort; (3) they can dissipate the animosity of those who oppose the teachings; (4) they cause even the indifferent to engage in the Dharma. (5) Those who are already so engaged they bring to maturity; (6) and those who are mature they bring to perfect liberation.

In one commentary, the following particular aspects are ascribed to the paramita of wisdom: skillful means, aspiration, strength, and primordial wisdom. On closer inspection, all these aspects are seen to pertain, of course, to the paramita of wisdom, but they can also be posited as separate paramitas. Given that on the seventh ground, skillful means are seen to have an extraordinary character, it is regarded as a paramita in itself, distinct from wisdom.

Here ends the seventh ground or stage in the cultivation of absolute bodhichitta.

VIII. THE EIGHTH GROUND: IMMOVABLE
A. The manner in which the eighth ground is attained
1   In order to acquire more merit than has been attained on the previous seven grounds, and through having fully accepted[237] that phenomena are without origin, the great Bodhisattvas enter the eighth ground, Immovable, and here the attainment of buddhahood is irreversible. For example, before setting sail upon the sea, one needs to walk to reach the boat. But once on board, there is no further need to walk, and the distance that it would take, let us say, a hundred years to traverse on foot can be covered in a single day! In just the same way, when faring upon the ocean of bodhisattva activities, spontaneously present primal wisdom can, in a single instant, master unfathomable omniscience, which could never have been attained previously, even after a hundred thousand kalpas of intentional effort. On the earlier seven grounds, Bodhisattvas journeyed toward omniscience by dint of arduous labor. They now progress spontaneously and without effort. Just like a man carried along by a river does not need to exert himself in order to reach the ocean, Bodhisattvas need make no effort as they move automatically toward omniscience. They never deviate from it, even slightly, and their progress is said to be irreversible. In general terms, the word "acceptance" is used to refer to the mental condition

of being able to see the ultimate truth. On the path of joining, acceptance is understood as a state that is in accordance with this realization. A greater kind of acceptance is gained on the path of seeing when the profound, ultimate truth is seen directly. The greatest kind of acceptance is said to be attained on the eighth ground because here there subsides the gross mental activity associated with a dual appearance.

B. The paramita of aspiration is preeminent on this ground

It is on this ground that the aspirations made from the first ground onward are utterly cleansed of all adverse factors. Countless[238] hundreds of thousands of aspirations are completely purified on this ground, and this explains the preeminence, here, of the aspiration paramita. At this stage, Bodhisattvas are like heirs to the throne. On the ninth ground they are regents of the Conqueror, while on the tenth they are empowered by the Buddhas as Chakravartins, universal sovereigns.

C. The qualities proper to this ground
1. Qualities referring to the arresting of samsaric existence
a. Even though Bodhisattvas have completely severed the links that bind them to samsara, the Buddhas exhort them to remain in samsara and to attain further enlightened qualities

Abiding in their past aspirations and the continuum of ultimate reality, the Buddhas arouse the Bodhisattvas from the cessation into which they have entered. They say: "Child of my lineage, this is excellent indeed. You have reached acceptance regarding the ultimate truth, but as for the qualities of buddhahood, you do not yet possess the ten strengths, the fourfold fearlessness, and the distinctive qualities of buddhahood. Strive therefore to gain these qualities in their totality! Be diligent! Do not abandon the acceptance you have gained! Child of my lineage, even though you abide in the complete deliverance of peace, be mindful of ordinary beings overpowered by their defiled emotion. Remember your past aspirations and the work that is to be accomplished for the sake of beings. Remember inconceivable wisdom—mere 'ultimate nature' is realized even by the Shravakas and Pratyekabuddhas!" It is thus that the Buddhas rouse them by virtue of their aspirations and the united level of ultimate reality. The Bodhisattvas attain primal wisdom beyond effort, which has the same taste or nature as cessation, and, thanks to the Teacher and their own compassion,* they do not remain in cessation.

b. The complete elimination of all stains

2   As the Bodhisattvas are roused from cessation, their wisdom, free from attachment, is "henceforth free from faults." As the sun of non-conceptual wisdom rises on the eighth ground, all stains (that is, the defiled afflictions experienced in the three worlds), together with their roots, completely subside. However, although these Bodhisattvas have no further defilements; and although in the three worlds (which they have wholly transcended) they have no superior, they are nevertheless still unable to achieve the spacelike, limitless wealth of a Buddha's qualities.

2. Samsaric existence ceases for such Bodhisattvas; nevertheless, they are able to display various forms within samsara

Given that samsaric birth is completely arrested, how is it that Bodhisattvas can perfect the qualities of buddhahood?   **3**   Samsara is indeed halted, but thanks to the ten powers, obtained on the eighth ground, it is said in the *Shrimaladevi-sutra* that they show themselves in various forms (which have the nature of mental body) for the sake of beings in samsara.

The ten powers are as follows: (1) power over life: such Bodhisattvas can bless their life span to last for countless kalpas; (2) power of mind: their unfathomable wisdom enters into meditative absorption whenever they wish; (3) power over material things: they can materialize anything and thus, so to speak, adorn the world with various ornaments; (4) power over karma: they can reveal the fully ripened effect of an action; (5) power over birth: they can take birth in any world; (6) power over the prayers of beings: they are able to display the attainment of buddhahood in any buddhafield and at any time they wish; (7) power over aspirations: in accordance with the aspirations of beings, they are able to manifest all the worlds of the universe filled with Buddhas; (8) power of miracles: they are able to display miracles in all worlds; (9) power of primal wisdom: they can display a Buddha's strengths, fearlessnesses, distinctive qualities, major and minor marks, and perfect

* *phyi nang yongs 'dzin.*

enlightenment; (10) power of Dharma: they can teach all the different sections of the Dharma, which is itself beyond center or periphery.

In respect of this so-called mental body, just as the mind can go wherever it wishes without impediment, the same is true of the mental body.

Here ends the eighth ground or stage in the cultivation of absolute bodhichitta.

IX. THE NINTH GROUND: PERFECT INTELLECT

1 On the ninth ground, not merely the ten strengths,[239] but also the entire paramita of strength become completely perfect and pure. The ten strengths, as explained in the sutra, are as follows. (1) The strength of thought is a total absence of afflictive emotion. (2) The strength of proficiency is the knowledge of how to define every empirical activity (supreme intention is a training in primal wisdom; *dharani* is the non-forgetting of the Dharma; and concentration is a constant freedom from distraction). (3) The strength of mastery refers to the fulfillment of all intentions. (4) The strength of fearless ability refers to the knowledge of how the Buddha's qualities are classified. (5) The strength of aspiration refers to the fact that the work of enlightened activities is never relinquished. (6) The strength of the paramitas means bringing to fruition the Doctrine and beings, never abandoning the activities that are of benefit to others. (7) The strength of love is never to give up actions that protect others. (8) The strength of compassion dispels the sufferings of beings. (9) The strength of ultimate reality refers to the actualization of the nature of "illusionlike" phenomena. (10) The strength of being blessed by all the Buddhas refers to irreversible advancement toward the wisdom of omniscience.

Bodhisattvas likewise gain the utterly pure qualities of the four aspects of perfect knowledge: (1) the knowledge of phenomena: they know perfectly the nature of each and every phenomenon; (2) the knowledge of meaning: they know perfectly how such phenomena should be classified; (3) the knowledge of expression: they know perfectly how this should be expressed; (4) the knowledge bestowed by intelligence and ability: they know the causes of phenomena perfectly and unceasingly.

Here ends the ninth ground or stage in the cultivation of absolute bodhichitta.

X. THE TENTH GROUND: CLOUD OF DHARMA
A. The qualities pertaining to this ground

1 The Bodhisattva on the tenth ground receives supreme empowerment by means of great rays of light emitted by the Buddhas of the ten
directions. The meaning of this is described in the *Dashabhumika-sutra*.
Having mastered the last of countless concentrations, such a Bodhisattva actualizes the concentration that is said to be the "empowerment indistinguishable from omniscient wisdom." At once, from the
precious "supreme" lotus, equal in size to a million three-thousandfold universes there appears a surrounding host of lotuses, as many as
there are particles of dust in a million three-thousandfold universes—
and the Bodhisattva's form is as large and numerous as they are. As
soon as this concentration is attained, the Bodhisattva appears seated
on a lotus. From the hair between the eyebrows of all the Buddhas
seated on their thrones in their respective buddhafields, rays of light
stream forth and empower the Bodhisattva. Such is the description of
this event.

B. The purity of the paramita of primordial wisdom
On this ground, the paramita of primordial wisdom is perfected. The
difference between wisdom (*shes rab*) and primordial wisdom (*ye shes*)
is said to consist in the presence or absence of dual appearance (that
is, a division between the perceiver and the perceived). However, in
the *Bodhisattvabhumi-shastra*, it is said: "The paramita of primordial
wisdom is the complete knowledge of every aspect of phenomena
(both ultimate and relative). It is wisdom that apprehends their ultimate nature, while it is primordial wisdom that apprehends the relative." In fact, when the ultimate truth is apprehended in one taste
with the relative, and when at the same time dual appearance subsides, no division can be made between the ultimate and the relative;
they are of one taste. The primordial wisdom therefore is the outcome of wisdom.

C. The qualities concordant with the definition of this ground
Just as in the ordinary world, gentle rain issues from rain clouds, in
the same way, from the great Bodhisattvas residing on the tenth
ground, there falls a spontaneous, effortless shower of the rain of

sacred Dharma, so that the excellent harvest of virtue might grow in the hearts of beings, bringing forth the fruit of their happiness. Therefore this ground is called *Cloud of Dharma*.

> *Here ends the tenth ground or stage in the cultivation of absolute bodhichitta.*

THE QUALITIES OF
THE TEN GROUNDS

I. AN EXPOSITION OF THE TWELVE GROUPS OF ONE HUNDRED QUALITIES THAT MANIFEST ON THE FIRST GROUND

1 When Bodhisattvas attain the first ground, in a single instant, (1) they behold a hundred Buddhas and (2) know that they are blessed by them. At that point, (3) they are able to remain upon this ground for a hundred kalpas and in addition, (4) they have, in their wisdom, a perfect knowledge also of what occurred before this period and what will occur after it. **2** (5) Bodhisattvas, possessing such wisdom, enter and relinquish a hundred kinds of concentration in a single instant. (6) Through their miraculous power, they are able to cause a hundred worlds in the ten directions to tremble and shake and (7) can illuminate them with their light. (8) Likewise their great miraculous powers are able in a single instant to bring a hundred beings to spiritual maturity.[240] Such Bodhisattvas can (9) travel to a hundred buddha-fields; **3** they can (10) perfectly open a hundred doors of Dharma;[241] they can (11) display a hundred bodies within their own bodies. And just as they are themselves surrounded by a retinue that serves to increase and intensify their beauty and majesty, so also (12) each of their hundred emanated bodes is likewise attended. **4** Thus the wise Bodhisattvas, who dwell on the ground of Perfect Joy, gain these twelve sets of a hundred-fold qualities, and these are the causes of their supreme joy.

II. THE ADAPTATION OF THESE QUALITIES TO THE FOLLOWING GROUNDS

A. On the following six impure grounds, the number of qualities is multiplied

Bodhisattvas dwelling on the second ground, the Immaculate, will acquire these same qualities but this time multiplied by a thousand. The same will subsequently apply for each of the five successive grounds. On the third ground, Bodhisattvas will thus perfectly gain these twelve qualities multiplied by a hundred thousand. **5** On the fourth ground, the twelve will be multiplied by a billion, on the fifth ground by ten billion, on the sixth by one trillion, and on the seventh by ten million trillions. All these qualities are perfectly gained.

B. On the pure grounds, the number of qualities is compared to particles of dust

1. The qualities of the eighth ground

From the eighth ground onward, the qualities gained are beyond counting. They are said to equal the number of particles of dust. **6** Bodhisattvas, who are now free from all conceptuality, dwell upon the eighth ground, the Immovable, where they obtain as many times the above-mentioned twelve qualities as there are particles of dust in a hundred thousand billion universes.

2. The qualities of the ninth ground

7 Bodhisattvas dwelling on the ninth ground, Perfect Intellect, gain as many qualities as the twelve previously mentioned, but this time multiplied by as many as ten times the particles of dust in one hundred thousand "countless" (10^{59}) billion-fold universes.

3. The qualities of the tenth ground

a. The multiplication of the twelve qualities

8 The expression "to say the least" in the root verse means that, although it is impossible to express completely all the qualities of the Bodhisattvas on the tenth ground (for they are beyond the reach of words), if one were to describe them just in part, one would say that if all the particles of dust in all the "countless" buddhafields were gathered together (a quantity well beyond all possibility of expression), so many would be the qualities that such Bodhisattvas obtain.

b. Other qualities

9   Free from all concepts, such Bodhisattvas are able to reveal in every pore of their bodies countless Bodhisattvas and their retinues, together with perfect Buddhas in infinite number, to say nothing of other beings: devas, asuras, humans, and so forth. The word "also" (in the third line of the stanza) indicates that the Bodhisattvas are able to assume, spontaneously and distinctly, in every instant and according to need, the form of Brahma, Ishvara, a Chakravartin, a Shravaka, or a Pratyekabuddha, and proceed to expound the Dharma.

THE ULTIMATE GROUND OF
BUDDHAHOOD

I. THE ATTAINMENT OF BUDDHAHOOD
A. How buddhahood is attained
1. When buddhahood is attained

10 "And thus because the moon shines brightest in a clear, un-clouded sky" (the earlier translation simply says: "Just as the moon shines brightly in a clear, unclouded sky"), the Bodhisattvas dwelling on the tenth ground cultivate the ten strengths, continually striving to attain the level of buddhahood. It should be noted that the translation of Nagtsho Lotsawa reads: "You strove again and again on the *preceding* grounds, to develop the ten strengths." In other words, because the im-maculate sky is an expanse of unobstructed openness, the moon ap-pears clearly therein and illuminates all beings. It could not do so, for example, if it were submerged in the sea, which is not unobstructed in the same way. Likewise the Bodhisattvas, while they were residing on the earlier grounds, were unable to cultivate fully the qualities of bud-dhahood (the strengths and so on). Now, however, they realize the spacelike wisdom of the tenth ground. All obstacles that hinder the at-tainment of a Buddha's qualities are removed, as a result of which the latter—the ten strengths and so forth—can appear clearly like the moon. Thus the tenth-ground Bodhisattvas, prior to the attainment of buddhahood, are able to cultivate the ten strengths and strive for the ultimate goal. The word "again" in the second line of the stanza refers to the fact that these Bodhisattvas are now very close to the attainment of buddhahood (which was not the case previously). This being so, the other grounds, now traversed, no longer lie between them and their goal. Their efforts are therefore much stronger as they aim exclusively at omniscience. On the first ground, Bodhisattvas strive for omniscience only in a general sense, while in reality focusing on the attainment of the wisdom of the second ground. On the tenth ground, the situation is different, for the Bodhisattvas are now aiming directly at omniscience.

2. The place where buddhahood is attained

The place of attainment is the buddhafield of Akanishta. This is where the unsurpassable objective, the fruit of the efforts of measureless kalpas, is achieved—the supreme level of peace with its ultimate and peerless qualities.

3. The manner in which buddhahood is attained

11 Just as different kinds of vessels (pitchers, bowls, and so on) do not hold within them different kinds of space, in the same way, whereas there are different categories of entity, like form and feeling, their ultimate reality is beyond all such distinctions. Therefore, in the very moment that "those possessed of perfect wisdom" understand that all phenomena are of a single taste, in that very instant they comprehend, in their omniscience, every object of knowledge.

B. An answer to objections
1. The objections themselves
a. It is inadmissible to say that the unborn nature is realized as an object

12 It could be objected that if the ultimate nature of phenomena is precisely the pacification of all conceptual designations of origin and cessation, this cannot be an object of apprehension or perception, because the mind cannot actively apprehend it. And if this is so, it is equally impossible to speak about the subject that perceives it—namely, the mind itself. For if the subject has absolutely no knowledge of an object, how can one talk of cognition? It is a contradiction in terms. Without origin and without cessation, the object is destitute of any referential feature, so what is there for the subject to refer to? Being unable to observe what is not present, it makes no sense to refer to it as an object. As there is nothing to understand, one cannot talk about understanding. One cannot recognize the face of a man one has never met!

b. If the subject (the mind) and the object (the unborn nature) are of a single taste (that is, the same nature), it follows that even when the unborn nature is understood, it cannot be taught to others

A further objection may be made to the effect that when a color (blue, for instance) is apprehended in a produced object, an apprehending subject is automatically implied. But how is it possible for an exalted being to know something that is not produced? Moreover, if the subject and object of cognition are indivisible, like water mixed with water, there is no perceiver able to define the object as such-and-such. Who, therefore, can point it out to his disciples? It is impossible.

2. An answer to the objections

a. It is admissible to talk about the realization of the unborn nature as an object

13   Since the unborn is the ultimate reality and the mind is also unborn, a cognition attuned to the unborn can be said to understand its object, namely, the dharmadhatu or suchness. But this is just a manner of speaking. In reality, the object and subject are not distinct. For example, it is said that when consciousness assumes the aspect of its object (such as a color), it thoroughly knows it. In the same way, using a similar kind of language, one speaks about "realizing ultimate reality." Of course, if one holds or considers *that* the object, namely, phenomena, is unborn,[242] this means that one's mind is *not* as yet attuned to ultimate reality. But when both object *and* subject are understood to be equally unborn, the mind is so attuned. One can then say that the latter realizes the former. In point of fact, however, this realization does not occur between a subject and object, distinct and separate from each other.[243] The Buddha's realization of ultimate reality is a matter of primordial wisdom (*ye shes*) where subject and object are of one taste. It is not simply wisdom (*shes rab*). For the latter discerns objects, whereas here there is nothing to be discerned as object. It is the Great Peace, the "one taste" of united subject and object, and this is not some definite, determined "object" that can be differentiated from other objects.

b. Even though the subject and object are not distinct, teachings can be given

i. Though the subject and object are not distinct, it is possible to expound the teachings

14   The Buddhas, who, while dwelling in a body of form, actualize the dharmakaya and who, by virtue of hundreds of accumulations of merit, assume a sambhogakaya, all expound the profound and ultimate reality. The same can be said of Bodhisattvas enjoying a continuous experience of the dharmata and who have an unmistaken realization of ultimate reality. This is also true for all the nirmanakaya emanations arising through the blessing of the sambhogakaya. It is, moreover, by their power that from the sky and elsewhere—mountains, cliffs, trees, and so forth—this same reality resounds and is revealed, so that even ordinary beings may realize it. Object and subject, ultimate reality and wisdom, are of a single taste. The Buddhas have no need to distinguish subject from object, saying: "Ultimate reality is like this." By virtue of the blessing-power of the ultimate nature, which is the great primordial wisdom of one taste, ultimate reality is not a mere vacuity.[244] How then do the Buddhas teach their disciples? The teachings of the Buddhas abiding in the sambhogakaya (the perfect maturation of the accumulation of merit) and the teachings of their nirmanakaya emanations and so forth, manifesting through the blessing of this ultimate nature, arise within a complete absence of concepts that apprehend subject and object as distinct entities.

ii. An example

15   Chandrakirti gives an example of how Buddhas help others, even though they have no conceptual mind and are beyond all exertion. The situation is like that of a potter's wheel, which through long effort has been set in motion so that it is turning with great momentum. The wheel will continue to turn without further effort on the part of the potter so that pots and so forth can be produced.   **16**   In the same way, the Buddhas exert not the slightest effort in teaching the Dharma (in the present moment in which they appear). Dwelling in the dharmakaya, their activities appear entirely through the merit of the beings[245] who receive the teaching, and through the power of their own extraordinary aspirations made in the past.[246] The actions of the Buddhas are thus inconceivable.

II. WHAT IS THE GOAL, NAMELY, BUDDHAHOOD?
A. A description of the kayas, which are the basis
1. The dharmakaya

17   When the tinder wood of knowledge objects (from forms right up to omniscience perceived in terms of dual appearance) is burned away by the fire of wisdom, all conceptual designations of subject and object subside—everything conceived in terms of "knower" and "known." This is what is called the dharmakaya of the Conquerors. Here there is no origin and no cessation, for the mind and mental factors have come to a halt. The dharmakaya is actualized on the basis of the sambhogakaya, which is to say that the dharmakaya is realized by the sambhogakaya. Referring to the fact that the tinder wood of all phenomena is entirely consumed by the fire of the wisdom kaya, Chandrakirti asserts in the autocommentary that all knowledge objects (in being devoid of inherent existence) are like firewood—suitable for burning. When the dharmakaya manifests, the fire of wisdom that directly realizes the ultimate nature of all phenomena consumes them all without exception. All distinction between the known object and the knowing subject, or mind, subsides. It is like pouring water into water. The mind, or subject, is of one taste with its object, the expanse of ultimate reality.

When this primordial wisdom (wherein there is not even the slightest concept regarding the perception or nonperception of objects) is described as being "without perception,"* the meaning is that appearance cannot be established (demonstrated) in or by wisdom. This, however, does not refer to a mere nonexistence of appearance, in the sense of an appearance understood in distinction from its contrary, nonappearance. Primordial wisdom possesses a knowledge that perceives all things in their multiplicity. Wherefore it is indeed said that wisdom is "with perception."† But this, be it noted, is a "wisdom perception," not the hallucinatory, fallacious perceptions that figure in the experience of ordinary beings. This is entirely beyond the mind's power to conceive. The expanse of ultimate nature is now manifest. There is no birth and no cessation. Beyond conception, beyond birth and death, the expanse of peace is manifest. The mind and mental fac-

---

* *snang med.*
† *snang bcas.*

tors come to a halt, for these are part and parcel of samsaric existence. If the mind did not come to a halt, wisdom, wherein subject and object are united in the same taste, could not manifest. By contrast, it is by halting the mind completely that the wisdom body is actualized. Therefore the root verse says that when the mind comes to a stop, the sambhogakaya actualizes the wisdom kaya.

2. The sambhogakaya

18 When all conceptual constructs of the mind and mental factors completely subside, the sambhogakaya arises, of one taste with the expanse that is free from concepts. It is effortless and free from all movement, whether of emanation or of dissolution. The sambhogakaya is radiant like a wish-fulfilling tree. And without any intention to do so, like a wishing-jewel, it sends forth a permanent supply of every enjoyment to beings until their liberation is gained.[247] It is perceptible only to those who realize the freedom from conceptual construction. Rendawa says that this kaya constantly provides beings, as numerous as space is vast, with the enjoyments of the higher realms and the definitive goodness of buddhahood. He says too that it is perceptible only to the Bodhisattvas on the pure grounds, who are themselves free from conceptuality, having gained immaculate mirrorlike wisdom, which arises from the two accumulations. It is not perceived by beings with conceptual minds*—which includes all the Bodhisattvas residing on the seven impure grounds.

3. The kaya similar to its cause
a. How Buddhas display all their activities within a single pore of their bodies

19 In a single instant, Buddhas, in a rupakaya attuned to its cause (that is, the dharmakaya and sambhogakaya), can reveal all the places of their births and deaths in samsara, from time without beginning until the attainment of omniscient wisdom. And they can do this with great clarity and without confusion. They can show spontaneously and in vivid detail all their past lives, in the manner of shapes reflected in a mirror. They can display also their activities as Bodhisattvas and how they performed them, practicing the paramita of generosity and

---

* *dmigs bcas.*

venerating the Buddhas. **20** They can show forth different universes and their inhabitants (the field of Lapis Lazuli and so on) and how they took birth there. They can demonstrate their sublime powers and the strength of their bodies and activities. They can recount how many Shravakas attended them as their Sangha, the character of each of them, and how they practiced the teachings. They can describe their accompaniment of Bodhisattvas—how they looked and whether their bodies were adorned with the major and minor marks. **21** They can reveal which teaching of the three vehicles they taught and to which caste (brahmin and so on) they belonged. They can describe their appearance whether as ordained monastics or laity. They can show how they practiced, starting from when they first listened to the teachings and so on up to their exploits as Bodhisattvas—all the offerings they made, in kind and quantity, to the Buddhas, Bodhisattvas, and Shravakas: food and drink, raiment and ornaments. All without exception they are able to display within their bodies. **22** In the same way, they can simultaneously reveal in their bodies all the situations in which they formerly practiced the paramitas of discipline, patience, diligence, concentration, and wisdom, without the omission of a single one. All their past activities they can display in every pore of their bodies.

b. They can display in a single pore of their bodies the activities of other Buddhas

23 Just as they display their own activities, they can clearly display in every one of their pores and all at once all the other Buddhas of the past, present, and future. They can show how the Buddhas live within the world and how they clearly proclaim the Dharma in every dimension of space, thus bringing solace to beings afflicted by sorrow. **24** In the knowledge that they are illusionlike and devoid of being, they can display in every pore of their bodies all the activities of the Buddhas of the three times, starting from their first cultivation of bodhichitta until the attainment of the heart of enlightenment—just like their own. If by the power of a magic spell a magician is able to cause to appear in his body various worlds and beings, it is hardly necessary to say that a Buddha can do the same. **25** In the same way, Buddhas are able to show all at once and in a single pore of their bodies the activities of all the Bodhisattvas of the three times, the activities of the Pratyekabuddhas and of the noble Shravakas, as well as all the worldly conduct of ordinary beings.

c. The power of Buddhas to accomplish all that they wish
i. With respect to space
26 Simply by wishing to do so, Buddhas, in whom all impurities have been cleansed away, are able to show that a single particle of dust is as large as a whole universe embracing the vast confines of space. Conversely, they can display the infinity of universes in all directions within a single particle of dust, and a speck of dust containing all the universes, and all this without the dust getting bigger or the universes smaller.

ii. With respect to time
27 Buddhas are utterly free of conceptuality. They can display in every instant, and as long as samsara endures, as many activities as the countless, infinitely small particles of the entire world.

B. The qualities based on the kayas
1. An explanation of the ten strengths, which are the principal qualities of buddhahood
a. A brief exposition
28 The level of buddhahood is characterized by the ten strengths. These are (1) the strength of knowing what is correct and what is incorrect; (2) the strength of knowing the fully ripened effects of actions; (3) the strength of knowing the various interests and aspirations of beings; (4) the strength of knowing the different dhatus; **29** (5) the strength of knowing the varying mental acumen of beings; (6) the strength of knowing all paths; (7) the strength of knowing all samadhis, perfect freedoms, concentrations, and absorptions; **30** (8) the strength of knowing past lives; (9) the strength of knowing the births and deaths of beings; (10) the strength of knowing the exhaustion of defilements.

b. A detailed explanation
Each of the ten strengths is now explained, following the root stanzas, each of which terminates in a conclusion containing the word "strength."

31   The omniscient Buddha has declared that correct knowledge consists in knowing that a specific cause will certainly produce a specific
result. For example, it is correct to say that virtue gives rise to happiness and that the contrary will not occur. In other words, suffering will
never result from virtue. Similarly, beings who attain the path of seeing
will not accumulate, by the power of karma, the eight kinds of existence. The Buddha has eliminated all incorrect knowledge objects,
which are an impediment to infinite wisdom. This is defined as his
strength of knowing what is correct and what is incorrect.

32   The knowledge of the Buddha penetrates strongly and unhindered all actions and their different effects: completely virtuous acts
that produce happy and desirable effects, completely negative acts that
produce undesirable effects, mixed actions (having both positive and
negative aspects) and utterly pure actions, unstained by belief in a self.
The Buddha knows all actions performed in the three times together
with their proper results. This is the strength of knowing the fully
ripened effects of actions.

33   The strength of knowing the various interests of beings embraces
all beings, past, present, and to come. The Buddha knows the different
aspirations of each and every one, developing from the negative emotions of craving and aversion and the rest (giving rise to samsara), and
from the positive emotions of faith and so forth (giving rise to nirvana). He knows all their interests and tendencies, base, mediocre, and
noble, including also their hidden aspirations, which do not appear
clearly in the way they behave.

34   The Buddha, versed in all the different categories of dhatus[248] or
elements, taught that the emptiness of the eighteen dhatus (like that
of sight) is also a dhatu. The unbounded cognition of the perfect Buddhas embraces all the different categories of such dhatus: the five elements, the two truths, the three worlds, and every kind of being
according to its character. This is the strength of knowing the different
dhatus.

35   Sharp faculties belonging to the side of purity (faith and so
forth), which overpower defiled thoughts and emotions, are described
as "supreme," whereas mediocre and dull faculties are regarded as "inferior." The twenty-two faculties, sight and the rest,[249] together with
their objects, are established through mutual interaction. The power
to do this is said to lie within the sense faculty, which is able to estab-

lish its object. It is also said that the faculties are established as mutually related cause and effect. For example, when one hears a knock, one looks in the direction of the sound. Similarly, the practice of generosity gives rise to the practice of discipline. The possession of an unimpeded knowledge of all this is said to be the fifth strength: the knowledge of different faculties, supreme or otherwise.

36   The knowledge of the Buddha embraces, without any attachment or hindrance, the objectives of all paths (in all their infinity). Buddhas know that some paths lead to buddhahood, some to the enlightenment of the Pratyekabuddhas, still others to the enlightenment of the Shravakas. They also know that other paths lead to the state of pretas, animals, gods, humans, and hell-beings. This is the strength of knowing all paths.

37   To know unhindered all the concentrations of shamatha, such as the different categories of the four levels of samadhi, the eight perfect freedoms, and the nine successive absorptions (the eight levels of samadhi and absorption, and the absorption of cessation, where perceptions and feelings are arrested) found within the minds of the all the yogis of infinite universes, is the strength of knowing all concentrations.[250]

38   To know unobstructedly each and every one of his past lives in beginningless samsara, as well as that of every other being, however many they are, transmigrating from life to life for as long as they are beneath the power of ignorance; to know also the causes of his own and others' lives, their countries, birthplaces, forms, colors, and so on, is the strength of knowing past lives.

39   The Buddha's knowledge, pure and infinite, free from all attachment, perceives the deaths and rebirths of each and every living being dwelling in every universe to the limits of space. The Buddha vividly perceives them in their every detail. This is the strength of knowing the births and deaths of beings.

40   The Buddha's ability to know without attachment or limitation that his omniscient wisdom has swiftly eliminated, in a single instant, all afflictive emotions, together with all habitual tendencies (even the most subtle ones), and to know that his disciples, Shravakas, Pratyekabuddhas, and others, have also brought their afflictions to an end through their stainless wisdom—this is the Buddha's strength of knowing the exhaustion of all stains.

2. The qualities of buddhahood are beyond telling
a. It is impossible to describe all the Buddha's qualities
Even if the Buddha himself had blessed his own life span so that he could remain alive for a measureless kalpa, and even if he employed his time exclusively in the description (at full speed) of the infinite qualities of buddhahood, without undertaking any other activities, he would be unable to complete such a discourse. No need therefore to mention the incapacity of the Bodhisattvas, still less that of the Shravakas and Pratyekabuddhas.   **41**   Birds turn back in their flight because they reach the end of their strength, not because they reach the edge of the sky. In the same way, not only the Shravakas, disciples of the Buddha, but even the Bodhisattvas fall silent, unable to describe the skylike, infinite qualities of the Buddha. The fact that they do so does not mean that there is nothing more to describe.

b. A brief description based on the scriptures
42   And so, Chandrakirti asks, how could someone like him know even a small part of the Buddha's qualities? How could he describe them? But since, he says, the noble Nagarjuna had partially discoursed upon them,[251] he has overcome his reticence and briefly mentioned them.

3. The benefits that result from knowing the qualities of buddhahood
43   To speak briefly, the "profound" quality of buddhahood is emptiness. This means the emptiness of the dharmakaya and the emptiness of the ground and path. All the other qualities (of the eleven grounds, the ten strengths, and so on) are referred to as "vast." (Rendawa, it should be noted, uses the words "profound" and "vast" to refer to the text in its entirety.) By understanding what these profound and vast qualities are and by meditating on them, we may also gain them for ourselves.

C. How, after achieving buddhahood, one may benefit others by means of nirmanakaya emanations
1. The deeds of the Buddha our Teacher, the supreme nirmanakaya
44   Possessing the immutable dharmakaya, which never stirs from the expanse of suchness, the Buddha's nirmanakaya went out once

more into the three dimensions of existence (above, upon, and below the earth). He descended into the human world from the heaven of Tushita. He took birth, displaying the link between mother and child. And having entered nirvana, the peaceful expanse of enlightenment, he turned the wheel of Dharma. It was thus that, in his compassion, he led "beyond suffering" all beings whose minds frisk and whirl like dancers, firmly caught in the lasso of their craving for objects of the senses.

2. The ultimate teaching of the Buddha is established as a single path
a. Reasoned proof that ultimately there is only one path to buddhahood

45 Except the knowledge of the ultimate nature of phenomena, there is no antidote able to remove the two obscurations. The ultimate condition of phenomena is not various as their different manifestations are. Ultimate reality is single and indivisible. Otherwise, primordial wisdom, the subject that cognizes ultimate reality, would have different object-assessing aspects. But this is not so; it too is indivisible. This is why the Buddha taught to beings a single, undivided vehicle, with which the other vehicles cannot compare. It is impossible for there to be a second vehicle—either in its aspect of ultimate fruit or in its aspect of path, whereon this vehicle proceeds to its destination. Neither can wisdom, the cognizing subject of ultimate reality, be distinguished from ultimate reality. If one fails to realize the ultimate as it is, omniscience has not yet been attained; obscurations have not yet been completely removed; the final path has not yet been followed. But when the ultimate *is* realized as it is, the two veils are removed and the Buddha's Mahayana stands revealed as the one and only vehicle.

The Buddha said: "If you understand, O Kashyapa, the state of equality of all phenomena, you will pass beyond suffering. All phenomena are one; they are not two or three." And Vimuktasena has said:

Because the dharmadhatu is without division,
Undivided also is your vehicle.
And yet three vehicles you have set forth
That beings might pursue the path.

b. The teaching that there are three paths is an expedient

This being so, one may wonder why it is said that the following of the Shravaka path will lead beyond suffering. **46** The answer is that beings are beset with unwholesome, defiled ideas, which serve only to compound their various shortcomings. Moreover, they live in the age of five kinds of degeneration, on account of which their aspirations are extinguished. It is impossible for them to enter, from the very first, the profound domain of buddhahood, the depth of which is so difficult to fathom. But, as Chandrakirti proclaims, the Sugata does not forsake beings simply because they are unsuitable vessels (for the ultimate teaching). The Buddha, Chandrakirti continues, possesses a wisdom that knows all the ways wherewith to bring benefit to beings, and in his compassion he is ever mindful of their need. While yet a Bodhisattva, he promised that he would bring them to liberation, which is certainly a task to be accomplished. **47** Therefore, just as a captain, skilled in wisdom and able to display a beautiful city so that his crew, laboring on their long journey to the isle of jewels, might refresh themselves, likewise the Blessed Lord set forth the lesser vehicles as means and aids to the undertaking of the great vehicle, soothing with peace the minds of the Shravakas and Pratyekabuddhas. Then, for those who train their minds in the emptiness of the emotions, separately from those who by temperament belong among the Shravakas and Pratyekabuddhas, the Buddha taught the great vehicle.

3. The Buddha our Teacher is beyond all limitation as concerns his perfect enlightenment and his sojourn in samsara
a. With respect to the moment of his perfect enlightenment

48 The blissful Sugata attains supreme enlightenment in as many kalpas as the specks of dust contained in the buddhafields covering every direction, which are the Buddhas' domain. But this is a "secret," utterly inconceivable, and is not revealed to those who do not have the requisite merit from the past and who are lacking in openness and the ability to understand. Yet the aspiration to know it is productive of great merit, and for this reason it is here explained. In the autocommentary, Chandrakirti says: "At what moment in time does the perfect enlightenment of the first nirmanakaya of the Buddha occur?" He is asking, in other words: "How many kalpas have elapsed since the first attainment of perfect buddhahood in this world of the supreme nir-manakaya?" It is written in the *Saddharmapundarika-sutra*:

> In kalpas millionfold and inconceivable,
> The span of which you cannot calculate,
> I have attained to perfect buddhahood
> And constantly the Dharma I explain.

As it is said, the Buddha is enlightened from beginningless time. Some commentators explain this by saying that once the Buddha reaches enlightenment, he reveals again his enlightenment in his nirmanakayas. Others say that this is inadmissible, even if the meaning is assumed to be that all "dharmakayas free from adventitious stains" of the Buddhas are identical. Commenting on this point, Gorampa says that the reference here is to the "dharmakaya of utterly pure nature." He says that if the nirmanakaya is beyond all limitation, its cause, the three kayas, must also be beyond limitation, as is also the first dharmakaya of a single Buddha. But to say this is to deny that there is a single dharmakaya for all future Buddhas, and so forth. This point obviously requires further examination. In his commentary, Rendawa says that the nirmanakaya attains perfect enlightenment in as many kalpas as there are grains of dust in the buddhafields of the ten directions.

b. With respect to the Buddha's sojourn in samsara
i. A brief explanation
49 The Victorious One, brought forth by mother Prajñaparamita, and with great compassion as his nurse, will remain until all ordinary beings attain enlightenment and until the disintegration of space itself. For how could the Buddha withdraw into the mere one-sided, partial peace of a "nirvana without remainder"?

ii. A detailed explanation
(1) The Buddha's unbounded compassion for beings
50 Due to ignorance, worldly beings swallow the food of the five objects of sense, impregnated as they are with the venom of sorrow. Taking such beings to himself as members of his family, so to speak, the Buddha feels great compassion for them. This compassion is far beyond even the anguish a mother might feel when her only child has

swallowed poison and is in torment. And this powerful compassion is directed to all mother sentient beings. Seeing that they are tormented, the Buddha never abandons them. The Lord never departs, withdrawing into the one-sided perfect peace of nirvana.

(2) The Buddha never departs into nirvana because the suffering of beings is endless

51   Beings are ignorant of the truth of ultimate reality. On the one hand they wrongly assume that phenomena are truly existent, while on the other hand they fail to recognize that the karmic law of cause and effect is ever operative. They suffer, passing endlessly through the process of birth and death, separated from what they long for, accompanied by what they do not want, obliged to sink into infernal realms and other lower destinies. All these beings, in their torment, are the object of the Buddha's compassion, and it is because of his love for them that the Lord shuns the one-sided peace of nirvana and remains within the world for as long as it lasts, without ever departing into nirvana.

CONCLUSION

I. THE CONCLUSION OF THE MAIN BODY OF THE TREATISE

A. How the text was composed

1. The composition of the text

a. On what it was based

52 This commentary, which comments unerringly upon the view of the Lord Nagarjuna, was distilled from the *Mulamadhyamaka-karikas*, *The Root Stanzas on the Middle Way*, and other Madhyamika treatises. The work was composed by the bhikshu Chandrakirti, who wrote it in accordance with the sutras of ultimate meaning, together with the practical essential instructions of Nagarjuna.

b. The shastra, thus composed, is indeed extraordinary

53 Those who are learned may be certain of the fact that aside from the *Mulamadhyamaka-karikas*, the full and unmistaken teaching on emptiness is not to be found in other treatises. Furthermore, the approach set forth in the present text, wherein no assertion is made as to the existence of phenomena "according to their own characteristics" on the relative level, is not to be found in other treatises, which consequently have only the appearance of Madhyamika texts.

2. Why this text was composed

a. Its purpose

54 Alarmed by such words as "unborn," "emptiness," and so on, which are like the darker color of the vast and deep waters of the wisdom of the Noble Nagarjuna, certain people in the past[252] have, like frightened children, rejected his excellent tradition and fled from it. But now the *Mulamadhyamaka-karikas*, like budding *kumuta* lilies moistened by the waters of the present shastra, have burst into flower. Thus the wishes of Chandrakirti are abundantly fulfilled.

Just as children are afraid of the sea and run away from it, Vasubandhu, Dignaga, the glorious Dharmapala, and others were alarmed by the meaning of terms like "unborn" and "emptiness," employed in the works of Nagarjuna, and shied away from them. However, just as in a pool, ravishing water lilies open in the white radiance of the full moon, Chandrakirti[253] has caused the lily buds of Nagarjuna's treatises to blossom into flower, so that now the lovely, lily-teeming waters of his lake of wisdom can fulfill the hopes and aspirations of beings.

Previously, some had turned away from the oceanic wisdom of Nagarjuna and were thus unable to imbibe its waters. But now, through a wonderful increase in their good fortune, they may enjoy the ocean of their aspirations' fulfillment.

Rendawa interprets this verse as meaning that it is the commentary of Chandrakirti that opens the profound truth as though it were the buds of water lilies; and it is through the nectarlike moisture of excellent instruction that Chandrakirti himself fulfills the wishes of beings. The *Mulamadhyamaka-karikas* arose from the ocean of Nagarjuna's wisdom like the buds of water lilies, and these have now blossomed in the light of Chandrakirti's wisdom. The nectar of the two truths contained thereby, endowed with eight qualities, fulfills the hopes and wishes of all beings according to their wish.

b. An injunction to uphold only this text

55   The profound and ultimate truth is realized only by those who possess a deeply ingrained longing for it. It is gained by no one else, no matter how well versed they may be in textual learning. It is indeed a source of fear to those of narrow mind.

Treatises contrived by the ordinary mind do not accord with the authentic tradition of the Buddha's wisdom. Therefore one should lay aside whatever inclination one might feel toward teachings and teachers who affirm the self of the person, and instead one should adhere to this text inspired by Nagarjuna.

B. The dedication of the merit accruing from the composition of the text

56   Here Chandrakirti dedicates the merit resulting from his text, in which, by quoting from the scriptures and through the use of reasoning, he clearly comments on the excellent tradition of Nagarjuna. He prays that it might spread to the limits of space. May the dark sky of the mind, tormented by negative emotions, become bright, he says, like the autumn stars. He prays also that the entire boundless multitude of beings might realize the profound and ultimate nature of phenomena—just as though they were to take the jewel from the head of the cobra (in other words, this mind of theirs)—and quickly come to the level of buddhahood. Rendawa interprets the verse as meaning that the dedication of such all-pervading merit is similar to the stars, brilliant upon the night sky, the mind obscured by defilement. And it is like the jewel on the crest of the cobra, the mind enveloped in the poison of thought and defilement.

> *May the merit I have gained through commenting the words*
>   *of master Nagarjuna grow in all directions to the limits of the sky!*
> *And may the mind enshrouded by defilement's gloom*
>   *be bright and shining like the autumn stars.*
> *And taking thus the jewel upon the forehead of the cobra of the mind,*
> *May all the world, through understanding suchness,*
>   *swiftly journey to the state of blissful buddhahood.*

II. CONCLUSION OF THE TREATISE

A. The author of the treatise

This introduction to the Middle Way elucidates the profound teaching on emptiness and the vast teaching on the qualities of the path and fruit. It was composed by the master Chandrakirti. Born in the land of Samanta, he was a *vidyadhara* immersed in the truth of the supreme vehicle. Wisdom and compassion were inalienably his, invulnerable to every adversity. He gained illusionlike concentration, thanks to which he could milk the painting of a cow and thus dispel the rigid belief of beings in the true existence of phenomena.

B. The translator

This text was translated using a Kashmiri text by the Indian abbot Tilaka Kalasha and the Tibetan translator, the monk Patsap Nyima Drak,* when residing in the Hidden Jewel temple in the center of the Kashimiri city of Anuparna, "Beyond Compare," during the reign of the king Shri Aryadeva. Subsequently, in the temple of Rasa Ramoche (Lhasa), a final, corrected version was made from a Magadha text by the Indian abbot Kanakavarman and the same translator Patsap Nyima Drak.

C. Colophon to the commentary

"Is" and "Is not," two extremes, when these are left aside,
The Middle Way appears,
Which stainless wisdom knows unerringly.
This soothes away the sorrows caused by dualistic views.
Some say "exists," some say "does not exist,"
While others claim that "Everything is naught."
People stray to one side or the other, and apprehending thus,
They keep an object when they "objectlessly" meditate!
But when "Is" and "Is not"—these imagined objects—
Are dispelled by reason of dependent origin,
Perfect certainty is gained that voidness and appearance coincide.
This is only found in Nagarjuna's excellent tradition.
This great profundity, this king of views, induced by reasoning,
May frighten feeble hearts,
Yet here the streams of Buddha's wisdom
Find their confluence.

All those who therefore thirst for this deep path,
Let them, endowed with fortune, understand
That Suchness should be realized.
And understanding thus, by study and reflection,
They should taste its meaning.

In general, textual outlines are but mere enumerations,
But some express the very essence of the text.

---

* *pa tshab nyi ma grags.*

The present outline, viewed with clear intelligence,
Will show itself supreme among all others!

This short concluding verse was composed during a detailed exposition of the *Madhyamakavatara* given by Mati,[254] a teacher of the five sciences and a member of the college of Dzogchen in Kham, a place where scriptures and reasoning resound like a lion's roar. By its merit may the doctrine of the Vajra Essence of Luminosity spread everywhere and always!

Mangalam

D. Colophon of the Tibetan editors

The Prasangika system is the ultimate tenet, for it embraces the meaning of dependent arising as emptiness, the inconceivable ultimate reality wherein there is no division between appearance and emptiness. Many there are who claim to uphold this view but are led astray by their strong habitual tendency to see the two truths as diverging. Therefore, in order to adorn the throats of those who aspire to the equality of all phenomena, here is a jeweled necklace with which to dispel the mire of the apprehension of extreme ontological positions—a garland of clear and spotless crystals, a wealth of elegant and incomparable explanations. It has arisen from the ocean of superior wisdom, profound and vast, and is an all-subduing reasoning, setting forth the primordial purity of all phenomena and proclaiming emptiness in all its glory. It is a marvelous banner of victory, whose pinnacle is ornamented by the ultimate wisdom of the Buddha. It should be given to those who are ready for the profound teachings. Even though the dualistic mind, which by proof and refutation uses correct assertion to penetrate the expanse that lies beyond it, where there is nothing to assert and nothing to deny, the fundamental nature of suchness is beyond all affirmation. This is the dharmakaya—the pacification of all conceptual constructs, the very secret space of all the Buddhas. This excellent path of the great sages, made lovely by many astonishing and wondrous qualities, is able to remove (for as long as sun and moon traverse the sky) the blinding scales and cataracts that cause us to apprehend phenomenal characteristics as real. To that end, may this perfect text resound like the sweet music of a drum. May it rouse all beings from the sleep of ignorance!

Performing thus Mañjushri's fearless work,
And placing thus all beings on the Middle Path,
Establishing the Buddha's vehicle as one and ultimate,
May this fulfill the wishes of the Buddhas and their heirs!

These notes and comments on the *Madhyamakavatara* composed by Mipham Rinpoche Jamyang Namgyal, a master who is like a lion of the Buddhist tradition, a pandita of the Middle Way of the Mahayana, were, with the help of Kunzang Pelden (the kind master of the Tripitaka), brought together and compiled into a book by Situpa Chökyi Gyamtso. This task was accomplished at the request of Zhechen Dentsap Rinpoche (the glory of the doctrine of the Old Translations), in the east of Tibet, at Kathog Dorje Den, in the monastery of Norbu'i Lhunpo, where the Buddha's teachings are explained and practiced.

Thanks to this, may all beings have a direct realization of the unerring wisdom of the Conqueror!

Notes

1 *Madhyamika* or *Madhyamaka*? Western scholars disagree on the use of these terms. Some use *Madhyamaka* to refer to the system and *Madhyamika* to refer to its proponents. Others use *Madhyamaka* as a noun and *Madhyamika* as an adjective; still others use one or the other term indifferently for both system and proponents. T. R. V. Murti (a member of the Sanskrit Commission set up by the Indian government in 1959) remarks as follows: "'Madhyamaka' or 'Madhyamaka Darsana' is an alternative, and perhaps an earlier term used for the Middle Way of Nagarjuna; it is derived from 'Madhya' (middle) by the addition of 'taddhita' suffixes. 'Madhyamika' is used both for the system and its advocates. . . . Nagarjuna or even Aryadeva do not seem to have used either of these terms." For reasons of simplicity, we shall follow Murti in using the single term "Madhyamika" in all cases. The stress falls on the second syllable.

2 See Georges B. J. Dreyfuss, *Recognizing Reality* (Albany: State University of New York Press, 1997), pp. 33–41.

3 The available bibliography in English is quite rich, and there is no doubt that modern scholarship had made and is making a valuable contribution. Interested readers will find that the work of D. S. Ruegg is an indispensable source of historical information, while the classic exposition of Madhyamika by T. R. V. Murti remains important especially for its treatment of the wider philosophical issues by a highly competent and interesting writer. Of the work of scholars who are themselves Buddhists, the most abundant and interesting, so far, has been that of Peter della Santina, of Jeffrey Hopkins and his students, and accessorily of Georges Dreyfuss. However, readers will find that for its clarity and compendiousness, as well as for its treatment of issues particularly relevant to an understanding of the work of Mipham Rinpoche, *The Beacon of Certainty*, translated and introduced by J. W. Pettit, is particularly valuable.

4 Nagarjuna is thought to have lived in the second century C.E.; Chandrakirti in the first part of the seventh.

5 Another translation of the title derives from an alternate interpretation of the element *avatara* (*'jug pa* in Tibetan) as meaning an addition or supplement. There is some justification for this, since, in presenting Nagarjuna's view, Chandrakirti adds further material of his own, elaborated through the application of Nagarjuna's dialectic to new questions and challenges that had been posed in the intervening period. See Jeffrey Hopkins, *Meditation on Emptiness* (London: Wisdom Publications, 1983), p. 867 n. 545.

6 The first two questions are sometimes formulated in terms of time and space, i.e., whether the universe is limited in time or extent.

7 *The Collection of Middle Length Sayings (Majjhima Nikaya), Volumes 1–3,* translated from the Pali by I. B. Horner (London: Pali Text Society, 1993, 1994, 1995).

8 Ibid.

9 *Mulamadhyamaka-karikas (rtsa ba shes rab)* (Varanasi: Pleasure of Elegant Sayings Press, 1974), xxiv, 12.

10 Ibid., xv, 7.

11 T. R. V. Murti, *The Central Philosophy of Buddhism* (London: George Allen and Unwin, 1968), p. 87.

12 See note 78.

13 See Mipham Rinpoche's commentary in the present volume and also Longchen Yeshe Dorje, *Treasury of Precious Qualities* (Boston: Shambhala Publications, 2000), pp. 252ff, 307ff.

14 See Bertrand Russell's *Problems of Philosophy* (Oxford: Oxford University Press, 1912) for a lively discussion of this matter.

15 *Bodhicharyavatara,* IX, 2. See Shantideva, *The Way of the Bodhisattva* (Boston: Shambhala Publications, 1997).

16 *Catuhsataka.* See Ruth Sonam, trans., *Yogic Deeds of Bodhisattvas* (Ithaca, N.Y.: Snow Lion Publications, 1994).

17 See Peter della Santina, *Madhyamaka Schools in India* (Delhi: Motilal Banarsidass, 1995), ch. 4.

18 See D. S. Ruegg, *The Literature of the Madhyamaka School of Philosophy in India* (Wiesbaden: Otto Harrassowitz, 1981). The most thorough exposition of this specific question is by Peter della Santina (*Madhyamaka Schools in India*), who bases himself on the Sakya teaching, particularly the view propounded by Gorampa. An extensive coverage of the subject is also to be found in Jeffrey Hopkins (*Meditation on Emptiness*), who bases himself on the writings of Jamyang Sheba and other masters of the Gelugpa tradition.

19 "Syllogism" is used loosely here to translate the Sanskrit term *prayoga* (Tib *sbyor ba*). In fact, the prayoga is structured differently from the syllogism of Aristotelian logic.

20 See Ruegg, *Literature*, p. 60.

21 See Immanuel Kant, *The Critique of Pure Reason* (London, 1929), A 252, pp. 270–71: "We have not, indeed, been able to prove that sensible intuition is the only possible intuition, but only that it is so for us. But neither have we been able to prove that another kind of intuition is possible. Consequently, although our thought can abstract from all sensibility, it is still an open question whether the notion of a noumenon be not a mere form of a concept, and whether, when this separation has been made, any object whatsoever is left."

22 Ibid., A 254: "If I remove from empirical knowledge all thought (through categories), no knowledge of any object remains. . . . But if, on the other hand, I leave aside all intuition, the form of thought still remains. . . . The categories accordingly extend further than sensible intuition, since they think objects in general without regard to the special mode (the sensibility) in which they may be given. But they do not thereby determine a greater sphere of objects. For we cannot assume that such objects can be given, *without presupposing the possibility of another kind of intuition than the sensible; and we are by no means justified in so doing.*"

23 See Murti, *Central Philosophy*, pp. 213, 297–301.

24 See M. Sprung, trans., *Lucid Exposition of the Middle Way* (London: Routledge & Kegan Paul, 1979).

25 See della Santina, *Madhyamaka Schools*, pp. 140ff.

26 Ibid., pp. 144, 149. See also Hopkins, *Meditation*, pp. 443ff. for a presentation of the "opposites of consequences (*thal bzlog*)" and "other-approved inferences."

27 Sprung, *Lucid Exposition*, I, 24 and see della Santina, *Madhyamaka Schools*, pp. 149–51.

28 Sprung, *Lucid Exposition*, 25.7–26.2.

29 See Bertrand Russell, *An Outline of Philosophy* (London: Routledge, 1995), ch. 1.

30 The incident is recounted by Shakya Chogden. See della Santina, *Madhyamaka Schools*, p. 85.

31 This kind of classification is to be found in the *lta ba khyad par* of Yeshe De. See Donald S. Lopez, *A Study of Svatantrika* (Ithaca, N.Y.: Snow Lion Publications, 1987), p. 56.

32 See Mipham, *Commentary on the Madhyamakalankara,* p 37 (Varanasi edition).

33 Ibid., pp. 41–43.

34 The main sources of biographical information on Mipham Rinpoche are to be found in Dudjom Rinpoche, *The Nyingma School of Tibetan Buddhism* (Boston: Wisdom Publications, 1999), and in *The Essential Biography* attributed to Khenpo Kunzang Pelden, on which Dudjom Rinpoche's account seems in part to be based. Another Tibetan source is *The Victorious Battle Drum* by Khenpo Jigme Phuntsok. Fortunately, Dudjom Rinpoche's account has been translated into English. See also E. Gene Smith Introduction to *Mipham's Answer to Blo bzang rab gsal's Refutation* (Gangtok: Sonam T. Kazi, 1969) and especially the relevant sections in the introduction to *Mipham's Beacon of Certainty* by John Pettit (Boston: Wisdom Publications, 1999), which brings together and summarizes all the available material.

35 See Khenpo Kunzang Pelden, quoted in Pettit, *Mipham's Beacon,* p. 26.

36 See Dudjom Rinpoche, *Nyingma School,* vol. 1, p. 872, and Pettit, *Mipham's Beacon,* p. 26, for two renderings of this inspiring passage.

37 With regard to the third turning, the sutras in question are, broadly speaking, the ones presenting the teachings on the Tathagatagarbha.

38 See Smith, Introduction to *Mipham's Answer.*

39 See Pettit, *Mipham's Beacon,* p. 27.

40 Ibid., p. 463 n. 16.

41 Ibid., pp. 182–84.

42 A translation of most of *The Essential Hagiography* is to be found in Pettit, *Mipham's Beacon,* pp. 23ff.

43 Kangyur Rinpoche, who died in exile in 1975, received Mipham Rinpoche's blessing when he was a child. Dilgo Khyentse Rinpoche, who died in 1991, was blessed shortly after his birth by Mipham Rinpoche and received from him the name Tashi Paljor (Mangala Shribhuti).

44 See Pettit, *Mipham's Beacon,* pp. 36–39.

45 See Pettit, *Mipham's Beacon,* pp. 141ff, for a detailed discussion.

46 See Dreyfuss, *Recognizing Reality,* pp. 106ff.

47 See Hopkins, *Meditation,* pp. 543ff.

48 Quoted in Longchen Yeshe Dorje, *Treasury of Precious Qualities,* p. 329.

49 A humorous reference to the Prajñaparamita, sometimes referred to as the Great Mother.

50 See Hopkins, *Meditation,* p. 544.

51 Ibid.; Elizabeth Napper, *Dependent Arising and Emptiness* (Boston: Wisdom Publications, 1989), p. 147; and Guy Newland, *The Two Truths: The Ma-*

dhyamika Philosophy of the Ge-luk-pa Order of Tibetan Buddhism (Ithaca, N.Y.: Snow Lion Publications, 1992), p. 12.

52   *Irreversibly Advancing* and *Clearly Manifest* are both names for the sixth ground.

53   Although the name is not specified here, this is called the *emptiness of all phenomena* (*chos thams cad stong pa nyid*).

54   "Countless," *grangs med*, is actually a number, defined in the Abhidharma as 10^{59}.

55   Jampel Gyepa'i Dorje is one of the names of Mipham Rinpoche.

56   *rtogs pa bzhi'i gtan tshigs*. Samsara and nirvana both derive from the same source: the unoriginated expanse of the mind's nature. When beings recognize this nature, nirvana occurs; when they fail to recognize it, samsara appears.

57   This introductory verse is the composition of the Tibetan editors.

58   As a convenient method of identifying the great wealth of Buddhist texts rendered into Tibetan, it was decided in the reign of the Dharma king Tri Ralpachen (866–901) that every translation would open with a specific salutation depending on the particular branch of teachings to which it belonged. Consequently all texts of sutra, the principal subject of which is meditative stabilization, traditionally open with a formula of homage to the Buddhas and Bodhisattvas. Vinaya texts, which deal with ethics and discipline, open with a homage to the Omniscient One. Finally, the texts of Abhidharma, expounding wisdom, begin with a homage to Mañjushri. Originally applied to translations, this rule is often followed by Tibetan writers generally, although in the latter case, the writer's yidam may also be invoked.

59   The last instant of the tenth ground before entering the path of no more learning (buddhahood).

60   The other seven links are: Consciousness, Name and Form, Sense Powers, Contact, Feeling, Birth, and Aging-and-Death.

61   See Longchen Yeshe Dorje, *Treasury of Precious Qualities,* pp. 85–93, for a detailed account of the twelve links of interdependent arising.

62   Ibid., p. 68.

63   See The Qualities of the Ten Grounds, p. 331.

64   *sbyor lam gyi bzod pa*. The path of joining is what links practitioners swiftly to the path of seeing and has four stages: "warmth," "peak," "acceptance," and "supreme mundane level." For "acceptance," see the eighth ground, p. 325.

65   See Longchen Yeshe Dorje, *Treasury of Precious Qualities*, ch. 6. The four kinds of Shravakas and Pratyekabuddhas are as follows:

(1) Stream Enterer (*rgyun du zhugs*). The Shravakas who abide in the understanding of the fifteen instants of the path of seeing, as described in the Hinayana Abhidharma, and the Shravakas who abide by the path of joining and the fifteen instants of the path of seeing, as described in the Mahayana Abhidharma, are all candidates for the degree of Stream Enterer. When they reach the sixteenth instant of the path of seeing, they become Stream Enterers who abide by the result. They are called Stream Enterers because they enter the stream of the path whereby they will attain the result.

(2) Once Returner (*lan gcig phyir 'ong ba*). The Stream Enterers who have rid themselves of the five degrees of obscurations in the desire realm eliminated by meditation are candidates for the state of Once Returner. On relinquishing the sixth degree, they become Once Returners abiding by the result. They are so called because they return only once more to the desire realm.

(3) Nonreturner (*phyir mi 'ong ba*). The Once Returners who have rid themselves of obscurations in the desire realm eliminated by meditation, to the seventh and eighth degree, but who have not yet eliminated those of the ninth, are candidates for the state of Nonreturner. When they discard all such obscurations, they become Nonreturners abiding by the result. They are so called because they will be reborn no more in the desire realm.

(4) Arhat (*dgra bcom pa*). The Nonreturners who are free of all the obscurations of the higher realms (i.e., form and formless) eliminated by meditation, right up to the eighth degree in the Peak of Existence, are candidates for arhatship. When they discard all the remaining obscurations of the three worlds, they become Arhats abiding by the result. Arhat means "Foe Destroyer." They are so called because they have destroyed their enemy, afflictive emotion.

66 For a detailed discussion of the obscurations eliminated on the path of seeing, see Longchen Yeshe Dorje, *Treasury of Precious Qualities*, p. 125.

67 Since wealth can appear in the lower realms, this shows that its cause, generosity, is not in itself a protection from lower rebirth.

68 A reference to the fact that the Bodhisattvas on this ground are approaching the elimination of the perception of dual appearance, even in the postmeditation stage.

69 Compare Shantideva, *The Way of the Bodhisattva*, ch. 6, 1.

70 This means to start their training in the paramitas from the beginning and continue the training for as many kalpas as moments of anger.

71 The prophecy referred to is that of impending buddhahood received by Bodhisattvas who are on the higher levels of the path of meditation, i.e., the eighth, ninth, and tenth grounds.

72 Indra is the king of the Heaven of the Thirty-three (gods). This divine
    realm is located on the summit of Mount Meru. According to traditional
    Buddhist cosmology, there exist an infinite number of universal systems,
    each of which has the same composition as our own, i.e. with its Mount
    Meru, four continents, etc. Consequently, every universe has its Heaven
    of the Thirty-three, each with its own "Indra."

73 Hard to Keep or Uphold (*sbyangs dka'*). This is the basis of the qualities of
    the extraordinary primordial wisdom of the lowest level of the middle
    Mahayana path of meditation. In the *Sutralankara* it is described thus:
    "Since bringing beings to complete maturity and taking care of one's
    own mind is difficult to achieve even for a wise Bodhisattva, this ground
    is called 'Hard to Keep or Uphold.'"

74 The sixth ground of realization has two names: Clearly Manifest (*mngon du
    gyur pa'i sa*) and Irreversibly Advancing (*mngon du phyogs pa'i sa*). Mipham
    Rinpoche uses both.

75 I.e., the five sensory consciousnesses, the mental consciousness, and the
    defiled emotional consciousness (*nyon yid*).

76 According to the Mahayoga tantra teachings, this is the eleventh ground
    and corresponds to buddhahood in the nirmanakaya aspect.

77 The upper fields are the Buddhas, the spiritual master, etc.; the lower
    fields are ordinary beings in the six realms.

78 In the following discussion, the use of the word "cause" must be clearly
    understood. Classical Western philosophy (for the present purposes,
    Aristotle and the Schoolmen) speaks of four kinds of cause: material or
    substantial, formal, efficient, and final. These may be defined using the
    example of a sculptor carving a statue. The substance carved, e.g., the
    marble, is the material cause; the shape and other features of the statue
    being carved are the formal cause; the sculptor or, more immediately,
    the chisel acting on the marble is the efficient cause; and the purpose
    for the work itself (e.g., that it will be used to adorn a public place) is
    the final cause. Although in modern English, "cause" is normally used
    only in the third sense (efficient cause), in the present context, and in
    Buddhist texts generally, it is used in the first sense: substantial or ma-
    terial cause. For example, an acorn is the cause of the oak tree into
    which it develops.

79 *gzhung gis bskyed pa'i bye brag gis chos can spang nas mkhas pa dang bud med
    byis pa'i bar dag la grags par gyur pa'i dngos po la ma lus yang dag 'jug par
    gyur.*

80 The followers of the Vedic tradition maintained that since the Vedas are
    eternal, the sounds that form them are also eternal and unchanging.

81 In the context of the present discussion, the expression "absolutist reasoning" should be understood as reasoning that investigates the ultimate status of phenomena, *don dam dpyod byed kyi rigs pa*.

82 There are three kinds of conventional valid cognition: direct sensory perception (*dbang po mngon sum*), inference (*rjes dpag*) and scriptural authority (*lung gi tshad ma*).

83 For example, candle flame and fire.

84 An extraneous true existence is as unreal as a barren woman's child. How can a phenomenon be empty of something that is itself a nullity?

85 These are the five great arguments (*gtan tshigs*) of the Madhyamikas (sometimes enumerated as four). See Kunzang Pelden, *Wisdom: Two Buddhist Commentaries* (Saint Léon-sur-Vézère: Editions Padmakara, 1993), pp. 105–18.

86 The answer given by the Samkhyas, to the effect that they are talking about two different states occurring in the same entity, in fact undermines an understanding of the causal process. If cause and effect are identical, act and potency coincide, which is impossible. The single underlying substance and the notion of evolution are incompatible. Either you assert unity, in which case you destroy causality, or you affirm causality, in which case the underlying unity is annihilated.

87 If self-production is true, there is no cogent reason that production should result in different things. Why not the same thing continuously?

88 Consider the classic Buddhist contention: "That is not one which is invested with conflicting characteristics."

89 In other words, causality is inferred from the coherence observable in production, even though the entities in question are separate and extraneous to each other.

90 I.e., the notion of otherness is only intelligible in a situation of contrast afforded by simultaneity. However, as a matter of experience, there is no simultaneity between seed and shoot.

91 I.e., no subject of the production process.

92 Other-production is a feature of the lower Buddhist tenet systems (including the Svatantrika Madhyamikas). The proponents of such systems naturally believe that their tenets provide an accurate account of the Buddha's teaching. But this is precisely what the Madhyamika questions. For Nagarjuna and Chandrakirti, other-production is a philosophical invention and falls short of the Buddha's view.

93 In the first case, the simultaneity of the process points to dependent arising, the seed and the shoot being dependent on each other.

94 If the content of consciousness is exactly simultaneous with its supposed

stimulus, the stimulus cannot be regarded as the origin of that content. The content is present already, independent of any such stimulus. The two are completely different things and there is no possible relation of dependence and consequently of causation. The nub of the problem is once again that of true existence, of two items that are inherently other. See Kunzang Pelden, *Wisdom: Two Buddhist Commentaries,* p. 97.

95 The difference is epistemic, not ontological.

96 This is the *rtag pa chen po* and *'dus ma byas pa chen po*, not to be confused with uncompounded space, etc. Nagarjuna said that this is inconceivable and not dependent on causes.

97 *thig le nyag gcig* or *chos dbying nyag gcig.*

98 A phenomenon possessing origin, duration, and cessation.

99 In other words, those who maintain that ultimate reality is a nonaffirming negative, *med dgag*. The expression "neither exist nor do not exist" looks, on the face of it like the fourth ontological extreme. But it should be understood in the sense of *med bzhin snang ba*, "not existing but yet appearing."

100 They have the same nature, but they are not simultaneous; rather they are to be found in two distinct moments, like the seed and its shoot.

101 Mental perceptions (as distinct from the other five sense perceptions) are dependent on the so-called mental organ, that is, the immediately preceding moment of sensory or mental cognition.

102 The argument, according to which the existence of phenomena is established by valid perception, is obviously circular.

103 A contrast is made here between *rtog pas brtags pa'i tshad grub* (the validly established phenomenon, which is just an imputation) as opposed to the Nyingmapa teaching of *rtog pas bzhag pa'i tshad grub* (the validly established phenomenon, which is the deposit—the long-term outcome—of mental habit).

104 The affirmations of false tenet systems are as illusory as the ordinary mistaken perceptions encountered in empirical experience. They have no reality on any level; the God of the theistic systems or the Self of the *atmyavada* correspond strictly to nothing at all. Moreover (see Murti on Bhavya, *Central Philosophy,* pp. 248–49), just as it is impossible to use mirages as a basis of life, in the same way false theories cannot be used as part of the path.

105 When informed of the recently published philosophy of Berkeley, disproving the existence of matter, Dr. Johnson kicked a boulder and exclaimed: "I refute it thus!"

106 On the face of it, a statement like "I have fathered this child" would seem
to indicate an example of other-production, not a contradiction of it. It
should be remembered that this argument about causality is being con-
ducted exclusively in the context of substantial causation and has to do
not so much with *causality* in the modern sense of word as with compet-
ing theories aimed at explaining the fact that phenomena arise, remain,
and cease. In contrast with the Samkhya doctrine, the Buddhist Abhidharmika theory (which Chandrakirti is in the process of refuting) states
that existence is momentary and that what appears as a single phenomenon is in fact a flux of instantaneous manifestations, each of which is
similar to, but totally separate from, the manifested entities that precede
and follow it. This doctrine, which is meant to account for the fact that
phenomena are not static things but series of separate events, is intended
to explain the impermanence of phenomena as well as to dispense with
the notion of enduring identity. Therefore when a man says that he fathered a child, the focus of interest is not the difference between himself
(the agent) and the baby (the result of the act), but between the item that
he contributed (the semen) and the finished product (the baby). Everyday language such as "I planted this tree" shows that ordinary people are
quite innocent of the kind of complicated metaphysical theories of the
kind just mentioned. The actual difference between the seed, which was
planted, and the tree, which is now observed, is usually ignored.

107 The three sovereign reasonings (*rigs pa'i rgyal po gsum*) are: (1) *'phags pa'i
mnyam bzhag dngos po ni 'jig gyur thal ba*; (2) *don dam par skye ba mi khegs pa'i
thal ba*; (3) *tha snyad bden pa rigs pa'i dpyad bzod du thal ba*. If there were
such a thing as other-production, naturally existent or according to
characteristics, it would follow that (1) the meditation of the Aryas
would destroy phenomena; (2) naturally existent production could not
be disproved on the ultimate level; and (3) the conventional truth would
resist analysis.

108 "Here things" (*dngos po*) only means "efficient phenomena." It is not understood in the wider sense of whatever is validly cognized by sight, hearing or mental activity. Sight refers to everything that is perceived directly
via the senses; hearing refers to what is learned indirectly by report from
other sources; mental activity refers to what is grasped inferentially.

109 I.e., valid cognition investigating the ultimate status of things (*don dam
dpyod byed kyi tshad ma*).

110 I.e., those, aside from the Svatantrikas, who refute only the true existence
of phenomena as distinct from phenomena themselves.

111   Such an analysis is out of place on the conventional level because it leads not to an explanation of the workings of phenomena but to the demonstration that they have no real existence. And, on the conventional level, the findings of such an analysis are irrelevant.

112   These words are addressed to those who entertain theories and elaborate formulas in order to explore the nature of phenomena. All such theories, at some point or other, fly in the face of ordinary, untutored experience.

113   That is, for the purposes of everyday existence.

114   See note 220 and Longchen Yeshe Dorje, *Treasury of Precious Qualities,* p. 329. "The objection might be raised that, without perception, it would be impossible to meditate on love and so forth, because the true existence of the referent must be apprehended as a basis of such a meditation—given that one must have a referent and the perception of it. To this we answer that that which apprehends objects as desirable or hateful is dualistic thought. It is this that brings forth the defilement and it is this that must therefore be removed. Aside from dualistic thought, there is no such thing as the so-called true existence of phenomena—somehow standing apart from them as a possible object of refutation."

115   "The pot is empty of true existence" looks like an assertion of extrinsic emptiness. This is not necessarily problematic. If the suggested distinction between the pot and its existence is understood as purely verbal, owing to the limitations of language, which necessarily makes a difference between subject and attribute, no difficulty ensues. In that case, *extrinsic* emptiness on the level of words is the equivalent of *intrinsic* emptiness on the level of meaning.

116   In other words, although the aggregates are multiple they are only empty of a truly existent oneness; although they are momentary, they are only empty of a truly existent permanence, etc.

117   The three points just mentioned, that phenomena are "without inherent nature" (*rgyu med pa*), that they are "without attributes" (*mtshan ma med pa),* and that they are "beyond expectation" (*smon pa med pa)* constitute the three doors of perfect liberation. See commentary on stanza 209 and Longchen Yeshe Dorje, *Treasury of Precious Qualities,* appendix 10.

118   And there would be nothing left to analyze.

119   As in the case of the reflection in a mirror.

120   *thob.* The Vaibhashikas explain the functioning of karma by saying that the performance of an action produces an entity (an "obtention," or *thob*), almost like a promissory note, that will provoke the resulting experience.

121 Something that is nonexistent does not exist (one negative). Something that is not nonexistent exists (two negatives making a positive). If the negation of nonexistence is once again negated, we come back to nonexistence (three negatives make a negative).

122 On the conventional level, phenomena lack true existence, but this does not mean that just anything can arise. There is, as a matter of fact, a discernible order in the universe, or at least in our perceptions of the same. Certain effects are invariably seen to arise from certain causes. In other words, experience on the conventional level evinces a certain "pattern." Chandrakirti is saying that the mechanism of karma partakes of this same pattern and is an expression of it.

123 I.e., will escape the karmic process.

124 By an appeal to valid cognition, either conventionally or ultimately speaking.

125 In that it partakes of the law of causality, karma functions with the same ineluctability as the causal sequences observable in everyday life. And it is just as inexplicable by rational means. Its "mysterious" character derives from the fact that its operation is occult and may extend over many lifetimes. Since, as unenlightened beings, we have only limited knowledge confined to the experience of a single existence at a time, we are unable to verify the karmic process for ourselves. Our knowledge of it derives ultimately from the Buddha's omniscience and not from direct perception or inference, as in the case of ordinary causes.

126 When considering the Madhyamika critique of the Chittamatra, it is important to realize that there is a difference between the mind-only teachings of the Buddha (bka'i sems tsam), recorded in the sutras and propounded by masters such as Asanga, Vasubandhu, and Sthiramati, and the Mind Only tenet system (grub mtha'i sems tsam) associated with the later elaboration of Dharmapala and others. The tenet system, which is primarily the object of Madhyamika attack, is a much more self-conscious form of philosophical idealism. See Janice Dean Willis, On Knowing Reality (Delhi: Motilal Banarsidass, 1982), pp. 20ff and 58, n. 74.

127 In his commentary on the Madhyamakalankara of Shantarakshita, Mipham Rinpoche says: "In different texts, the dependent nature is presented either from an ultimate or from a relative point of view. If considered from the point of view of its ultimate status (namely, the way of being of the dependent nature itself), it is ultimate. If, however, it is considered from the side of its appearing mode, it is proper to include it in the relative."

128 For the Madhyamikas, consciousness is a dependent arising.

129 The example given does not carry equal weight for both parties. The fact of dreaming does not prove that the mind is a really existent entity—more real than what it is dreaming about.

130 In appealing to the example of dreaming, the Chittamatrins are basing themselves on the common conviction that dreams are illusory while waking life is real. They argue that the fact that one can dream of wholly absent objects shows that the mind, the dreaming subject, is real and can experience mental contents that have no external referent. For the Madhyamikas, this is not a convincing demonstration of the reality of the mind as compared with extramental objects, because, when the dream occurs, i.e., within the dream, there is nothing to show that the dreaming subject is in fact more real than the object dreamed about. In order to defend themselves against this charge, the Chittamatrins naturally try to establish a link between the dreaming mind and the waking mind—given that the waking state is generally thought of as having more reality than the dreaming state. If there is a continuity between the two, this should be enough to show that (even granted the Madhyamika objection) the dreaming subject is more real than the dream. The proof of continuity between the dream and waking states is the fact of memory. One can remember that one has dreamed: the subject that is awake now is the same subject that was dreaming in the course of sleep. Chandrakirti reduces the argument to absurdity by saying that if memory is sufficient to prove continuity, the same should hold good not only for the subject but also for the object.

131 Chandrakirti's argument envisages two men. One has an eye disease; the other does not. The former sees black lines before his eyes (and for him the experience corresponds to waking reality). The healthy man of course sees nothing. We are thus faced with two alternatives. In the first, the mind is a dependent arising, in which case the consciousness of black lines or whatever depends on circumstances (a disease in the present case). In the second of the alternatives, consciousness is not a dependent arising and the mind is something inherently real. If consciousness does not depend on circumstances, it must function irrespective of them, regardless of whether, for example, the eyes are healthy or not. If the presence of illness makes no difference to the perceptions of the mind, the experience of the sick man should be equally available to the healthy man. Neither of these alternatives fits the position of the Chittamatrins. In the first case, the independence of the mind is disproved; in the second it is an undeniable fact that floating black lines are not seen by healthy people.

132 *bdag gcig 'brel.* As in "the roundness of a circle." This excludes a relation of causality.

133 *de byung 'brel.* See Daniel Perdue, *Debate in Tibetan Buddhism* (Ithaca, N.Y.: Snow Lion Publications, 1993), p. 617.

134 An interdependent proof of real existence, as proposed by Chandrakirti's opponent, is a contradiction in terms. For real existence to be proved, evidence must be supplied from *outside* the closed circle of the interdependent relationship. Two interdependent terms are incapable of mutually proving their individual, real existence. This is precisely the Madhyamika point: interdependence precludes real existence by definition.

135 The Chittamatrins do not in fact assert other-production as an element of their tenet system. However when the Chittamatra position is subject to analysis, it can be shown to exemplify this same extreme position.

136 In other words, the Chittamatrins cannot have it both ways. Either the dreamer and the blind man both see, or neither of them does. The first alternative does not fit experience; the second alternative does not fit the Chittamatra theory.

137 They are thus caught in a manifest contradiction. The argument has four stages: (1) Being asleep and being blind are equal states in that in both cases the eyesight does not function. (2) Seeing, according to the Chittamatrins, is the result of ripening potential. Ostensibly, it has nothing to do with the function or nonfunction of the eyes. (3) This being so, since the absence of sight (in the case of the waking blind man) is not regarded as the triggering circumstance for the unfolding of the seeing potential (he cannot see), there is no reason the absence of sight (in the case of the sleeping man) should be so regarded (allowing him to see things in his dreams). (4) Therefore, the Chittamatrins are contradicting themselves.

138 This is a reference to the nonconceptual, mental consciousness. This operates during the dream state.

139 Debate can only take place between people who are willing to subject their own views to the findings of impartial reason. No discussion is possible with dogmatism—the mere assertion of a position without evidence or reasoned proof.

140 Prakriti can be refuted by both kinds of reasoning. Insofar as it is a supposedly inherently existent thing, it can, like other phenomena, be refuted by absolutist arguments. Insofar as it is a mistaken notion, it is to be disproved like other illusions (water seen in a mirage, for example) by reasoning operating on the conventional level.

141 I.e., a meditative technique intended to counteract lust, such as visualizing desirable human beings as skeletons.

142 *rtog pas bzhag pa tsam.* The approach described here is typically Nyingmapa, as distinct from that of the Gelugpas (*rtog pas brtags pa tsam*). See note 103.

143 In other words, if there is no substrate (even an occult one) underlying appearances, there can be no objective coherence in the universe in general and specifically in the causal sequence.

144 If fire is validly established by imputation (i.e., by the act of imputing) and not simply through the outcome of long-term habitual patterns, it ought to be objectively hot and should burn indiscriminately in all situations, which is not the case.

145 These three principles of reasoned investigation are: *chos nyid kyi rigs pa, bya byed kyi rigs pa,* and *ltos pa sgrub pa'i rigs pa.* To these a fourth principle is normally added, *'thad pa sgrub pa'i rigs pa* (the principle of valid proof). See Dalai Lama, *The World of Tibetan Buddhism* (Boston: Wisdom Publications, 1995), pp. 48–49.

146 The categorization of actions as positive or negative arises from their incontrovertible effects, not from the dictates of a moral code.

147 Seen from the point of view of the effect.

148 When they purify their defilements to the point where their status is commensurate with that of the animal or human realms. If such beings acquire even greater merit, corresponding, for example, with the divine realm, they will encounter not water but nectar. And as a result of high accomplishment, "water" appears as the female Buddha Mamaki.

149 In other words, that there are no objective facts; there is nothing beyond subjective experience.

150 I.e., according to similar karma shared by, for example, the human race. In our world, it is generally accepted, according to invariable experience, that snow is white. Therefore, if one sees blue snow, one knows that something is amiss.

151 The object is recalled with the thought "I have seen *such-and-such.*" The subject is recalled with the thought "*I* have seen such-and-such."

152 One can only remember something that one was conscious of.

153 If, in any given experience, there is no aspect of reflexive awareness, it would be impossible to recollect the experience as having been one's own.

154 See also Kunzang Pelden, *Wisdom*, p. 52 n. 1.

155 I.e., instances of sound. These are all, as it happens, impermanent, but the evidence of individual examples, however numerous, does not amount to a *logical* demonstration of the impossibility of permanent sound.

156 To do so would be to fall into a circularity. Since the two terms are inter-dependent, one of them cannot be cited as a proof of the other's existence.

157 The fire crystal and water crystal are legendary substances able to pro-duce fire and water respectively.

158 If they are truly and independently existent, the past experience and the present memory are as extraneous and alien to each other as the mental events of two different mind streams. And just as Upagupta cannot be said to remember Maitreya's experiences, neither (if moments of con-sciousness are independent existents) can the present Maitreya be said to remember what the past Maitreya did. The Chittamatra theory is an ex-ample of the doctrine of "other-production." But see note 135.

159 Memory is an undeniable fact of experience, but the Prasangikas do not construct a theory about it.

160 The discussion now returns to the earlier question of stanza 72.

161 Combination implies contact, and contact implies parts. Therefore, part-less particles could never combine together to form larger objects.

162 I.e., as a sort of discrete, partless entity.

163 Earlier on, Chandrakirti refuted both the Buddhist and non-Buddhist account of relative phenomena. How can he now espouse the ideas of or-dinary people as his view of conventional truth?

164 For Mipham Rinpoche, conventional discourse is not simply for the pur-pose of communication with others. The Prasangikas make use of it also on their own account. This concerns the question whether the Prasangikas adopt a theoretical position of their own. According to the Nyingma un-derstanding, the Prasangikas make no positive assertion when they are en-gaged in debate and establishing the view (in the sense of *rnam grangs ma yin pa'i don dam*). On the other the hand, when reflecting on the path and expounding it, they do make assertions, in the sense of explaining the path and the fruit. Chandrakirti's text itself furnishes an example of this, for in addition to establishing emptiness according to the Prasangika method, it sets forth the bodhisattva bhumis and discusses the qualities of buddha-hood, etc.

165 In other words, the Buddha was not laying the foundations for an ideal-istic philosophy.

166 See Longchen Yeshe Dorje, *Treasury of Precious Qualities,* p. 90, for a pres-entation of the twelve interdependent links in forward and reverse order.

167 I.e., not shared by other minds.

168 This is probably a reference to the hills in the peripheral hells on which the shalmali trees grow.

169   In other words, it can be seen that both the Svatantrika and the Prasangika methods have their utility and place, the former acting as a propaedeutic for the latter. But this scheme of things is disrupted by an ill-advised retention of the Svatantrika method and terms in a Prasangika context. Confusion is the result, and the difficulty of gaining realization is aggravated.

170   This explains the structure of Chandrakirti's sixth chapter. The personal no-self is set forth in the Hinayana texts and constitutes the realization of the Arhats, whereas the phenomenal no-self is the preserve of the Mahayana. Given this apparent hierarchy of views, one might have expected Chandrakirti to discuss these two "no-selves" in the same order. The fact that he did not do so has important implications. With regard to a personal self, it is important to bear in mind that Buddhism draws a distinction between the "imputed self" (the product of reflection, or a belief instilled by religious and philosophical teaching), which is learned anew in any given life, and the "innate self," a deep-rooted feeling that forms part of one's basic psychological orientation, which accompanies the mind from life to life and is present in every moment of consciousness. Of these two selves, the first or "imputed self" is easier to deal with, since it can be called into question and disproved through the application of logical argument. By contrast, the profoundly habitual tendency represented by the "innate self" is far more difficult to dislodge and can only be dispelled by long training on the path. The innate sense of self is activated, confirmed, and intensified in the course of everyday experience, and this is in turn grounded in the naïve and unexamined conviction that the external world is intrinsically real. It stands to reason therefore that, as a means of coming to grips with the problem of the self (which is after all the *fons et origo* of samsara and its suffering) it is important to deal first with the "phenomenal self." This is a comparatively easy matter, since in the course of experience, we receive plenty of indications (dreams, for instance, or the fact that our senses often deceive us) that lead us to doubt that the world really is as it actually appears. Thus the structure of the sixth chapter is essentially pragmatic. The phenomenal self is discussed first because it is, in practice, the first thing that must be dealt with. This in turn suggests that in order to realize the personal no-self, it is also necessary to realize the phenomenal no-self. This leads to the vexed question whether the Arhats, in realizing the personal no-self, must also realize the phenomenal no-self. It is sometimes said that Chandrakirti believes that they must, and we are faced with the paradox that in attaining their nirvana, the Arhats must realize a truth that is set forth in the Mahayana and

is not accounted for in their Hinayana tenets. As will be shown later, Mipham Rinpoche does not agree that the Arhats have full realization of the phenomenal no-self and believes that Chandrakirti is misinterpreted on this point. See the commentary to stanza 179.

171 Since self-production and other-production are both indemonstrable, the combination of the two is equally indemonstrable.

172 The expression here, *ngo bos byung bar smra ba* appears to be a translation of the Skt. *svabhavavada*, which was an early designation of the materialist school. The implication of this expression is that the Charvakas "traced whatever character an object might manifest to that very object and not to any extraneous agent." See M. Hiriyanna, *The Essentials of Indian Philosophy* (Delhi: Motil Banarsidass, 1995), p. 57. The natural world of experience is simply what it is; it does not reveal the presence or activity of any creative agency, divine or otherwise, a creator God, or a principle of causal concomitance.

173 This is the logical implication of uncaused production. On the other hand, experience shows that the universe is coherent and appears to function predictably according to stable principles.

174 The sky-lotus, i.e., a lotus literally growing in space, is the stock example of something never experienced.

175 Mind is simply an epiphenomenon of matter and the two are not separable; therefore, talk of lives before or after the present one is meaningless.

176 For the Charvakas have said that direct perception of an object furnishes the only grounds for belief in the existence of that object.

177 If the difference between existence and nonexistence is annihilated, the Charvaka position collapses. However convoluted this argument may seem, it has the merit of showing that, despite its claims to rationality, the assertion of materialism, that there are no past and future lives, is not logically coherent.

178 For on their own admission they only accept direct perception as a valid source of knowledge.

179 Divine sight, i.e., the knowledge of past and future lives, is one of the qualities possessed by a Buddha. It is also possessed by highly accomplished humans as a kind of clairvoyance. For beings thus equipped, past and future existences are directly perceived. For ordinary mortals, among whom the Charvakas are certainly to be numbered, direct perception in these matters is impossible—not because the object of such perception is nonexistent but because the requisite powers of detection are not available.

180 The Buddhist approach to this question is based on the teaching of no-

self and on the doctrine of dependent arising. When these two points are understood, it becomes apparent that there is absolutely no reason for thinking that this present existence is the only reality or that past and future "lives" do not exist. The succession of lives is no different from the succession of moments within a given so-called existence—a beginningless and endless fabric of interdependent relationships. Whether or not a present state of consciousness is able to envision, through memory or clairvoyance, the sequence of past lives and future lives, or whether indeed it is able to embrace past or future moments of the present existence, is simply a matter of mental acuity.

181   The brilliant sheen of a peacock's feathers can create a three-dimensional effect, and a swarm of bees looks like a homogeneous, almost liquid body, whereas of course it is just a grouping of individual insects.

182   The opponent believes that appearance proves existence: if a thing appears, it must exist. For the opponent, to say that something ultimately does not exist is to place it in the same category as a rabbit's horns or a barren woman's son, i.e., something that has absolutely no existence and can never be encountered. In reply to this, Chandrakirti points out that appearance is not a criterion for existence. In the case of someone suffering from an eye disease, we have an example of something appearing that is universally recognized as being nonexistent. The same applies to the hallucinations of a drug addict. In being without existence, these hallucinations are on a level with a rabbit's horns. Nevertheless they appear, and their appearance is something that depends on the condition of the perceiving subject. In perceiving things for which there is no objective referent, Chandrakirti contends, those who suffer from an eye disease, are comparable to ordinary beings generally. In other words, the opponent's argument from appearance is as useless in convincing Chandrakirti of the reality of phenomena as it is in refuting the hallucination of the drug addict. Phenomena appear, *but they do not exist*; the hallucinatory objects do not exist, *yet they appear*.

183   Being nonexistent, they are beyond assessment as being good or bad.

184   At first sight, it may seem strange that illusions, mirages, and so on are said to be without existence *on the ultimate level*. Surely ordinary investigation on the conventional level is enough to reveal their falsity. It is important to bear in mind that illusions have two aspects. In a mirage of an oasis, for example, the water, palm trees, and so on are completely illusory. As water and trees, they are uncaused (no atoms of hydrogen and oxygen have combined, no palm saplings have been planted, etc.), and

their existence is disproved by conventional empirical investigation. As an optical illusion, however, the mirage itself does have causes (the heat and atmospheric conditions of the desert, the fatigue of the traveler, etc.). From this point of view, the mirage is like every other phenomenon and is disproved on the ultimate level accordingly (by reasoning). In short, the mirage of an *oasis* is disproved on the conventional level; the *mirage* of an oasis is disproved on the ultimate level.

185 The child of a barren woman is a logical impossibility (unproduced on the ultimate level) and as a matter of fact is never born or encountered (unproduced on the conventional level). It is perhaps significant that Chandrakirti only mentions the barren woman's child here. It is interesting to reflect that in this respect, the two stock images of the child of a barren woman and the horns of a rabbit are not the same. The idea of the child of a barren woman contains a contradiction and its occurrence is thus a logical impossibility. By contrast, to say that the horns of a rabbit do not exist is a an empirical generalization. In practice, horned rabbits are not met with, but there is nothing logically impossible in the idea of a rabbit having horns—and for all we know there may be, lurking in the jungles of Borneo and waiting to be discovered, a hitherto unknown species of horned rabbits. But given that horned rabbits, as a matter of fact, are not encountered, the nonexistence of rabbit's horns is proved, or rather supposed, empirically on the conventional level. Whereas the nonexistence of the barren woman's child is proved by both reasoning and experience, the rabbit's horns are disproved only by experiment. However, insofar as the expressions "barren woman's child" and "rabbit's horns" correspond to nothing on the empirical level (the former certainly, the latter probably), the arguments proper to their refutation are confined to the level of conventional reasoning. As Mipham Rinpoche observes on several occasions, it is inappropriate to try to disprove them with absolutist reasoning, for the simple reason that they are not phenomena.

186 In other words, that a pot is not a cloth and a cow's horns are not a rabbit's horns—i.e., a completely trivial and irrelevant conclusion.

187 In other words, although the syllogism is necessarily couched in sentences composed of subject and predicate, true existence is not to be understood as a predicate in the normal sense of the word, implying that the subject can be considered in isolation of it. The statement "The rabbit's horns do not exist" simply means that the rabbit has no horns. It does not mean that the rabbit has horns and these are nonexistent. In

the same way, it is nonsense to say that the proposition "The pot is empty of true existence" means that the pot is separable from its true existence and can somehow survive its removal.

188 Only the indivisible particles of matter and the indivisible instants of consciousness are ultimately real for the Vaibhashikas, while gross objects have a relative existence only. The Sautrantikas accept only specifically characterized phenomena (i.e., impermanent phenomena able to function) as ultimately existent, while generally characterized phenomena (i.e., mental objects) have a relative existence. A forest, for example, is a mere conceptual imputation made in dependence on individual trees. As such, it has only a relative existence.

189 See note 218.

190 As when one says, for instance, that a cup is empty of water.

191 "Form is emptiness, emptiness is form, form is not other than emptiness, and emptiness is not other than form."

192 To say that something is produced by something else suggests a relationship of dependence in the ordinary sense of the word. But the meaning of dependent arising is more subtle than this.

193 It is therefore totally at variance with the view it is intended to express.

194 I.e., in its natural state. See S. Radhakrishnan, *Indian Philosophy* vol. 2 (Delhi: Oxford University Press, 1923), p. 266.

195 "Mahat, or the Great, the cause of the whole universe, is the first product of the evolution of prakriti. It is the basis of the intelligence of the individual. While the term *mahat* brings out the cosmic aspect, *buddhi*, which is used as a synonym for it, refers to the psychological counterpart appertaining to each individual. In the Samkhya, stress is laid on the psychological aspect of *mahat*. From the synonyms of *buddhi*, . . . it is clear that *buddhi* is to be taken in the psychological sense. But the designations of *mahat* (the Great, Brahma, etc.) imply that it is used in the cosmic sense also. *Buddhi* is not to be confused with the incorporeal *purusha*. It is regarded as the subtle substance of all mental processes. It is the faculty by which we distinguish objects and perceive what they are. The functions of *buddhi* are ascertainment and decision. All other organs function for the intellect (*buddhi*), which works directly for *purusha*, enabling the latter to experience all existence and discriminate between itself and *prakriti*." Ibid., pp. 266–67.

196 "From the subtle element of smell proceeds earth; from the subtle element of form proceeds luminosity; from the subtle element of taste proceeds water; from the subtle element of contact proceeds wind; and from

the subtle element of sound proceeds ether." Translated from *Les strophes de Samkhya, avec le commentaire de Gaudapada* (Paris: Société d'Edition "Les Belles Lettres," 1964).

197 See Radhakrishnan, *Indian Philosophy*, pp. 270ff. "The world as the object of perception has the five *tanmatras*, corresponding to the five sense-organs. These are the essences of sound, touch, color, taste and smell, conceived as physical principles, imperceptible to ordinary beings. . . . These invisible essences are inferred from visible objects, though they are said to be open to the perception of the yogis. The fine (subtle) elements are said to be devoid of difference, while the gross elements arising from them have a definite quality . . ."

198 There are different ways of assigning the functions of the three aspects of ahamkara. In contrast to the arrangement given here, both Radhakrishnan and Hiriyanna say that manas and the five organs of sense and action derive from the sattvika aspect; the subtle and gross elements derive from the tamasa aspect, while both are pervaded by the rajasa aspect. But Radhakrishnan acknowledges that there are different ways of enumeration other than the one that he adopts. See Hiriyanna, *Essentials*, p. 110, and Radhakrishnan, *Indian Philosophy*, p. 263 and note.

199 The cuckoo represents the imputed permanent self (e.g., purusha), which is completely unconnected and alien to the five impermanent aggregates. As such, it cannot be what experiences the objects of sense. Consequently, even though the existence of such a self is disproved by reasoning, the apprehension of and clinging to the sense objects remains unchanged.

200 According to Gorampa, this point is a unique feature of Chandrakirti's teaching. Without the realization of the emptiness of the phenomenal self, there can be no realization of the emptiness of the personal self.

201 This is an important point. We may think that the five aggregates *as a whole* constitute the self. But Chandrakirti points out that a whole, made up of parts, enjoys only an imputed existence. It is just an idea, like "forest," of which only the individual trees exist materially and can be used. This at least is the position of the Sammitiyas and others. Of course, for Chandrakirti himself, an individual tree is also composed of parts, and it too has no more than an imputed existence. The Sammitiyas and other substantialist schools up to and including the Svatantrikas (i.e., followers of Bhavaviveka) make a distinction between the real, material existence (*rdzas yod*) of substances, e.g., a man, and the merely conceptual existence (*btags yod*) of abstract ideas or universals, e.g., mankind. For them the basis of imputation (*gdags gzhi*) has a substantial existence

(*rdzas yod*), whereas the imputed thing (*btags chos*) has only an imputed existence (*btags yod*). The basis of imputation is real; the imputation itself is merely conceptual. The Prasangikas, by contrast, consider that the ground of imputation is also *btags yod,* that it is no more than a thought. They consider that the mind grasps only at baseless concepts, and for them, accordingly, the self is nothing but a name. Theoreticians, on the other hand, may inquire about the basis to which such a name is applied, and produce different answers. And the substantialist schools (of Buddhism) consider that the ground to which the label "self" is applied is indeed the five aggregates. To illustrate this point, one may imagine, for example, that when a hiker in the countryside sees a scarecrow in the distance and thinks that it is the local farmer, the scarecrow is the substantial basis for the hiker's mistaken idea. By contrast, Chandrakirti says that a more accurate description of the situation is that when the hiker sees the sticks, coat, hat, and so on, the idea "farmer" arising in his mind is due simply to a disposition grounded in past experience and habit. In other words, the scarecrow is not the *real basis* for the erroneous idea; it only acts as the occasion of the idea's occurrence. The illusory farmer has no real material basis, either in the scarecrow or anywhere else. Neither is there any real link between the object standing in the field and the farmer that the hiker thinks he sees. To be sure, in the moment of illusion when the hiker believes that the farmer is there, it is not that he is detecting something present in the scarecrow, for there is certainly no trace of the farmer contained in it. The farmer is just a baseless illusion, which does not in any way consist of, or in, the scarecrow. If the situation were otherwise, we would have to explain where the farmer went to when, on approaching, the hiker discovers a pair of sticks and some old clothes. In just the same way, for Chandrakirti, the illusion of the self is *gzhi med*; it has no real basis. The aggregates are only the occasion of a mistaken conception. Indeed, if the aggregates were the real basis for the self, one would have to conclude absurdly that when the former are meditated upon and discovered for what they are, the self is actually being destroyed. But in fact there is no self to be destroyed.

202 It is not a concrete, autonomous entity and cannot function.

203 In which case it would be possible to point to water and say, "This is hydrogen and oxygen."

204 *yid nye bar rgyu ba bco brgyad.* According to Khenpo Zhenga, this refers to the pleasant, unpleasant, or neutral movements of the mind toward the six objects of sense.

205 Chandrakirti emphasizes that the object of reference for our ego-clinging is not the five aggregates but rather the idea of "I" that we entertain.

206 In other words, the false philosophical concept.

207 These words of the root text are in fact a quotation from the *Suhrllekha* of Nagarjuna.

208 Note that the twenty views of the self are part of innate ego-clinging. They are naturally part of one's "mind-set"; one does not need to subscribe to a tenet system to be under their influence.

209 In a way, the Vatsiputriyas (*gnas ma bu ba*) resemble the Prasangikas in saying that the basis of ego-grasping is the (supposed) self and not the aggregates. But the similarity ends there. For the Vatsiputriyas the self is a real entity; for the Prasangikas it is a mere idea. Other Buddhist substantialists say that while the self is just an imputation, the basis of imputation—namely, the aggregates—is real. The Prasangikas correct this by denying the reality not only of the imputation or label, but also of the basis of labeling. The Vatsiputriyas proceed in a diametrically opposite direction. They assert the reality not only of the basis of labeling but of the label itself.

210 Compare the remark of the philosopher David Hume: "For my part, when I enter most intimately into what I call *myself*, I always stumble on some particular perception or other, of heat or cold, light or shade, love or hatred, pain or pleasure. I never catch *myself* at any time without a perception and never can observe anything but the perception. When my perceptions are remov'd for any time, as by sound-sleep; so long am I insensible of *myself*, and may truly be said not to exist." *A Treatise of Human Nature*, Book 1, part IV, section VI (London: Penguin Classics, 1984), p. 300.

211 I.e., in identity or difference. See commentary to stanza 143.

212 Of the sevenfold reasoning, the first five points were already current in Chandrakirti's time, whereas the last two represent his own personal insights. This is no doubt why he deals with them here at some length, while the previous five have been dealt with summarily and by implication in the foregoing stanzas.

213 In other words, the opponent is caught in a circularity. All talk of "chariot parts" presupposes the prior existence of the chariot, but this is precisely what is supposedly produced *subsequent* to the juxtaposition of items that, *in and of themselves*, cannot be qualified as chariot parts.

214 It is just an idea, an imputation—just as a forest is imputed in dependence on individual trees.

215 The wheels are still round and so on.

216 When looking at the round object, we identify a wheel; we do not see the form of a chariot. The question is, when all the disparate "constitutive" elements, each with its own shape, are assembled and a new overall shape has emerged, do we have the shape of a chariot? To answer in the affirmative is to fall into a manifest contradiction. As will be shown in the commentary to the following stanza, to say "this is the shape of a chariot" is to make "chariot" the prius or first idea of the logical sequence, whereas, according to the opponent, the shape comes first and the identification "chariot" follows. To say that the shape is a chariot is to turn the logical process on its head and is no more than a careless, in fact meaningless, expression. The terms of reference are, of course, entirely relative. The same argument could be equally applied to the wheel (or any other of the chariot's constituents) if this were made the object of analysis. The wheel itself is not the shape of its assembled constituents and is just as elusive and unfindable as the chariot itself.

217 The opponent's view is incoherent. The opponent does not in fact ascribe real existence to collections. A collection does not exist as such; it is but a name. It has a merely imputed existence and is nothing real or substantial. As such, it cannot have a shape. This notion of the chariot being the newly assumed shape of the arrangement of parts goes against the opponent's fundamental principle that only the basis of imputation (*gdags gzhi*) is materially existent (*rdzas yod*), while the thing imputed (*btags chos*) is only a name (*btags yod*).

218 According to the Vaibhashikas, phenomena require the interaction of eight really existent particles (earth, air, fire, water, form, odor, taste, and touch). These particles are not perceptible to the ordinary senses; their existence is inferred from their functions. The impenetrability of an earthenware pot manifests the earth element; the fact that it coheres shows the presence of the water element; the air element allows it to be transported from place to place, etc. The Vaibhashikas say that when all the particles are assembled and a thing appears, the idea or name of the thing arises too. Chandrakirti denies this. The idea of a pot, he says, cannot be based on such putative particles, because when these are investigated as to their origin, it will be found that none of the four theories of production can be applied to them. Therefore, they have no real or substantial existence. By the same token, gross phenomena are equally unreal.

219 This statement is very characteristic of Chandrakirti's Prasangika approach, according to which the relative truth is defined simply as what

appears to unreflective experience. No philosophical or scientific explanation of the relative is put forward, and no theory is entertained about
it. Although it is true that a chariot is a mere dependent arising based on
its parts, ordinary people take its existence for granted and certainly do
not think in terms of shape, assemblage, and so on when they say, for instance, that they need a taxi. By contrast, the Buddhist opponents of the
Prasangikas not only uphold the view that the personal self does not exist (*bdag med*), but they elaborate a philosophical theory in order to "explain the situation." They say, for instance, that the parts (aggregates)
have a real existence, but that the whole (the self) is only a label. It is
thus, as Chandrakirti points out, that they contradict the commonsense
experience of ordinary people.

220 See Longchen Yeshe Dorje, *Treasury of Precious Qualities,* p. 331: "The personal self, or ego, is the name given to what is assumed to be our inherently existing person; the 'phenomenal self' is what is assumed to be the
inherently existing phenomenon. These are the conceived objects apprehended in the two kinds of self-clinging. In the example of the rope mis-
takenly apprehended as a snake, they correspond to the snake. They are
as nonexistent as a rabbit's horns, even on the relative level. In addition
to this, there is self-*apprehension* or self-*clinging*. To cling to the personal
self means to believe that one's self is truly existent. To cling to the phenomenal self means to believe that phenomena are truly existent. The
person and phenomena are thus the referents of these two self-clingings.
In the example given, they are like the colored rope that acts as the basis
for the mistaken perception of the snake." In other words, the *inherently
existent* ego and phenomena are purely imaginary. On the relative level,
there is only a "person" and "phenomena," which are nothing but imputations projected onto the appropriate constituents, and the latter are, of
course, transitory phenomena. In other words, although "clinging to
self" is real enough, the object of clinging (an *inherently existent self*) is a
mere figment, as nonexistent as the apparent snake.

221 To say "This is a cause" is only another way of saying "This has an effect";
to say "This is an effect" is only another way of saying "This has been
brought about by something." In other words, language itself may be
seen to imply interdependence.

222 If they are in genuine contact, at what point does the cause end and the
effect begin?

223 In an estuary, where does the river end and the sea begin?

224 Stream Enterer, Once Returner, Nonreturner, and Arhat.

225 People already suffer because of their innate notion of self. Their predicament is compounded by the addition of ideas and theories about the imputed self.

226 The distinction between the personal self and the phenomenal self is made only from the subjective viewpoint of the individual. The personal self refers only to the subject; the phenomenal self refers to everything else, including other living beings as well as the subject's own aggregates. In fact, however, the personal self is just a category of the phenomenal self.

227 A whole is mentioned, but only a part or aspect is intended. Thus the Shravakas and Pratyekabuddhas are said by Chandra to understand the phenomenal no-self, but in reality, they do so only partially, indeed only slightly.

228 One of these misconceptions is precisely the clinging to a nonaffirming negative (*med dgag*).

229 Which presumably would be the case if the Shravakas really did have a full realization of emptiness.

230 *khog pa*. These are the actual material supports of the senses and are not to be confused with the senses themselves. According to the Abhidharma, they are subtle objects, possess different shapes, and are located respectively within the eyes, ears, tongue, and so on.

231 *don ldog*. The meaning-isolate, or meaning distinguisher, of a phenomenon is its defining property expressed conceptually. See Dreyfuss, *Recognizing Reality*, p. 117.

232 According to the Abhidharma (see Mipham Rinpoche's *mkhas 'jug*), perception is defined as "that which grasps, or identifies, characteristics" (*mtshan mar 'dzin pa*). Perception is related to the six senses: the five physical senses which are nonconceptual, and the mind or "mental sense," which functions by means of concepts. These two categories of conceptual and nonconceptual perceptions are themselves divided into two groups according to whether, in the course of their activity, they succeed in discerning the characteristics of their objects. If they do so, they are referred to as *mtshan bcas* (discerning); if they fail to do so, they are called *mtshan med* (nondiscerning).

233 See Longchen Yeshe Dorje, *Treasury of Precious Qualities*, appendix 9.

234 The knowledge of the Buddhas is never inferential; they know everything by direct cognition. This characteristic is not shared even by Bodhisattvas on the tenth ground.

235 On the side of ultimate truth or *chos nyid* (emptiness itself), there is no such thing as "twenty emptinesses." It is only from the point of view of

the subject or *chos can* (i.e., empty phenomena) that emptiness can be approached, as it were, from different angles (according to the various ways in which people experience things and fixate on them). This gives rise to the present twentyfold classification. In the same way, an individual man may be qualified in twenty ways, while remaining, from his own point of view, a single reality.

236 The kyurura fruit being transparent, the lines of one's hand are visible through it.

237 The word translated as acceptance is *bzod pa*, which also suggests fearlessness.

238 See note 54.

239 These ten strengths, which are specifically associated with the ninth ground, are not to be confused with the ten strengths of the Buddha.

240 This means that the Bodhisattva can enable them to enter the path of seeing through having abandoned all that obstructs this realization (*mthong spangs*).

241 I.e., different subjects (elements, ayatanas, paramitas, etc.).

242 I.e., still in conceptual terms, so that "unborn" is understood as being in contrast with "born."

243 This same point is discussed in Kunzang Pelden, *Wisdom: Two Buddhist Commentaries*, p. 37.

244 The Buddhas have realized the equality status of phenomena.

245 This is the main cause (*rgyu*).

246 This is the contributary cause (*rkyen*).

247 See the song of Yeshe Tsogyal in Gyalwa Changchub and Namkhai Nyingpo, *Lady of the Lotus-Born* (Boston: Shambhala Publications, 1999), p. 161.

248 *Dhatu* or *khams* refers to *yul can gyis bcad pa*, i.e., all that the mind can consider or investigate. This includes the "postmeditation" experience of a Bodhisattva residing on the grounds of realization.

249 The six sense faculties, sexual organs, and so on.

250 See Longchen Yeshe Dorje, *Treasury of Precious Qualities*, pp. 239–42, 341–42.

251 For example in the *Stotras* (*stod tshogs*).

252 A reference to the Chittamatrins.

253 Note the play on words. The flowers in question are said to flower in the light of the moon, in Sanskrit, *chandra*.

254 Mati is *blo gros* in Tibetan. *blo gros dri med* was one of Mipham Rinpoche's names.

Glossary

ABSOLUTIST REASONING, *don dam dpyod byed kyi rigs pa*. This is reasoning that investigates the absolute or ultimate status of phenomena, employing the four or five Madhyamika arguments.

ACCEPTANCE, *bzod pa*, lit. patience. Fearless acceptance of the ultimate nature of things.

AFFIRMING NEGATIVE, *ma yin dgag*. A negation in which the possibility of another (positive) value is implied. For example, in the statement "It isn't a cat that is on the roof," the presence of a cat is denied, but in such a way as to suggest that there might be something else. Compare this with the statement "There is nothing on the roof." This is a nonaffirming negative (*med dgag*), which negates without implying anything else.

AGGREGATES, *phung po*, Skt *skandhas*. These are the five psychophysical constituents of the individual person: form, feelings, perceptions, conditioning factors, and consciousness.

ALAYA, Skt, *kun gzhi*, lit. the ground-of-all, universal ground. According to the Chittamatra school, this is the fundamental level of the mind, in which karmic imprints are stored.

ARGUMENT OF NEITHER ONE NOR MANY, *gcig du bral gyi gtan tshigs*. One of the four great Madhyamika arguments, which investigates the nature of phenomena. All phenomena both inside and outside the mind are devoid of real existence because it can be shown that neither a single, discrete, truly existent thing, nor a plurality of such things, exists.

ARYA, *'phags pa*, lit. superior, sublime, or noble one. One who has transcended samsaric existence. There are four classes of sublime beings: Arhats, Pratyekabuddhas, Bodhisattvas, and Buddhas.

ATMYAVADA, Skt. A general term for the traditions of Indian philosophy that assert the existence of the self, or atman—that is, the orthodox schools of Hinduism. It is opposed by the *nairatmyavada* (in other words, Buddhadharma), which denies the atman.

AYATANA, Skt, *skye mched*, sense fields. The six inner ayatanas refer exclusively to the sense organs (the mind being the sixth); the twelve ayatanas comprise these six plus their outer corresponding objects. (The outer and inner ayatana of the mind is the mental sense organ and mental objects. In this case, the mental organ is the immediately preceding moment of consciousness.) From the interaction of the six sense organs and their six objects, the six consciousnesses are engendered.

CESSATION, *'gog pa*. This term has different meanings. In the Hinayana context, it refers to the cessation of afflictive emotion brought about by wisdom. The cessation itself is the "small nirvana" of the Shravakas and the Pratyekabuddhas.

CHAKRAVARTIN, Skt, *'khor lo sgyur ba'i rgyal po*. The wheel-turning king. The name given to a special kind of exalted being who has dominion over a greater or smaller part of the three-thousandfold universe, so called because he is said to possess a great wheel-shaped weapon with which he subdues his enemies. According to traditional cosmology, such beings appear only when the human life span surpasses eighty thousand years. By analogy, the word is also used as a title for a great king.

CHARVAKA, *rgyang 'phen pa*. Name of an ancient Indian philosophical school professing materialistic nihilism. The Charvakas denied causality, the law of karma, and the existence of past and future lives.

CHITTAMATRA, *sems tsam pa*. Also called Yogachara, this philosophical school of the Mahayana asserts the self-cognizing mind as the ultimate reality and identifies emptiness as the absence of the subject-object dualism that overspreads and obscures the underlying pure consciousness. Although this school is usually traced back to Asanga and his brother Vasubandhu (fourth century C.E.), who base themselves on the scriptures of the third turning of the Dharma wheel, such as the *Sandhinirmochana-sutra*, the Chittamatra, as a tenet system, is more accurately associated with the sixth-century master Dharmapala.

COGNITIVE OBSCURATIONS, *shes sgrib*. Dualistic thought processes that apprehend subject, object, and action as being truly existent and that thus act as obstructions to the mind's omniscience.

COMPOUNDED PHENOMENON, *'dus byas.* A phenomenon belonging to the relative level, brought about by causes and conditions, and which appears to originate, remain, and eventually cease.

CONCEIVED OBJECT, *zhen yul.* A technical term in Buddhist logic, used to refer to objects of the conceptual mental consciousness that identifies and names things. It refers to sense objects as apprehended by this consciousness, but also to objects wrongly assumed to exist (e.g., the self).

DHARANI, Skt, *gzungs.* The term is used to refer to the accomplishment of different kinds of unfailing memory. It is also a verbal formula, often quite long, blessed by a Buddha or a Bodhisattva, belonging to the sutra tradition and similar to the mantras of the Vajrayana.

DHARMAKAYA, *chos sku. See* Kaya.

DHARMAKIRTI, *chos kyi grags pa* (seventh century C.E.). One of the greatest masters of logic in the tradition of Dignaga. He was the author of numerous works, the most celebrated of which is the *Pramanavarttika (tshad ma rnam 'grel).*

DHARMAPALA, *chos skyong.* A master of the Chittamatra tradition and disciple of Dignaga, whom he followed as the abbot of Nalanda. He was a brilliant scholar and logician and was one of the teachers of Dharmakirti. He composed commentaries on the works of Vasubandhu and also on Aryadeva's *Four Hundred,* which have been preserved in Chinese translation.

DHATU, Skt, *khams.* This term has a very wide range of meanings. In general, it refers to all the "elements" that the mind can consider or investigate—from the senses and their objects to the postmeditation experience of a Bodhisattva residing on the grounds of realization.

DIGNAGA, *mchog glang.* A disciple of Vasubandhu; one of the great figures in the Buddhist logical tradition and a formidable defender of Buddhist doctrines against Hindu opponents. Together with Dharmakirti, who appeared a generation later, he effected a far-reaching reform in Buddhist logic along epistemological lines.

DOMINANT CONDITION, *bdag po'i rkyen.* One of the four conditions systematized by Vasubandhu in his *Abhidharmakosha* to explain how causality functions. The other three are the causal condition (*rgyu'i rkyen*) the immediately preceding condition (*de ma thag pa'i rkyen*), and the objective condition (*dmigs pa'i rkyen*).

DUAL APPEARANCE, *gnyis snang.* The perception of an object as separate from the perceiver. Despite the fact that they realize emptiness on attaining the path of seeing, Bodhisattvas traversing the path of meditation continue to experience, when not absorbed in meditative equipoise, the percept and the perceiving mind as two separate entities. This is the residue of dualistic habit and continues until full enlightenment even though, by virtue of their realization, the Bodhisattvas in question have long abandoned any belief in the reality of this appearance.

EXISTENCE ACCORDING TO CHARACTERISTICS, *rang mtshan nyid kyis grub pa.* A term coined by the Sautrantika-Svatantrikas to refer to phenomena considered as conventionally existent by virtue of their defining properties and functional efficiency.

EXPEDIENT MEANING, *drang don.* The teachings of expedient meaning are, for example, the instructions on the Four Noble Truths, the aggregates, the dhatus, and so forth, which insofar as they do not express the ultimate truth are of provisional validity only. They are nevertheless indispensable in that their purpose is to lead beings gradually on the path, bringing them to greater understanding and final accomplishment. Contrasted with the ultimate or definitive meaning *(nges don).*

FIVE KINDS OF PRETERNATURAL KNOWLEDGE, *mngon shes lnga.* These are: (1) the knowledge and ability to perform wonders; (2) the knowledge of births and deaths of all beings; (3) the ability to hear all sounds throughout the three-thousandfold universe; (4) the knowledge of one's own and others' past lives; and (5) the knowledge of the minds of others.

FOUR ARGUMENTS, *dbu ma'i gtan tshigs bzhi.* The four great Madhyamika arguments used to prove that phenomena are without intrinsic being. The first is the so-called diamond splinters argument. This addresses the question of causes and shows that it is impossible for phenomena to arise produced from themselves, from something else, from both self and other or uncaused. The second argument deals with effects and demonstrates that it is impossible for effects, whether existent or nonexistent, to be produced. The third examines both cause and effect together and refutes the production from any of the four alternatives. The fourth investigates the nature of phenomena and is divided in two separate arguments: the argument of dependent arising and the argument of neither one nor many.

FOUR BOUNDLESS ATTITUDES, *tshad med bzhi.* Translated also as boundless thoughts, they are four highly virtuous states of mind, regarded as immeasurable because they focus on all beings without exception and are productive of boundless merits. They are: love, compassion, sympathetic joy, and impartiality.

GENERALLY CHARACTERIZED PHENOMENA, *spyi mtshan*. Universal ideas and mental images of phenomena (*don spyi*), as contrasted with real, individual, concrete objects. See also *Specifically characterized phenomena*.

GORAMPA, *go ram pa bsod nams seng ge* (1429–1489). A major scholar of the Sakya school and one of the most important commentators of the writings of Sakya Pandita. His works greatly contributed to the final shaping of the Sakya system in the domain of logic and epistemology and clearly defined the philosophical differences separating the Sakya and Gelug schools.

IGNORANCE, *ma rig pa*, Skt *avidya*. In a Buddhist context, ignorance is not mere nescience but mistaken apprehension. It is the incorrect understanding of, or failure to recognize, the ultimate nature of the person and phenomena, and the false ascription of true existence to them.

ISOLATE, *ldog pa*. A term used in Buddhist logic and epistemology. Literally, the Tibetan word *ldog pa* means "reverse." An isolate of an object (sometimes also called "distinguisher") is defined as "that which is the reverse of what is not that object." In other words, it is the equivalent of a given object in purely conceptual terms. There are different kinds of isolates, and, generally speaking, they are used in Buddhist logic to explain the possibility of predication in the absence of universals, the reality of which, on the whole, is denied, in Buddhism.

JAINA, *gcer bu pa*. An important Indian religious system founded in the sixth century B.C.E.) by Jina (whence Jaina or Jain), also known as Vardhamana. The Jains advocate a very pure ethical system involving, in particular, an extreme form of *ahimsa* or nonviolence. They are subdivided in two groups, the naked ones (*gcer bu pa*) and the white-robed ones.

KATHOK SITU CHOKYI GYAMTSO, *ka thog si tu chos kyi rgya mtsho* (1880–1925). A nephew and disciple of Jamyang Khyentse Wangpo (in the transmission of whose teachings he was instrumental) and a disciple of Mipham Rinpoche.

KAYA, *sku*. According to the teachings of the Mahayana, the transcendent reality of perfect buddhahood is described in terms of two, three, four, or five kayas, or bodies. The two bodies, in the first case, are the dharmakaya, the Body of Truth, and the rupakaya, the Body of Form. The dharmakaya is the absolute, "emptiness" aspect of buddhahood and is perceptible only to beings on that level. The rupakaya is subdivided (thus giving rise to three bodies) into the sambhogakaya, the Body of Perfect Enjoyment, and the nirmanakaya, the Body of Manifestation. The sambhogakaya, or the spontaneous clarity aspect of buddhahood, is perceptible only to highly realized beings. The nirmanakaya, the compassionate aspect, is perceptible to ordinary beings and appears in the world usually, though not necessarily, in human form. The system of four bodies consists of the three just described together with the svabhavikakaya, or Body of Suchness, which refers to the union of the previous three. When five bodies are mentioned, this means the first three kayas together with the Immutable Diamond (or Vajra) Body (the indestructible aspect of buddhahood) and the Body of Complete Enlightenment (the aspect of enlightened qualities).

KUNZANG PELDEN, *kun bzang dpal ldan* (c.1870–c.1940). A greatly respected Nyingma master in eastern Tibet, also known as Khenpo Kunpel. He was a disciple of both Patrul Rinpoche and Mipham Rinpoche. He wrote a commentary on the latter's *Beacon of Certainty (nges shes sgron me)* and on Shantideva's *Bodhicharyavatara* in which he closely follows the interpretation of Mipham Rinpoche. He founded the *shedra,* or college of higher studies, at Kathok monastery.

LONGCHENPA, *klong chen rab 'byams.* Longchen Rabjam (1308–1363) is regarded as the greatest genius of the Nyingma tradition, an incomparable master and author of over two hundred and fifty treatises. Longchenpa's wide-ranging commentaries cover the whole field of Sutra and Mantra, in particular the teachings of the Great Perfection, but also such topics as history and literature.

MAIN MIND, *gtso sems.* A technical term of Buddhist epistemology, referring to the consciousness that detects globally the presence of an object, while the different types of mental factors (*sems byung*) apprehend and react to particular aspects of that object.

MENTAL FACTORS, *sems byung.* These are innumerable mental factors or events concomitant with the consciousness (the main mind), which can be gathered, according to Asanga, in fifty-one principal ones. These are again subdivided into six groups: (1) five omnipresent factors; (2) five object-ascertaining factors; (3) eleven wholesome factors; (4) six root defilements; (5) twenty lesser defilements; and (6) four variable factors.

MIMAMSA. Name of two distinct Hindu tenet systems based on the exegesis of the Vedic texts.

NAGTSO LOTSAWA, *nag tsho tshul khrims rgyal ba* (b. 1011). A translator and minister of the king Changchub Ö, sent to India in 1037 to invite Atisha Dipamkara to Tibet.

NEITHER ONE NOR MANY. *See* Argument of neither one nor many.

NONAFFIRMING NEGATIVE, *med dgag. See* Affirming negative.

PEAK OF EXISTENCE, *srid pa'i rtse mo.* The highest level in the formless realm and thus the summit of all possible states in the dimension of samsaric existence.

PERSONAL SELF, *gang zag gi bdag.* Innate and conceptual apprehension of an inherently existent I, ego. It is a mere assumption of what does not in fact exist.

PHENOMENAL SELF, *chos kyi bdag.* Innate and conceptual apprehension of the inherent existence of phenomena, which in fact lack such existence.

QUALITIES OF ELIMINATION AND REALIZATION, *spangs rtogs kyi yon tan.* Spiritual qualities (e.g., the realization of the five kinds of enlightened vision) that shine forth in proportion as the emotional and cognitive veils are removed from the mind's nature.

RENDAWA, *red mda' ba gzhon nu blo gros* (1348–1412). An important Sakya master from whom Je Tsongkhapa received the Madhyamika teachings.

RUPAKAYA, *gzugs sku. See* Kaya.

SAMKHYA, *grangs can pa.* One of the oldest and most important systems of the Indian philosophy, of which Kapila was the first exponent. It is a rationalistic interpretation of the Upanishads and posits two fundamental principles of matter (prakriti) and of mind (purusha), both of which are regarded as ultimately real.

SAMMITIYAS, *mang bos skur ba,* the followers of Sammita. This Hinayana group (of which no original writings have survived) seems to have been large and, to judge by the Tibetan name ("honored by many"), prestigious. It is divided into three subgroups or lineages: (1) Kaurukullaka *(sa sgron ril gnas pa'i sde)*; (2) Avantava *(rung ba pa'i sde)*; and (3) Vatsiputriya *(gnas ma bu ba'i sde)*.

SAUTRANTIKA, *mdo sde pa.* One of the four systems of Buddhist tenets. Together with the Vaibhashika school, the Sautrantika is considered as belonging to the Hinayana. The Sautrantikas are divided into two subgroups: the Sautrantikas following scripture *(lung gi rjes 'brang)* and the Sautrantikas following reasoning (*rigs kyi rjes 'brang*). The former group is quite close in outlook to the Vaibhashikas; the latter is particularly associated with Dharmakirti and is remarkable for its elaborate epistemology and logic. It is widely studied and utilized in Tibetan Buddhism.

SHANTIDEVA, *zhi ba lha*. (flourished in the first half of the eighth century C.E.) A member of Nalanda University and the celebrated author of the *Bodhicharyavatara*. He upheld the view of the Prasangika Madhyamika in the tradition of Chandrakirti.

SPECIFICALLY CHARACTERIZED PHENOMENA, *rang mtshan*. Concrete individual phenomena characterized by impermanence and ability to function. *See also* Generally characterized phenomena.

THIRTY-SEVEN ELEMENTS LEADING TO ENLIGHTENMENT, *byang chub yan lag so bdun*. A system of thirty-seven factors practiced on the paths of accumulation, joining, seeing, and meditation, by means of which progress is made toward enlightenment.

TSONGKHAPA, *tshong kha pa* (1357–1419). Also known as Lozang Drakpa and, more honorifically, as Je Rinpoche. A major scholar and master of the Tibetan tradition, considered to be an emanation of the Bodhisattva Manjushri. He was the founder of the Gelug school.

ULTIMATE MEANING, *nges don*. The teachings of the ultimate or definitive meaning expound the ultimate truth, or emptiness, in direct terms. They are contrasted with the teachings of expedient meaning.

ULTIMATE TRUTH, *don dam bden pa*. The ultimate nature of the mind and the true status of all phenomena, the state beyond all conceptual constructs which can be seen only by the primordial wisdom in a nondual manner. This is the so-called ultimate truth in itself (*rnam grangs ma yin pa'i don dam*). The Svatantrika Madhyamikas speak also of the approximate ultimate truth (*rnam grangs pa'i don dam*), which is the conceptual assessment of and an approach to the ultimate truth in itself. The approximate ultimate truth is a mental image posited in contrast with conventional truth.

VAISHESHIKA, *bye brag pa*. A non-Vedic doctrinal system generally linked with the Nyaya school and laying great emphasis on analysis and reason.

VALID COGNITION, *tshad ma*. A cognition that correctly knows its object, a nondeceptive cognition that brings about certainty regarding its object.

VASUBANDHU, *dbyig gnyen* (280–360 C.E.). The only Buddhist master to enjoy equal prestige as an exponent of the Hinayana and the Mahayana. During his Sarvastivadin phase he composed the *Abhidharmakosha-bhasya*, which is the most systematic and complete exposition of the Abhidharma and is one of the summits of Hinayana scholarship. Later in life, through his own inner development and under the influence of his elder brother Asanga, Vasubandhu adopted the Mahayana Yogachara view and composed many works of which the *Trimsikavijnapti-karika* (*Thirty Stanzas on the Mind*) is the most outstanding.

VATSIPUTRIYA, *gnas ma bu ba'i sde*. Subdivision of the Sammitiya school, the distinctive tenet of which was the assertion of a quasi-permanent self, neither different from nor identical with the five aggregates. It was for this reason universally attacked by other Buddhist schools.

Bibliography

Tibetan Sources

Chandrakirti *(zla ba grags pa). Madhyamakavatara (dbu ma la 'jug pa).* Varanasi: Pleasure of Elegant Sayings Press, 1975.

Mipham *('jam mgon 'ju mi pham rgya mtsho). A commentary on [Chandrakirti's] Madhyamakavatara entitled The Word of Chandra, the Garland of Spotless Crystal. (dbu ma la 'jug pa'i 'grel ba zla ba'i zhal lung dri med shel 'phreng).* Collected Works, volume 1. Derge Gonchen *(sde dge dgon chen)* prints. pp. 497–816.

——. *An explanation of [Shantarakshita's] Diadem of the Middle Way entitled Words Pleasing to the Guru Mañjushri. (dbu ma rgyan gyi rnam bshad 'jam dbyangs bla ma dgyes pa'i zhal lung).*

Nagarjuna *(klu grab). Mulamadhyamaka-karikas (rtsa ba shes rab).* Varanasi: Pleasure of Elegant Sayings Press, 1974.

Western-Language Sources

Dalai Lama. *The World of Tibetan Buddhism.* Boston: Wisdom Publications, 1995.

Della Santina, Peter. *Madhyamaka Schools in India.* Delhi: Motilal Banarsidass, 1995.

——. "The Madhyamaka and Modern Western Philosophy." *Philosophy East and West* 36, no. 1 (January 1986).

Dreyfuss, Georges B. J. *Recognizing Reality.* Albany: State University of New York Press, 1997.

Driessens, Georges, trans. *Traité du Milieu.* Translation of Nagarjuna's *Mulamadhyamaka-karika.* Paris: Editions du Seuil, 1995.

Dudjom Rinpoche. *The Nyingma School of Tibetan Buddhism.* Boston: Wisdom Publications, 1999.

Gyalwa Changchub and Namkhai Nyingpo. *Lady of the Lotus-Born.* Translated by Padmakara Translation Group. Boston: Shambhala Publications, 1999.

Hiriyanna, M. *The Essentials of Indian Philosophy.* Delhi: Motilal Banarsidass, 1995.

Hopkins, Jeffrey. *Emptiness Yoga: The Tibetan Middle Way.* Ithaca, N. Y.: Snow Lion Publications, 1987.

———. *Meditation on Emptiness.* London: Wisdom Publications, 1983.

Horner, I. B., trans. *The Collection of Middle Length Sayings (Majjhima Nikaya), Volumes 1–3.* London: Pali Text Society, 1993, 1994, 1995.

Hume, David. *A Treatise of Human Nature.* (1739) London: Penguin Classics, 1984.

Jamgön Kongtrul Lodrö Tayé. *Myriad Worlds.* Ithaca, N.Y.: Snow Lion Publications, 1995.

Kant, Immanuel. *Critique of Pure Reason.* Translated by Norman Kemp Smith. London, 1929.

Kunzang Pelden. *Wisdom: Two Buddhist Commentaries,* Book 1: *The Nectar of Mañjushri's Speech,* commentary on *Bodhicharyavatara,* chapter 9. Saint Léonsur-Vézère: Editions Padmakara, 1993, 1999.

Longchen Yeshe Dorje, Kangyur Rinpoche. *Treasury of Precious Qualities.* Translated by Padmakara Translation Group. Boston: Shambhala Publications, 2001.

Lopez, Donald S. *A Study of Svatantrika.* Ithaca, N.Y.: Snow Lion Publications, 1987.

Murti, T. R. V. *The Central Philosophy of Buddhism.* London: George Allen and Unwin, 1968.

———. "Samvrti and Paramartha in Madhyamika and Advaita Vedanta." In *The Problem of Two Truths in Buddhism and Vedanta,* edited by M. Sprung. Dordrecht/Boston: D. Reidel Publishing, 1973.

Nagao, Gadjin M. *Madhyamika and Yogachara.* Delhi: Sri Satguru Publications, 1992.

Napper, Elizabeth. *Dependent Arising and Emptiness.* Boston: Wisdom Publications, 1989.

Newland, Guy. *The Two Truths: the Madhyamika Philosophy of the Ge-luk-pa Order of Tibetan Buddhism.* Ithaca, N.Y.: Snow Lion Publications, 1992.

Perdue, Daniel E. *Debate in Tibetan Buddhism.* Ithaca, N.Y.: Snow Lion Publications, 1993.

Pettit, John W. *Mipham's Beacon of Certainty: Illuminating the View of Dzogchen, the Great Perfection.* Boston: Wisdom Publications, 1999.

Radhakrishnan, S. *Indian Philosophy.* Delhi: Oxford University Press, 1923; George Allen and Unwin, 1994.

Ruegg, David Seyfort. *The Literature of the Madhyamaka School of Philosophy in India*. Wiesbaden: Otto Harrassowitz, 1981.

——. "On the Reception and Early History of the dbu ma (Madhyamaka) in Tibet." In *Tibetan Studies in Honor of Hugh Richardson*. Edited by M. Aris and A. Suu Kyi. New Delhi: Vikas, 1980.

Russell, Bertrand. *An Outline of Philosophy*. Revised edition. London: Routledge, 1995.

——. *The Problems of Philosophy*. Oxford: Oxford University Press, 1912.

Scruton, Roger. *Kant*. Oxford: Oxford University Press, 1982.

Shantideva. *The Way of the Bodhisattva (Bodhicharyavatara)*. Translated by Padmakara Translation Group. Boston: Shambhala Publications, 1997.

Smith, E. Gene. Introduction to *Gzhan gyis brtsad pa'i lan mdor bsdus pa rigs lam rab gsal de nyid snang byed, by Mi-pham rgya-tsho: An Answer to Blo-bzang-rab-gsal's Refutation of the Author's "Sher le nor bu ke ta ka" and Its Defence, the Brgal lan nyin byed snang ba*. Gangtok: Sonam T. Kazi, 1969.

Sonam, Ruth, trans. *Yogic Deeds of Bodhisattvas, Gyel-tsap on Aryadeva's Four Hundred*. Commentary by Geshe Sonam Rinchen. Ithaca, N.Y.: Snow Lion Publications, 1994.

Sprung, Mervyn, trans. *Lucid Exposition of the Middle Way*. Translation of essential chapters of Chandrakirti's *Prasannapada*. London and Henley: Routledge and Kegan Paul, 1979.

Stcherbatsky, T. *Buddhist Logic*. Leningrad, 1930; Delhi: Motilal Banarsidass, 1994.

Les Strophes de Samkhya, avec le commentaire de Gaudapada. Paris: Société d'Edition "Les Belles Lettres," 1964.

Thurman, Robert A. F. *The Central Philosophy of Tibet*. Princeton: Princeton University Press, 1991.

Willis, Janice Dean. *On Knowing Reality: The Tattvârtha Chapter of Asanga's Bodhisattvabhûmi*. Delhi: Motilal Banarsidass, 1982.

Index

Page numbers in boldface refer to the root verses. The outlines (sabche) have not been included in this index.

dependent reality (impure), **78**,
    228–29, 237, 245–50, 366 n. 127
    compared to conventional reality,
        251–53
desire, **65**, 159
Dharma rain, **103**, 329–30
Dharma wheel, turnings of, 44, 358
    n. 37
dharmadhatu, 143, 195, 336
    See also ultimate truth
dharmakaya, **106–7**, 317, 337–39, 347
Dharmakirti, 21, 33, 49
dharmata, 193
dhatus, **108**, 342, 382 n. 248
Dignaga, 21, 33, 49
Dilgo Khyentse Rinpoche, 358 n. 43
diligence, **66**, 160
direct perception. *See under* perception
discursive thought, **84**, 245
disintegration as a positive entity,
    223–25
discipline, **62–63, 69**, 149, 153–56
divine sight, 263, 372 n. 179
doubt, 149, 302–3
dream example (selected instances),
    74–75, 229–31, 367 n. 129
Dreyfuss, Georges, 355 n. 3
dual appearance, 156, 216, 338, 360
    n. 68
Dzongsar Khyentse Rinpoche, 1,
    2–4

ego-clinging. *See* self-clinging
eleventh ground, 361 n. 76
emotional obscurations, 282
empirical experience. *See* ordinary ex-
    perience

emptiness *(shunyata)*
    according to Tsongkhapa, 49–50,
        174–75
    and appearance, 192–93, 251,
        274–78
    categories of, **93**, 210, 309, 314–19,
        322–23, 381–82 n. 235
    and compassion, 4
    extrinsic, 365 n. 115
    four modes, 277–78, 375 n. 191
    objections to, 18–19
    of both out and in, **94**, 316
    of the compounded, **95**, 317
    of defining attributes, **96–97**,
        319–21
    of emptiness, **94**, 316
    of essential nature, **96**, 318
    of immensity, **94**, 316
    of inner, **93–94**, 314
    of the nature itself, **99**, 322
    of "nonthings," **98**, 322
    of outer, **94**, 316
    of phenomena, 21–22, **96**, 163–83,
        317–19, 359 n. 53
    of the transcendent quality, **99**,
        323
    of the ultimate, **94**, 317
    of the uncompounded, **95**, 317
    of the "unobservable," **98**, 321
    of things, **98**, 322
    of "what is beyond extremes," **95**,
        317
    of "what is endless and beginning-
        less," **95**, 317–18
    of "what should not be spurned,"
        95, 318
    realization of, 25, 50, 176, 211–12,
        216, 313–14, 376 n. 200

The Padmakara Translation Group

THE PADMAKARA TRANSLATION GROUP *is devoted to the accurate and literary translation of Tibetan texts and spoken material into Western languages by trained Western translators, under the guidance of authoritative Tibetan scholars, principally Taklung Tsetrul Pema Wangyal Rinpoche and Jigme Khyentse Rinpoche, in a context of sustained study and discussion.*

TRANSLATIONS INTO ENGLISH

The Excellent Path of Enlightenment, Dilgo Khyentse, Editions Padmakara, 1987

The Wish-Fulfilling Jewel, Dilgo Khyentse, Shambhala, 1988

Dilgo Khyentse Rinpoche, Editions Padmakara, 1990

Enlightened Courage, Dilgo Khyentse, Ed. Padmakara, 1992 (North American edition: Snow Lion Publications, 1994)

The Heart Treasure of the Enlightened Ones, Dilgo Khyentse and Patrul Rinpoche, Shambhala, 1992

A Flash of Lightning in the Dark of Night, the Dalai Lama, Shambhala, 1993

Wisdom: Two Buddhist Commentaries, Khenchen Kunzang Pelden and Minyak Kunzang Sönam, Editions Padmakara, 1993, 1999

The Words of My Perfect Teacher, Patrul Rinpoche, International Sacred Literature Trust—HarperCollins, 1994, 2nd edition Sage AltaMira, 1998, Shambhala, 1999

The Life of Shabkar: Autobiography of a Tibetan Yogi, SUNY Press, 1994

Journey to Enlightenment, Matthieu Ricard, Aperture, 1996

The Way of the Bodhisattva (Bodhicharyavatara), Shantideva, Shambhala, 1997

Lady of the Lotus-Born, Gyalwa Changchub and Namkhai Nyingpo, Shambhala, 1999

Treasury of Precious Qualities, Longchen Yeshe Dorje, Kangyur Rinpoche, Shambhala, 2001

Counsels from my Heart, Dudjom Rinpoche, Shambhala, 2001

WITHDRAWN